Rock climbing in Scotland

Second Edition

Kevin Howett

Constable London

Constable Publishers
3 The Lanchesters
162 Fulham Palace Road,
London W6 9ER
www.constablerobinson.com

This second edition published in the UK by Constable,
an imprint of Constable & Robinson Ltd 2001
First published by Constable 1990
Copyright © 1990 Kevin Howett

A copy of the British Library Cataloguing in Publication Data is available from
the British Library.

ISBN 1–094–79610–6

Printed and bound in the UK

Dedicated to Catherine

Contents

Illustrations

Key to symbols used on maps

$\boxed{i}$	Information Centre
∧	Camp Site
▲	Youth Hostel
🏰	Castle
†	Church
P	Parking
T	Telephone
△	Mountain Peak
☀	Viewpoint
MRP	Mountain Rescue Post
🗼	Lighthouse
⚓	Ferry with crossing time
⇌	Railway Station
– — –	Railway line
··········	Footpath
– – –	Track
———	Road
▬▬▬	Motorway
⌄⌄⌄⌄	Cliffs
▲▲▲▲	Crags described in text
🌳ᚼ🌳	Trees

Acknowledgements

I must thank Dave Cuthbertson, Gary Latter, Alan Moist, Mark Charlton and Andy Nelson, with whom I have enjoyed most of my climbing in Scotland. I should also like to express my gratitude to the following people:

To Mary and John Griffiths for their outstanding diagrams, and Gary and Susannah Haley for producing excellent maps from the basic scribbles. Their work has added considerably to the quality of the book.

To Liz Paul for deciphering my handwriting and keeping pace with all the last-minute changes whilst typing the manuscript.

To Colin Moody, Steve Kennedy, Andy Nisbet, Dave Cuthbertson, and Gary Latter for their invaluable help and advice on routes, grades, descriptions, and even whole new areas of which I was ignorant.

To Catherine Howett for moral support, ideas, and considerable assistance with the English language.

The following people have also provided the help needed to complete this book in various ways from advice to supplying information: Alan Winton, Alan Thomson, Raymond Simpson, Chris Bonington, Paul Laughlan, Paul Nunn, Davy Gunn, Grant Farquhar, Fiona Gunn, Ken Crocket, Rab Anderson, Geoff Cohen, Arthur Paul, Cynthia Grindley, Terry Doe, Ed Grindley, Ian Sykes, Noel Williams, Ben Ankers, Ian Sutherland, Carol Fettes, Chalky White, Sandra White, Neil Morrison, Martin Moran, Molly Gibb, John Spencer, Alistair Todd, Alistair Walker, Stephan Harrison, Andy Tibbs, Greg Strange, Nick Sharpe, Graham Little, Tom Prentice and Mick Fowler.

K.H.
1989

Rab Anderson on The Giant, Crag on Dubh Loch p. 464

Foreword

Why selected climbs?

When I compiled the first edition of my *Scottish Climbs* in 1971, there was a certain lack of interest in my attempt to encompass, in the two volumes, a selection of routes from all the main climbing areas of Scotland.

My argument then was that visiting climbers, and indeed even Scottish climbers, would not necessarily wish to purchase all the detailed local climbing guidebooks, at considerable expense. If they had a special interest in a particular region, then they obviously would invest in a more detailed work. Meanwhile, a comprehensive and selective guide would serve them well. The popularity of such guides today has vindicated my early convictions.

This is a well thought-out rock-climbing guidebook in one volume, and is an up-to-date passport to many happy days on a galaxy of crags, cliffs, and mountains. It is a book to take along.

Hamish MacInnes

Pete Whillance and Pete Rotterill on The Naked Ape, Creag an Dubh Loch p. 466

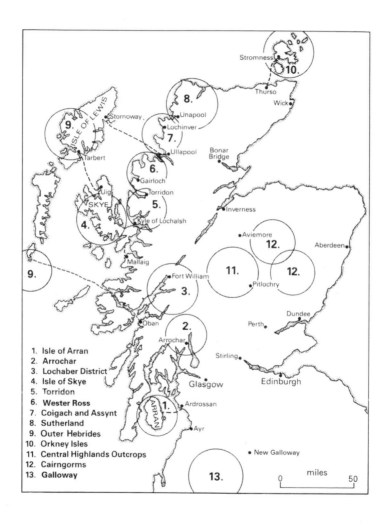

1. Isle of Arran
2. Arrochar
3. Lochaber District
4. Isle of Skye
5. Torridon
6. Wester Ross
7. Coigach and Assynt
8. Sutherland
9. Outer Hebrides
10. Orkney Isles
11. Central Highlands Outcrops
12. Cairngorms
13. Galloway

Preface to the 2ᴺᴰ Edition

In the period since this guide was published (1990) there have been a great many changes to rock climbing in Scotland. There has been an exponential growth in new routes on smaller outcrops across the northern and western Highlands as more and more activists have realised the wealth of clean rock that remained unclimbed. Only a few significant additions have been made to the traditional mountain haunts, although Arran, parts of Cairngorm and Sron Ulladale on the Isle of Lewis are exceptions. Sea cliffs have also seen much interest, particularly on the Outer Hebrides and a rapid but limited and localised development of 'sport' climbs has occurred in the Central Highland area.

All these developments reflect the changing priorities of climbers today. As a result some routes regarded as worthwhile for a selected guide in 1990 have seen few repeats and nature is taking hold again, whilst it is now recognised that some areas do not offer as good a quality climbing as some of the new developments. This new edition of the guide has catered for these changes and you will find some climbs (and even cliffs) removed to enable these new areas to be included.

I have also decided to remove the star ratings previously given to the climbs. ALL the routes in this selected guide are worth doing for their own particular reason and making comparisons between them seems superfluous.

Scottish rock climbing is undergoing a boom, a new (even frenetic) heyday, and I hope you can share in the experience by getting a taster of it here.

I would like to thank all those people who have helped in the updating of this guide and particularly to Andy Cunningham, Lawrence Hughes, Graham Nicoll, John Mackenzie, Blyth Wright, Bob Reid, Rick Campbell, Steve Reid and Alistair Todd.

Kevin Howett 1998

Introduction

Ethics

Modern protection devices mean that the continuing use of pegs on established routes is unacceptable and will unnecessarily damage the rock. Such acts of vandalism do still occur! In-situ pegs should, therefore, be left in place and offenders should buy a rack of nuts.

Although the development of sport climbs has occurred in Scotland, the venues are still few in number. When their development began in earnest in Scotland it was feared by some climbers that indiscriminate bolting would destroy future advances in traditional climbing. To help give guidance for the future development of this side of the sport a bolts policy was established in 1991 by the Mountaineering Council of Scotland and endorsed by its members and most Scottish climbers and has more or less been adhered to (bar a few notable exceptions). It is reproduced here for information. Scotland's true wealth in climbing (and something of a diminishing resource elsewhere in the world) remains concentrated on boldness and adventure. Most sport venues so far developed are not up to the quality of the best in England or Wales but one venue stands out as good as any in the UK and is described.

Bolting Guidelines for Scotland

This compromise statement developed from the views of most of the active climbers in Scotland by the Mountaineering Council of Scotland should act as a guideline:

'The MCofS acknowledges that there is a place for bolts in the future development of Scottish climbing. However, to ensure that the highly regarded ethos of, and future development of, traditional climbing (involving leader-placed and second-removed protection) is not threatened, it is felt that the use of bolts should be limited to the production of "Sport" climbs. There should be no retrospective bolting of established climbs for protection or belays, and there should be no minimalist bolting.

The production of Sport climbs with bolts is acceptable on natural rock only when all the following conditions have been satisfied:

1) On low-lying cliffs, provided that such development is not against the wishes of the landowner. Bolts are inappropriate on mountain and seacliffs.
2) On routes where natural protection is absent or is inadequate for the repeated falls that such routes necessitate.
3) Where the rock is steep and provides climbs of a high order of difficulty, at the forefront of developments of the day.
4) Where there is no anti-bolt ethic.

Concerning quarried rock, it is felt that any future development should be constrained only by points (2) and (4) above. Finally it is felt that bolts should be located to ensure minimum visual impact and should be placed according to current best practices.

It is intended that these principles are not seen as simply restrictive rules, but as a guide to promote the positive development of Scottish climbing, where Sport climbing, rather than becoming a substitute for traditional climbing, grows alongside it.'

Mountaineering Council of Scotland, 1991

Grading

The nationally accepted adjectival/numerical system is used. Foreign visitors and even many British climbers have trouble with it. The adjectival is an 'overall' grade, which takes into account not only the hardest move but the amount and quality of protection, difficulty placing it, strenuousness, quality of rock and general situation.

For each adjectival grade there is a combined standard technical grade indicating well-protected normality. Deviations from this indicate either that it is more or less serious, or more or less sustained. Technical grades start at 1a, but have been omitted below 4a as the adjectival grade is sufficient to describe routes from Moderate to Very Difficult. At the upper end of the scale there appears to be a compacting of the technical grades. In fact, the absolute technical limit has probably been reached at 7a, since such grading at this elevated standard becomes subjective and dependent on an individual's physical characteristics. The adjectival grade then takes over and expresses a progressively more sustained succession of difficult moves in a more strenuous or more serious situation.

European grades correspond generally only with British technical grades, since their protection is normally good (in-situ bolts).

Comparisons are therefore difficult, but an attempt has been made by the UIAA and is included in the table below.

Adjectival	Abbrev.	Serious or Sustained	Standard	Safer and/or short and hard	UIAA	French
Moderate	M				I	1
Difficult	D				II	2
Very Difficult	VD				III	3
Severe	S		4a	4b	IV	4
Hard Severe	HS	4a	4b	4c	V	5
Very Severe	VS	4b	4c	5a	VI	5
Hard Very Severe	HVS	4c	5a	5b	VI+	5/6a
Extremely Severe	E1	5a	5b	5c	VII−	6a
Extremely Severe	E2	5b	5c	6a	VII	6b
Extremely Severe	E3	5b	5c/6a	6b	VIII	6b/6c
Extremely Severe	E4	5c	6a	6b	IX−	6c/7a
Extremely Severe	E5	5c/6a	6b	6c	IX	7a/7b
Extremely Severe	E6	6a	6b/6c	7a	X−	7b/7c
Extremely Severe	E7	6b	6c	7a	X	7c/8a

Abbreviations

The following abbreviations are used throughout the guide:

FA: first ascent

FFA: first free ascent

PA: peg for aid

L: left

R: right

tr.: traverse

diag.: diagonal/diagonally
OH: overhang
OH-crack/wall, etc.: overhanging crack/wall, etc
PR: peg runner
NR: nut runner (vital or in-situ)
PB: peg belay
N, S, E, W: North, South, East, West
NTS: National Trust for Scotland

'Right' and 'left' in route and descent descriptions refer to climbers facing the cliffs, unless otherwise stated.

Maps

The sketch maps are detailed enough to be used on their own for the more accessible crags. It is advisable, however, to refer to Ordnance Survey maps when visiting the more remote mountain cliffs, for safety reasons. All cliffs have an associated six-figure reference applicable to the OS Landranger Series 1:50 000 maps. A key to the symbols on the maps is on page vii.

There are alternative maps for some of the more popular areas produced independently by Harvey Maps Ltd. There are two scales available, Walker Series (1:40 000) and Super Walker (1:25 000). The Super Walker maps in particular contain excellent detailed information.

Transport and accommodation

Relevant bus / air / rail / ferry routes are briefly outlined in the introduction to each area. Concise information is available from the transport operators or from the tourist publications detailed briefly in the Appendix, on page 493.

The nearest accommodation for climbers has been described, in each section. Information about hotels, B & B and self-catering accommodation can be obtained from Tourist Information Centres.

Access and Conservation

Most people believe they have a common law right to walk, climb and to camp wild for short periods over the Scottish mountains, a

'Freedom To Roam'. In reality there is a written law of trespass but the overall situtation is open to interpretation. There is one clear law, the 1865 Trespass Act, which makes 'encampment' and the 'lighting of fires' without the permission of the landowner an offence. However, a low impact approach to 'wild camping' in remote areas will, in most cases, be accepted. Since early in 1996 a voluntary 'Concordat' has been agreed between Access Groups and Landowners in Scotland on this issue. This informal agreement beholds both groups of people to acknowledge the legitimate desires and needs of the other. In essence this means that climbers and walkers should expect a welcome onto the hills and crags of Scotland as long as they act sensibly, respect the people who own and work in the hills and have due regard for the plants and wildlife that surrounds them. The 4 main principles of the 'Access Concordat' are reproduced below.

The Mountaineering Council of Scotland (MCofS) is the body that represents the views of climbers and hill walkers. One of its primary concerns is the continued free access to the hills and crags that we all enjoy and it played an instrumental part in formulating 'The Access Concordat' and is actively involved in developing advice to government on future access legislation based on the freedom to roam.

One of the issues regarding access in the hills concerns sporting shooting of deer and grouse and possible disturbance to these activities by mountaineers. To help, the MCofS brings climbers and land managers together to plan their activities so as not to conflict; The book 'Heading for the Scottish Hills' gives Deer Forest Estate contact addresses and 'The Hillphones' system gives recorded information messages about stalking activity for popular areas. Details of both are available from the MCofS. The important times for stalking are usually September to November and will vary in location across the hill. The shooting of grouse starts on 12th August till October. The shooting butts are obvious on the hills and the areas around these should be avoided during this time. Neither activities should prevent you from enjoying your climbing. Land owned by the National Trust for Scotland, the Forest Enterprise, Scottish Natural Heritage (National Nature Reserves) or John Muir Trust have no requirment for visitors to contact them about stalking activity.

Should climbers encounter situations that are contrary to the concordat then they should contact the MCofS with full details.

THE ACCESS CONCORDAT
The parties to the Concordat agree that the basis of access to the hills for informal recreation should be as follows:

Freedom of access exercised with responsibility and subject to reasonable restraints for management and conservation purposes.

Acceptance by visitors of the needs of land management, and understanding of how this sustains the livelihood, culture and community interests of those who live and work in the hills.

Acceptance by land managers of the public's expectation of having access to the hills.

Acknowledgement of a common interest in the natural beauty and special qualities of Scotland's hills, and of the need to work together for their protection and enhancement.

Another issue concerns conservation. Climbers should be particularly aware of possible disturbance to nesting birds. There are various rare species that share the cliffs and crags including, Peregrine Falcon, Golden Eagle and Sea Eagle; Puffin, Guillimot and Razorbill. It is an offence to disturb these (indeed all birds) at their nests. Further information is contained in an Information Sheet 'Climbers and Nesting Birds' available free from the MCofS. Some cliffs also hold rare plant species and care should be taken not to destroy flowers of any kind (the picking of wild flowers is in any case illegal).

Other information available from the MCofS includes the following *leaflets* – 'Freedom To Roam'; 'Wild Camping'; 'Sanitation in the Hills' and a range of *Information Sheets* including 'Health Issues' which gives advice about the growing problem of tick-borne diseases.

Safety Information

Climbers should be self sufficient in all aspects of what they do; self rescue (particularly from mountain and sea cliffs), emergency first aid, benightment, navigation and general health when in remote areas. Some of the cliffs and climbs detailed here offer serious expeditions and should not be undertaken lightly, especially considering the fickle nature of Scottish weather which can change from sunshine to snow, even in summer!

Mountain Rescue

There is a well organised voluntary Mountain Rescue Service in Scotland represented by the Mountain Rescue Committee of Scotland. In the event of an accident contact should be made with the Police in the first instance (by telephone; dial free on 999). The Police will decide whether to employ a voluntary civilian team and whether help is needed from RAF or Naval helicopters. It is vital that details of the location of the casualty (6 figure grid reference), a description of the location, the accident and the time it occurred, the name of the casualty and next of kin, and the nature of the injuries are given to the Police.

Names of civilian rescue teams and the nearest telephones for summoning help are given for each area. Do not rely on mobile phones in remote hills as coverage is patchy and reception in corries can be non-existent.

Weather

The best periods of settled good weather occur in spring and autumn (April, May, June, September, October). Some mountain cliffs, however, often come into condition only in July and August.

The following sources of weather information are specific to Scotland.

Climbline Telephone and Fax Service:
West Highlands 09001 333 111 601; East Highlands 09001 333 111 602 (calls cost 45p/min cheap rate; 50p/min at other times)

Metcall Telephone and Fax Service:
West Highlands 09068 500 441; East Highlands 09068 500 442
(calls cost 39p/min cheap rate; 49p/min at other times)

BBC TV Scotland: Mountaineering forecast, Friday evenings at
6.45pm.

Radio Forecasts:
BBC Radio Scotland 92.4–94.7 FM (regular coverage including
walkers specific forecast 6.45am); Nevis Independent Radio 96.6 FM;
Moray Firth Independent Radio 96.6–97.4

Health Hazards
The stream water in the Scottish hills is currently free of the Guardia
parasite and can be safely drunk fresh without treatment. A current
increase in the numbers of ticks has also led to more cases of Lyme's
disease being reported. In some places ticks have reached plague
proportions and should be avoided.

   The other threat is midges, which occur from June till September in
varying degrees of unpleasantness. A midge-rating system is included
where applicable, and refers to the worst months of July and August.

 Bearable

 Nasty (repellent necessary)

 Excruciating

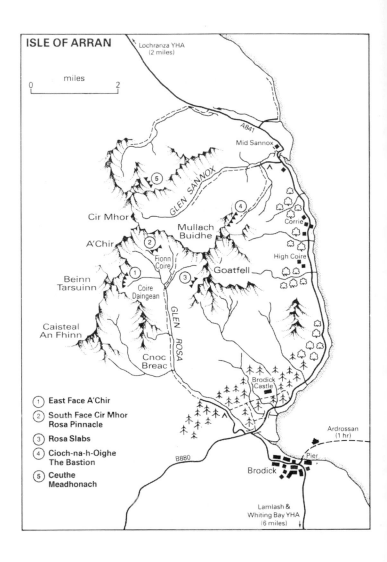

ISLE OF ARRAN

miles
0   2

Lochranza YHA
(2 miles)

A841

Mid Sannox

GLEN SANNOX

⑤

Cir Mhor

④

Corrie

Mullach
Buidhe

A'Chir

②

Fionn
Coire

High Coire

①

Goatfell

Beinn
Tarsuinn

Coire
Daingean

③

GLEN ROSA

Caisteal
An Fhinn

Cnoc
Breac

Brodick
Castle

Ardrossan
(1 hr)

① East Face A'Chir

② South Face Cir Mhor
   Rosa Pinnacle

③ Rosa Slabs

④ Cioch-na-h-Oighe
   The Bastion

⑤ Ceuthe
   Meadhonach

Pier

B880

Brodick

Lamlash &
Whiting Bay YHA
(6 miles)

1 ARRAN

Introduction

Arran is the unmistakable mountain island basking in the Firth of Clyde. The highest point is Goatfell at 2,866 ft (860 m), but despite this height the hills do not have a 'mountain harshness' as on the mainland, and allow climbing from March onwards. The climbing described here is confined to the major peaks which make up the north-east massif of Goatfell: Cir Mhor, A 'Chir and Beinn Tarsuinn. Unfortunately, perhaps, for the 'crag rats', the cliffs tend to be on or near the top of the hills. The views, however, are excellent and the midges few, making it an ideal choice for midsummer.

The rock is a coarse-grained granite. Cracks are uncommon and usually rounded, whilst the flakes can seem very hollow. The quality of the granite varies from a sort of 'Weetabix' at its worst, to excellent solid stuff, but even then the slabs retain a gritty surface texture. Apart from occasionally sticking to your boots, this does not hamper what can be outstanding climbing – where else are pocket holds found in seemingly blank granite walls?

History

In 1628 'Lugless' Willie Lithgow walked up Goatfell and marvelled at the fact of viewing 'Three Kingdoms at one sight', namely Northern Ireland, the Isle of Man and Cumbria. W. W. Naismith and Gilbert Thomson, SMC founders, explored Cir Mhor in 1891 and the A 'Chir Ridge was traversed a year later by G. A. Gibson and party. By 1895 the North-East Face of Cir Mhor was proving popular, with James Horst Brunneman Bell's route, Big Rib the classic, albeit dirty route.

Oppenheimer Chimney on Beinn Nuis, climbed in 1901 by Baker, Puttrell and Oppenheimer, was the best-known and most notorious route of the time, with its loose rock and dripping interior. The early pioneers seemed to relish such places and only in the 1930s did they venture on to the exposed buttresses.

In 1933 J. A. Ramsey and party found a way up the Rosa
Pinnacle of Cir Mhor by a wandering line. They returned two
years later and climbed the layback crack to rectify this in the
upper half. In 1940 Hamish Hamilton tackled a direct line up
the lower half of the ridge, over three visits with different
parties, finally linking it all together with D. Paterson,
producing a great route. The 1940s were the preserve of two
naval engineers stationed at Largs, G. H. Townend and G. C.
Curtis. They produced routes all over the island, including
Sou'wester Slabs and Labyrinth on Cir Mhor, the excellent
Pagoda Ridge on A 'Chir, and a route on Cioch-na-h-Oighe
which enhanced an earlier view that the Cioch was an unstable
mass of rubble and vegetation – even Bell had trouble finding
any rock on it. It was decades before this belief was dispelled.
However, Townend and Curtis did much to establish Arran as a
worthy rock-climbing centre.

After the War little fresh was reported till the late 1950s
when J. Johnston and others recorded some routes in
preparation for the first guidebook. The most significant ascent
was the bold Sickle in 1957 by J. Ashford and D. Burke. The
guidebook sparked off much interest, and the 1960s were very
productive, with the less popular cliffs receiving most
attention.

Andrew Maxfield loved Arran, and particularly Cioch-na-
h-Oighe where he discovered that the rock on the Bastion was
excellent: his Tidemark (Severe) is a stunning, very exposed jaunt
across this steep face. Klepht, Ziggurat and Galway Slabs were
his, too. Joe Brown visited the Bastion and commented that Klepht
could go free, but mysteriously he didn't try it. The Meadow
face of Beinn Tarsuinn, a big wall by any standards, had its
main lines climbed, though unfortunately the numerous grass
ledges and poor quality of the rock were not up to the stature of
the cliff itself. Rab Carrington then climbed the formidable slab
of Insertion on Cir Mhor in 1969. This unprotected 5c horror
was the hardest route on the island, and lay unrepeated for more
than ten years. J. M. Shaw and Ian Fulton climbed on the East
Face of A 'Chir, Minaret and Mosque resulting; whilst A.

'Bugs' McKeith climbed some excellent routes up the Rosa Slabs on the other side of the valley.

Bill Skidmore's first new route on Arran was The Rake on Beinn Tarsuinn, but soon he produced the great West Flank Route on Cir Mhor. In the 1970s he became its main devotee, and many big lines bear his name. Fearful of English raiders, he became obsessive in his eagerness to climb a huge corner on the Meadow face, and it took two attempts to produce The Blinder. Skidmore then initiated the third phase of the Bastion's development with Gazebo on the left wing, before venturing onto the 'unflawed wall' to give Armadillo. Climbed with a little aid in blazing sun, it was compared with a Glen Coe route for some reason!

Graham Little noted the potential of the Bastion and, climbing solo, he forced the massive horn of rock in the centre (Rhino) with one point of aid. He repeated it, free, later that year with Skidmore. In 1980 he inspected the most striking line up the centre, cleaned it on abseil and placed bolt belays. The ascent employed twelve aid points, and was controversial, but it was five years before anyone took up the challenge. On a hot June day in 1985, Gary Latter, Kevin Howett and Dave Cuthbertson arrived to free Abraxas, only to find Craig MacAdam had beaten them to it by a day. In 1981 Little attacked the impressive prow on Upper East face of Cir Mhor. Skydiver is a brilliant route but it required aid. It was led free and straightened out three years later by Colin McLean and Andy Nisbet. Also on the Rosa Pinnacle, the thin line next to Sickle became Vanishing Point for Macadam in 1985, who also made a free ascent of Skidmore's Armadillo. In 1985 on a very humid day in June, Cuthbertson and Howett climbed the big wall right of Rhino on the Bastion to give the hard Token Gesture with two hard pitches of 6b.

There was little activity in 1986 except for a fleeting visit to The Rosa slabs by Howett and Mark Charlton. Charlton pulled out the stops in repeating Insertion, adding a completely unprotected direct version in the process which warrants E5. He also led the slightly better protected West Point (E4). The early

1990's was quiet. It was not until the long hot summer of 1995 that the pace increased again. Howett and Little concentrated on Cuithe Mheadhonach, climbing the desperate and sustained Icarus (E5) as well as bringing to a fitting close the saga of a route called Achilles. This had been previously climbed by Little in 1984 utilising aid from rivets (replaced by a bolt). The bolt was later removed but the route remained unclimbed. Howett succeeded by a slightly variant line at E5 6c. That same weekend the pair on-sight led Blundecral (E3) up the obvious big gap on the Meadow Face finishing by jumping onto a ledge to escape. The logical direct finish was nabbed the following year by Robin McAllister and Dave McGimpsey at E5. This pair also climbed the longest extreme route (300 m) on the island with Gulliver's Travels (E2) also on the Meadow Face. Interest waned again after this except for Howett and Little's ascent of The Brigand (E6) in 1996 (accompanied by Lawrence Hughes); a striking and serious arete on Cioch-na-h-Oighe.

Access

Car ferry: Ardrossan, Ayr to Brodick (Caldedonian MacBrayne Ltd), 55 mins; 5 sailings daily; 4 on Sundays; last sailing 18.00 hrs. Claonaig, Kintyre, in Argyll to Lochranza (Caledonian MacBrayne), 30 mins; mid-April to September; daily including Sundays. For a short stay it is worth considering that the crags can be easily reached by foot. The Glen Rosa crags can be walked to from Brodick, whilst Cioch-na-h-Oighe can be approached from Mid Sannox village via the local bus service.

Accommodation

Camping – Glen Rosa site (995380), at entrance to glen, has basic facilities. Outside this area camping is discouraged but 'roughing it' at head of valley seems to be tolerated. Glen Sannox site (010453), at end of track heading into the glen, has no facilities but brilliant natural pools and nude bathers. Unrestricted camping further up the glen.

Bivvy sites – Large boulders below South Face of Cir Mhor give primitive shelter. At Devil's Punchbowl (002439),

Cioch-na-h-Oighe, a large howff accommodates two people and
has a good supply of spring water.
Youth hostel – Whiting Bay in the S of the island and
Lochranza in the N.

Provisions
Brodick has cafés and ample shopping facilities which provide
everything from food to frisbees. Beware Sundays and
Wednesdays when everything seems to close, and Mid Sannox
village where the only thing you can buy any day of the week
is an ice-cream! The nearby village of Corrie has a post office
and a shop, as well as a good hostelry for the addicted.

Mountain Rescue
Arran Rescue Team – Post: police station, Brodick (013358).
Public telephone boxes are located at Cladach (the path to
Goatfell), Corrie village (beside the hotel), and Mid Sannox
(opposite the campsite entrance).

Guidebooks
*Arran, Arrochar and the Southern Highlands, Rock and Ice
Climbs*, G. E. Little, T. Prentice and K. Crocket, SMC, 1997

Map
Landranger Series: Arran, 69
Harvey Maps: Walker and Super Walker Series, North Arran

A'CHIR   (966419) Alt. 1,500 ft (450 m) East facing 🦋 🦋
A'Chir (pronounced A Keer) is the highest point on the ridge
between Beinn Tarsuinn and Cir Mhor. The climbing interest is
contained on the series of seven overlapping buttresses on the E
flank, from whose appearance the name 'The Comb' is derived.
They face SE towards Coire Daingean, a subsidiary Coire of
Glen Rosa. The accompanying gullies can best be described as
horrible – the infamous Gully 3 having the dubious accolade of
being the 'best' of its kind on Arran.
    Descent – Down hillside well to L of the buttresses.

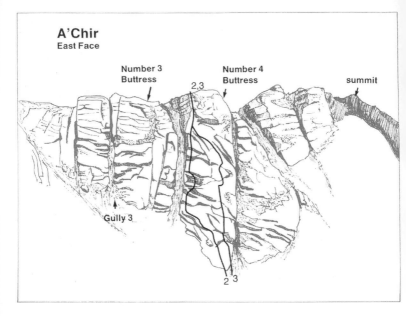

A'Chir
East Face

Number 3 Buttress

Number 4 Buttress

summit

2,3

Gully 3

2 3

---

1 **A 'Chir Ridge** *1 mile (1.6 km)* M-VD
FA: *J. A. Gibson and party, 1892*
An excellent outing, one of the best ridges outside Skye. The difference in grade is due to one either avoiding all avoidable sections or encountering short pitches on the true ridge. Start from Glen Rosa and take a route up Cnoc Breac, then up to Beinn a'Chliabhain. Follow this ridge to a col and take a path branching R below a rocky wall to join the ridge proper.

The first obstacle is 'the gap' where the ridge levels out after a steep step. This can be turned on the W flank. A few yards further at a cairn (and red arrow), descend the steep E wall for 15 ft (3 m) on good holds (exposed) to gain a grassy, part rocky trench heading down and out of sight. This leads to a small col, the 'mauvais pas', an O H-wall, has just been passed. The final section, keeping to the crest, is the best part of the ridge.

2 **Pagoda Ridge** *700 ft (210 m)* S
FA: *C. H. Townend and G. C. Curtis, 1943*
One of the best climbs on the face mainly following the L edge
of Number 4 Buttress.
Start: Near bottom R corner of the buttress just L of the lowest
slab (Arrow).
1. 90 ft (27 m) Start R up a grassy crack ending in a sharp
   flake. Tr. L up a heather patch, then cross a slab L to stance
   below an overlap.
2. 90 ft (27 m) Move up on to a sloping shelf above (delicate)
   and go L to the edge. Up this for 30 ft (9 m) to nut
   belay.
3. 60 ft (18 m) Follow the edge, with one short excursion on the
   R, to a pile of blocks.
4. 60 ft (18 m) Up past heather ledge and climb short steep wall
   to good stance behind large block overlooking the gully (nut
   belay).
5. 110 ft (33 m) Tr. R to small corner with spikes. Swing R and
   tr. a slab until the wall above can be climbed R'wards. Move
   back L to edge to a jammed flake. Good belay.
6. 110 ft (33 m) Crack above and the edge to a steep wall up to
   a belay on large boulders.
7. 180 ft (54 m) Finish up the edge overlooking the gully (about
   D standard).

3 **Mosque** *700 ft (210 m)* VS
FA: *I. Fulton and J. M. Shaw, 1968*
An excellent route more or less directly up the centre of
Buttress 4.
Start: 20 ft (6 m) R of Pagoda Ridge at the lowest slab. 'PR'
inscribed on rock.
1. 130 ft (39 m) 4c Straight up steep slabs R of Pagoda to
   overlap. Tr. L to a jutting block. Over overlap and head
   R'wards to a stance (PB).
2. 100 ft (30 m) 4c Up slab above and move R to a flake in the
   next overlap. Mantelshelf over and up to another overlap.
   Climb this and the slab above to a flake, belay.

3. 80 ft (24 m) 4b Up the bulging wall to the R and follow a slab and grass to another overlap (nut belay).

4. 70 ft (21 m) 4b Over this one also and slab (*déjà vu!*) R'wards on pocket holds. Go round on edge and up to a peg belay in small corner.

5. 130 ft (39 m) 4b Up the corner and tr. R to a crack in an overlap. The crack contains a loose block, but carry on regardless, then R'wards on to a slab which leads straight up to a block.

6. 110 ft (33 m) 4 b Go L over slabs to join Pagoda.

7. 70 ft (21 m) Up Pagoda easy slabs to finish.

SOUTH FACE CIR MHOR, THE ROSA PINNACLE.   (975429) Alt. 1,500 ft (450 m) ✗

Rosa Pinnacle is the massive buttress S of the Ridge of Cir Mhor (pronounced Keer Vor). It commands a magnificent view down Glen Rosa.

Approach – It most easily reached via a long boggy walk up the main Glen Rosa path following the stream N to the col between Cir Mhor and Goatfell. A reasonably well-trodden path branches off to the L, following the small stream issuing from the Fionn Choire, and leads to the base of the buttress.

Topography – The clean, impressive slabs on the L (W) side of the almost 1,200 ft (360 m) South Ridge provide the most obvious feature. The R (E) side is less impressive, big and broken in its lower reaches, until higher up the Sub Rosa Gully it forms the vertical wall of the Upper East Face (see diagram opposite). The West Face Slabs are split by two R-facing parallel chimney/corner lines which curve R'wards to form overlaps. The R-hand one is the general line of Sickle. Smooth slabs lead further R to the jumble of roofs and corners near the ridge itself. An obvious L-facing corner splits this section: this is West Flank Route (see diagram on p. 12).

Descent – From the summit it is easiest to descend just to the L of the Far West Buttress. Do not be tempted to descend the gully further L, which is unstable. Most of the routes on the West Face Slabs finish on the grass terrace below the upper

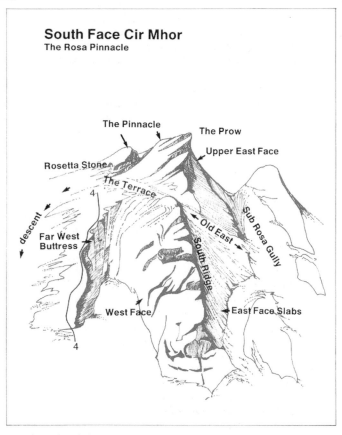

South Face Cir Mhor
The Rosa Pinnacle

The Pinnacle

The Prow

Upper East Face

Rosetta Stone

The Terrace

descent

Far West Buttress

4

Old East

Sub Rosa Gully

South Ridge

West Face

East Face Slabs

4

pinnacle of the ridge. An easy scramble (**Old East Route, D**) allows one to gain the Upper East Buttress.

Far West Buttress:
The buttress lying opposite the slabs of the west face. Not as impressive as its neighbouring buttress but it offers one classic route (see diagram above).

4 **Caliban's Creep**   *475 ft (139 m)   VD*
FA: *G. C. Curtis and G. H. Townend, 1943*
Atmospheric climbing. Start at R toe of buttress below
square-cut OH.
1. 80 ft (24 m) Take a L diagonal line across slabs to boulders
   lying below an OH.
2. 80 ft (24 m) Tr R across wall. Move down and round edge to
   gain easy chimney leading to easy slabs and sloping roof.
   Belay.
3. 50 ft (15 m) Cross slabs to below a vertical wall. Belay at
   the R edge.
4. 65 ft (20 m) Crawl through a narrow 'tunnel' (the creep) on
   the R. Follow a narrow exposed ledge on the east face to
   gain chimney. Follow this into the base of a deep fissure.
5–6. 200 ft (60 m) Exit the fissure and climb pleasant slabs near
   R edge to top.

The West Face:

5 **Arctic Way**   *540 ft (164 m)   VS*
FA: *W. Hood and C. Moody, 1982*
Start at the foot of a long L-slanting groove, level with the
vertical wall of Caliban's Buttress. The first two pitches are
shared with the easy line of Fourth Wall (Severe).
1. 165 ft (50 m) Follow the groove and a steeper continuation to
   block belay.
2. 165 ft (50 m) Continue in the same general line by cracks
   and grooves to shattered ledges below a large plinth.
3. 130 ft (40 m) 4c Gain the obvious L-facing corner in the slab
   just to R. Follow the corner then continuation crack over two
   bulges. Then direct up slab above to beneath OH.
4. 80 ft (24 m) 4c Move L to climb crack through OH. Go L
   again to bulge (PR). Climb this and go L on slab for 2 m
   then R to gain thin crack. Climb this then trend L to block
   belay.

Sou Wester Slabs, Cir Mhor, Arran

6 **Sou Wester Slabs**   *540 ft (162 m)   VD*
FA: *G. H. Townend, G. Curtis, H. Hare and M. Hawkins, 1944*
A classic and popular route.
Start: About 15 ft (5 m) down from the top of the wall at a
large ramp/groove slanting L.
1. 60 ft (18 m) Up the groove to a grass platform.
2. 60 ft (18 m) Up continuation groove (steeper) to a stance and
    block belay.
3. 40 ft (12 m) Gain the grooved rib on the L and climb to
    another block belay.
4. 50 ft (15 m) Tr. R easily, descending slightly to the foot of
    an open chimney. Up this to a spike belay below prominent
    parallel flake cracks.
5. 90 ft (27 m) Follow twin flake cracks to the edge of the slab.
    Descend R on to a lower slab (thread runner), and diag. R up
    the cracked slab to below a great OH-wall.

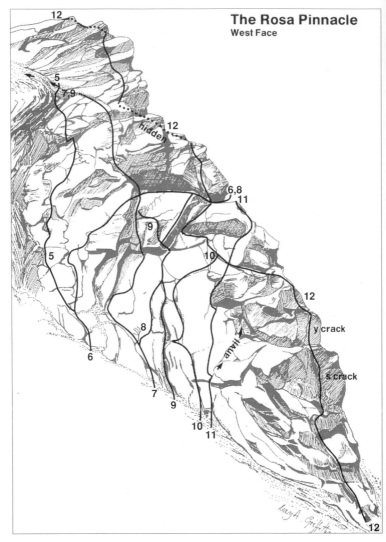

The Rosa Pinnacle
West Face

6. 40 ft (12 m) Tr. R below O H and round corner to big ledge
   below a three-tier chimney (South Ridge Route).
7–8. 200 ft (60 m) Finish up this.

7 **The Sickle**   *450 ft (135 m)   HVS*
FA: *J. Ashford and D. Burke, 1957*
An excellent route, poorly protected and high in its grade.
Start: Midway between Sou Wester Slabs and West Flank Route
at a L-trending flake.
1. 100 ft (30 m) Up the L-slanting flake to a poor block belay
   on a grass ledge just below the narrow chimney.
2. 90 ft (27 m) 5a Up the chimney for 15 ft (3 m), then tr. R
   across the bare slab to gain an obvious flake at its halfway
   point. Follow this almost to the overlap. Move R and
   delicately up to narrow groove splitting it. Pull through and
   up twin grooves to a good stance. Bollard belay.
3. 70 ft (21 m) 4c Up groove to join Sou Wester Slabs at its
   thread belay, then follow groove above to below O H-wall.
4. 70 ft (21 m) Semi hand-tr. L round the rib to good holds and
   on to small stance and P B.
5. 120 ft (36 m) Up broken slabs to block and L diag. fault.
   Above to terrace.

8 **Vanishing Point**   *500 ft (150 m)   E5*
FA: *C. MacAdam, 1985*
A brilliant route, bold and technical.
Start: As for Sickle.
1. 120 ft (36 m) 6a Up the L-trending flake as for Sickle for
   15 ft (4 m). Step out R via small flakes on to the slab. Tr. R
   to gain the obvious large flake at its base. Climb this till it
   fades. The blank slab above succumbs via two pockets to
   gain the continuation flake which leads to a stance.
2. 90 ft (27 m) 4c A crack in the slab leads to the R end of
   the large overlap. Tr. R to belay in the base of large
   corner.
3. 90 ft (27 m) 5c Climb the corner for a few feet until possible
   to pull L on to sandwiched slab. Up this as for West Flank

Hammer, Cir Mhor, Arran

Route to spike, then the edge of the slab via a quartz band,
then bold moves to belay below a large OH-wall.

4–5. 200 ft (60 m) Tr. out R as for Sou Wester Slabs, and finish
up the ridge.

9 **West Flank Route**   *490 ft (148 m)   E1*
FA: *W. Skidmore, R. Richardson, J. Madden and J. Crawford,
1963*
This is the L-facing tapering chimney system splitting the lower
slabs just R of Vanishing Point.
Start: Below the chimney.

1. 110 ft (33 m) 5a Up the lower chimney, strenuous, to
   possible stance. The narrowing second chimney is awkward
   and even more strenuous, and leads to ledges.
2. 90 ft (27 m) 4b Up flake crack in slab above to overlap. Tr. R
   to niche in base of large corner.
3. 100 ft (30 m) 5a Round arete on L, into groove. Follow over
   bulge and up layback corner to spike. L out of groove and
   up to horizontal crack. Descend L down slab beneath a small

overlap to join Sickle. Up this groove, through overlap to
thread on Sou Wester Slab. Belay.
4. 70 ft (21 m) 4c Up corner above. Step L to platform with
   block on edge of slab. Up this to big OH then hand-tr. L,
   gaining better holds and small stance (PB).
5. 120 ft (36 m) 4a Up broken slab and L diag. fault to terrace.

10 **Hammer**   *540 ft (162 m)*   *VS*
FA: *R. Simm and D. Cameron, 1960*
Good climbing. Tenuous on its second pitch.
Start: 30 ft (9 m) lower than West Flank Route, just R of its
fault line.
1. 100 ft (30 m) 4b up the crack in the slab to a ledge at 25 ft
   (7 m). Move L on to the steep slab overlooking West Flank
   Route. Continue up to a large stance on the L (common with
   West Flank Route).
2. 80 ft (24 m) 4c Tr. R a few feet, then climb a steep, thin,
   grass-filled crack to a ledge.
3. 100 ft (30 m) 4b Follow a shallow groove in the same line
   for 40 ft (12 m). Go diag. R up a line of dimples and cracks
   to join South Ridge Route on a long spacious ledge.
4/5/6. 260 ft (78 m) Finish up the Lovats Layback corner and
   chimney pitches of South Ridge Route.

11 **Insertion (Direct)**   *350 ft (105 m)*   *E5*
FA: *R. Carrington and I. Fulton, 1969*
FA: *M. Charlton and K. Howett, 1988 (direct)*
A daunting slab climb with only one runner on the crux pitch.
Not for the faint-hearted!
Start: Right of Hammer an intermittent stepped corner runs
down the slab to cut back L as an overlap across the lower
section of slabs. Splitting this overlap is the obvious crack of
Anvil, which finishes up the corners (VS). Start directly below
the crack.
1. 50 ft (15 m) 5 c Up the casy slab to the overlap. Over this
   via crack, then L on to the slab. Anvil continues up the
   crack. Move up with more faith than friction, passing a

horizontal line of pockets to gain shallow scoop. Up scoop, trending slightly L into centre of slab. When just below the large overlap, and before gravity overcomes ambition, gibber R'wards to a hanging stance on Friends under overlap.

2. 130 ft (39 m) 5b Undercling L into rounded corner. Pull out R under roof at top and up slab L'wards to a large ledge (South Ridge).

3. 50 ft (15 m) 5c Directly up steep wall via large obvious pockets (TR) to gain R end of large roof. Swing round arete and up to ledge. Easy scrambling remains.

12 **The South Ridge**   *1,060 ft (318 m)   VS*
FA: *J. F. Hamilton and D. Patterson, 1941*
On an azure, sun-drenched day this ranks as one of the best lower-grade outings in Britain. Not sustained but continuously interesting.
Start: Directly below obvious darkly etched 'S' crack in steep wall near base of ridge.

1. 350 ft (105 m) Scramble up lower broken slabs to rock crevasse 60 ft (18 m) below and R of the 'S' crack. Go up L-slanting groove to ledge.

2. 40 ft (12 m) 4c The 'S' crack and bucket holds lead to ledge.

3. 90 ft (27 m) 4c The 'Y' crack in OH-wall above (crux). Continue up slabs to boulder-strewn terrace.

4. 100 ft (30 m) Tr. L across top of Western Slabs via ledge to overlap. Up its R side to roof, tr. L into large corner.

5. 60 ft (18 m) 4b (**Lovat's Layback**) Up corner to spike. Out R along fine granite dyke footholds. When these finish a further line of holds allows one to climb slab direct to big platform.

4/5a. **Direct Variation, VS**: From boulder-strewn terrace climb direct up deep-cut chimney and slabs above to platform. Harder, but not as good.

6. 50 ft (15 m) 4a Climb three-tier chimney above, then two short slabs separated by a short wall. Belay on crest of ridge.

7. 100 ft (30 m) Easily up crest to terrace.

The Upper Pinnacle:

8. 90 ft (27 m) From a flake at the base of the first slab, using

knob-like holds, gain L-trending fault. This leads to foot of chimney.

9. 40 ft (12 m) The chimney to grass ledge.
10. 140 ft (42 m) Along ledge until possible to gain and climb slab to the R of small chimney. Up to crest. When slab becomes holdless, tr. on to East Face and climb corner past outward sloping shelf. Short slab leads to summit.

The Upper East Face:
The gully bounding the E side of the ridge is followed past the broken and vegetated East Slabs. Rearing above these is the compact Upper East Face. A rising grassy rake (**Old East Route, D**) divides the two from bottom R to top L. The most prominent feature is a twin groove capped by an amazing nose, hanging above the bottom of Old East Route, known as Skydiver. The next route starts part-way up Old East Route.

13 **Bluff**   *250 ft (75 m)   E1*
FA: *H. Donahue and E. McLellan, 1968*
FFA: *C. Dale and partner, 1970s*
Start: the wall L of Skydiver is criss-crossed by two vertical and horizontal cracks (small cairn).

1. 55 ft (17 m) 5a Climb the crack over a bulge to gain a ledge leading to a spike in corner on L. Up corner to grass ledge. Up the corner above to another ledge.
2. 35 ft (10 m) 5b Up past a sling to gain shallow chimney which is followed to a bulge. Move R across a steep wall below overlap to down-sloping ledge. Follow to stance.
3. 90 ft (27 m) 5b Follow scoop above to a corner (NR). Move R on steep slab, using holds on overlap above. Round corner of overlap (PR) and on to crack in edge of slab. Up crack and tr. R into corner. Small stance.
4. 90 ft (27 m) Go L and climb groove to join South Ridge. Easily up final pitch of ridge to pinnacle summit.

14 **Skydiver**   *260 ft (78 m)   E3*
FA: *G. E. Little and C. Ritchie, 1981 (4 PA)*

FFA: *C. McLean and A. Nisbet, 1984 (and direct finish)*
This superb route climbs the amazing prow.
Start: Directly below the nose and just L of the main arete.

1. 80 ft (24 m) 5b Enter a short corner from the L and climb it until a pull R gains a tiny stance on the arete. Up the superb twin-cracked corner to a sloping stance below roof.
2. 30 ft (9 m) 5c A contorted move L behind the huge prow and a further few difficult feet to a small stance (detached flake).
3. 100 ft (30 m) 4c Stand on flake and up a crack to horizontal break. Move R to another flake. Climb the flake and twin roofs above to recess. Pull out R and up slab to a good ledge.
4. 50 ft (15 m) A slab and short OH-corner leads to the pinnacle crest.

To the R of the prow of Skydiver is a deep-set chimney curving up and R: this is **Minotaur (VS)**. It bounds the L side of what appears to be a 100 ft (30 m) 'boulder'. The R side of the 'boulder' is defined by a vertical chimney fault, which gives the next route:

15 **Labyrinth (Direct)**   *400 ft (120 m)   VD (HS)*
FA: *G. C. Curtis and H. K. Moneypenny, 1943*
FA: *J. S. Orr and J. C. MacLaurin, 1951 (direct finish)*
Varied with some vegetation, but a classic route of considerable character.
Start: In the recess below the vertical chimney.

1. 70 ft (21 m) Up the recess of wide chimney and exit through hole on L under massive capping boulder. Up to grass platform.
2. 30 ft (9 m) Ascend chimney above to a cockpit. Block belay.
3. 50 ft (15 m) Groove above to grassy patch. Tr. L along a small horizontal ledge to small stance below small undercut corner.
4. 70 ft (21 m) Straddle up the groove to turf clump. Go R to deep chimney. Grapple up to grass ledge.

5. 30 ft (9 m) The long chimney above, going over first chockstone and under second to a rock ledge (the Eyrie).

6. 40 ft (12 m) Climb up over massive blocks to base of huge corner capped by roof. (Original finish escaped R up grassy rake, VD.)

7. 100 ft (30 m) 4b Layback up corner, helped by flake on L wall for 15 ft (5 m), and gain two parallel grooves rising L'wards. Use these to go round corner and short slab, gaining the crest.

THE ROSA SLABS OF GOATFELL   (987414) Alt. 1,150 ft (345 m) West facing 🦋 🦋

To anyone walking up Glen Rosa the huge expanse of slabs on the W slopes of Goatfell directly below the summit are immediately obvious.

Topography – There are two separate areas. The main slabs are a roughly triangular shape and nearly 700 ft (210 m) high. They are split into three sections by two parallel terraces slanting down R to L. Unfortunately these slabs are less continuous than appears at first glance, and contain large areas of vegetation and some gritty rock.

However the South Slabs, about 400 metres S of the main area, although slightly smaller, are of excellent rough granite. These slabs lie more than 1000 ft (300 m) above the glen floor. There are few prominent natural lines and it may well be possible to climb almost anywhere, but the routes described provide great slab climbing, including some pure friction. The slabs are roughly pear-shaped. From the central base an obvious and broken vegetated fault runs up diag. L. This was the original route up the slabs (Route 1). The first route described starts just L of the base of this fault, and takes a direct line to the top.

16 **Pochmahone**   *400 ft (120 m)   VS*
FA: *A. McKeith and M. Kelsey, 1966*
Sustained at start with short sections a bit harder.
Start: A few feet L of Route 1.

Blank, Rosa Slabs of Goatfell, Arran: climber, Derek Bearhop

1. 35 ft (11 m) 4b/c Climb straight up the steep slab and cross
   Route 1. Take a belay on a big spike just above.
2. 120 ft (36 m) Continue up steep slabs over a small overlap,
   followed by smooth slabs to a heather ledge. Block belay.
3. 100 ft (30 m) 4c A few feet to the R is a rib forming the L
   side of a scoop (Blank). Climb the steep wall above the
   belay (or the rib at HVS 5a) and directly up the steep slab,
   over an overlap, and up to a quartz band. Move L into the
   foot of a corner. Small spike belay.
4. 140 ft (42 m) Tr. back R and follow slab just to R of
   cornerline to top.

17 **Blank** *400 ft (120 m) S*
FA: *B. Kennelly and A. McKeith, 1963*
Fine slab climbing.
Start: 12 ft (4 m) R of Route 1.
1. 100 ft (30 m) Climb straight up smooth slab with a tricky bit

at 20 ft (7 m), passing the R side of a small overlap. Go slightly R to poor stance (PB).

2. 100 ft (30 m) Follow a line of pocks diag. L across steep slab, then a groove line to heather ledge. Block belay, shared with Pochmahone.
3. 100 ft (30 m) Go R round the rib into a steepening scoop. At its top, tr. 10 ft (3 m) right. Surmount a bulge and follow a line of pockets up to stance (PB).
4. 100 ft (30 m) Easy slabs to top.

18 **Blankist**   *110 m   HVS*
FA: *D. Bathgate and J. Renny, 1964 (pitch 1)*
FA: *G. E. Little and K. Howett, 1995 (pitch 2–4)*
The best route on the slabs giving memorable 'padding'. Start 15 ft (5 m) R of Blank in the centre of the slab, immediately R of a black streak.

1. 100 ft (30 m) 4c Up holdless slab to flakes. These lead to heathery groove and gravel ledge.
2. 82 ft (25 m) 4b Step L and climb line of pockets. Move L to gain long thin flake. Thin moves above this lead to flake belay on ledge.
3. 150 ft (45 m) 4b Climb direct up bare slab to gain rib. Follow this then easier angled slabs to rock ledge in base of banana-shaped groove.
4. 30 ft (10 m) Easier up broken slabs.

CIOCH-NA-H-OIGHE, THE BASTION   (999440) Alt. 2,000 ft (600 m) South-east facing ✖
This 'breast of the eagle' (pronounced Kee Ok Na Hoyk) thrusts out of the N spur of Mullach Buidhe. Its slopes are precipitous but very heathery, except, that is, the SE face. Almost hidden amongst the tiers of unstable vegetation and unsound rock of this dangerous hillside is one of Arran's true gems. The Bastion is a compact 400 ft (120 m) mass of rock, comparable to the best in Britain.

Approach – From the ruined mine buildings beside the campsite in Glen Sannox follow a small path up the side of a small stream on the L. The stream leads into the Devil's Punchbowl, the corrie below the Bastion.

The whole hillside is bisected by five roughly parallel diagonal ledge systems. Composed of collapsible rock and vegetation, they were climbed by Naismith and friends in 1894, when such horrendous sport was fashionable; nowadays it is merely unjustifiable. However, ledge 3 is the least messy and provides an easy approach to the base of the Bastion. It is about 1¾ miles (2.8 km); allow 1 hr.

Topography – The Bastion starts as a compact area of slabs distinguished by a niche in the centre, capped by a huge roof. To the R are two massive corners and aretes, leading to the main face. Prominent here are two gigantic flakes which form amazing horns of rock staring at each other across a blank wall. R again is a large vertical corner. A ledge cuts across the upper section of the face just above the horns, which yields the line of *Tidemark*, the only easy climb here.

Descent – The climbs finish on ledge 4. The cliff above contains other less worthy routes. Follow the ledge up to the spur of the hill. Descend this ridge to regain the top of ledge 3 (see diagram opposite).

19 **Digitalis**   *230 ft (69 m)   E2*
FA: *G. Little and W. Skidmore, 1981 (3* PA*)*
FFA: *P. Linning and C. Ritchie, 1983*
This climbs the first (L-hand) arete bounding the slabs of Gazebo.
Start: In base of huge corner to the R of the arete.
1. 60 ft (18 m) 5b/c Up OH-corner for 30 ft (9 m) to small ledge. Move L across blank slab to small hold. Round arete to belay in grass niche.
2. 100 ft (30 m) 5b Up corner above a detached pillar to roof. Skirt on R, and up cracks trending L to small ledge. Up awkward corner above, then direct to small ledge below twin roofs.
3. 70 ft (21 m) 5b Tr. R onto L wall of Klepht. Climb crack, then gain groove on L. Go L and up to easier rock and ledge

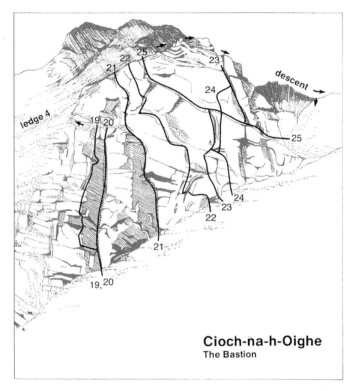

Cioch-na-h-Oighe
The Bastion

(flake). Up slabby groove to terrace (thread belay). Walk off
L to gain ledge 4.

20 **Klepht**   *210 ft (63 m)   E2 5c 5c*
FA: *A. J. Maxfield and A. Wilde, 1967 (Aid)*
FA: *G. E. Little and C. Ritchie, 1981 (direct, 4 PA)*
This climbs the large corner above the start of Digitalis in two
pitches. There is some crumbly rock on the first pitch but the
line is compelling. On the second pitch, beyond a recess, a

small crack in L wall allows the final corner to be climbed to ledges (thread belay). Walk off L to ledge 4.

21 **Armadillo**   *360 ft (108 m)   E3*
FA: *W. Skidmore and R. Richardson, 1977 (2 P A)*
FFA: *C. MacAdam and S. Steer, 1985*
The second huge corner whose R wall contains three prominent roofs.
Start: Directly below the corner.
1. 80 ft (24 m) 6a Up to the first roof. Awkward moves past old P R to reach the middle roof. Turn this on the L with hard moves to gain the ledge above (crux).
2. 140 ft (42 m) 5b Continue up the groove past throwaway flakes to its end at a small bulge. Tr. R to gain a crackline and corner which is followed to a large ledge. (Bolt belay – nothing else exists.)
3. 140 ft (42 m) 5a Climb a series of short O H-corners on the L (hard move on R to start). Tr. L then either go R into final grassy groove or follow crumbly rock up L, both rather gripping, to top.

22 **Abraxas**   *300 ft (90 m)   E4 ****
FA: *G. E. Little, R. J. Little, 1980 (12 P A , bolt belay)*
FFA: *C. Macadam, D. Austin, 1985 (in-situ gear)*
G. Latter, D. Cuthbertson, 1985 (led with no in-situ gear)
A controversial history. Climbed initially with much aid and a bolt stance in the centre of a blank wall, thereby splitting a natural pitch. MacAdam freed the route, but used the in-situ protection and bolts. Two days later these were dispensed with on the third and fourth ascents. As described, it is absorbing.
Start: 30 ft (9 m) R of Armadillo a R-facing corner curls down the wall. Begin up and R on ledge 3.
1. 60 ft (18 m) 6a Tr. L over slab to corner. Swing L round arete into further corner. Pull through overlap above, via hidden pocket in wall above (crux). Trend R across slab to belay.

Abraxas, Cioch-na-h-Oighe, Arran: climber, Kevin Howett

2. 140 ft (42 m) 6a Crack above to ledge leading L into space. Undercling round its end (exposure explosion!) to gain waterworn groove. Move L at the top to small ledge. Follow diag. ramp L (awkward but well protected) and thin ledge to stance.

3. 100 ft (30 m) 5b Up into hanging crack (rotten rock). When it veers R, swing L round arete into groove, then top.

23 **Rhino** *270 ft (71 m) E2*
FA: *G. E. Little (solo, 1 PA), 1979*
FFA: *G. E. Little and W. Skidmore, 1979*
The wall R of Abraxas leads to the obvious R-hand horn.
Start: 20 ft (6 m) R of Abraxas at an elevated grassy ledge.

1. 70 ft (21 m) 5b Gain and climb a 10 ft (3 m) L-facing flake. Mantelshelf and up direct to bulge. Pull L to gain small heather ledge. Climb up to hole (PR), step R to grass ledge.

2. 70 ft (21 m) 5b Up on good flakes and a crack leading to chimney of The Horn (PR). The chimney, passing a chockstone, gains slab of Tidemark.

3. 100 ft (30 m) 5b Walk R to large block. Large corner above with hard detour on L wall to grass ledge.

4. 30 ft (9 m) 4c OH-corner and a strenuous finish to ledge. Scramble to ledge 4.

24 **Token Gesture**   *320 ft (96 m) E5*
FA: *D. Cuthbertson and K. Howett, 1985*
FA: *P. Whillance and Party, 1983 (pitch 3)*
Follow a line just R of Rhino, the second pitch climbing the striking groove in the arete of the Horn.
Start: Just R of start to Rhino below obvious undercling 10 ft (3 m) up bulging wall.

1. 90 ft (27 m) 6b Pull up and R via wild move through bulge to gain flake. Stand on this with difficulty, then tr. R to flakes. These lead L to good hold then back R. Continue up until level with grass ledge of Rhino, Pitch 1. Tr. L via large pockets in bulge to grass ledge.

2. 80 ft (24 m) 6b Back along the pockets and up the hanging

groove. Pull R with much difficulty on to slab of Tidemark.
3. 80 ft (24 m) 5c Climb pocketed wall above L'wards to flakes which lead to ramp on R. Step up short corner at end to slab. Then R into corner of Rhino.
4. 70 ft (21 m) 4c Rhino to top.

25 **Tidemark**   *230 ft (69 m)*   S
FA: *A. J. Maxfield and J. Peacock, 1960*
Essentially a girdle of the upper reaches of The Bastion. Stunning position.
Start: Nearly at top of ledge 3, a gully defines the R side of the wall. Begin at a spike sitting at its base beside gravelly slab.
1. 90 ft (27 m) Cross two steep slabs L'wards via horizontal breaks (poor rock) and up to a grassy corner with huge block at base, at start of tapering gangway.
2. 90 ft (27 m) The gangway is increasingly more exposed, with a brilliant finale. Stance on small ledge, flake belay.
3. 50 ft (15 m) A few feet L of the belay go up until one can tr. L and up over slabs and grooves to finish.

CUITHE MHEADHONACH   (970451) Alt. 1,900 ft (570 m)
South East facing 🦋🦋
A magnificent 250 ft (75 m) wall hidden away from the hustle and bustle of the main hills. It lies on the east flank of the northern ridge of Caisteal Abhail within Coire nan Ceum.
Approach – It is best approached from North Glen Sannox. Leave the road at the small bridge over the North Sannox river and follow a muddy path along its south bank, through conifer plantations, then following the left fork of the river into the Coire. The wall is obvious high on the right.
Topography – There are two separate sections. The R-hand side is bigger but more broken. The L-hand wall is compact and looks impregnable. A shattered lower tier is bypassed on the L to gain a heathery terrace below this wall. The routes described are on the L-hand wall (from L to R).

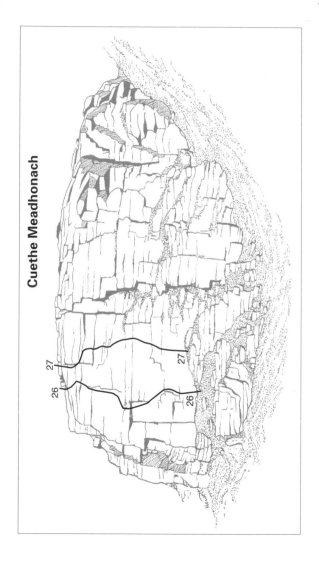

Cuethe Meadhonach

26 **Ulysses**   *165 ft (50 m)   E3*
FA: *G. E. Little and W. Skidmore, 1982*
Takes a line through the low overlap L of centre. Start 20 ft
(6 m) R of a vertical vegetated crack.

1. 82 ft (25 m) 5c Climb up and R passing the R end of a tiny
   OH to gain a R-facing scoop. Move up then L to under the
   overlap. Pull through directly and up with difficulty before tr.
   L to gain a grass ledge. Hollow block and small RP,s belay
   (or a bolt for the less brave!).
2. 82 ft (25 m) 5c Tr. Back R to gain a crack-line. Follow it to
   a jug below the bulging upper wall. Tr. R some distance to a
   shallow groove and pull through the bulges by a 10 ft (3 m)
   L-wards Tr. and on strenuously to ledges.

27 **Achilles**   *165 ft (50 m)   E5*
FA: *G. E. Little (2* PA*), 1984*
FFA: G. E. Little and K. Howett (alt), 1995
A magnificent central line up L-hand wall. Start at the highest
point of heathery terrace 30 ft (10 m) R of Ulysses.

1. 65 ft (20 m) 5c Climb slabby wall to gain easy L-facing
   flake. From its top gain fragile flake above with difficulty
   and secure belay in deep crack above.
2. 100 (30 m) 6c Follow deep crack as it curves L into
   horizontal break until possible to move up to further break.
   Make desperate moves to gain a small (fat) L-facing flake
   above. Reach horizontal break above, then another flake on
   L. Follow horizontal rail L'wards with difficulty into a final
   flake and crack system to the top.

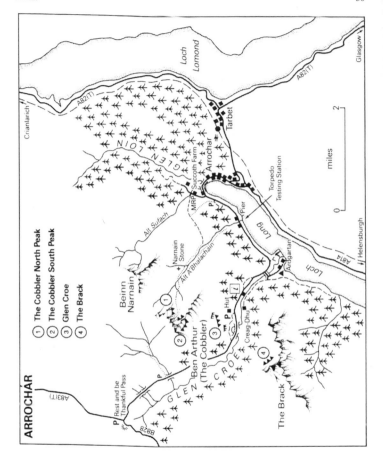

ARROCHAR

① The Cobbler North Peak
② The Cobbler South Peak
③ Glen Croe
④ The Brack

2   ARROCHAR

Introduction
The main cliffs are centred around the adjacent hills, Ben
Arthur (known as the Cobbler) and the Brack, which are
separated by Glen Croe and the Rest and be Thankful pass.
They are only 35 miles (56 km) N of Glasgow but are often
overlooked by climbers in their rush N.

The rock is a form of mica-schist with generally poor friction
and a liberal growth of lichen. When wet this lichen renders the
frictional properties almost non-existent, but this is really only a
problem on the harder and/or less well-known routes. The
schists are wrinkled and contorted, with a great variety of holds,
from small sloping ones to large jugs, from quartz to finger
pockets, from cavities to knobbles. Any cracks tend to be
hostile to human fingers and conventional protection, so
camming devices prove their worth. However protection still
tends to be sparse at all grades, creating a sense of seriousness,
further heightened by incredible exposure. This is especially
true in the lower grades and results in some of the best such
routes in the W of Scotland.

History
Development in the Arrochar area has been characterized by
short bursts of activity, interspersed by periods of neglect. Its
proximity to Glasgow allowed the early SMC members to visit
it, from the 1890s onwards. Harold Raeburn, William Wilson
Naismith and Mike Rennie all climbed here, but their routes
were not up to the quality they achieved elsewhere.

A lull followed until the Depression of 1930. At Craigallion a
few miles from Glasgow near the Campsie Fells, Andy Sanders
formed the Creagh Dhu Club. Consisting mostly of unemployed
Clydeside shipworkers, the Club took to the hills in search of
adventure. About the same time the Ptarmigan Club appeared.
Its leading light was a Glaswegian crane-driver called Jock
Nimlin. Teaming up with Sanders, he produced Recess Route

(one of the most enjoyable from this period), Nimlin's Direct Route and Ardgartan Wall. Other members of the Creagh Dhu thrutched their way up Ramshead Gully.

The Second World War interrupted exploration but the emerging Creagh Dhu were to dominate Scottish climbing for the next decade. During this Scottish heyday, standards rose above anything south of the Border. John Cunningham, Mick Noon, Bill Smith and Pat Walsh were most active, and teaming up with a local Greenock lad, Hamish MacInnes, they took over the Cobbler and Glen Coe. Gladiator's Groove on the Cobbler's South Peak succumbed in 1951 to Smith and MacInnes, with the bold direct pitch (HVS) completed the following year, again by Smith. In 1954 Walsh succeeded on an overhanging crack on the Cobbler's North Peak, after various club members had failed. On one occasion he fell on to a poor peg and was lowered semi-conscious and propped up in a cave whilst his mates went off climbing. He recovered and descended to the Narnain Stone, where they found him asleep. Club Crack is a brilliant E2, at that time matched only by Chris Preston's Suicide Wall in Wales for difficulty.

A month after Club Crack, Edinburgh climber Robin Smith did Glueless Groove (E2). Smith, university-educated, was not only a good climber but wrote marvellous accounts of his exploits and was drawn to the SMC. A healthy competition sprang up with the Creagh Dhu, channelled towards Glen Coe, leaving the Cobbler to sleep again for a while.

Over 1967/68 Bill Skidmore forced Mainline and Mammoth on The Brack, resorting to a few pulls on pegs, and Rab Carrington and Jimmy Gardiner did McLean's Folly on the Cobbler, another E2.

The 70s saw a breakthrough in standards in England and Wales, and a corresponding jump occurred in Scotland, although lagging a few years behind; Dave Cuthbertson and Murray Hamilton were prominent in this. While they were busy in Dunkeld and Newtonmore, the only significant ascent in Arrochar was the free ascent of Mammoth, on its second ascent, by Dougie Mullin and Alan Petit. Then in 1979 Wild Country fell to Cuthbertson and Rob Kerr. This was a free trip up the banana wall of the Cobbler's North Peak and was Scotland's first E5. It was 7 years before a repeat confirmed it as Scotland's first E6! In 1980, after a brief scrub on abseil, Cuthbertson attacked the sensational hanging groove in the main arete of the South Peak, expecting a reasonable middle-grade extreme. It turned out to be desperate and he struggled up to the belay wishing he had made a better job of cleaning it. Ruskoline was another E5. Rest and be Thankful (E5) soon followed on the wall left of Club Crack, a serious outing which took him two visits before he succeeded, and which is compared with Right Wall in Wales. Earlier that year Pete Whillance climbed his very serious Edge of Extinction on the Brack. With scant protection and technical difficulty it remains one of the more frightening leads in the area.

Dave Griffiths had been the main activist at Glen Croe which he had been developing with friends through the mid 1980's. In 1989 he ventured up the hill to the Cobbler's South Face and nabbed the excellent Osiris (E4), the only route of note for some time. This spurred Gary Latter into action, taking over from Cuthbertson as the peak's major activist, repeating Osiris and adding Horus (E6), Ra (E4) and Gib (E4) to this wall. He also completed the left arete of the Punster's Crack wall with Wild at Heart (E6).

The stunning overhanging off-width crack above Punster's Crack itself had spurred advances for years. The Creag Dubh Club had apparently tried it using cut-down chair legs for protection and Cuthbertson had a series of huge drilled-out 'tubes' made to fit the crack. However, it was left to Rick Campbell and Paul Thorburn to climb this plumb line in 1995 at E5 with large camming devices for protection. This spate of activity was continued with Thorburn adding Ethereal and Sleeping Gas, both E6, and Latter completing the huge overhanging prow of Baillie's Overhang that is the major feature of the North Peak to give Dalriada (E8) utilising a collection of in-situ peg protection.

Access
The nearest villages are Arrochar, at the head of Loch Long, and Tarbet, 1 mile (1.61 km) E on the shores of Loch Lomond. The A814 and the A82(T) go directly to these villages respectively from Glasgow.
Bus: Glasgow to Oban daily, via Tarbet; Tarbet to Arrochar (over the Rest and be Thankful Pass at the head of Glen Croe), intermittent service.
Train: Glasgow to Tarbet, even on Sundays.

Accommodation
Camping – Ardgartan (274030) Forestry Commission site at base of Glen Croe. Camping elsewhere in the Glen is discouraged, but is unrestricted at higher altitudes along the Alt. a' Bhalachain leading up the Cobbler.
Youth hostel – At Ardgartan (274030) next to the campsite.
Bivvy sites – The famous Narnain Stone half-way up the Alt. a' Bhalachain, where many a latter-day tiger bouldered, gives frugal comfort. Better are the two caves under the largest boulders below the N peak of the Cobbler up in the E corrie itself. On the Brack a large cave skulks below the main face.

Provisions
Arrochar has several small shops for general foods, welcoming ale houses and some good cafés. One of the latter seems to open for business every day of the year and closes late evening.

Mountain Rescue
Arrochar Rescue Team – Post: Succoth Farm (295053), 1 mile (1.61 km) N of Arrochar.

Guidebooks
Arran, Arrochar and the Southern Highlands, Rock and Ice Climbs, G. E. Little, T. Prentice and K. Crocket, SMC 1997

Map
Landranger Series: Loch Lomond, 56
Harvey Maps: Walker and Super Walker Series, Arrochar Alps

THE COBBLER   (259059) Alt. 2,600 ft (780 m) 🦋
Seen so clearly across the head of Loch Long from Arrochar
village, Ben Arthur is composed of three distinct peaks of bare
rock: N is the Cobbler, Centre is the Summit, and S is the
Cobbler's wife, Jean! They circle the bowl-like E. Corrie just
below Ben Arthur's summit. The cliffs are very exposed to winds
and low cloud, so fine, dry weather is advantageous. It is usually
possible, however, to find a wall in the sun, or sheltered from the
Westerlies. They are the most popular cliffs in the Arrochar area.
   Approach – There are two ways in:
1. The A83(T) circles the head of Loch Long from Arrochar
   village. Just after a small R turn to Succoth Farm there is a
   lay-by on the L (294048). Opposite, a short track runs into
   the trees. Follow this, and then a path which first goes
   through thick forest, then open ground up the hill, following
   the concrete remains of a cable railway, to a junction with a
   good track circling the hillside. Follow this L to the Alt. a'
   Bhalachain (Buttermilk Burn), then up to the base of the N
   peak. Allow 2 hrs 15 mins.
2. The Alt. a' Chothruim stream issuing from the Coire of the
   Bealach a' Mhaim (Coire a' Chothruim – not named on the
   map), just N of Ben Arthur, runs into Glen Croe. There is a
   small parking area where the main road crosses it (242061).
   A small path follows the stream to an old dam. Strike up the
   shallow corrie on the R to gain the top of the Cobbler –
   steep but short, 1½ miles (2.4 kms), allow 1 hr 30 mins.

The South Peak
A high pinnacle-type summit completely bounded by rock faces.
The South Face, which is the wall overlooking Glen Croe, has a
sunny aspect, and so is clean and sound and dries quickly after
rain. By contrast the North Face is continually shaded and has a
strong lichen growth, but the routes have a big powerful feel

The Cobbler
South Peak   South Face

Porcupine Wall

and are well worth struggling with. The top of the South peak can be gained by a moderate scramble up the SE ridge, or a short scramble through the summit boulders from the South/ Centre Peak col.

South Face

Topography – The upper L-hand side of the face is somewhat broken with many grass ledges. However, as the wall drops down the hillside to form a tongue of steep slabs at its base, the rock becomes clean and unbroken. Half-way down the face a L-leaning grassy corner with an OH-R wall defines the junction between the two sections. All the routes described are to the R of this corner.

Descent – Tr. off R along terrace to descend the SE ridge by an easy scramble.

Thin cracks in the short OH-wall of the corner were climbed with aid by Hamish MacInnes in 1951, giving Porcupine Wall. The most obvious feature in the centre of the wall is a large L-facing corner. The wall to its L is formed into a large scoop. The next route climbs this:

28 **Glueless Groove**   *150 ft (45 m)   E2 5b*
FA: *R. Smith, 1957*
Start below ramp-like grooves that form the scoop R of the base of Porcupine Wall. Up the cracked grooves that trend R to gain a ledge just R of the central corner-line. Climb the wall out left for 20 ft (6 m) to quartz blotches. Continue up to large ledge. Climb OH-groove above, passing flake to top.

29 **Ithuriel's Wall**   *145 ft (45 m)   E2*
FA: *H. MacInnes, 1952*
FA: *Direct line, (unknown)*
A steep route up the central L-facing corner-line.
Start: 30 ft (9 m) lower than Glueless Groove at a broken grassy fault leading up R to base of corner.
1. 30 ft (10 m) 4a Climb the fault up R to large ledges below the corner. Block Belay.

2. 80 ft (25 m) 5b Follow the excellent corner direct past bulges to large ledge. Belay at R side of ledge below corner (shared with Gladiators Groove).
3. 30 ft (10 m) 4c Climb the arete to R of corner.

30 **Gladiators Groove Direct** *200 ft (65 m)* *E1*
FA: *W. Smith and H. MacInnes, 1951/52*
An excellent route, sustained and poorly protected on pitch 1 but on fine rock.
Start: 20 ft (6 m) L and above the 'pit' at the base of the wall, level with a quartz band.
1. 110 ft (35 m) 5a Climb up steeply to gain the L end of the quartz (unprotected). Continue up steep slab to ledge then tr. delicately R to large block near arete. Continue up (PR) to ledges below corner.
2. 60 ft (20 m) 5b Climb the corner until step L gains steep R-facing groove. Up this with a difficult exit out left to reach ledge. Belay below corner to R.
3. 30 ft (10 m) 4c Climb the corner to the terrace.

31 **Osiris** *120 ft (36 m)* *E4 6a*
FA: *D. Griffiths, 1988*
A brilliant one-pitch route up the smooth slab in base of wall.
Start: In the 'pit' below the face. Pull on to ledge below bulge. Up to holds under it (PR), and tr. L till possible to pull over on pockets (PR). Continue past good holds (TR). Step L and up to large pockets (Friend 1), then up faint crackline just L of small overlap to quartz (PR). Tr. up and R, then direct to blocks on arete. PB above.

32 **Ardgarten Arete** *180 ft (54 m)* *VS*
FA: *J. Cunningham, 1948*
Essentially climbs the R prow of the face. A great outing.
Start: 20 ft (6 m) up R of the 'pit' at the base of the wall.
1. 90 ft (27 m) 4b Climb up and over a bulge at 15 ft (3 m) into scoop, then go diag. L across slab to join the arete below large blocks (PB above).

2. 35 ft (11 m) 4a Step R on to wall and up two parallel cracks. Then go L to block belay.
3. 55 ft (17 m) 4a Crack above to top.

North Face
The North Face of the South Peak is rather rambling and covered in lichen. There are some good lines, spoilt by being dirty and usually wet. In the centre is a huge O H -arete containing a small groove. This is **Ruskoline, 260 ft (78 m) E5 6a, 5a**. Although offering stunning climbing it is unfortunately rarely repeated and covered in lichen. R of Ruskoline's upper section are several corner lines. The first is **Deadman's Groove, 150 ft (45 m) VS 4c** and the second **McLean's Folly 260 ft (78 m) E15b**. The R arete of the North Face offers a classic, atmospheric mountaineering outing, climbed on its R side and is described next:

33 **Nimlin's Direct Route**   *240 ft (72 m)   VD*
FA: *J. B. Nimlin and A. Sanders*
Start: Up R of a short deep chimney near the L edge of the wall.
1. 110 ft (32 m) Climb up L across the wall to the arete. Follow the arete and easy ground to a terrace below the final arete.
2. 130 ft (40 m) Follow a series of cracks and corners to R of arete to gain the summit block.

The North Peak   South facing
This is the most striking of the three peaks, and offers the finest climbing, particularly in the lower grades. Although mainly short, the walls are steep with plenty of good holds, and their alarming situation, perched high above the coire compensates admirably for the walk up. Lichen poses no real problem here, except in damp conditions when it can become very greasy.

Topography – The North Peak is complex, composed of two distinct sections. First is an upper tier of soaring aretes and jutting right-angled buttresses, the most prominent being those of Wild Country and the impressive stepped prow of Baillie's

Overhang at the R end. Below Baillie's Overhang a gully marks the L side of the lower tier (Ramshead Gully).

Routes on the lower tier can be combined with those on the wall to the R of Baillie's Overhang, (Whither Whether Wall) on the upper tier: see diagram on p. 48.

Upper Tier
The cliff increases in length from the L, forming four distinct buttresses, separated by chimneys or recesses. The first route climbs the L arete of the first chimney (Right Angled Chimney): see diagram on p. 42.

34 **Chimney Arete**   *80 ft (24 m)   VS 4b*
FA: *J. Cunningham and I. Dingwall, 1947*
The steep arete on the first buttress is surprisingly delicate and poorly protected. Take a short excursion to the L or R about mid-height.

The obvious chimney topped by a roof on R is **Right Angled Chimney (D ***)**. It exits up slabby wall L of roof on polished holds, and is well worth doing.

35 **Cat Crawl**   *120 ft (36 m)   VS*
FA: *A. Lavery, 1936*
This climbs the second buttress immediately R of Right Angled Chimney. Varied and interesting, it follows part of an obvious fault from L to R into the main groove.
1. 60 ft (18 m) 4c Climb direct into the start of the fault. Tr. this by foot or by stomach, depending on your bravery, to a spike belay.
2. 60 ft (18 m) 4b Climb the bulge above and go L across the lip of OH in L wall. Continue up the wall, with moves back R, to take the obvious line to the top.

Nimlin's Direct Route, The Cobbler, South Peak: climber, Colin Moody

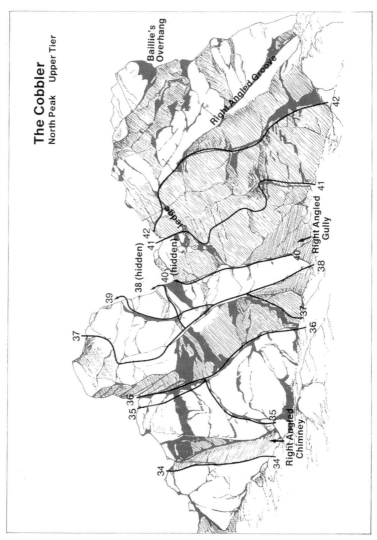

The Cobbler
North Peak Upper Tier

Baillie's Overhang

Right Angled Groove

36 **Direct Direct**   *110 ft (33 m)   HVS*
FA: *J. Cunningham, 1948* (direct start)
FA: *R. Muir and J. Wilton*, 1930s (final crack)
A direct line on Cat Crawl, taking the groove/fault separating
buttresses 2 and 3.
Start: In recess below fault.
1. 70 ft (21 m) 5a/b There are two cracks issuing from the
   recess. Climb the wall to L of L-hand crack through bulge to
   large hold. Continue up and R into corner, and then to join
   Cat Crawl at spike belay.
2. 40 ft (12 m) 5a The steep crack above to top.

37 **Wild Country**   *160 ft (48 m)   E6*
FA: *D. Cuthbertson and R. Kerr, 1979*
Climbs a compelling line up the centre of the third buttress (the
acutely OH-Dinner Plate Wall). It follows, in part, an old aid
route called The Nook.
Start: In the recess of Direct Direct.
1. 70 ft (21 m) 5c Struggle up the R diag. crack from the recess
   and up slabs to ledge and belay (common with Punster's
   Crack).
2. 90 ft (27 m) 6b Climb L up slab and steepening
   quartz-blotched wall to ledge (NRS in thin crack on R). Tr. R
   along diminishing ledges. Where they diminish completely,
   gain good hold above in base of acutely OH-crack. Thug
   style laybacking gains better holds in recess just below top.

38 **Punster's Crack**   *160 ft (48 m)   S*
FA: *J. Cunningham and W. Smith, 1949*
A fine route, open and spectacular on the last pitch.
Start: In base of short corner between Wild Country and gully
on R.
1. 50 ft (15 m) Layback up corner to easy ground. Trend diag.
   L past grass ledges to ledge near L arete. Block belay.
2. 50 ft (15 m) 4b Climb up and R to obvious ramp. Follow R
   until blocked by bulge and gap. Step sensationally across gap
   to belay at end of ramp overlooking gully.

3. 60 ft (18 m) The steep wall following shallow crack to top.

39 **Wide Country**   *165 ft (50 m)   E5 6b*
FA: *R. Campbell and P. Thorburn, 1994*
The meat of this is the striking off-width crack above the tr. of
Punster's Crack. Large camming devices are a must. Start up
Punster's Crack and continue direct to OH-off-width crack. Lots
of grunting will gain rest in niche. Swing R (spectacular) onto
easy slab to top.

40 **Evening Stroll**   *140 ft (42 m)   E2*
FA: *D. Cuthbertson and R. Kerr, 1979*
A steep first pitch up the OH-arete just R of Punster's Crack
(5a/b) leads to belay on Punster's Crack. The second pitch (4c)
climbs up wall to shallow crack as far as Punster's Crack, then
takes the line of the L-curving overlap, finishing at L end of
slab in a spectacular position.
The gully/recess R of Evening Stroll separates the third and
fourth buttresses. It gives a popular route (**Right Angled Gully,
VD ****), escaping R at two-thirds height along obvious ledge.
The wall to the R contains two excellent climbs.

41 **Rest and be Thankful**   *120 ft (36 m)   E5 6a*
FA: *D. Cuthbertson and K. Johnstone, 1980*
This climbs up the centre of the wall. The obvious crack further
R is Club Crack. Start below a short groove in centre of wall.
    Gain the groove direct with tricky moves. From its top swing
L round bulge, and tr. down and L to good footholds. Step
slightly L then directly up wall to R end of bulge at two-thirds
height (intricate). Pull over slightly R on huge pockets to
foot-ledge. Tr. L and pull on to ledge of Right Angled Gully.

42 **Club Crack**   *110 ft (33 m)   E2 5c*
FA: *P. Walsh and others, 1954*
This is the crack R of Rest and be Thankful.
    Start: In the cave in base of R-side of wall. Climb direct
through its apex then a further roof to gain crack. Strenuous and

Punster's Crack,
The Cobbler,
North Peak

sustained, and named in honour of the aspiring first
ascensionists, members of the Creagh Dhu Club. About eight
followed on the first ascent.

Right Angled Groove (S) escapes R from the Club Crack cave
on to grass terrace below an attractive continuation groove
bounding L side of Baillie's Overhang. This terrace can also be
gained by grovelling through the back of the cave.

The grass terrace continues R underneath Baillie's Overhang
(aided in 1967 by Rusty Baillie). Round to the R of Baillie's
Overhang is a stunning wall with three excellent routes. They
can be gained along the terrace or by descending from the top

of Ramshead Gully. It is better, however, to combine them with
Ramshead Gully and Whither Wall on the lower tier.

43 **Whither Whether**   *120 ft (36 m)   VS 4b*
FA: *H. MacInnes and W. Smith, 1952*
FA: *W. Smith and T. Paul, 1952 (variant finish)*
A steep route with a pronounced sense of exposure, this is one
of the finest routes of its grade in Scotland!
Start: Below the prow of Baillie's Overhang. Step on to steep
wall (Bolt R) and go up R round edge on to wall. Climb up
close to the L edge of the wall for approx. 70 ft (21 m) to R
side of niche. Step slightly R, and then to top of ridge. Easily
then to summit.
Or: Step L from the niche and climb the edge to the top (4b)
extremely airy and with poor protection.

44 **Grey Wall**   *120 ft (36 m)   HS 4b*
FA: *W. Rowney and M. Noon, 1952*
An excellent route up the wall R of Whither Whether.
Start: On the narrow grass ledge at base of wall about the
central point. Climb up and slightly R for 40 ft (12 m), then
direct on small holds up wall to top.

The Lower Tier
Ramshead Gully, 200 ft (60 m) D, an excellent example of
Cobbler chimney-climbing splits the L edge of the Lower Tier,
and where it opens out it leads to Grey Wall and Whither
Whether. The next route climbs the L wall of the lower part of
the gully:

45 **Whether Wall**   *100 ft (30 m)   VS 4c*
FA: *J. Cunningham and H. MacInnes, 1951*
A great climb, giving poorly protected balance work typical of
the Cobbler.
Start: From a grass ledge in Ramshead Gully above chockstones
and below deep chimney of gully. Step L on to wall and make
mantelshelf moves heading up to L-pointing flake. Pull over this

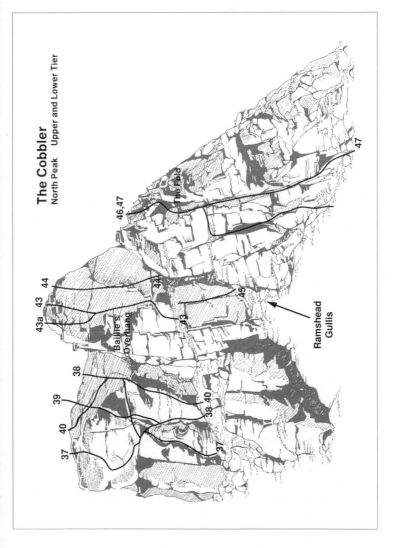

and climb groove above to terrace below Whither Whether, which gives the logical continuation.

46 **Recess Route**   *275 ft (85 m)   S*
FA: *J. Nimlin, J. Fox and R. Ewing, 1935*
Very popular, and perhaps the best of its grade.
Start: At the lowest rocks there is an OH-recess (Fold Direct). Just to its L is a cracked slab. Start here.
1. 65 ft (20 m) Climb the cracked slab until it steepens. Tr. hard R into a corner and over a short wall. The short slanting crack on the L leads to a belay in a deep chimney.
2. 100 ft (30 m) Up this chimney, passing OH on R (or direct). Deep chimney above to a terrace striking R 'wards from base of Ramshead Gully. Tr, Easily R along terrace to belay.
3. 30 ft (10 m) from R end of terrace step into the steep groove of The Fold, which is climbed on the L wall to a cave. Belay.
4. 80 ft (25 m) The OH above can be climbed on L or R to a platform. The recess above is climbed on the L wall to summit slopes.

47 **Fold Direct**   *275 ft (75 m)   VS*
FA: *J. B. Nimlin and R. Browning, 1936*
This is a direct line into the groove of The Fold, climbing the fault which runs up to the R-hand end of the terrace. It is climbed in three pitches, the second, a scoop, being the hardest.
Start: below corner 30 ft (10 m) R of Recess Route.
1. 80 ft (25 m) Follow corner to bulge. Avoid on L and gain ledge below steep scoop.
2. 50 ft (15 m) 4c Climb scoop to chimney.
3. 65 ft (20 m) Climb chimney to half-way terrace below The Fold. Continue up steep groove (The Fold) and belay in cave above.
4. 80 ft (25 m) Finish as for Recess Route.

THE BRACK   (345031) Alt. 2,000 ft (600 m) North facing ✗
The Brack lies across Glen Croe from the Cobbler. Its very impressive N face is the best piece of rock in the area.

However, like the Cobbler, the rock with its covering of lichen is greasy when damp and the face receives no sun.

Approach – From the entrance to the Ardgartan campsite cross a bridge and follow a forestry road R for about ½ mile (800 m). Just past a L and R loop, the track crosses a burn; take a path up its E side on to the open hillside below the coire. Follow the burn until convenient to break out R on to the alp below the lower buttress: allow 1 hr 30 mins.

Topography – On the E side of the coire are small outcrops. The main upper buttress is obvious. There are broken rocks below it and access is via a sloping ramp along its base going from L to R. The main wall consists of two large square-cut buttresses separated by a groove of dreadful rock. The described route climbs the impressive arete in the centre of the L hand buttress.

Descent – Go L and follow burn down into the coire E of the buttress.

48   **Edge of Extinction**   *300 ft (90 m)*   *E6*
FA: *P. Whillance and P. Botterill, 1980*
One of the best mountain routes in Scotland.
Start: As for Mammoth
1. 140 ft (42 m) 6a Climb the OH-recess as for Mammoth then direct up crack above to ledge at 40 ft (12 m). Move on to the wall just R of arete (Rurp Runner and PR), and up diag. R to flake. Steep wall above on small holds to ledge. Take hanging corner above PR, exiting L at top to ledges on the arete. Step down L to PB.
2. 150 ft (45 m) 6a R. side of arete for 20 ft (6 m) to small ledge. Up ramp on L side of arete till it merges with steep wall (2 PRS, one hand placed in pocket just above). Wall L to a ledge. Continue on good holds leading back to arete at 90 ft (27 m). Turn overlap above on R. Step back L on to arete and easily to top. Serious.

GLEN CROE   258044 Alt. 500 ft (150 m) South facing 🦋🦋
Only recently has the quality of climbs on the small crags of

Glen Croc been realized. Although short, these offer very steep climbing on easily accessible, quick-drying rock, and are a perfect choice when the 'clag' encircles the hilltops. The rock is liberally covered in small pockets, and has been brushed clean by local devotees.

Approach – About ½ mile (800 m) beyond the Creag-dhu Information Centre, there is a loop section of the old road on the R. Park here.

The crags can be seen, one above the other, on the spur of the hillside directly ahead. Upper Crag, the third and most distinctive outcrop encountered as one walks up the spur, is severely OH, split by arching roofs and up to 80 ft (24 m) high. This steepness ensures that it dries surprisingly quickly and may even rescue a rainy day! The lower outcrops provide good solo problems.

Upper Crag
Topography – The crag is split centrally by a large recess-cum-groove which is itself broken by two roofs (Hooded Groove). The routes are described L to R.

49 **Zig Zag**   *40 ft (12 m)   VD*
Bounding the L side is a cracked slab. Start up the slope a little and climb the cracks.

50 **Outside Edge**   *60 ft (18 m)   HVS 4c*
FA: *D. Griffiths and C. Bell, 1986*
Climbs directly up the L edge of the front face, just R of Zig Zag, passing a thread runner.

51 **All Heroes Die Young**   *60 ft (18 m)   E3 6a*
FA: *D. Griffiths, 1986*
This climbs a line of slim grooves in the L side of the wall, just round from outside Edge.
Start: On grass ledge 15 ft (5 m) up and L from base of face.

The Edge of Insanity, Glen Croe, Upper Crag: climber, Kevin Howett

Take the diag. crack R to large holds in horizontal break. PR. Climb direct (PR) to a large hold in L edge. Pull L to join top of Outside Edge (thread runner). Fingery blind climbing.

52 **The Hooded Groove** *80 ft (24 m)* *E2*
FA: *Creagh Dhu Members, 1930s*
FFA: *unknown*
Climbs through 12 ft (4 m) of horizontal rock.
1. 24 ft (7 m) 5c The deep inset recess is guarded by a 6 ft (2 m) roof. Climb directly through the crack to a stance.
2. 55 ft (17 m) 5b Climb the groove and layback round the R end of the upper roof to finish.

53 **The Edge of Insanity** *75 ft (23 m)* *E4 5c*
FA: *D. Griffiths, 1987* (bolt runner)
FA: *G. Latter, 1987* (bolt removed)
A poorly protected but sensational little route up the R arete of Hooded Groove.
Start: On the wall 15 ft (5 m) R of Hooded Groove. Pull up the steeply impending wall with an initial stretch move to blocky jugs, leading to an impasse below very steep upper wall. Tr. L to recess. Immediately pull up R arete to hanging ledge (loose block). Stand on ledge and swing wildly R to jugs.
Pose for photos and scuttle to top.

54 **Short Sharp Shock** *70 ft (21 m)* *E4 6a*
FA: *R. Bruce, 1986*
Further R the wall is more like a roof. R again are two vertical cracks. Climb the L-hand crack on stretchy finger-plugging with good protection. Feet seem redundant.
   The R-hand crack is **Double Clutching (E3 6a)** which has a fierce start.

3   LOCHABER

Introduction

Although not all strictly within the bounds of Lochaber, the
following cliffs are most conveniently grouped together.

Glen Coe provides a large number of good quality, high
mountain cliffs easily reached from the road, and comparisons
have been made with Llanberis Pass. However solitude is the
norm in Glen Coe, and the situations are far more impressive.
The weather is as reliable as in Wales, and only time will tell if
weekend queues for routes will become normal here too.

Ben Nevis offers both the massive brooding faces of the N
corries, with long mountain routes which are rarely in condition,
and a multitude of low-level crags in Glen Nevis. The latter is now
arguably the most important hard rock climbing centre in Scotland.

Also included are the 'Alpine' cliffs of Garbh Bheinn in
Ardgour, and the unique Etive Slabs on the E slopes of Beinn
Trilleachan, S of Glen Coe.

Finally, should the weather preclude any outdoor activity,
there is the climbing wall in Fort William to stave off boredom
and accelerate arthritis.

Access

Rail – King's Cross, London to Fort William, via Glasgow.
Bus – Glasgow to Fort William (City Link), BR connection at
Crianlarich; Fort William to Glencoe (local bus); Fort William
to Glen Nevis (local bus), summer only. Garbh Bheinn and
Glen Etive have no public transport.

Provisions

Fort William – supermarkets (late-closing Thursday), three
outdoor shops, and petrol station just N of town, which is
late-closing, open Sundays. *Glencoe/Ballachulish* – post offices/
shops in both villages, and late-closing grocer in Ballachulish.
Outdoor shop in Tighphuirst, near Glencoe. Most petrol stations
open Sundays.

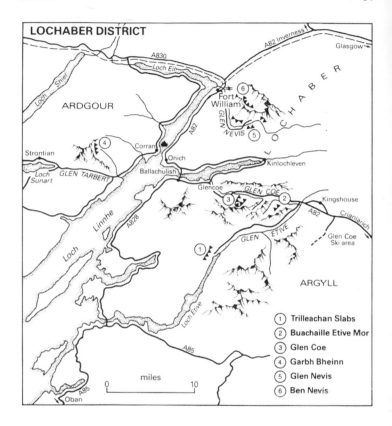

LOCHABER DISTRICT

1. Trilleachan Slabs
2. Buachaille Etive Mor
3. Glen Coe
4. Garbh Bheinn
5. Glen Nevis
6. Ben Nevis

Mountain Rescue

Glen Coe Mountain Rescue Team – Posts: Achnacon (119566), Kingshouse (259546) and Achnambeithach (140565) – all in or near Glen Coe.

Lochaber Mountain Rescue Team – Posts: police station, Fort
William (009736); CIC Hut, Coire Leis, Ben Nevis (167722)
has direct radio link to police. Steall Hut, Glen Nevis (177684).

Guidebooks
See individual areas

Maps
Landranger Series: for Glen Coe, Glen Nevis and Ben Nevis –
Ben Nevis, 41; for Glen Etive – Glen Orchy, 50; for Garbh
Bheinn – Loch Shiel, 40 and Oban and East Mull, 49.
Harvey Maps: Walker and Super Walker Series: Glen Coe, Ben
Nevis

Glen Coe and Buachaille Etive Mór

Introduction
The area is mainly composed of ice-scoured lava flows of
andesite and rhyolite. The climbing is mainly confined to the
latter, which is weather resistant and clean. The Etive Slabs, of
granite, lie outside the main area but have similar access, so
they are included in this section.

History
The earliest recorded climb occurred in 1868 when Neil
Marquis, a local shepherd, scrambled into Ossian's Cave.
Twenty-one years later the SMC was formed, but because of
difficult access to Glen Coe it concentrated initially on Skye. In
1894, however, the Fort William railway was built, and Norman
Collie recorded the first route on Buachaille Etive Mór.
Subsequent pioneers included James H. B. Bell, William Wilson
Naismith, the Abraham Brothers and, notably, Harold Raeburn.
    The war years intervened but when a new road was built into
Glen Coe in 1935, the recently formed Creagh Dhu Club
arrived to find acres of virgin rock. Although they would later
dominate the scene (monopolizing in particular the Buachaille),
in the early 1930s the SMC were still the major activists. One

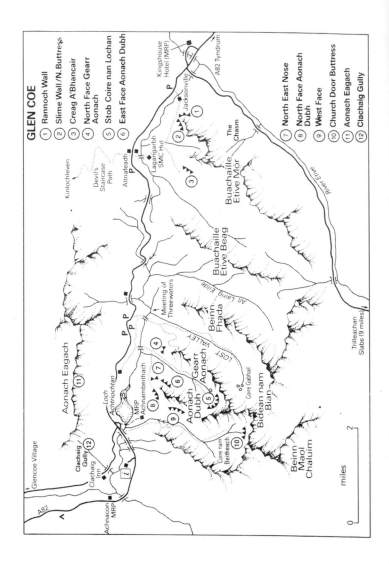

GLEN COE

1. Rannoch Wall
2. Slime Wall / N. Buttress
3. Creag A'Bhancair
4. North Face Gearr Aonach
5. Stob Coire nan Lochan
6. East Face Aonach Dubh

7. North East Nose
8. North Face Aonach Dubh
9. West Face
10. Church Door Buttress
11. Aonach Eagach
12. Clachaig Gully

of the talented youngsters, Hamish Hamilton, did Agag's
Groove in 1936, beating Bill MacKenzie to it by half an hour.
This must have been an intimidating on-sight lead on the
deceptively blank-looking Rannoch Wall. Ian H. Ogilvie of the
Junior Mountaineering Club of Scotland also put up some
brilliant routes on Rannoch Wall including Red Slab (VS),
which he led in plimsolls in 1939.

By 1946 the Creagh Dhu were making their mark. John
Cunningham climbed Gallow's Route on the Buachaille.
Strenuous, poorly protected and climbed in gym shoes, it still
warrants E1 5b. The same year Bill Murray found the classic
easy route Archer Ridge on the East Face of Aonach Dubh.
Slime Walls's apparent impregnability was breached in 1948
when Cunningham, seconded by Bill Smith, climbed Guerdon
Grooves (HVS), tying two ropes together in order to reach a
spike belay high up the face. Forty members of the Creagh Dhu
watched, and some described it as unjustifiable, but it led the
way for Pat Walsh and J. R. Marshall (an East-coaster), to blitz
it with routes in the 1950s.

The Etive Slabs were explored by a Cambridge University
party led by Eric Langmuir in 1954, giving Spartan Slab (VS).
Three years later the Creagh Dhu arrived and the main lines,
including Swastika, fell to Mick Noon, Cunningham and others.
This burst of activity peaked in 1958/9. The Cunningham/Noon
partnership succeeded on Carnivore (E2) on Creag a' Bhancair
in 1958, after Don Whillans had earlier cracked the entry pitch.
Then Cunningham did Bluebell Grooves next to Gallow's Route
on the Buachaille. Even with plenty of aid it was regarded by
Cunningham as his hardest route.

The Creagh Dhu's dominance began to be toppled when
East-coasters Robin Smith and Dougal Haston entered the
scene. Smith climbed Shibboleth (E2) next to Guerdon Grooves
in 1958. This poorly protected route was one of the hardest in
the country (Vector in Wales being still two years away). Smith
and others worked at routes for several days, and Shibboleth's
true finish in 1959 was a result of this approach. Also in 1959
Smith and D. Hughes succeeded where Whillans had retreated

on Aonach Dubh's North Face, to give Yo Yo (E1). 'E' Buttress gave Haston Hee Haw (E1), then a race for the great corner of Trapeze (E1) ensued between Smith and Marshall, with Marshall topping out first. This was reversed a year later when Smith climbed Marshall's Wall (E2) on Gearr Aonach after his rival had failed.

In 1961 Smith and Jimmy Gardner did the stunning Big Top (E1) on 'E' Buttress, whilst Whillans returned to Carnivore, enjoying revenge with a fine direct finish. But the 1960s was a decade of change, clouded by Smith's death in the Pamirs. Haston moved to Switzerland and Walsh to Manchester. Despite this, Scotland received its first E3 when John Jackson and Rab Carrington, two talented new members of the Creagh Dhu, climbed The Pinch on Etive.

The 1970s produced new names and new styles, local climbers being influenced by events in England. Sight-leads of hard lines continued, with Ed and Cynthia Grindley's Clearances (E3), Ken Johnstone's impressive lead of Eldorado and Spacewalk (E5), Tut Braithwaite's ascent of the lichenous Scansor (E2), and Dougie Mullins's free ascent of Freakout (E4), a saga started by Walsh in 1960. Indeed Nick Coltons Le Monde on Creag a' Bhancair (E5), was regarded as the hardest route in the area.

Gradually abseil cleaning caught on. Willy Todd inspected Flyman in 1976, and in 1980 Lakelander Pete Whillance did likewise to the major line of The Risk Business (E5) on Creag a' Bhancair. In 1981 Dave Cuthbertson climbed Revengance on Aonach Dubh, after inspection to establish Scotland's first recorded E6, but took a 70 ft (21 m) fall on the relatively easier second pitch. In complete contrast, he blindly sight-led Prophet of Purism (E6) that same year. In 1984, Cuthbertson with Kevin Howett breached the left side of Creag a' Bhancair with Romantic Reality (E7). With sport climbing becoming more prevalent in England some Scots climbers began searching for possible venues in Scotland. As a result the Tunnel Wall on Creag a'Bhancair was breached in 1986 with a limited number of bolts or other in-situ gear to produce two routes whose character was both sport and bold. Cuthbertson climbed Uncertain Emotions (E6) using some hammered nuts (later replaced by bolts) and Graeme Livingston produced Fated Path (E6) on bolts, the names reflecting the polarised feelings of these two climbers towards their placement (polarised views shared by many of Scotland's leading climbers ever since).

Creag a'Bhancair became the main centre of interest over the following years and saw several more 'traditional' routes climbed by this pair, including Waltzing Ostriches and Gone With the Wind (both E6) from Cuthbertson and The Twighlight Zone (E6) from Livingston. More lines with in-situ gear followed with Admission (E6, Livingston), and The Railway Children (E6, Cuthbertson). The only other additions of note to other crags in Glen Coe were Howett's Salome (E5) on Aonach Dubh and Fringe Benefits (E5) on Gear Aonach; The Chant of Jimmy Blacksmith (E5) on Aonach Dubh and Creag Dhont Woll (E5) on the very traditional venue of North Buttress on Buachaille Etive Mor, both from Mark McGowan. Further additions to the Tunnel Wall started in 1990 with Paul Laughlan's Tribeswoman (E6 with some bolts) and in 1991, Up With The Sun (E6) from Grant Farquhar and Gary Latter. Cuthbertson showed he wasn't finished with the adventurous side of climbing on the Buachaille when he added The New Testament (E4) to Slime Wall and Symbiosis (E8) to the Tunnel Wall.

Very recent additions to Glen Coe have included the discovery of Yosemite Walls and the retro-bolting of the Tunnel Wall routes to create sport style lines rather than the original hybrids – an act that is sure to reactivate the whole debate of bolts on mountain crags.

Accommodation
Camping – Invercoe Camping and Caravan site (099595), Glencoe village on the lochside; Forestry Commission site (112578) 1 mile (1.6 km) SE of Glencoe village; Red Squirrel site (116578) Leacantium on old road between Glencoe village and Clachaig Inn.

Rough Camping – Kingshouse Hotel (260547); banks of River Etive; Glen Etive (109450) road-head car-park.

Bunkhouses – Red Squirrel (116578), Leacantium, tel: 01855 811256; Inchree, Onich (024632), P. Heron, tel: 01885 821287 (with a café); Glencoe Mountain Cottages at Gleann-leac-na-muidhe (112551), tel: 01855 811598: The Glencoe Outdoor Centre in the village, tel: 01855 811350; In nearby Kinlochleven are West Highland Lodge, tel: 01855 831471 and Manmore Lodge Hotel Bunkhouse, tel: 01855 831213.

Club Huts – Bookable through the club secretaries. Blackrock Cottage (267531), Ladies' Scottish Climbing Club, by White Corries Ski Area; Lagangarbh Cottage (222559), SMC, Altnafeadh, below Buachaille Etive Mór; MacIntyre Memorial Hut (045611), MCofS/BMC, North Ballachulish; Manse Barn (033613), Lomond CC Hut. Onich Hotel; Inbhirfhaolain House (158507), Grampian Club Hut, Glen Etive.

Youth Hostel – Leacantium (116576), on old road by Red Squirrel Bunkhouse.

Hotels – The Clachaig Inn (128568), traditional climbers' pub with real ale (plus yearly festival) and food, regular slide shows and good accommodation (B&B and Chalets); The Kingshouse (260547), another traditional climbers' hotel at the opposite end of Glen Coe offers usual hotel food and accommodation, climbers' bar and live music; Creag Mhor Hotel, North Ballachulish also offers facilities for climbers.

Guidebook
Glen Coe, Rock and Ice Climbs, K. V. Crocket, R. Anderson and D. Cuthbertson, SMC, 1992. Update due 2000.

ETIVE SLABS   (097446) Alt. 1,100 ft (300 m) South-east facing 🦋 🦋 🦋
Magnificent sheets of smooth granite lying 1¼ miles (2 km) beyond the road-head car-park down Glen Etive. Most of the harder routes are pure friction, but the more amenable classics follow flakes, corners and cracks, with only short stretches of

poorly protected uncertainty. It has been said that if they inclined one degree more steeply, then some routes would be unclimbable, and if one degree less steeply, then they could be walked up. As it is, the climbing can be described as extreme walking. The major threat on a visit is the midge, which makes grown men run, young men weep, and knowledgeable men abstain on calm days in July and August.

Approach – A boggy path from the road-head leads to the R end of the slabs and the 'Coffin Stone': 30 mins.

Topography – The 'Coffin Stone' lies at the base of the main sweep of slabs. These are crossed by two horizontal curving overlaps and capped by a vertical headwall. To the L the slabs are bounded by the huge corner of Agony rising the full height of the wall. The even larger corner L again is taken by Hammer. Routes are described R to L.

Descent – A good path down a heather rake on the R side of the main slabs, separating them from the less impressive upper slabs.

55 **The Long Reach**   *653 ft (198 m)*   *E1*
FA: *J. McLean and W. Smith, 1963*
A brilliant sustained route, with some serious slab sections.
Start: Off the 'Coffin Stone'.
1. 120 ft (36 m) 5b Climb the middle of the slab into a corner curving R as an overlap. Pull over to gain ledge (Spartan Slab belay).
2. 140 ft (42 m) 5b Undercling R along diag. twin overlaps above to large pocket in slab above; gain horizontal quartz band. Follow L into tiny L-facing corner (NR). Up and L across slab to gain R end of small overlap, then up to corner. Near its top, exit L to ledge and tree below main overlap. (Junction with Swastika).
3. 50 ft (15 m) 5a Up to main overlap. Pull over (PR). Move R a little and up to ledge in base of short corner.
4. 140 ft (42 m) 5b Move out L of corner and up slabs past quartz pocket to gain small corner. 'Reach' L for flat hold and crack, then up direct to mini marooned overlap.
5. 80 ft (24 m) 5b Step on to lip of overlap. Black bulging slab

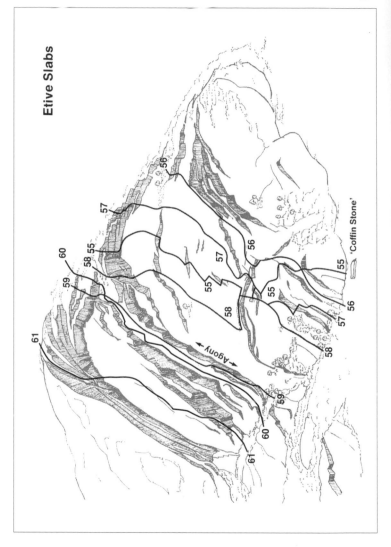

Etive Slabs

above easing to gain large overlap. Move R to below diag. crack splitting it.

6. 130 ft (39 m) 5b Crack through overlap and groove above to obvious line leading L to a sentry box in L end of upper walls. Exit this via crack on the R to grass ledges.

56 **Spartan Slab**   *624 ft (189 m)   VS*
FA: *E. Langmuir, M. J. O'Hara and J. Mallinson, 1954*
This climbs up the R side of the main slab.
Start: 12 ft (3 m) L of the 'Coffin Stone' at a shallow R-facing groove with lodged blocks at 30 ft (9 m).

1. 125 ft (38 m) 4a Up groove past blocks till it peters out. Step R over corner and lower slab. Up flake to ledge.

2. 85 ft (26 m) 4a Climb slab off R end of ledge to flake overlap. Follow flake corner above until possible to step R past arete, then up over step to ledge and tree.

3. 109 ft (33 m) 4c Up under overlap. L into recess. Pull over (hard) and up crack to crevasse ledge. Up thin vertical crack to horizontal crack; follow R to easier ledges leading L, and up to ledge. Tree belay near edge.

4. 105 ft (32 m) 4c Up crack into corner. Pull round L arete into crack (PR), and then to bulge. Step R under bulge to block in lip on R. Crack above through bulging rock to slab and small ledge. A lovely pitch.

5. 119 ft (36 m) 4b Up cracks and shallow R-facing corner to grass ledge.

6. 80 ft (24 m) Scramble up directly above, then L along ledge into short exit chimney.

57 **The Pause**   *630 ft (190 m)   HVS*
FA: *J. R. and R. Marshall, G. J. Ritchie and G. Tiso, 1960*
Sustained, with one section a little harder.
Start: 20 ft (6 m) L of 'Coffin Stone', at thin groove up slab L of Spartan.

1. 80 ft (24 m) 4c Up thin groove (peg scars), then out L on to bigger groove (PR). Up this for 20 ft (6 m), then swing out L by large spike to gain heather ledges and tree.

2. 60 ft (18 m) 4c Back R to edge of bigger groove, and follow layback flake along its lip and easier slab to small heather ledge.
3. 70 ft (21 m) 5b Straight up to small overlap (as for Swastika). Tr. R into corner leading up to main overlap. Tr. R under it (crux) to 'crevasse'.
4. 130 ft (39 m) 5b Gain slab above and enter groove on L. This leads over overlap to ledge (PR). Tr. R to faint line of cracks leading to small bulge. Move R to stance.
5. 140 ft (42 m) 4c Continue R to R end of higher overlap, and climb thin crack to easy groove leading to grass ledge at R end of second main overlap.
6. 100 ft (30 m) 5a Climb overlaps on L to final slab. Tr. L to an undercut edge. Up this to grass ledge.
7. 50 ft (15 m) 5a Vertical corner on L to top.

58 **Swastika**   *625 ft (187 m)*   E2
FA: *M. Noon and E. Taylor, 1957*
FFA: *W. Todd and J. Wilson, 1977*
The long-time classic of the slabs, this is particularly good on the crucial quartz-band pitches.
Start: From the 'Coffin Stone' go L past an area of grass and trees to the next clean slab, and start at R-hand of two parallel cracks.
1. 110 ft (33 m) 5a Climb crack to ledge.
2. 110 ft (33 m) 4c Move R across ledges and up to highest heather ledge. Up slab to small overlap above. Pull over direct, and up to ledge and tree under main overlap.
3. 75 ft (22 m) 5a Move slightly R and pull over overlap (PR, common with The Long Reach). Tr. L along the break in lip and remains of The Moustache to a ledge.
4. 110 ft (33 m) 4c The quartz band runs up the slab R'wards to a grass ledge.
5. 100 ft (30 m) 4c The quartz band continues up to the upper main overlap, by which time the leader is in extremis. This pitch has been climbed without the use of hands.
6. 60 ft (18 m) 5b Pull through the hanging corner, through overlap. Slab leads up to tree below upper wall.

7. 60 ft (18 m) 5c Climb a smaller corner L of main corner to top. Well protected.

The great corner bounding the L side of the main slab is **Agony** (**E2 5c 5c 5c**). It climbs the corner for 50 ft (15 m), then tr. R to recess in slab (PR). Then slab L'wards over small overlap to corner again, belay. This is climbed to grass, then goes diag. R up slab to overlap, and up to nut belay. Directly up to next overlap, then move 15 ft (4 m) R to good holds and stance. The corner above leads to small overlap. Then a tr. L across slab to tree. The OH-wall leads to final slabs. Good climb, but slow to dry.

59 **Pinch Direct**   *640 ft (192 m)   E3*
  FA: *R. Carrington and J. Jackson, 1968*
  FA: *M. Hamilton, B. Duff and D. Jameson, 1978 (direct)*
  FA: *R. Anderson and K. Spence, 1984 (true finish)*
  The huge corner to L of that of Agony is Hammer. The Pinch climbs up the R edge of the slab of Hammer, via a small inset corner.
  Start: As at the foot of the Agony corner.
  1. 120 ft (36 m) 5c Climb the first 10 ft (3 m) of corner, then move up L into inset slab. Continue past a constriction when corner is only inches wide to stance (PB).
  2. 70 ft (21 m) 5c The continuation corner to heather ledge of Hammer in centre of slab.
  3. 65 ft (19 m) 5c The slab trending R to a steepening The Pinch gives the key to reach large pocket (Friends 2 and 3). Cleaned crack on R leads to foothold stance on edge.
  4. 130 ft (39 m) 5b Climb straight up long clean crack, easy at first until it fades. Step R with a hard move to thin crack leading to guarding overlap; pull over on jugs and along Moustache above overlap to stance of Hammer above a chimney.
  5. 115 ft (34 m) 4c Slabs and two steep corners through overlaps to below final wall.
  6. 80 ft (24 m) 5b/c Tr. L to a chimney. Up this and walls above to tree.
  7. 60 ft (18 m) Cracks to finish.

60 **Hammer**   *495 ft (150 m)*   *HVS*
FA: *M. Noon and J. Cunningham, 1957 (with tension aid in scoop)*
FFA: *Unknown*
Climbs the huge corner up and L of the Agony Corner.
Generally well-protected classic. Start by scramble to base of corner.

1. 50 ft (15 m) 4a Corner to tree.
2. 115 ft (35 m) 4b Climb cracked slab R of corner to stance near top of heather patch.
3. 80 ft (25 m) 5a Above is a shallow 'scoop' in slab. A forceful approach is needed to get up it to gain main corner-line again. Continue to belay halfway up corner.
4. 135 ft (40 m) 5a Corner for 65 ft (20 m) (PR). Out R across slab for 10 ft (3 m) to gain cracks leading to large OH. Move R into recess and pull over OH into base of main corner-line.
5. 115 ft (35 m) 4b Corner, then undercuts R under overlap, then diag. R to exit onto descent path.

61 **Jaywalk**   *640 ft (190 m)*   *E1*
FA: *J. R. Marshall, J. Moriarty and J. Stenhouse, 1960 (4PA)*
FFA: Unknown
Climbs slab L of Corner of Hammer. Start near R edge of slab on heather rake L of Hammer.

1. 120 ft (35 m) 5b Climb two-tiered groove in bulging slab and R-trending continuation onto upper slab. Step L then up to belay.
2. 150 ft (45 m) 5a Step R and follow grooves to further belay.
3. 150 ft (45 m) 5a Follow grooves to grass patch. Move L 3 ft (1 m) and up slab to grass ledge.
4. 120 ft (35 m) 5b From grass ledge above, climb short wall (spike) and up crack and groove. Move R and into grassy groove. Belay.
5. 100 ft (30 m) Vegetated ground leads to top.

The Pinch, Etive Slabs

BUACHAILLE ETIVE MOR   (223543)

Known popularly as 'the Buachaille' (the big shepherd), and pronounced Bookle Etiv Mor, it is essentially a 2½ mile (4 km) ridge whose NE summit, Stob Dearg 3,403 ft (1,022 m) overlooks Rannoch Moor. The flanks of Stob Dearg contain numerous cliffs in a complex layout. The main ones are the following (see diagram opposite):

Central Buttress – forms the L side of Easy Gully opposite the waterslide. Its E wall is a prominent smooth red face. Rannoch Wall – Crowberry Ridge defines the L side of Crowberry Gully. Its L (E) face is the impressive Rannoch Wall.

North Buttress, East Wall – lies immediately R of the base of Crowberry Gully.

Slime Wall – the W wall of North Buttress overlooking Great Gully.

Great Gully Buttress – directly opposite Slime Wall, across Great Gully.

Creag A'Bhancair – separate from main mass, and lying on W side of Stob Coire nan Tulaich, which is the subsidiary (N) summit of the Buachaille, W of Stob Dearg.

Approach – There are two paths. One leads from large car-park ½ mile (1 km) W of the Etive/Kingshouse junction. Stepping-stones cross River Coupal to Jacksonville Hut, and path leads up to waterslide. The second goes from lay-by at Altnafeadh, via a footbridge across River Coupall to Lagangarbh Hut. A path leads up into Coire na Tuilach. Another path branches off L, skirting base of hill to the waterslide.

Descent off summit – Follow path S from summit for ½ mile (1 km) and descend Coire na Tuilach (216542), or down Curved Ridge (M).

Central Buttress   (227545) Alt. 1,900 ft (600 m) East facing 🦋🦋

The E (L) face clearly seen from the Kingshouse is smooth and red. It forms a narrow buttress on its R known as the North Face. The L side of the buttress is defined by a grassy gully which disappears higher up at a terrace skirting buttress.

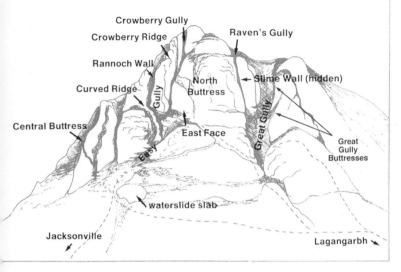

Buachaille Etive Mor

Crowberry Gully

Crowberry Ridge

Raven's Gully

Rannoch Wall

North Buttress

← Slime Wall (hidden)

Curved Ridge

Easy Gully

Great Gully

Central Buttress

East Face

Great Gully Buttresses

waterslide slab

Jacksonville

Lagangarbh ↘

62 **North Face Route**   *726 ft (220 m)   VD*
FA: *J. H. B. Bell and A. Hanson, 1929*
Start: At bottom L toe of this grassy gully. Scramble up easy
slabs to main rocks (spike belay L of rock niche). Climb series
of corners and walls, negotiating final steep wall via L hand
crack. Easy scrambling, bearing slightly L, gains heather ledge.
Climb up for 5 ft (1 m), to obvious tr. R round edge. Up to
recess. Go up R to ledge, then up awkward wall to R-slanting

ledge. Follow to chimney. Climb chimney to gain grass ledge.
Tr. L on sloping holds to short steep crack near edge of
buttress. Follow this to top. Belay where necessary.

Descent – Go R above a gully and buttress to gain Curved
Ridge beside Rannoch Wall. Down this, or combine with
Crowberry Ridge Direct Route to top Route No. 68.

The Rannoch Wall   (226544) Alt. 2,700 ft (800 m) East facing ✻
This is probably the best-known face on the Buachaille. Its
steepness and profusion of holds and alarming exposure give
reasonably graded routes in situations normally associated with
extreme routes. Dries quickly and receives sun all morning.

Approach – Follow wandering path up Easy Gully on L of
waterslide to open bowl below base of Crowberry Gully. Easy
Gully deepens and narrows above bowl to run up L under L
side of Crowberry Ridge. Follow its rocky rib (Curved Ridge,
M) to below wall: 1 hr 15 mins.

Topography – Easy Gully separates Curved Ridge from the
wall. The gully is blocked half-way up by a cave. Above the
cave, the gully and the ridge meet as a level platform before
rearing up and becoming separate again. Above the platform the
wall is split in two by an area of broken grassy rock. The most
obvious feature of the whole wall is a snaking groove-line up
the R-hand edge (Agag's Groove). At the far L end of the wall
Easy Gully forms another cave.

Descent – All routes finish on easy upper section of
Crowberry Ridge. Scramble up this to tower which can be
by-passed easily on L (E) to gain top of Curved Ridge.
Scramble down this to base of wall.

63 **Grooved Arete**   *(65 m)   HS*
FA: *J. Cunningham and W. Smith, 1946*
Excellent exposed and poorly protected climbing up R edge of
wall. Start at small groove immediately R of edge (L of small
chimney marking start of Crowberry Ridge Direct Route).

North Face Route, Buachaille Etive Mór

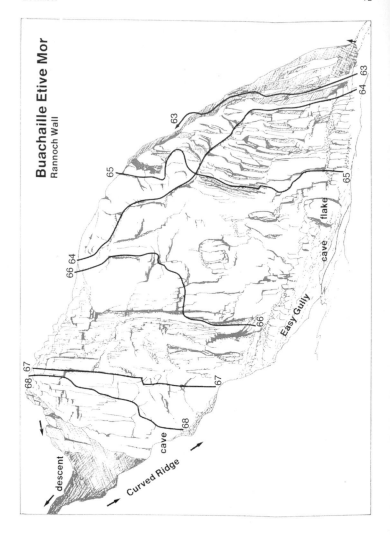

Buachaille Etive Mor
Rannoch Wall

63

65

66 64

67
68

descent

66

Easy Gully

cave

flake

65

64 63

67

68

cave

Curved Ridge

1. 80 ft (25 m) Climb groove on small holds until move L possible to block belay in base of groove of Agag's Groove.
2. 135 ft (40 m) Gain arete on R and make delicate tr. R to regain line of original groove. Follow this trending R across the wall to below the more defined part of Crowberry Ridge. Follow this to top, 250 ft (75 m).

64 **Agag's Groove**   *330 ft (99 m)   VD*
FA: *J. G. Hamilton, A. Anderson, A. and D. Small, 1936*
The snaking L'ward-leaning groove rising from bottom R to top L can be seen from the road. Probably the most frequently climbed route on the Buachaille – but tread as delicately as the biblical character who gave it its name.
Start: At a large detached rectangular block at the extreme R end of the face (R round the corner is a smooth slabby groove (Grooved Arete, S)).
1. 90 ft (27 m) Crack behind the block soon becomes a corner. Follow it until one can reach a block belay at the start of the groove line (crux).
2. 100 ft (30 m) Easily follow the groove to another block belay.
3. 75 ft (23 m) Continue up the groove until an easy tr. L leads on to the exposed face below a projecting nose of rock. Climb the nose by a narrow groove and go L to a block belay.
4. 65 ft (20 m) Move L and up the face to the ridge.

65 **January Jigsaw**   *225 ft (68 m)   S*
FA: *H. I. Ogilvy and Miss E. Speakman, 1940*
A better companion route to Agag's Groove. Hard, excellent climbing, interest increasing with height. There is a large semi-detached flake in the bed of the gully about midway between Agag's Groove and the cave pitch of Easy Gully.
Start: At a pinnacle on grass ledge midway between Agag's Groove and this flake.
1. 65 ft (20 m) Straight up a crack for 20 ft (6 m), then up and L by large rock steps to big flake. Tr. R along a ledge to obvious flake belay.

2. 65 ft (20 m) Move R and climb flake, then a wall, and straight up to the block belay below the nose of Agag's.
3. 50 ft (15 m) From the top of the block tr. R round an edge into a slanting groove; follow this into triangular niche of The Haven then tr. L to reach PB below on OH-crack.
4. 60 ft (19 m) Tr. up and R (wild). Swing round an edge and into groove, up this a short distance until one can climb L on to steep wall (crux). From its top either an easy groove on R or final section of the OH-crack.

66 **Red Slab**   *270 ft (85 m)   VS*
FA: *H. I. Ogilvy and Miss E. Speakman, 1939*
Start: 15 ft (3 m) above the cave pitch of Easy Gully at an OH-groove.
1. 65 ft (20 m) 4b Up the groove and wall above to small stance at bottom L of rock nose.
2. 100 ft (30 m) 5a Step to R round nose, tr. across a ledge and climb the Red Slab on small holds. Tr. round OH and continue up 15 ft (3 m) to a corner. Up it and vertical wall above (crux) then easier to nut belay.
3. 100 ft (30 m) Easy rock to finish about 15 ft (4 m) L of Agag's Groove.

67 **Line Up**   *240 ft (72 m)   HVS*
FA: *C. Higgins and I. Nicholson, 1969*
One of the best routes on the wall. About 45 ft (13 m) above the cave pitch of Easy Gully is a short vegetated chimney (start of Route 1, the first breach of the wall in 1934 by G. G. McPhee and party). To its L is a large red slab with a small overlapping slab on its top.
Start: At bottom R of this red slab.
1. 80 ft (24 m) 4c Up the R side of the slab, climbing a small corner and stepping L above the small overlapping slab. Step R and belay.

January Jigsaw, Buachaille Etive Mór

   2. 80 ft (24 m) 5a The corner above for 15 ft (4 m). Step L and
      up to foot of groove.

   3. 80 ft (24 m) 5a Climb the groove and the roof above direct
      to top.

68 **Peasant's Passage**   *230 ft (69 m)   HVS*
    FA: *W. Rowney and H. MacInnes, 1952*
    Between Line Up and the second cave of Easy Gully on the L
    is a shallow corner – this is it.

   1. 50 ft (15 m) 4c Up corner for 15 ft (4 m), and swing R on to
      a rib. Tr. slabs on the R to narrow rock ledge. Follow it R to
      a stance.

   2. 60 ft (18 m) 4c Up round an edge to steep wall with shallow
      crack. Climb to the L for a few feet, with easier broken
      rocks leading to nut belay.

   3. 120 ft (36 m) 4b Above and R climb a steep corner to white
      rock spike. Swing on to rib on the R and continue to top.

69 **Crowberry Ridge**   *675 ft (202 m)   S*
    FA: *W. W. Naismith, W. Douglas, 1896 (original route)*
    FA: *Abraham Bros, Putrell, Baker, 1900 (direct route)*
    A route of historical interest climbed by bald men in tweeds. At
    R end of Rannoch Wall (round R of Agag's Groove) is a
    well-marked 20 ft (6 m) chimney (M), leading to the first
    platform.
    Start: At the R end of this platform near Crowberry Gully (at
    the 2nd large pinnacle leaning against the wall).

   1. 120 ft (36 m) Climb shallow chimney facing L side of
      pinnacle to its top. Wall above leads to Abraham's Ledge.

   2. 60 ft (18 m) Tr. L in exposed position. Balance up on slopies
      to gain a scoop (crux). Go diag. R, gaining large holds
      leading to upper ledge (can be avoided by descending R
      from Abraham's Ledge down a chimney on to lower part of
      upper ledge – Naismith's Route).

   3. 60 ft (18 m) Tr. L and go round an edge.

   4. 250 ft (75 m) Two long slabs (M) lead to easy ground. From
      here scrambling leads to Crowberry Tower, easily climbed

direct on its N side. Descent is down a spiral from top of W flank into gap (gully down L back to top of Curved Ridge, or cross gap and up path to summit).

North Buttress – East Face   (225545) Alt. 2,700 ft (800 m) ✗
The large flat face to the R of Crowberry Gully. The rock is clean and solid, and gives one- or two-pitch climbs. Remains dry over most of its length after heavy rain.

Approach – Up Easy Gully on L of waterslide to open bowl below start of Curved Ridge. Break out R and gain the terrace below the wall: 1 hr 10 mins.

Topography – The wall is split into two tiers by a diag. grassy gully (Green gully). 25 ft (8 m) from L end of wall is area of rough red rock 15 ft (5 m) up, split by hanging crack (Brevity Crack, VS 5a). To its L is a shallow, slanting groove (VD). The upper tier's most prominent feature is a large open corner (Hangman's Crack): see diagram on p. 78.

Descent – Tr. R down Green Gully, or R above upper tier to descend easy rocks of North Buttress.

About 6 ft (2 m) R of Brevity Crack is another very prominent crack which gives the following excellent classic route, which ascends both tiers:

70 **Shackle Route**   *280 ft (85 m)*   S
FA: *S. H. Cross and Miss A. M. Nelson, 1936*
In case you've missed the obvious line, 'Shackle' is etched into its base.
1. 130 ft (40 m) Climb crack for 60 ft (18 m), then move on to L wall. Up this (crux), and gain sentry box. Continue up the crack. After 45 ft (14 m), easy rocks lead to Green Gully.
2. 150 ft (45 m) Directly above, a tall pinnacle flake is set against a corner with a jammed block between it and the L wall. Either up the black groove on R of pinnacle, or up over block to gain slanting groove. At its top a steep wall and easy rocks gain high ledge.

Buachaille Etive Mor
North Buttress   East Face

71 **Crow's Nest Crack**   *255 ft (68 m)   VS*
FA: *J. Cunningham and P. McGonagle, 1946*
15 ft (4 m) R of Shackle Route is a grassy recess at base of
crag. A long narrow crack springs up from its overhung top.
This is the line. Good sustained climbing.
Start: Just L of recess at thin vertical line (Shattered Crack,
VS).
1. 150 ft (45 m) 4c Climb up on good holds for 10 ft (3 m).
    Diag. R for another 25 ft (8 m). Make an awkward step at a
    corner and tr. R into narrow crack. Follow this until a long
    step L below small roof can be made on to a slab. The slab,
    then regain the crack. Where it divides over O H-nose, follow
    L branch to Green Gully.
2. 75 ft (23 m) 4b On the upper tier climb the black groove on
    R side of pinnacle of Shackle Route, and go R to gain
    obvious crack. Follow it to high ledge.

72 **Mainbrace Crack**   *150 ft (45 m)   HVS 5a*
FA: *P. Walsh and W. Smith, 1955*
Continuing R from the grassy O H-recess, there is an obvious
deep recess (Bottleneck Chimney) after 35 ft (10 m).
Start: Between these two, at a groove. Climb the groove to an
O H at 10 ft (3 m). Gain a crack. Up this for 30 ft (8 m), gaining
a groove part way, then quit this L'wards up wall for 12 ft
(4 m) to gain an open groove. Follow it to beneath the O H.
Gain a foothold on edge on R (hard – crux). Climb the steep
delicate groove above, then move R and finish up steep wall on
good holds to Green Gully.

73 **Bottleneck Chimney**   *130 ft (39 m)   HS*
FA: *R. G. Donaldson, J. R. B. McCarter, 1941*
Takes the obvious bottle-shaped deep recess about 15 ft (5 m)
from the R end of the terrace. It can be seen from the road.
Closer acquaintance shows it not to be a true chimney but a
recessed crack. Recommended.

74 **Gallow's Route**   *100 ft (30 m)   E1   5c*
FA: *J. Cunningham and I. Dingwall, 1947*
Tortuous, poorly protected climbing with a delicate crux. R of
Bottleneck Chimney a broad nose projects from the face,
forming a corner. R of this is a shallow chimney leading up to a
platform. Gain the platform either up chimney or easy rock to
R. Step on to face and tr. L (crux) to reach steep scoop. Up
this, taking OH on L. Up another scoop to roof. Breach it on R
by shelf. A third scoop is followed till a tr. L gains better holds,
leading to stance. Scramble up to Green Gully.

The following climbs are on the upper tier above Green Gully.
They are good as continuations to the climbs listed above:

75 **Hangman's Crack**   *110 ft (35 m)   VS 4c*
FA: *R. G. Donaldson and G. M. B. McCarter, 1941*
The original continuation to Bottleneck Chimney.
Start: Below obvious steep, clean-cut corner about 40 ft (12 m)
above and R of Bottleneck Chimney. Scramble up to sloping
ledge and belay. Go up and slightly R. An awkward mantelshelf
follows (crux). Move L into the corner crack and up it until a
tr. on to the R wall can be made (long stretch – gibbons only).
Steep climbing to top.

76 **Garotte**   *110 ft (33 m)   VS 5a*
FA: *J. Cunningham and M. Noon, 1955*
A hard route taking the slabs R of Hangman's Corner.
Start: 10 ft (3 m) R of Hangman's at obvious thin crack. Up
crack to grass ledge (crux). Continue above over OH and rock
ledges to the top.

Mainbrace Crack, Buachaille Etive Mór: climber, Billy Hood

Buachaille Etive Mor

Slime Wall

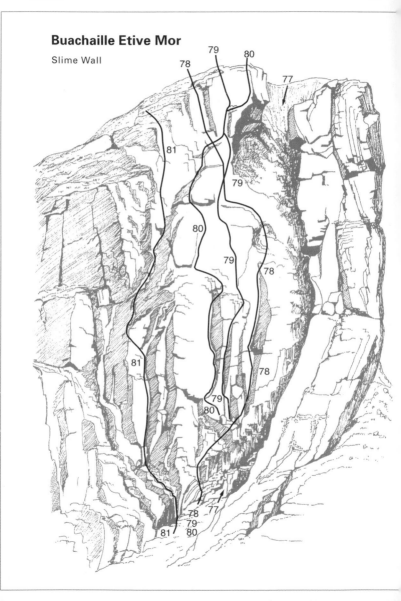

North Buttress – West Face (Slime Wall)   (225546) Alt.
2,500 ft (750 m)
Steep and gloomy, but awe-inspiring. It is misnamed, there being
little vegetation, but it weeps somewhat and requires a dry spell. It
is composed of steep slim grooves with sloping holds, and with
less protection than one would like. Receives little sun.

Approach – Cross River Coupal by bridge at Lagangarbh. Big
path leads up into Coire na Tulaich. Branch off L just behind
hut, and follow another path till below the start of Great Gully.
Either the L or R bank can be followed, until you can enter
Great Gully's broad upper section, and so to base of wall: 1 hr.

Topography – The deep chimney gully of Raven's is obvious.
The main wall lies to its L. Prominent in the centre of the wall
are two parallel grooves (Bludgers and Lecher's Routes). R of
these are a series of slimmer grooves, the larger being
Shibboleth, streaked black and usually wet.

Descent – Follow a descending shelf R across top of Raven's
Gully into Great Gully. Scramble down this with care (loose
rubble).

77 **Raven's Gully (Direct)**   *420 ft (135 m)   HVS (E1)*
FA: *J. Nimlin, B. Braithwaite, N. Millar and J. Macfarlane,
1937*
FA: *J. Cunningham, W. Smith and I. Paul, 1948 (direct finish)*
An epic Scottish gully, but harder than most. A drought is
desirable, but not essential for the insane.

There are eleven short pitches. Pitch 4 is crux (5a). A huge
chockstone. Climb the L wall, smooth and exposed, to find a
good jug high on the R. Nut belay well up scree slope above
Pitch 5 (4c), has a narrow chimney with a jammed chockstone.
Above this climb a groove in the L wall. Pitch 6 (4c), 'Bicycle
Pitch', on the L wall on small holds. Pitch 8 finishes below a
rib and shelf which rises steeply on the L. Pitch 9/10, tr. L
round foot of rib into grooves parallel with the gully. Up these;
easier rock for 150 ft (45 m), to a grass platform.
Direct Finish 160 ft (48 m) E1 5a
Pitch 9/10, instead of tr. L continue up gully towards impressive

arch (which higher up bristles with caves, OHS and chockstones). Climb first chockstone on R wall, tr. to L wall and gain a dark cave. Bridge wildly upwards until rock shelves allow, tr. L under huge chockstones to grass ledge. Pitch 11, finish by narrow holdless chimney on R, or on L via slabs, chimney and groove.

The wall to the L of Raven's Gully contains some stunning routes. The first few climbs all have a common first pitch to reach a ledge at 75 ft (23 m). This is gained up a series of R-trending grooves leading to the L end of the ledge which contains a large flake belay. **Guerdon Grooves (HVS 4c)** climbs off the R side of the ledge and takes a rising line R'wards across the wall to near the top of Raven's Gully. It is generally scrappy after the second pitch.

78 **Apparition**   *565 ft (170 m)   E1*
FA: *J. R. Marshall and J. MacLean, 1959*
An intimidating climb, direct up wall R of Shibboleth, finishing just L of the true finish.
Start: 20 ft (6 m) L of the base of Raven's Gully at the groove of the common start.
1. 75 ft (23 m) Up grooves trending R to gain large flakes and thus gain ledge.
2. 100 ft (30 m) 5a Tr. 10 ft (3 m) horizontally R round awkward square-cut edge to reach nut belay.
3. 150 ft (45 m) 5b Groove above to its top. Step L into parallel groove leading to OH. Over this, and steep groove above to ledge. Slab and groove on R lead to nut-belay just below grass ledge.
4. 120 ft (36 m) 5a Up to ledge. Move L and up steep L-trending crack to easier ground leading to Shibboleth ramp.
5. 120 ft (36 m) 4c Take groove line above and L to top. (Obvious groove on R is Shibboleth.)

79 **The New Testament**   *435 ft (135 m)   E4*
FA: *D. Cuthbertson and J. George, 1995*
An excellent route and one of the best in the region. Takes
direct line between Apparition and Shibboleth.
Start: As for Guerdon Grooves / Apparition.
1. 75 ft (23 m) Up grooves and flakes to grass ledge.
2. 90 ft (27 m) 6a Climb the corner above the R end of the
   ledge for 20 ft (6 m), then small stepped overlap going L to
   enter slim hanging groove (immediately R of Shibboleth). At
   its top move R into corner and climb this and its R edge,
   then another slim corner on R near top. Final cracks to belay
   on L.
3. 90 ft (27 m) 5c Go up slightly L then R into crack in slim
   groove. Follow this then trend L and up a shallow groove
   with rib leading to isolated OH (on Shibboleth Pitch 4).
   From a handrail R of OH climb wall to enter small L-facing
   corner leading to ledge.
4. 90 ft (27 m) 5c Step R, and climb twin tapering cracks to
   ledge. Go up R to sloping shelf leading to R edge of steep
   wall. Climb up L to good hold and good side-pull higher
   beneath bulge. Move L onto a ledge (shared with Shibboleth
   True Finish).
5. 90 ft (27 m) 5c Tr. R along ledge and climb brown streak
   into cracks trending R leading to easier ground.

80 **Shibboleth**   *535 ft (163 m)   E2*
FA: *R. Smith and A. Fraser, 1958*
FA: *R. Smith and J. MacLean, 1959 (True Finish)*
An all-time great that every climber should aspire to. It has
been soloed in the rain! Protection is reasonable, using small
wires.
Start: As for Guerdon Grooves / Apparition.
1. 75 ft (23 m) 4b Up grooves trending R to gain ledge.
2. 75 ft (23 m) 5c From near the R end of ledge climb obvious
   crack for 15 ft (4 m). Tr. 10 ft (3 m) L, then diag. R along
   small ramp to prominent groove (often wet). Up this to small
   ledge.

3. 70 ft (21 m) 5a Continue up groove. Step R at top and follow
   obvious continuation line diag. L across wall to small stance
   20 ft (6 m) below large obvious flake up on L (Revelations
   Flake). PR and Thread.
4. 100 ft (30 m) 5b Climb slim groove above on R (usually PR
   with sling in-situ) till holds on R lead up wall to small
   isolated OH. Tr. horizontally L to gain base of glacis leading
   diag. up R to stance below steep wall.
5. 65 ft (20 m) 5a Up slim corner in steep wall to gain ramp
   and belay at its R end.
6. 75 ft (23 m) 5b (the Original Finish, 4b, goes up wall above
   trending R up grooves to finish in short OH-corner). Tr. R to
   spike. Step up R into bottomless groove. Follow this to
   ledge.
7. 75 ft (23 m) 5b Tr. R across wall on lip of 'The Great Cave'
   to enter recess. Exit up crack that sprouts from its top.

81 **Bludgers Revelation**   *400 ft (120 m)   HVS*
    FA: *P. Walsh, H. MacInnes and T. Laurie, 1952 (Bludgers)*
    FA: *J. R. Marshall, Griffin Adams, 1957 (link)*
    FA: *P. Walsh and C. Vigano, 1956 (Revelation)*
    L of Guerdon Grooves start are two prominent parallel grooves.
    This combination generally follows L groove and wall above.
    Start: At a small corner directly below groove.
    1. 95 ft (16 m) 5a Up corner and L to foot of groove.
    2. 75 ft (23 m) 4c Up detached flake to R of groove. Step L
       into it and continue up good holds to ledge. Steep and
       sustained.
    3. 100 ft (30 m) 4c Move L to the edge. Up for 6 ft (2 m) then
       tr. L into vertical crack. Up this to ledge and corner. Move R
       round edge on to wall. Slabby rock follows to a move L on
       to ledge 20 ft (6 m) below obvious large flake (Shibboleth
       belay over to R).
    4. 70 ft (21 m) 4b Directly up to gain the flake. Follow it to
       below OH. Round this on L and up to ledge.
    5. 100 ft (30 m) Follow crest of large flake up to R and finish
       easily.

Great Gully Buttresses   (224546) Alt. 2,500 ft (750 m) North East Facing

Two smooth clean walls on the west side of Great Gully, directly opposite Slime Wall. The larger lower buttress (Great Gully Buttress) is mainly slabby. The Upper Buttress, some distance up the hillside above Great Gully Buttress, is smaller but steeper. The rock is clean and the climbing amongst the best in Glen Coe.

Approach – as for Slime Wall into broad upper section of Great Gully. Base of crag is up and R.

Descent – Scramble down to L for Great Gully Buttress, down R for Upper Buttress.

Great Gully Lower Buttress

The most prominent features are three parallel crack-lines in the upper L section; a slight 30 ft (10 m) rib forming a lower central toe to the cliff with a small grass ledge at its top; and a prominent slim slab up to R (**Sundown Slab, 165 ft (50 m) S**, starting up L-hand of two grooves to reach slab). Routes are described L to R.

82 **July Crack**   *165 ft (50 m)   VS*
FA: *R. Smith and A. Fraser, 1958*
Climbs the excellent central crack of the three parallel cracks (the L-hand crack is **August Crack, 165 ft (50 m) VS 4a, 4b** gained from top of first pitch of July Crack by descending tr.). Start up and L of toe of cliff at grass ledge about 30 ft (10 m) from L end.
1. 45 ft (15 m) 4a Up to ledge below thin crack.
2. 115 ft (35 m) 5a Climb the thin crack above to top. Sustained.

Playmate of the Month 195 ft (60 m) E3 6a. Climbs obvious very thin crack in wall immediately R of July crack gained from top of pitch 1 of June Crack (with crux through bulge at half height). The following routes start up groove just R of rib at toe of buttress.

83 **June Crack** *195 ft (60 m)* VS
FA: *W. Smith and J. Cunningham, 1948*
1. 30 ft (10 m) Climb groove to grass ledge at top of rib.
2. 75 ft (20 m) 4c From L end of ledge climb up L to crack. Climb it to rock shelf on L.
3. 100 ft (30 m) 5a OH-crack above by nose on R to start (harder direct). Easier to top.

84 **Ledgeway** *195 ft (60 m)* HS
FA: *W. Smith and R. Hope, 1952*
Climbs the centre of the buttress above the toe. Start as for June Crack.
1. 30 ft (10 m) Climb groove to grass ledge at top of rib.
2. 75 ft (20 m) From R end of ledge, tr. R and up to white scarred fault. Follow fault to bulge. Pass on L and up to belay on large pointed flake.
3. 80 ft (25 m) Climb flake then crack and groove above to top.

85 **The Whip** *245 ft (75 m)* E1
FA: *J. R. Marshall, R. Marshall, 1966 (1PA)*
Start down and R of rib in toe below small OH.
1. 115 ft (35 m) 4c Direct to OH. Turn on R by small groove and up to grass ledge.
2. 50 ft (15 m) 5b Climb brown groove above to spike belay.
3. 80 ft (25 m) 4c Tr. L to gain gangway, then easier to top.

Great Gully Upper Buttress
The most prominent feature is chimney crack splitting centre of face (**Yam 130 ft (40 m) E1 5b**, with crux over OH). To R of Yam is wide crack giving good climbing (**Happy Valley 100 ft (30 m) E1 5b**). Routes described L to R.

86 **Yamay** *135 ft (40 m)* E2 5b
FA: *I. Nicholson and K. Spence, 1968*
Steep, well-protected crack and corner to R of Yam. Climb to small OH. Tr. R and up corner to top.
Direct Start: E2 5c climbs crack to R direct into corner.

87 **May Crack** *(35 m)   VS 4c*
FA: *R. Hope and W. Smith, 1952*
Crack above detached block 15 ft (5 m) R of Yamay.

Creag A'Bhancair   (215550) Alt. 1,650 ft (500 m) North-west
facing 🦋 🦋
Directly above Lagangarbh Hut is the prominent Coire na
Tulaich. To its W, facing towards Glen Coe, are two obvious
walls. The lower one, Creag A' Bhancair, catches the late
afternoon sun in summer.
   Approach – From Altnafeadh via Lagangarbh, contour R from
path round base of coire and so to wall: 30 mins.
   Descent – To the L of the cliff, looking out.

88 **Carnivore**   *540 ft (162 m)   E3(2)*
FA: *J. Cunningham and M. Noon, 1958*
FA: *D. Whillans and D. Walker, 1961 (**The Villains' Finish**)*
FFA: *E. Cleasby and partner 1978*
The first route to breach the wall.
Start: Near L end of wall below short hanging groove.
1. 145 ft (43 m) 5b/c Up on good holds, slightly R to rest place.
   Direct (tricky) to large sloping hold (PR). Make descending
   tr. R for 10 ft (3 m) to gain descending fault line.
   Horizontally now along good holds and continuation shelf to
   gain big horizontal ledge. Nut belay at R end below green
   groove.
2. 120 ft (36 m) 5a Up green corner, then ledges and fault
   line to crack (PR); crack leads to glacis in black OH-recess
   (PB).
3. 75 ft (22 m) 6a Tr. R across slab to crack under roof. Follow
   this and continuation crack R, to gain ledge (numerous old
   PR); follow ledge R to recess. (The Villains' Finish breaks
   through crack above the belay on to upper wall, where easy
   ground leads to top – E2 5c.)
4. 30 ft (9 m) 5c Continue R on underclings to large grass
   ledge.
5. 75 ft (22 m) 4c Tr. L above roofs for 30 ft (9 m). Move L

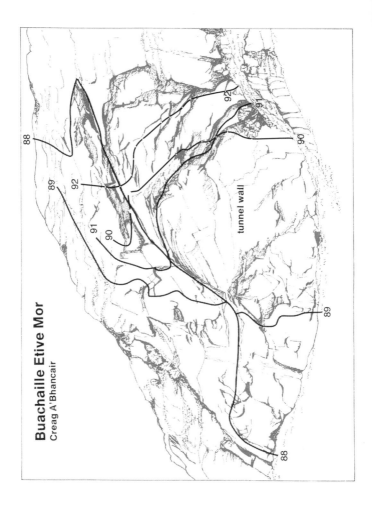

Buachaille Etive Mor
Creag A'Bhancair

under bulge, then up to grass ledge and up easily to small ledge.

6. 100 ft (30 m) Easy rocks to top.

89 **Romantic Reality** *330 ft (96 m) E7*
FA: *P. Whillance and D. Jameson, 1980 (pitch 1)*
FA: *D. Cuthbertson and K. Howett, 1984*
A stunning and serious route tackling the black OH-wall above Carnivore's first pitch.
Start: Below the belay ledge at end of Carnivore's first pitch. The red tunnel wall begins just to R. Diag. crack runs down from ledge L'wards to stop in lip of bulge 50 ft (15 m) up.
1. 70 ft (21 m) 6a Climb direct through bulging wall to slight recess of light rock. Climb diag. L to roof and pull through to crack. Grovel up this to end spectacularly on ledge.
2. 100 ft (30 m) 6b Directly above stance to small glacis below small overlap. Pull over (RP2), and palm up sloping holds in a desperate bid to reach diag. crack. Pull L into shallow groove leading to roof. Swing wildly R through the bulging roof (gulp) to big jug. Struggle with small roof above leading slightly L to safety.
3. 150 ft (45 m) 5b Diag. R and up wall of recess awkwardly. Then move easily to top.

To the R is the Tunnel Wall bounded on its R by an OH-corner system (The Risk Business).

90 **Up With The Sun** *385 ft (115 m) E6*
A direct line cutting through Risk Business, offering scary climbing.
Start: 20 ft (6 m) L of tree at start of Risk Business at distinctive triangular foothold.
1. 165 ft (50 m) 6b Climb up L'wards to gain thin crack. Climb difficult bulge R'wards to better holds. Side protection used on R and L. Climb up and R onto small ledge on pitch 1 Risk Business (PR). Climb that routes crux up and L then enter and climb groove in arete above on R, past overlaps, to

pull onto capping wall with difficulty. Continue more easily
to belay on shelf below recess (below crack in OH –
Villain's Finish) shared with Carnivore.
2. 70 ft (20 m) 6b Move out L to prominent undercling. Climb
   direct (hard) to in-situ sling (old). Step L and up to OH then
   tr. diag. L to easier ground at top of Risk Business.
3. 150 ft (45 m) Easily to top.

91 **The Risk Business**   *370 ft (111 m)   E5*
   FA: *P. Whillance, P. Botterill and R. Parker, 1980*
   An absolute classic up the huge L-arching groove line bounding
   the R side of the tunnel wall. Pitch 1 is bold.
   Start: At foot of the line at a tree.
   1. 75 ft (22 m) 6a Up L to a small ledge (Poor PR, Friend
      under roof above). Step L; either pull up and tr. L or stay
      low and then up (both hard). Continue up L to better holds.
      Follow line L to large ledge.
   2. 45 ft (14 m) 5c The big groove above to ledges on Carnivore.
   3. 100 ft (30 m) 6a Go 20 ft (6 m) L down ledges of Carnivore.
      Up a short wall to small ledge below small roof. Pull round
      its L side and up groove to bigger roof. Pull through direct,
      with difficult move on a jug to ledge. Shallow groove above
      to grass ledge.
   4. 150 ft (45 m) Easily to top.

92 **Bloodline**   *315ft (95 m)   E3*
   FA: *M. Hamilton, R. Anderson and P. Whillance, 1984*
   Good route taking a R to L diag. crack in wall above Risk
   Business. Start below the corner bounding the R edge of the
   Tunnel Wall.
   1. 150 ft (45 m) 5c Climb corner to break out L onto wall and
      diag. crack. Follow it (strenuous) to easing in angle. Up and
      L (bold) to small ledge (PB).
   2. 80 ft (25 m) 5c Tr. hanging slab L, then up to shelf below
      OH-recess (Carnivore).

Carnivore, Buachaille Etive Mór: climber, Paul Farrell

3. 80 ft (25 m) 5c The Villain's Finish to Carnivore through the
    OH-recess via layback crack.

Glen Coe

The S side of Glen Coe is formed by the huge mass of Bidean
nam Bian, the highest peak of Argyll at 3,795 ft (1,150 m). Its
four main ridges project N, three of them being the buttresses
of the Three Sisters of Glen Coe, Beinn Fhada, Gearr Aonach a
nd Aonach Dubh. The majority of the climbs are on the flanks
and noses of the latter two, whilst others are found on
cliffs enclosed within Coire nan Lochan and Coire nam
Beitheach.

  Approach – All the cliffs except those in Coire nam
Beitheach (Church Door and West Face, Aonach Dubh) are
reached from two large car-parks 500 yds/metres down from
Meeting of The Three Waters (172568). Below each are
footbridges crossing the River Coe. Good paths radiate from
here. Church Door and West Face, Aonach Dubh are
approached from Clachaig Junction (138566): see map, p. 56.

GEARR AONACH
High above the flat section of Coire Gabhail (the Lost Valley)
is the E face or Mom Rath Face. Excellent in winter but
herbaceous in summer. The biggest cliff is at the nose itself, the
North Face.

Gearr Aonach, North Face   (167562) Alt. 1,200 ft (400 m) ✗
An imposing face, unfortunately guarded by a wet and
vegetated andesite tier. The routes chosen, however, are clean
and are incredibly exposed.

  Approach – As the path into Coire Gabhail cuts into the
gorge, branch off up and R towards rock in the nose. A
prominent zig-zag path cuts up face just E of the nose onto the
top of the ridge. From the base of the zig-zag contour W on the
terrace to below nose.

  Descent – Head back along the ridge to descend the zig-zags.

A large chimney system with caves defines the L side of the main wall (**Chimney and Face Route, S**). To the R is a prominent red wall with black streaks, below which is a grey slabby tongue of rock, bounded on R by grassy chimney.

93 **Preamble**   *450 ft (135 m)   S*
FA: *J. R. Marshall, L. S. Lovat and G. L. Ritchie, 1957*
Start: At the tongue of rock 30 ft (9 m) L of obvious boulder.
1. 75 ft (23 m) Climb the grey tongue to small chimney just L of horrible grassy chimney.
2. 75 ft (23 m) Climb small chimney.
3. 125 ft (38 m) Follow the line of black stained groove in upper red wall to slabby ledge. Traverse R along it (PB).
4. 75 ft (23 m) Steep black wall on R, then easier to a nut belay.
5. 100 ft (30 m) Easy scrambling to top.

The next routes are on the W side of the main nose. They start from the girdle ledge. Gain the ledge by scrambling up to the R end. The climbs are on good rock, in very exposed positions:

94 **Marathon Man**   *315 ft (95 m)   S*
FA: *A. Crocket and K. V. Crocket, 1978*
Follows steep rib of clean rock towards R side of wall. Start 30 ft (10 m) L of R end of ledge below steep black wall with grooves.
1. 150 ft (45 m) Climb direct to ledge.
2. 135 ft (40 m) Above is L-trending gully bounded on L by steep rib. Climb up to rib. Step L onto it and follow direct to ledge (flake belay).
3. 30 ft (10 m) Step L and up short hard wall to easier scramble to top.

95 **The Cheek**   *300 ft (90 m)   S*
FA: *H. MacInnes and M. C. MacInnes, 1968*
Start: About 100 ft (30 m) L of the R end of ledge is a recess beyond a large rowan tree.

1. 15 ft (4 m) Climb the chimney above the recess to a small bay.
2. 70 ft (21 m) Move L round steep corner. Go diag. L to small ledge on the edge of the wall. Tr. round L down to a groove. Up this to block belay. (**The Prowl, VD**, takes the line of cracks out of the L side of the bay to the top.)
3. 60 ft (18 m) The chimney above to ledge.
4. 155 ft (46 m) Finish easily by a wall on L, up good rock.

AONACH DUBH

The most westerly of the Three Sisters of Glen Coe, its cliffs contain some of the best routes in the area, in spectacular settings. These are: the upper and lower tiers of the East Face flanking the glen leading to Coire nan Lochan; the imposing North-East nose overlooking the entrance; the complex North Face up and R of the nose, dominated by Ossian's Cave; and finally the West Face, where six buttresses overlook the entrance to Coire nam Beitheach and the Clachaig Inn see map on p. 56 and diagram opposite.

The East Face   (156558) Alt. 1,800 ft (600 m) 🦋
Approach – From either car-park take lower footbridge over River Coe, and follow path rising up into Coire nan Lochan, and so to base of lower tier.
   Topography – The Weeping Wall, characterized by red and black streaks, lies up to the L. An upper tier lies above a terrace and its R end is smooth and impressive (Archer Ridge). The cliffs descend diag. R down the valley in a series of tiered walls and terraces. The lowest is only 200 ft (60 m) above the stream. The first route climbs the clean slabby wall L of the Weeping Wall.
   Descent – see diagram on p. 98.

96 **Rowan Tree Wall**   *230 ft (75 m)   VD*
FA: *W. H. Murray and D. B. McIntyre, 1947*
This clean wall is separated from the Weeping Wall by a vegetated groove, and contains three cracks and a small

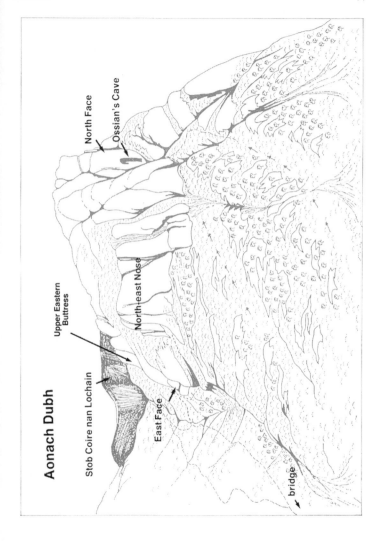

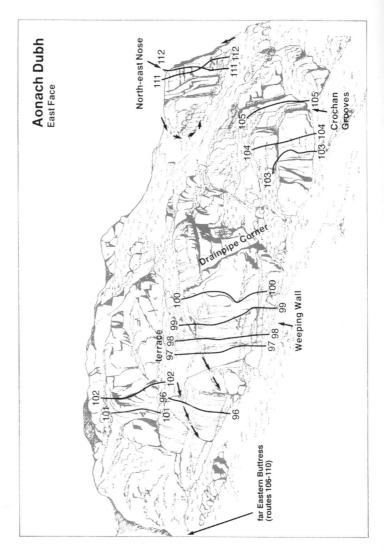

Aonach Dubh
East Face

North-east Nose

Crochan Grooves

Drainpipe Corner

terrace

Weeping Wall

far Eastern Buttress
(routes 106-110)

pot-hole. Climb any of the cracks for 75 ft (23 m), then easier to a ledge. Slabs lead to the terrace.

The Weeping Wall

Smooth and scoured by vertical water streaks and faint grooves. Separated by a vegetated groove from Rowan Tree Wall and defined on its R by a deep inset corner (Drainpipe Corner).

97 **The Spider**   *200 ft (60 m)   HVS*
FA: *J. R. and R. Marshall, and A. H. Hendry, 1957*
A lovely route up the groove and crackline immediately L of the L-most water streak.
Start: Directly below the water streak.
1. 20 ft (6 m) Scramble up the lower wall to a large ledge.
2. 130 ft (40 m) 5a Up the wall above the ledge for 30 ft (9 m) until possible to tr. R into groove bordering the edge of the water streak. Up groove for 20 ft (6 m), then move L to thin crack. Up this (crux) to narrow ledge. Continue up wall to reach a ledge.
3. 50 ft (15 m) Easier slabs to terrace.

98 **Solitude**   *220 ft (66 m)   E2*
FA: *D. Cuthbertson, R. Anderson and W. Todd, 1977*
A great route up the red wall between the two L-hand water streaks. Serious, but on excellent rock.
Start: As for Spider.
1. 20 ft (6 m) Scramble up to ledge.
2. 140 ft (42 m) 5b From R end of ledge climb short corner to higher ledge and large block. Up wall above with very bold moves to reach base of diag. crack running out L (small wires). Continue direct above to narrow ledge, then obvious line direct to ledge.
3. 60 ft (18 m) Continue easily up to terrace (or escape along slim grass ledge to L to gain base of crag).

99 **Quietude**   *205 ft (62 m)   HVS*
FA: *D. Cuthbertson and W. Todd, 1977*
This takes the line of cracks up the R-hand water streak.
Start: 15 ft (4 m) L of an obvious large boulder sitting at base
of wall to R of water-streaked area.
1. 30 ft (9 m) Scramble up broken rocks to ledge below black
    cracked OH.
2. 40 ft (12 m) 5a Through OH by L-slanting crack to ledge.
3. 75 ft (23 m) 4c Continue up wall via general line of
    L-slanting cracks leading to a shallow groove. This leads to
    ledges.
4. 60 ft (18 m) Wall above to terrace.

R of Quietude, the wall has no streaks. It is split by a diag.
cracked fault beginning above the large boulder at the base of
the wall, and running L parallel with Quietude. This is
Weeping Wall Route, 300 ft (90 m), S.

100 **The Long Crack**   *280 ft (84 m)   S*
FA: *L. S. Lovat and J. Johnstone, 1953*
A prominent feature of this section of the wall is a crack
beginning half-way up the wall, slanting R then vertically, to
finish near a small tree at top. Good to combine with Archer
Ridge above and to the L.
Start: Just R of detached boulder at base of wall.
1. 100 ft (30 m) Up broken rocks to gain short bulging wall.
    Through this to obvious diag. fault line (which continues L,
    parallel to Weeping Wall Route) and gain ledge.
2. 130 ft (39 m) Gain the long crack which is up and R and
    follow it, using the wall on the R to ledge and tree.
3. 50 ft (15 m) Easy slabs to terrace.

The wall now turns an arete and runs up into a deep-set corner
stained black by water-seepage. This is **Drainpipe Corner
(S **)** and is excellent when dry. It can be climbed when wet,
when it is a little more daunting.

Upper Tier
The following routes climb the clean upper section above the R end of the terrace. Reach them by climbing Rowan Tree Wall or scrambling up rocks to its L (M), or by climbing the Long Crack on Lower Tier.

101 **Quiver Rib**   *200 ft (60 m)*   D
FA: *D. B. McIntyre and W. H. Murray, 1947*
At the L end of the terrace is a damp chimney. This climbs the rib and wall immediately R.
1. 100 ft (30 m) Up rib to stance below steep wall.
2. 100 ft (30 m) Follow narrow groove trending L up steep wall with crux just above the belay.

102 **Archer Ridge (Direct)**   *200 ft (60 m)*   S
FA: *W. H. Murray and D. McIntyre, 1947*
FA: *L. S. Lovat, I. D. McNicol and A. Way, 1957 (direct)*
A steep wall leads R of Quiver Rib, terminating at a blunt ridge. This gives a serious route. The wall is climbed by **Arrow Wall (VD)**, which keeps just R of Quiver Rib, sharing its belay and climbing a narrow black groove R to finish.
Start: Below ridge at lowest rocks.
1. 80 ft (24 m) Follow ridge to good stance on crest.
2. 120 ft (36 m) Steep corner on crest above. Follow ridge to a formidable bulge, then move L below it. Ascend back R above it on to steep exposed crest leading to the top. Both the steep corner and the bulge can be turned on the R to gain the final steep crest. Easier, but not as good.

Lower Tier
Below and R of Drainpipe Corner a smooth, vertical, two-tiered wall runs down to R and forms the lowest climbable rocks of the East Face. It increases in height R 'wards to form a blunt nose as it cuts up the hillside into a deep, wet corner/chimney. In the nose is a huge open groove leading to a large grass ledge with trees: this is **Grochan Grooves (150 ft (45 m), S)**.

103 **Lady Jane**   *120 ft (36 m)*   *E2 5b*
FA: *D. Cuthbertson and D. Jameson, 1977*
The L side of the front face is continually wet, and is split by
two large corners – two deep, wet cracks to their R. The red
cracked wall R again is the line of Lady Jane.
Start: Just R of the wet black streak issuing from the large
crack. Climb the wall to reach thin R diag. crack. Up this to
deep horizontal crack just to L of another black streak line.
Climb up slightly L, then back R to finish on ledge just R of a
tree. Walk off L to finish.

104 **Sir Chancealot**   *180 ft (54 m)*   *E2*
FA: *B. Duff and K. McLuskey, 1978*
Climbs the wall just R of Lady Jane to another tree in
horizontal break, then groove through OH above.
Start: Below cracked wall midway between the black streak R of
Lady Jane and a shallow stepped corner leading up to the tree.
1. 120 ft (36 m) 5b Up wall direct, keeping R of black streak to
   gain sloping shelf. Up wall above over tiny OH to break. Tr.
   R to tree.
2. 60 ft (18 m) 5c Climb the groove through the roof to gain
   better holds on L. Continue up upper tier to grass ledges and
   spike belay.

105 **Lament**   *200 ft (60 m)*   *VD*
FA: *J. Cullen and C. Vigano, 1951*
An excellent steep route on perfect rock up the centre of the
wall between Grochan Grooves and the deep wet corner. R of
Grochan Grooves are L-slanting slabs.
Start: At the R-most of these, where a small vertical corner runs
up the steep wall.
1. 120 ft (36 m) Gain a ledge a few feet off the ground then
   enter corner. Up this trending L, pull out R at top (crux), and
   gain shallow groove above. Follow it to large recess in wall.
2. 80 ft (24 m) Easily up same line to top.

Lady Jane, Aonach Dubh, East Face: climber, Alan Winton

Far Eastern Buttress
Just L of Rowan Tree Wall is a larger more rambling buttress (Barn Wall). About 500 yds/m above and L of here is another slabby wall of excellent rock.

Topography – In the centre is a lower slabby section above which sits a high central wall characterised by a thin crack cleaving its full height. The buttress is bounded on the R by a deeply cut gully (Hole and Corner Gully). L of this is a smaller wall with twin R-diagonal cracks. L of this and bounding the main central wall is a chimney. To the L of the central wall is a ramp running up and L. The face then turns into the hillside into a broken gully.

Descent – Either tr. L (looking out) above the wall (exposed) and continue beyond Hole and Corner Gully or make longer but less daunting trek R. Routes are described R to L. The first two routes start by a scramble of 45 ft (15 m) to stance at base of chimney bounding R side of main wall.

106 **Shibumi**   *135 ft (40 m)   VS 4b*
FA: *K. V. Crocket and G. Jefferies, 1990*
From base of chimney go R to good footholds below corner crack of R-hand of twin diag. cracks. Climb these to easier ground then edge to top.

107 **Satori**   *135 ft (40 m)   VS 4b*
FA: *K. V. Crocket and G. Jefferies, 1990*
Climb the L-hand of twin diag. cracks. Step onto wall, move R and up to block at R end of small OH. Climb L and follow crack to top.

108 **Nirvana Wall**   *245 ft (75 m)   S*
FA: *I. Clough, C. Kynaston and J. G. Garster, 1966*
Climbs thin central crackline up highest section of wall cutting through final OH on R. Start near L end of lower slabs near start of crack and thin streaks of quartz. Excellent climbing.

109 **Eastern Promise**   *245 ft (75 m)   E1*
FA: *R. Anderson and C. Anderson, 1991*
Climbs arete and thin crack L of Nirvana Wall. Start at base of
grassy groove.
1. 165 ft (50 m) 5a Grassy groove for short way until possible
    to pull into crack-line on R-wall. Follow this, then arete to
    block belay below upper wall.
2. 80 ft (25 m) 5b Step down R into thin crack. Climb this past
    R side of block to OH. Pull through R, then back L above
    OH to top.

110 **Rough Slab**   *165 ft (50 m)   S*
FA: *R. T. Richardson, P. Mckenzie and W. Skidmore, 1962*
At L end of buttress, rocks turn into broken gully. Clean wall
overlooks gully. Start at groove in this wall. Climb groove past
block to good ledge below OHS. Tr. R and climb OH by slight
groove. Exit round L onto steep clean slab leading to top.

The North-East Nose   (158563) Alt. 1,850 ft (525 m) East
facing 🦋
This is the smooth, pale-coloured tower lying up to the R of the
East Face in the nose of Aonoch Dubh, and facing up the glen.
    Approach – Follow the path up towards Coire nan Lochan
and branch off as for the East Face. From below the lower tier,
contour R and then up the hillside to the base of the wall: 1 hr
15 mins.
    Topography – The wall is cleaved by two huge curving
corner lines on the L. The L-hand corner is more broken and
often wet. The L-hand corner is **Boomerang (VS 5a, 4a)** and
gives an easy line up an impressive face.

111 **Freakout**   *220 ft (66 m)   E4*
FA: *D. Bathgate and A. McKeith, around 1967*
FFA: *D. Mullin and J. Melrose, 1979*
A stunning route up the centre of the pale wall passing through
the A-shaped niche hanging in the middle of nowhere.

Start: Scramble up broken rocks to a flake belay by a tree below the centre of the wall.
1. 70 ft (21 m) 5c Up the wall to gain the vertical crack. This thins, after which it's possible to tr. R to a ledge (PB).
2. 90 ft (27 m) 6a Tr. back L into crack line. Up into 'A' roof. From jug in lip, make tricky layback over lip (PB). Crack continues to down pointing flake. Pull through roof above, R'wards on to ledge.
3. 60 ft (18 m) Wall above to top.

112 **Spacewalk**   *155 ft (46 m)   E4*
FA: *K. Johnstone and P. Ogden, 1978*
FFA: *M. Hamilton and D. Cuthbertson, 1980*
Takes a line up the R side of the wall. The second pitch is a strenuous proposition and harder for the short.
Start: 30 ft (9 m) R of Freakout below crack in steep wall.
1. 80 ft (24 m) 5c Crack leads up to R side of L-curving line of OH. Climb through and tr. L until strenuous moves up gain ledge (PR). Up short corner to stance on Freakout (PB).
2. 75 ft (23 m) 6b Continue up the groove line on R (PR) to below roofs. Step L and pull through roof into short groove. A puzzling move past an in-situ NR, usually with heavy arms, constitutes the crux. Up R to tree. Abseil off.

North Face   (152562) Alt. 2,470 ft (750 m)
This massive brooding face overlooks Loch Achtriochtan and is split by a diag. grassy terrace running L to R. The terrace dwindles beyond Ossian's Cave and is known as 'the Shelf'. The climbing is centred on the wall above this. Slow to dry, and very steep; is sunlit in the evenings.
   Approach – Follow path leading into Coire nan Lochan but branch off just after crossing River Coe and gain the big terrace. Follow it, keeping very close to the cliffs where they are cut by two large gullies. The path is loose and steep when

Spacewalk, Aonach Dubh, North Nose: climber, Calum Frazer

passing Ossian's Cave. Alternatively take the lower but parallel line – see diagram on p. 97. 1 hr 30 mins.

Topography – R of Ossian's Cave are two parallel chimney lines. The main wall R of this is split by two obvious vertical corners. The first leans L, its slabby L wall enclosed by a roof-like R wall (Tober). The second is clean-cut and continuous (Yo Yo).

Descent – All routes finish on a ledge system (Pleasant Terrace) below upper wall. Follow it R to descent by abseil (PB in situ).

The R-hand chimney is most prominent and is **Fingal's Chimney (550 ft (170 m) VS)**. This is a prolonged excursion for devotees of grovelling, gained from the R. **Tober (380 ft (114 m)   VS 4c, 4c, 4b** climbs line of big open corner slanting L with red L wall firstly by a slab leading L then into a short groove L again. This leads to slabs and grass rake to a final rib just R of Fingal's Chimney. Between Tober and Yo Yo is an OH-wall split by two cracklines. The R one is The Clearances. The L cuts through roofs and gives Eldorado. Both start at same place, below the curving overlap below The Clearances crackline.

113   **Eldorado**   *380 ft (115 m)*   *E5 ****
FA: *K. Johnstone and M. Worsley, 1997*
FFA: *M. Hamilton and D. Mullin, 1980*
FA: *D. Cuthbertson and K. Johnstone, 1980 (pitch 3)*
A very strenuous route with a thin crux.
1. 50 ft (15 m) 5b Climb slabby ramp leading L below overlap. Tr. L to ledge. Alternatively, loose crack on left (5c) to ledge.
2. 120 ft (36 m) 6b Follow slim groove to OH. Up short corner, stepping out L over roof. Follow thin crack over smaller OH. Up and L to ledge. Continue up crack to rock terrace.
3. 130 ft (40 m) 5c Climb groove just R of arete above – the second most obvious groove to L of the prominent groove of The Clearances – until an obvious tr. R leads to The Clearances (PB).

Yo Yo, Aonach Dubh, North Face: climber, Alan Taylor

  4. 80 ft (24 m) 5a Climb rib above to Pleasant Terrace as for
     The Clearances.

114 **The Clearances**   *350 ft (105 m)   E3*
FA: *E. and C. Grindley and J. Main, 1976*
An ace route with two contrasting pitches. First pitch takes the
hanging crack up the red wall R of Eldorado.
Start: Below a curving overlap directly below the crackline as
for Eldorado.
  1. 130 ft (39 m) 5c Climb slabby ramp that leads L below
     overlap across wall, for 30 ft (9 m), until flat holds on wall
     on R can be gained (PR). Up wall steeply, then head R (PR)
     into crack. Up this with surprising difficulty, to land panting
     on a large rock ledge.
  2. 140 ft (42 m) 5c Up into large corner above. Up its L wall
     past two NR. A tricky move R from top nut gains roof. Pull
     round it on R on huge flat holds (PR in lip). Continue up
     groove to open wall (single PB by small ledge common with
     Eldorado).
  3. 80 ft (24 m) 5a Climb direct up rib above to Pleasant Terrace.

115 **Yo Yo**   *320 ft (96 m)   E1*
FA: *R. Smith and D. Hughes, 1959*
Start: Below a huge undercut flake which grants entrance to the
corner 20 ft (6 m) R of The Clearances.
  1. 120 ft (36 m) 5b Using underclings, gain slab above on L
     (harder than most will encounter on a mild extreme). Up
     steep wall on R to ledges. Up curving corner to rock terrace
     (PB on L).
  2. 100 ft (30 m) 5b Back into the groove and up to a chimney.
     Grovel, squeeze or bridge up it in a superb position to a belay.
  3. 100 ft (30 m) 5b Continue in same line, keeping to the main
     corner crack to Pleasant Terrace.

West Face   (143556) Alt. 1,790 ft (550 m) South-west facing
A complex face lying above the entrance to Coire nam
Beitheach. It is composed of six clean red buttresses separated

by a series of deep-set gullies, and split horizontally by a prominent terrace. The best section for rock climbing is the R-hand face of E Buttress which forms the L retaining wall of No. 4 Gully, obvious from the road as the largest gully just R of centre. The rock on E Buttress in particular is superbly weathered rhyolite, mainly sound and the face is sunlit in late afternoon and evening, and is sheltered.

Approach – Car-parking at Clachaig Hotel junction. Follow track towards Achnambeithach. Skirt farm on R through gate. Follow L bank of stream till level with waterfalls. No. 2 Gully descends Aonach Dubh to join the waterfalls. Cross the gully's base and follow B Buttress (just R of gully) via faint path to middle ledge; follow this R into No. 4 Gully and the wall, see diagram on p. 112. 1 hr 15 mins.

Topography – The L edge is an impressive arete (The Big Top). In the centre of the wall is a huge open corner (Trapeze) and further up the gully is a vertical crackline (Hee Haw), immediately R of which is an arete taken by Flyman (E1 5b).

Descent – Walk back along top of cliff and descend slabs into ampitheatre at back of No. 4 Gully.

116 **The Big Top**   *500 ft (150 m)   E1*
FA: *R. Smith and J. Gardner, 1961*
Takes the challenge of the edge. Great position.
Start: Scramble up off the path to a ledge just L of the main arete.
1. 110 ft (33 m) 4c Tr. L along ledge into large R-facing slabby corner. Up it and tr. slab R to short chimney. Belay on top of chimney.
2. 100 ft (30 m) 5a Up to roof. Swing R round arete (PR), rush up steep wall just R of arete (ignoring stunning views into Glencoe post office) and back on to slabby L side of edge. Flake crack in edge above leads to below steeper upper wall (PB).
3. 140 ft (42 m) 5a Move R into diag. line of slabby ramps to long horizontal ledge. Take R-most leaning groove (PR). Swing L at its top via flake crack to large grass bay. Belay in base of huge flake.

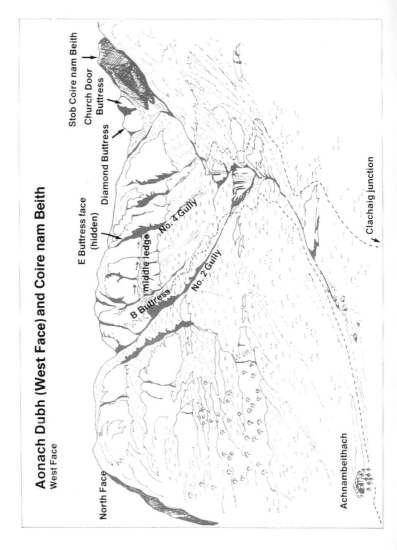

Aonach Dubh (West Face) and Coire nam Beith
West Face

North Face

E Buttress face
(hidden)

B Buttress

middle ledge

No. 4 Gully

No. 2 Gully

Diamond Buttress

Church Door
Buttress

Stob Coire nam Beith

Clachaig junction

Achnambeithach

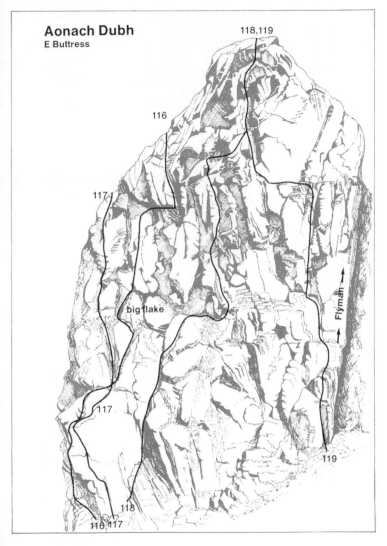

Aonach Dubh
E Buttress

118,119

116

117

big flake

Flyman

117

118

116,117

119

4. 150 ft (45 m) 5a/b The big flake. From its top, step on to
    wall (PR). Up, first R then L, into slight recess. Tr. R into
    second small niche, then up groove to top.

117 Salome/Prophet of Purism/Bannockburn   *430 ft (129 m)   E5*
FA (Banockburn): *D. Cuthbertson and W. Todd, 1977*
FA (Prophet): *D. Cuthbertson, 1981*
FA (Salome): *K. Howett and G. Latter, 1987*
This is a combination of routes up the wall R of Big Top giving
sustained intimidating climbing.
Start: On ledge above the rowan tree R of the edge. Scramble
on to ledge below leaning wall.
1. 80 ft (24 m) 5c Step off large flake embedded in ledge and
    follow twin cracks up wall. Step L as they disappear and
    gain handrail leading L. Pull directly up into shallow niche.
    Exit direct above this on suspect rock to impasse after 15 ft
    (5 m). Move L on to arete and flake crack (nut belay).
2. 120 ft (36 m) 5c Up flake crack then tr. R into thin diag.
    crack. Follow this with deviations on wall above to block
    and line of holds leading R above crack, to gain little ledge
    and flake crack. Up this for one move, then groove on L to
    long horizontal ledge (junction with Big Top).
3. 100 ft (30 m) 5a/b Up twin grooves in wall above to L of
    groove of Big Top to large grass bay.
4. 130 ft (39 m) 5c On the R is the great flake of Big Top.
    Above are two groove lines. Climb the steeper L-hand
    groove, then easier groove to top.

118 Trapeze   *455 ft (138 m)   E1*
FA: *J. R. Marshall and D. Leaver, 1958*
A complex wander across the highest part of the cliff.
Start: Up the massive corner R of Big Top and Salome.
Scramble up behind the rowan tree to ledge which leads R into
base of corner.
1. 65 ft (19 m) 5b The corner (strenuous laybacking) to below
    roof. Nut belay.
2. 140 ft (42 m) 4c Turn OH on L. Continue up easy corner,

then easier slab into a mossy bay below steep upper wall (poorest belay in glen).

3. 70 ft (21 m) Skitter round corner to R, to spacious platform.
4. 130 ft (39 m) 5a Leave platform on L via steep wall to ledge (hard). Above is large clean corner (Direct Finish HVS 5a), turn it on R. Rising tr. R to gain groove. Up crack in L wall on to slab cowering beneath OH. Tr. R to bay.
5. 50 ft (15 m) Leave bay by a slab on R and gain a crack. Follow it steeply to top.

119 **Hee Haw**   *435 ft (130 m)*   *E1*
FA: *D. Haston and J. Moriarty, 1959*
Completes the trilogy.
Start: Below the R arete of the face (Flyman).
1. 55 ft (17 m) 5b Climb steep groove just L of the arete to large grass ledge.
2. 90 ft (27 m) 4c Up corner crack above for 20 ft (6 m), and steep wall above to detached block under obvious crack line (PB).
3. 90 ft (27 m) 5a Climb the OH-crack to below large OH. Up R through OH by steep wall, and to ledge.
4. 130 ft (39 m) 4c Tr. L across wall (exposed) to steep groove line. Up to its top, then L to slab and small stance.
5. 70 ft (21 m) 4c Up slab and finish by OH-crack near top of buttress.

STOB COIRE NAN LOCHAN   (153551) Alt. 2,300 ft (780 m)
North-east facing
In the back of the coire formed by the ridges of Gearr Aonach and Aonach Dubh lies this impressive columnar cliff of andesite. It contains some fine corner lines. Receiving the sun only in the morning and late evening, it is a little lichenous, but it dries surprisingly quickly. Greasy when damp.

Approach – From the Glen Coe car-parks take lower bridge over River Coe, and follow path up past East Face Aonach Dubh and into the Coire: see diagram p. 97.

Topography – The most obvious buttresses in the centre of

the face are South and Central, separated by deep cleft of 'SC' Gully.

Descent – Broad Gully to the L (E) of South Buttress, between it and the summit buttress. Steep and loose near top.

South Buttress

The L-hand of the two steep middle buttresses. Its L wall is riddled by corner and chimney lines. The front nose is a steep pillar containing the gigantic corner of Unicorn. A grass ledge circles the foot of the wall.

120   **Unicorn**   *360 ft (105 m)   El*
FA: *J. R. Marshall and R. Campbell, 1967*
The magnificent corner.
1. 100 ft (30 m) 5b Up corner for 20 ft (7 m), then move R on to rib. Up this for 15 ft (5 m), crux. Re-enter corner and up to stance.
2. 60 ft (18 m) 5a Follow the corner to stance.
3. 120 ft (36 m) 5a Continue up the sustained corner to terrace. *Take Care*: massive loose blocks at top of corner.
4. 65 ft (20 m) 5a Corner and chimney above for a few feet. Swing R onto wall. Steep moves lead to top.

BIDEAN NAM BIAN, CHURCH DOOR BUTTRESS   (144544)
Alt. 3,000 ft (900 m) North-west facing
Skulking high up in Coire nam Beitheach below the summit of Bidean nam Bian itself are two relatively small twin buttresses, Diamond and Church Door. Diamond is disappointing, but Church Door compares with the best elsewhere in Glen Coe. It was named by W. Tough who had a vivid imagination. Sunlit in the late afternoon, dries slowly.

Approach – Car-parking at Clachaig Hotel junction. Follow path from Bridge up R (W) side of stream till well past West Face of Aonach Dubh. Coire nam Beitheach lies straight ahead. Cross stream and follow L branch into upper Coire below Church Door Buttress. 2½ hrs.

Topography – Diamond is separated from Church Door by Central Gully, a prominent lump of rock sitting at its base

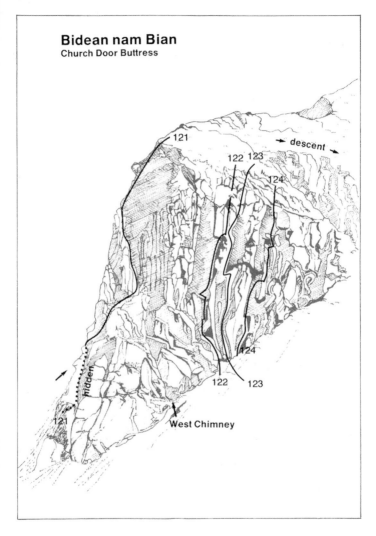

Bidean nam Bian
Church Door Buttress

(Collie's Pinnacle). Church Door's East Face overlooks the gully, and contains Crypt Route. The front prow is generally broken, but turns into the striking, grooved West Face.

Descent – Down the hillside to R of face.

121 Crypt Route   *405 ft (135 m)   VD*
FA: *M. Wood, J. Wilding and A. S. Pigott, 1920*
An esoteric excursion through the bowels of Bidean, climbed day or night at no change in grade!
Start: Opposite neck of Collie's Pinnacle a chimney runs up to R-hand end of 'the Arch', an exposed ledge formed by two huge jammed boulders.
1. 65 ft (20 m) Up the chimney to a corridor cutting into centre of the earth. Journey to the dark end. The choice now depends on the party's stomach dimensions and supply of batteries.
a). the Tunnel – through narrow passage in L wall to rock chamber (total oblivion). Tunnel leads to second chamber, then a 10½ inch (45 cm) diameter escape hatch on to front face. 15 ft (5 m) slab leads to the hole in lower R end of 'the Arch'.
b). the Through Route – up to cave end of corridor. Gain smaller cave. Exit direct (sensational), the top of the chockstone providing good holds. Beyond is grass ledge, jumble of boulders and 'the Arch'.
c). the Gallery – take through route to second cave and enter chimney in same fault line to third smaller cave. The gallery is 6 ft × 3 ft × 20 ft (2 m × 1 m × 6 m). Enter it. Descend for few metres, and, facing out, tr. R for 45 ft (14 m), till possible to climb up to 'the Arch'.
2. All routes finish up chimney and steep wall above 'the Arch'.

West Face
Towards the L side of the West Face there is a small bay in the angle formed by the projecting spur of the buttress and the face. Above is a deep chimney which is best avoided in summer. To the R the wall is steep and split by several large corners. In the

centre of the wall is a large smooth wall split centrally by a groove leading up to a short hanging chimney in the steepest section. This is Kingpin. To its R are several corner lines, each one characterized by its colour.

122 **Kingpin**   *344 ft (103 m)*   *E3*
FA: *J. Hardie and W. Thomson, 1968*
FFA: *D. Cuthbertson and D. Mullin, 1978*
FFA: *M. Hamilton, D. Cuthbertson, 1977 (Pitch 1)*
Start: Just L of the R end of a sloping ramp below the flared groove (about 60 ft (18 m) R of the above-mentioned chimney).
1. 60 ft (18 m) 6a Gain ramp. Tr. L up it a little, to below L-facing groove. Up this using R arete (hard) until a swing R can be made into casket-shaped niche. Hanging belay.
2. 60 ft (18 m) 5c Go up R wall of niche and move into black groove. Up this a few feet then step R on to face. Mantel on to peculiar projecting ledge. Gain short hanging chimney above.
   Awkward moves gain small stance out on L at top (PB).
3. 100 ft (30 m) 5b Tr. R across top of chimney and up ramp-cum-groove to recess. Exit L and then up to ledge (some variation possible). A crack leads to ledge below big corner.
4. 90 ft (27 m) 5a The corner up to roof. Hand tr. R under roof and round arete on to face. Up to ledge (PB).
5. 40 ft (12 m) A groove leads to top.

123 **The Lost Ark**   *E4*
FA: *P. Whillance and R. Parker, 1983*
The obvious groove / corner system R of Kingpin. Start at foot of white-speckled groove.
1. 135 ft (40 m) 6a Climb groove for 60 ft (20 m) to small OH. Up and L onto arete. Up this with difficulty for 15 ft (5 m) then move back R and up to ledge. Tr. R 3 ft (1 m) and up to OH. R across OH and up to good ledge. Belay below big corner.
2. 150 ft (45 m) 5b Step R, climb crack then R wall for 36 ft

(12 m) before moving back L to climb easy groove to top of pillar. Groove above to top.

124 **Temple of Doom**   *220 ft (66 m)   E3*
FA: *K. Howett and M. Charlton, 1984 (Pitch 1)*
FA: *M. Hamilton, G. Livingston and R. Anderson, 1984 (Pitch 2)*
Climbs an obvious deep black V groove, and hanging stepped corner system R of Lost Ark. Tried on sight, but darkness and lichen ended attempts in stepped corner. After a clean it succumbed to Hamilton and party. Immediately R of The Lost Ark, a slim V-groove peters out at 50 ft (15 m). R of this is a further groove trending R initially.
Start: Below this.
1. 80 ft (24 m) 6a Up groove to ledge. More open groove above via crack in R wall, then move across groove to L and up with difficulty to reach belay.
2. 140 ft (42 m) 5c Step R to climb a crack for 20 ft (6 m). Step back L and pull over into foot of stepped corner system. Climb this (sustained) and continuation crack for a short way until possible to step R into corner on R. This to top.

AONACH EAGACH

This is the mountainous ridge forming the north side of Glen Coe. There are huge buttresses of rock along its entire length, unfortunately none of good quality rock. However, there are two routes that are worthwhile, both offering mountain excursions rivalling anything in Scotland.

125 **Aonach Eagach Ridge Traverse**   *1.6 miles (4 km)   Moderate*
FA: *A. R. Wilson, A. W. Russell and A. Fraser, 1895*
The longest ridge on the mainland which involves some climbing. Start at east end of ridge at usual car-parks (173567). Follow well-defined path up south ridge of Am Bodach. From its top tricky descent on its north side before tr. back to south side where reverse of short pitch is required to continue (abseil ?). About half-way along between Meall Dearg and Stob Coire Leith are series of pinnacles on narrow ridge which offer

dramatic exposure. Descend down badly eroded (and difficult to locate) path to west of Clachaig Gully (same descent as for anyone completing the gully). Please note that there is no safe or easy descent on Glen Coe side between Am Bodach and Stob Coire Leith. This route should not be underestimated and is a long day out.

126 **Clachaig Gully** *1,700 ft (520 m) S*

FA: *W. H. Murray, A. M. MacAlpine, J. K. W. Dunn and W. G. Marskell, 1938*

The best of series of gullies throughout Scotland. This offers very long expedition on clean and compact waterworn rock which, unusually for a gully, catches sun. The gully is obvious cleaving hillside of Sgorr nam Fiannaidh at west end of Aonach Eagach ridge above Clachaig Inn. The way is obvious to the first obstacle at 500 ft (150 m).

1. The Great Cave. Climb R wall and slab to tree. Tr. down, round rib. Climb L to red wall leading back into gully bed.
2. The next pitch above Great Cave is climbed by slabby shelf on R into corner.
3. Short chockstone pitch.
4. Jericho Wall. To R of waterfall. Climb by smooth corner until possible to trend L and up to top.

5/6/7. Several good pitches including The Red Chimney 65 ft (20 m), a shallow cave with 15 ft (5 m) chimney above. Climb R wall of cave to ledge near foot of chimney. Exposed move into this then chimney to slab leading to gully bed.

8. The last pitch is climbed by R side of wall, then tr. L to centre of wall with awkward pull to finish.

GARBH BHEINN, ARDGOUR (904622) Alt. 2,600 ft (780 m) South facing

Ardgour is the district W of Loch Linnhe. There are several peaks in the area named Garbh Bheinn, but the one in question is the highest peak and can be clearly seen from the Ballachulish Bridge. The most popular cliff is the South Face, which lies in two tiers directly below the summit and forms one flank of the upper section of the Great Ridge, which drops from the summit for 1,000 ft (325 m).

Access
Cross Loch Linnhe via Corran Ferry and take A861 S towards Strontian. Crossing times: 7 am – 9 pm, summer every 20 mins.

There are two ways in 1) For Great Ridge, a long walk up Coire an Iubhair from the car-park near Inversanda House (928597): 2 hrs. 2) For South Face, a short steep flog up Coire a'Chothouium (unnamed on map). This is due S of the summit. Start from lay-by near top of Glen Tarbet (897603), follow path up E bank into coire, then up hillside to top: 1 hr 30 mins.

Accommodation
Camping – Entrance to Coire an Iubhair by car-park; it is courteous to ask at Inversanda House.
Hotels/Self Catering – Corran Hotel; chalets in Salen and Strontian on A861.

Provisions
Spar shop and fuel at Clovullin, 1 mile (2 km) S of Corran.

Guidebook
Glen Coe, *Rock and Ice Climbs*, K. V. Crocket, R. Anderson and D. Cuthbertson, SMC, 1992. Update due 2000.

Mountain Rescue
Lochaber Mountain Rescue team – nearest post in Fort William; nearest telephone at Inversanda House (928597) or public telephone at Clovullin, 1 mile S of Corran.

127 **The Great Ridge Direct**   *1,000 ft (325 m)   VD*
FA: *J. H. Bell and W. Brown, 1897*
FA: *D. D. Stewart and D. N. Mill, 1952, (direct)*
The lower part of the Ridge is a mass of slabby rock split part

of the way up by two horizontal grassy rakes. The most prominent feature is a slabby ramp with a continuously steep L wall in the lower section.

Start: Below this feature at the lowest rocks, 10 ft (3 m) R of a twisting crack.

Climb a steep slab with difficulty to gain the slabby ramp. Follow this in two pitches to broad grass ledge. Move L round edge and climb direct to second grass ledge with a conspicuous flake chimney above. Up this to a grass rake. Tr. R along this till below the well-defined ridge. This is followed on good holds, with superb views, to the summit.

The South Face, Lower Tier

The terrace below this tier can be tr. R to gain the upper rocks of the ridge if so desired.

  Topography – A broken ledge cuts across the face at about 60 ft (18 m). At the R end is a continuous corner system (Butterknife). Just to its L is a conspicuous pyramidal pillar heading up to the main section of the corner, and just L of the pillar is a large jumble of boulders laying against the wall.

128 **Butterknife** *325 ft (106 m)* *VS*
   FA: *J. R. Marshall, A. H. Hendry, G. J. Ritchie and I. D. Haig, 1956*
   The classic climb of the cliff up steep rock in an intimidating situation. Up the R side of both tiers.
   Start: At the chimney which forms the R side of the pyramidal pillar.
   1. 75 ft (23 m) Up chimney and corner to ledge above top of pillar.
   2. 50 ft (15 m) 4a Up and R across wall into main corner line. Leads to large grass ledge.
   3. 80 ft (24 m) Easier walls and ledges lead up and L to belay below roof near R end of upper tier.
   4. 120 ft (36 m) 4b Pull over small roof and steep wall on jugs. Easier rocks lead L beneath short, cracked leaning wall and so to top.

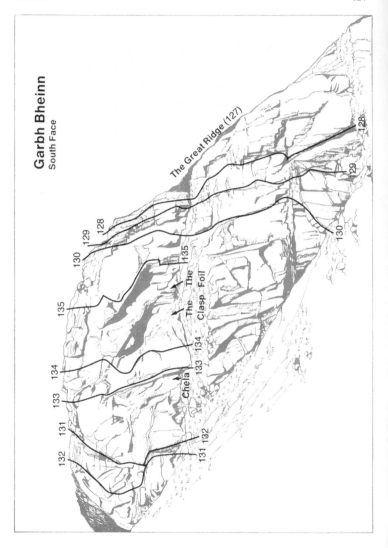

Garbh Bheinn
South Face

The Great Ridge (127)

129 **The Golden Lance**   *320 ft (105 m)   E2*
FA: *R. Anderson and A. Russell, 1984*
This ascends both tiers via a crackline up wall L of Butterknife.
Start: At the jumble of boulders to L of pyramidal pillar.
1. 60 ft (18 m) 5c From top of boulders climb cracked wall
   above leading L then up to long ledge.
2. 130 ft (39 m) 5c Up thin diag. crack leading R to large hollow
   block. The short steep wall above then same line to terrace.
3. 130 ft (39 m) 5b 30 ft (9 m) L of R end of upper tier is short
   corner capped by roof. Up corner and pull out R to gain
   easier rocks. Up to short leaning wall. Pull through this, then
   easy rocks to top.

130 **Scimitar**   *330 ft (108 m)   VS*
FA: *D. D. Stewart and D. N. Mill, 1952*
Near the L end of the lower tier are roofs bounded on R by a
large hanging corner. Broken rocks lead up R to the horizontal
ledge cutting across the wall. Start here.
1. 100 ft (30 m) 4c Gain horizontal ledge from its L end, and
   climb steep crack past spikes to small OH. Step R to smooth
   slab leading up L to a nut belay.
2. 70 ft (21 m) 4b Continue directly above into prominent
   chimney leading to terrace.
3. 160 ft (50 m) 4c To the L is a deep L-facing corner, and on the
   R is a horizontal roof. Climb the smooth vertical groove
   between these to wall. Move up R to a flake, then on L sloping
   corner with slabs on L side. The corner on the slabs lead to
   easier slabs and top. Belay can be taken on flake if desired.

The large open corner in lower tier L of Scimitar is **Gralloch**
(**E2 5b**), gained from Scimitar via thin cracks and ramps.

South Face, Upper Tier
Generally one-pitch routes.
   Topography – The L end is dominated by a smooth OH-wall.
It is defined on its L by a deep chimney (Sgian Dubh), and on
its R by a L-facing corner (**Chela, E3 6a**). The wall above and

L of Sgian Dubh is split by cracks (The Peeler). In the centre of the face is a smooth white wall (White Hope), R of which are two parallel diag. roofs. The routes are described L to R.

131 **The Peeler**   *150 ft (45 m)   HVS 5b*
FA: *R. Smith and J. Moriarty, 1961*
Start: Just L of Sgian Dubh chimney. Climb crest of flake which forms the chimney to platform. Up groove on R and pull up L over small roof. Go up short steep crack into prominent V-groove. Up this to top.

132 **Sgian Dubh**   *150 ft (45 m)   S*
FA: *J. R. Marshall and L. S. Lovat, 1956*
A sustained little route.
Ascend the chimney with difficulty to a platform: nut belay at its L end. Tr. up L via ledges to a stance. Then move L and over OH. Then back R and up a nose and steep rock to top.

133 **The Pincer**   *150 ft (45 m)   E2 5b*
FA: *D. Dinwoodie and R. A. Smith, 1978*
A brilliant sustained pitch.
Start: Below the corner of Chela. Climb up a crack in the R wall to swing out R on to white face. Up the slight groove just R of the arete with continuous interest, passing a bulge on the L to small OH. Pull round its L side and enter steep corner. This and its L arete to top.

134 **White Hope**   *150 ft (45 m)   E4 6a*
FA: *P. Whillance, R. Anderson and M. Hamilton, 1984*
An intricate line up the centre of the white wall, taking the general line of a thin vertical quartz vein up to a R-slanting flake to 40 ft (13 m). From its R end hard moves gain jugs below small isolated OH. Thin diag. crack from above roof L into centre of wall. Up groove and wall R to block below final leaning wall. This leads to ledge. Scramble to top.

The Clasp (HVS 5a) follows a L-trending line below the first roof starting near its R end, then tr. L across slab from below its L end, crossing White Hope into shallow groove and finishing up a chimney on L. It is quite bold. **The Foil (E1 5b)** is another serious route up the sandwiched wall between the roofs. It begins up wall L of groove leading to R end of roof. From the L end it exits L on to slabs and final cracks to top.

135 **Excalibur**   *250 ft (75 m)   VS*
FA: *K. V. Crocket and C. Stead, 1972*
Climbs a very exposed line along the lip of the second roof above Foil.
Start: At orange-streaked groove leading up to R end of large roof, just R of Foil.
1. 130 ft (39 m) 4c Up the groove until tr. R leads to rib. Go up then L along lip of roof to steep corner. Up this to ledge on L (PB).
2. 120 ft (36 m) 4a Go L for 10 ft (3 m) and climb walls above to top.

Glen Nevis

Introduction
Glen Nevis is the large valley running S from Fort William round the S flank of Ben Nevis, to melt into the great expanse of the Mamore forest close to Rannoch Moor. This truly beautiful glen attracts an ever-increasing number of tourists to its road-head car-park and hamburger van, to glimpse Steall Falls, the second largest in Britain. But still relatively few climbers pay it a visit.

The rock is very clean, rough mica-schist. Cracks tend to be small or incipient, so protection involves the intricate use of RP nuts. A number of the harder routes completed during the 1980s and early 1990s used Skyhooks for protection rather than resort to bolts or marginal pegs: a practice that never really caught on, although a small number of devotees have taken the ethic further afield. When the glen becomes infested with midges, the higher more exposed crags are the best option.

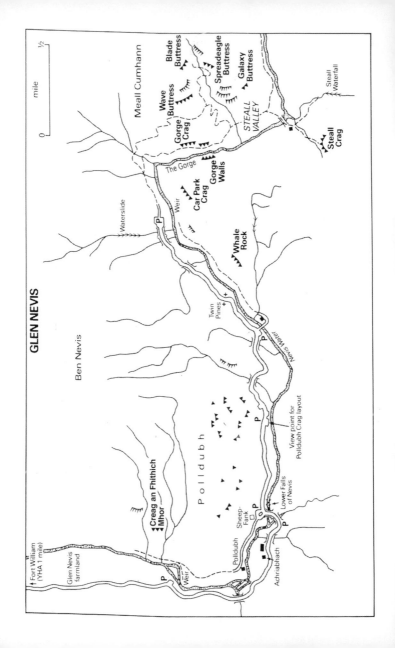

GLEN NEVIS

Ben Nevis

Meall Cumhann

Blade Buttress

Wave Buttress

Spreadeagle Buttress

Galaxy Buttress

Gorge Crag

STEALL VALLEY

Steall Waterfall

The Gorge

Gorge Walls

Car Park Crag

Steall Crag

Waterslide

Weir

Whale Rock

Nevis Water

Twin Pines

Polldubh

Creag an Fhithich Mhor

Fort William
(YHA 1 mile)

Glen Nevis farmland

Weir

Polldubh

Sheep-Fank

Lower Falls of Nevis

View point for Polldubh Crag layout

Achriabhach

0   mile   ½

History

Pioneering climbers, who had to provide their own hamburgers, have been active in the glen since 1940. Brian Pinder Kellet was known to have soloed routes here but left no record of his ascents. Predominant in the late 1940s were the local Lochaber Mountaineering Club, under whose auspices Jimmy Ness produced Pine Wall (S), Pinnacle Ridge (S) and others. After a lull through the 1950s when the only visitors were the RAF for training, Ian Clough and Terry Sullivan blitzed the main section of Polldubh in 1958/59. Their routes remain amongst the best here – Resurrection, Phantom Slab, Damnation, Flying Dutchman, and Kinloss Grooves.

The 1960s were quiet, outcrops being spurned for the mountain cliffs apart from brief visits from John Cunningham, while he was resident at Glenmore Lodge, and Yorkshireman Allan Austin, who with Jenny Austin freed Storm and Crag Lough Grooves, (both HVS).

From 1969 Klaus Schwartz, when free from the local Outward Bound Centre, was at large amongst the Polldubh Crags, producing nearly sixty routes, including Foil, Kyanite, Cervix, Autobahnausfahrt and others with a German theme.

The first of the visiting Lakelanders Ed Grindley, removed Schwartz's aid indiscretions on such routes as The Web, Withering Crack, Kaos and Foil (now E2 or E3) in the late 1970s, as well as producing a few of his own. There had been occasional forays by Clough and Schwartz to Car-Park and Gorge Crags, but the full potential of Steall was not investigated until the early 1980s. Pete Whillance and Dave Armstrong, the second invasion of Lakelanders, with Murray Hamilton and Alan Murray dug Car-Park Crag free of its thick lichen in 1981. The best route was the stunning Quality Street (E3). Meanwhile Whale Rock, Wave Buttress and Gorge Crag were developed by Dave Armstrong (from Nottingham), Grindley and Dave Cuthbertson respectively. The hard climbs produced during this period were Edgehog, Earthstrip and Cuthbertson's Cosmopolitan. On Creag an Fhithich Beag, Cuthbertson climbed the hardest route to date with Exocet (E6).

In 1984, Achintee was the birthplace of the 'Glen Nevis Cruisers'. Under the parental guidance of the then owners Bill and Mo Wright, Cuthbertson, Kevin Howett and Gary Latter, assisted by Alan Moist and the 'Bistro Boys', made a clean sweep of many remaining good lines over the next few years. The walls of the gorge were attacked with Latter producing Rats in Paradise (E5), Howett climbing Chimera (E4) on the opposite side and Cuthbertson climbing Aquarian Rebel (E4), The Amusement Arcade (E5) and If Looks Could Kill (E5), all to the amazed tourists stumbling along the gorge path. Howett breached the ridiculous Steall Wall with Lame Beaver (E7) as well as the amazing pillar of Blade Buttress to give Flight of the Snowgoose (E6); this latter route using skyhooks for dubious protection. The upside-down groove to the L of 'Snowgoose' became the subject of a race with Latter succeeding to give Cruisability (E5). Other new faces started to contribute with Mark 'Face' McGowan adding Stage Fright (E5) to Pinnacle Ridge, again using a skyhook for protection, soon followed by Jodicus Direct (E6) on Wave Buttress. Colin Gilchrist repeated many of the hard routes in good style before producing The Nuns of Navarone (E5) on Whale Rock.

However, the hardest addition was Femme Fatale (E8) on Whale Rock in 1986 by Cuthbertson and although unconfirmed, this route still marks the high point in the glen's standards. The only routes to rival this came in 1987 with Liminality (E7), again by Cuthbertson and in 1988 Howett completed Chiaroscuro (E7) on Spreadeagle Crag.

Various new venues were discovered thereafter particularly amongst the trees of the south side, but Steall Wall quickly became the centre of attention. Here McGowan started it off with The Trick of the Tail (E6) in 1989 after drying a perpetual weep with a blow-torch. Murray Hamilton then succeeded on the stunning R diag. crack after pre-placing the natural protection to give Leopold (E7). It remains un-repeated. Its neighbouring crack was then led by Latter in red-point style at E7 (Arcadia). Controversy erupted in 1993 when bolts appeared, some of which intruded on established routes. Some were removed but others still remain on Leopold.

The Glen boasts the highest concentration of quality routes in Scotland and remains the premier venue for hard traditional climbing.

Accommodation
Camping – Glen Nevis Campsite (125722) open March to October, tel: (01397 702191) beside youth hostel 3 miles (5 km) from Fort William; '*Savage Camping*' below Polldubh or in Steall (discouraged on Glen Nevis farmland between Fort William and Polldubh).

Bunkhouses – Ben Nevis Bunkhouse, Achintee (125731) at beginning of pony track up the Ben, tel: (01397) 702240; The Smiddy, Corpach, on the road out to Mallaig, tel: (01397) 772467

Club Huts – Steall Hut (178683), Lochaber MC (JMCS) in Steall Meadow.

Youth hostel – Glen Nevis (128718), 3 miles (5 km) from Fort William.

Guidebooks
Highland Outcrops, K. Howett, SMC, 1998

Topography of Glen Nevis
There are four distinct sections. Also see map. p. 128.
1. Creag an Fhithich: the first encountered past the youth hostel.
2. Polldubh: half-mile stretch of scattered buttresses along a ridge from lower falls of Nevis at Achriabhach.
3. Car Park: all the crags around the road-end car-park.
4. Steall: the numerous crags in and above the Gorge and in Steall Meadow.

CREAG AN FHITHICH   (146694) Alt. 400 ft (120 m)
West-facing 🦋 🦋
This nestles among trees above the flat Glen Nevis farmland in the lower stretch of the Glen. There are two buttresses, the

lower one (Creag nan Fhithich Beag) being the most impressive. It contains nothing but hard routes, but they are some of the best in the area. They are typical Dave Cuthbertson creations – sustained, strenuous, and very technical.

Approach – Dry feet: from the lower falls, follow the track past sheep pens and Polldubh cottages, then the river bank until below crag. Wet feet/wellies: park opposite the crag at end of flat section of farmland, and wade the river via a small weir.

Topography – The crag's main feature is an OH-orange wall, with a steep arete on L and a higher prow on the R.

Descent – To L of crag.

136 **Liminality**   *100 ft (30 m)*   E7 6c ***
FA: *D. Cuthbertson and A. de Klerk, 1987*
The striking arete on the L of the main wall (acutely OH and adorned with in-situ pegs). An unusual exercise in laybacking in two directions at once.

137 **The Handren Effect**   *120 ft (36 m)*   E6 6b
FA: *D. Cuthbertson, 1983*
This climbs up the centre of the orange wall via an obvious quartz line. Start at a short vertical crack 25 ft (7 m) R of Liminality. From the top of the crack tr. diag. L (PR) to base of faint groove. Up this (NR), usually in extremis, to easy ground.
The Monster (E5 6a) starts off end of ledge to R of Handren and climbs direct to roof; then it pulls through L via faint crack. **Exocet (E6 6b)** climbs through roof just R and up centre of magnificent prow above.

138 **Spring Fever**   *180 ft (54 m)*   E3
FA: *D. Cuthbertson, K. Howett and C. Henderson, 1985*
This follows an older route Steerpike (E2 5c 5b) for much of the way, but where this route escapes out R Spring Fever launches on to the wildly hanging prow.
Start: As for Monster at R end of ledge.
1. 60 ft (18 m) 5c Up the wall to sloping ledge (PR). Monster climbs directly up. Tr. R along gangway with puzzling

moves under a nose. Then up and L to belay on top of nose.

2. 120 ft (36 m) 5c Pull over OH just R of stance to slab (Steerpike escapes R from here). Step down and grope L round hideously exposed arete for a jug. An obvious diag. line leads L in a castrated position to top. Belay well back.

POLLDUBH CRAGS   (153686) Alt. 640 ft (200 m) South facing

From Achriabhach Bridge over the Lower Falls of Nevis, the crags are spread in a complex manner for half a mile (800 m) along the lower slopes of Ben Nevis. Consequently routes have been chosen for ease of recognition as well as quality. Regular visitors should buy the concise guide, if they want to explore the delights of Polldubh fully.

Topography – The crags of the L-hand section are generally small and rather scattered, but contain a few gems worth searching out once the bigger crags have been exhausted.

The main area (R-hand section) has more to offer, on larger crags. Nearly all the buttresses form a slabby front wall, bounded by a steep L-hand wall with clean-cut aretes or shoulders between. The longest is High Crag, almost on the skyline, whose L wall forms a massive 'skull' staring down the valley. Below this the jumble of crags almost reaches the road, Pinnacle Ridge being the lowest.

All the crags are best approached from here, where there is ample parking and a good spot for camping (152684), although this is currently being discouraged due to litter problems. The first approach to the crags can be confusing, thick trees obscuring minor crags and sheep paths criss-crossing the hillside. Study the diagram on p. 134, carefully (the crags described are all quite distinctive) and follow the paths that are marked.

Pinnacle Ridge 🦋 🦋 🦋

Not really a ridge, but a two-tiered wall whose R bounding edge gives the route of the buttress's name. It is extremely popular because of its proximity to the road, and is used by locals for training.

Polldubh
(R-hand section)

1. Pinnacle Ridge
2. Pandora's Buttress
3. Cavalry Crack Buttress
4. Secretaries' Buttress
5. Nameless Crag
6. High Crag
7. Pine Wall
8. Styx Buttress
9. Black's Buttress

P Parking and crag viewpoint
SW South-west Buttress
B The 'Block'

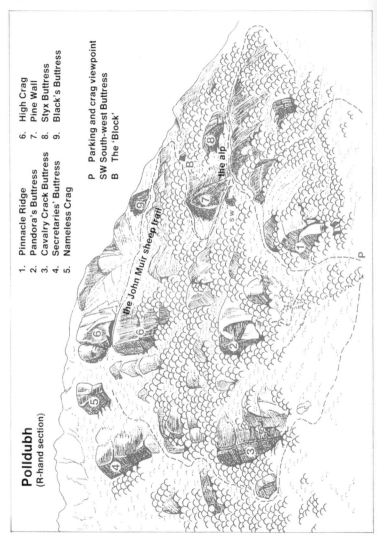

Lower Left Wall
The crack in the centre is **Clapham Junction (VS 5a)**, while
the wider crack on the R (**Severe Crack, MVS 4c**) has a tricky
start. **Soap Suds (E4 6a)** climbs through the overlap at L end
and is poorly protected.

139 **Pinnacle Ridge**   *145 ft (44 m)*   S
FA: *J. Ness, 1947*
Start at the toe of the ridge R of Severe Crack. Climb the edge
to a tree. An easy angled scoop leads to a terrace. From the tree
up on the R, move along the top of a big flake and up rough
slabs of the upper tier to the top.

140 **Tip Toe**   *75 ft (23 m)*   HS
FA: *J. Ness, 1947*
On the slabby R face, R of the ridge from the base of a
L-leading staircase, climb the slabs R to a small foothold.
Tiptoe L to good hand holds. Tr. L until possible to climb niche
to terrace on Pinnacle Ridge. A direct version climbs through
the break in O H R of the niche and on up slabs (E1 5b).

Pandora's Buttress 🦋 🦋 🦋
Sits up and L of Pinnacle Ridge. Characterized by two large
diag. cracks running R to L round the steep face which
separates the R-hand slabs and the steep L wall. The R wall
descends into the trees as two slabby tongues.
    The routes have considerable character, Flying Dutchman in
particular being a fine outing. Routes are described from R to L.

141 **Flying Dutchman**   *210 ft (63 m)*   S
FA: *T. Sullivan and I. Clough, 1959*
Start: At the base of the higher R-hand tongue.
1. 90 ft (27 m) Easily up the tongue to a large terrace. Tree
    belay.
2. 90 ft (27 m) Climb the large corner past slight bulge, till
    about 15 ft (4 m) below main roof. Tr. across slab, heading

diag. up to a short corner in L side of roof. Pull over and crack, then L round rib to stance. Awkward belay.

3. 30 ft (9 m) Scramble to top, or climb thin diag. crack in slab on R (VS 4c).

Tomag (E3/4 5c) climbs the twin diag. cracks up the OH-wall and is a midget's misfortune.

142 **Pandora**   *220 ft (66 m)*   S
FA: *T. Sullivan and E. Buckley, 1959*
Start: As for Tomag, then it climbs the major fault in the L face.

1. 80 ft (24 m) Up the L tongue to the terrace.
2. 70 ft (21 m) Continue up the rib on the L leading into the steep L wall, to a tree on R wall of big corner.
3. 70 ft (21 m) Go up the corner under the big roof, and then slabs lead to top.
3a. **Phantom Slab**, 60 ft (18 m) VS 4c. Drop down to another tree. Tr. out L on to slab and climb delicately by a vague crack line. Great climbing but poorly protected.

Cavalry Crack Buttress 🦋 🦋 🦋
One of the largest buttresses in the lower tiers of Polldubh. The imposing L wall is criss-crossed by cracks and a grassy break line at two-thirds height containing two big Caledonian pines. Down to the R, facing the road, is a smooth wall identified by two more big pines.

143 **Fang**   *145 ft (44 m)*   E2
FA: *W. Skidmore, P. MacKenzie and J. Crawford, 1963*
FFA: *E. Grindley and I. Nicholson, 1978*
This climbs up the centre of the clean wall at the R end which faces the road.
Start: About 25 ft (8 m) R of base of buttress, below a shallow groove with a roof 15 ft (5 m) up, guarding the base.

Flying Dutchman, Pandora's Buttress, Glen Nevis: climber, Alistair Todd

1. 70 ft (21 m) 5b Up to the roof (PR over lip). Continue up shallow groove to resting place. Break up the wall on R via tenuous blind moves, to gain ledge on edge. Gain and follow diag. crack L to nut belay on grass break.
2. 75 ft (23 m) 5a Up the large corner above to OH, then swing out R. Follow slabby groove to top.

L of Fang, two slabby ribs descend to the toe of the buttress. The next route starts up the L-hand rib:

144 **Drizzle**   *160 ft (48 m)   HS*
FA: *I. Sykes and party, 1959 (pitch 1)*
FA: *T. Sullivan, 1963 (pitch 2)*
Start: 10 ft (3 m) R of toe of buttress, by a holly tree.
1. 85 ft (26 m) Climb the L-hand rib above and behind the holly to the big pines.
2. 75 ft (23 m) Climb up the open corner behind pines with awkward step, and pull on to slab on R. Gain open vertical diedre running L to top.

145 **Heatwave**   *270 ft (82 m)   S*
FA: *I. Clough, and party, 1959*
Climbs line around slabby arete between the two faces of crag.
Start just L of toe of buttress at base of twin groove/ramps.
1. 70 ft (21 m) Follow either groove to belay at horizontal break.
2. 30 ft (10 m) Walk along break to R round edge then up to holly tree in base of gully.
3. 80 ft (25 m) Climb slabby L wall of gully close to edge to gain large terrace.
4. 90 ft (27 m) Climb slabs above trending L into short groove. Finish direct above.

Just L is another groove/ramp: The next route starts here:

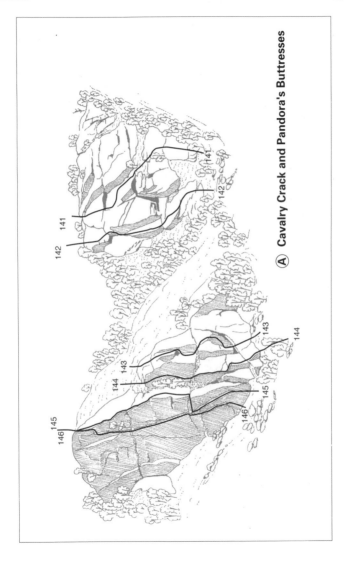

Ⓐ Cavalry Crack and Pandora's Buttresses

146 **Storm**   *250 ft (75 m)*   *HVS*
FA: *I. Clough and T. Sullivan, 1959*
FFA: *A. Austin and J. M. Austin, 1962*
The Polldubh classic.
1. 70 ft (21 m) 4b Climb the groove and ramp to belay below
   small tree at base of deep diag. crack.
2. 90 ft (27 m) 4c The diag. crack to large pine. Nut belay just
   R of R pine.
3. 90 ft (27 m) 5a Climb the groove above with hard moves
   over a bulge to easier ground. Either continue up groove in
   the R edge (great position) or tr. L into obvious corner with
   a roof (**True Finish** E1 5b).

To the L a wide crack runs up the centre of the wall to the
large pine on Storm. Not surprisingly this is known as **The
Long Crack (HVS 5a)**. From the pine it avoids the bulge
above via the wall on the L, regaining the continuation crack
just above.

Secretaries' Buttress 🦋 🦋
A big buttress high on hillside, level with base of High Crag.
Easily recognizable from the road by its steep L wall split into
three tiers by two oblique faults. One of the best buttresses in
Polldubh, with immaculate rock. Approach it most easily via a
faint path up the L-hand side of Cavalry Crack Buttress (see
diagram on p. 134).
   The base of the crag is guarded by a diag. roof. The
first route starts beyond the R end of this and climbs up the
slabs:

147 **Secretaries' Direct Route**   *260 ft (78 m)*   *MS*
FA: *I. Clough and E. Buckley, 1959*
Highly enjoyable.
Start: Just R of the 'Knoll' below the wall's arete at the large
L-facing slabby corner.
1. 45 ft (14 m) Up the corner to ledge of first fault. Tr. R to end
   of overlap above.

2. 55 ft (17 m) Climb the crack on superb quartz holds to the second fault.
3. 160 ft (48 m) Follow the slab and ridge to top.

148 **Super Direct**   *160 ft (48 m)*   *HVS*
FA: *K. Schwartz, J. Mount and A. Fulton, 1969*
Excellent thin work in a very exposed position. Start as for Direct Route.
1. 55 ft (17 m) 4c Step on to the sandwiched slab on L and tr. L Cross the overlap above, near the L edge, and up this first break. A surprising pitch.
2. 50 ft (15 m) 5a Follow the very smooth slab above keeping just L of a slight curving overlap to second break (daunting).
3. 55 ft (17 m) Cross the wide cleft, and easy slabs to top.

149 **Vincent**   *20 ft (60 m)*   *E3*
FA: *D. Cuthbertson and I. Sykes, 1981*
This climbs through all three tiers on the steep L wall. Not quite a tr. line, but with lots of diag. climbing. The top pitch is stunning.
Start: 20 ft (6 m) up R of the very toe of the L wall.
1. 80 ft (24 m) 5b Swing on to main face and follow diag. crack until large holds lead up to a nut belay on the shoulder of the first break.
2. 40 ft (12 m) 5c Move down break L for a few feet. Pull on to wall, then up with hard moves to gain thin crack near the shoulder. Follow, difficulties easing, to second break.
3. 80 ft (24 m) 5c Descend L to obvious break in roof. Swing on to wall with difficulty and follow crack until a line of good holds lead L to a small ledge. Thin diag. crack leads R with further interest, then direct to top.

Nameless Crag 🦋 🦋
A lovely airy crag in open surroundings between the top of Secretaries' and the 'Skull' of High Crag. It has two faces of quite different character, both offering bold climbing.

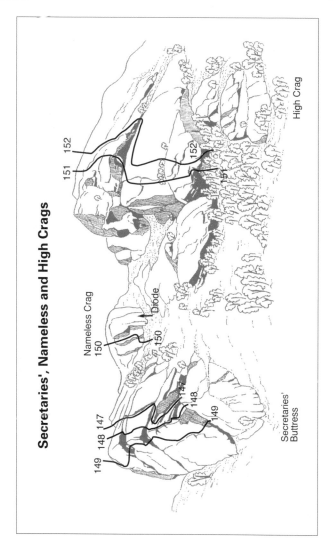

Secretaries', Nameless and High Crags

The West Face
This is split by two diag. slabby grooves. Between them is a conspicuous wide slab giving an excellent route:

150 **Risque Grapefruit** *100 ft (30 m) E4 5c*
FA: *D. Jameson and D. Cuthbertson, 1981*
Aptly named. Start below the R hand (undercut) groove. Pull into it and move L on to the slab. Climb diag. L over small overlap to resting footholds and poor runners. Thinly up right on to glacis in small corner. Follow this L to the top.

The East Face
A smooth blank-looking sheet of rock, staring across at the 'Skull' of High Crag, is split by two mossy vertical breaks into three distinct walls. The centre of the L wall is **Quadrode (E2 5b)**. The central wall gives **(Cathode Smiles (E2 5c)**. The R wall contains a prominent crack, **Diode (E2 5c)**, and the blank wall to its L, finishing up the stepped overlap, is **Triode (E5 6a)**. All are excellent.

High Crag 🦋 🦋
The biggest crag here, almost 500 ft (155 m), but its complex structure consists of several tiers of slabs culminating in the stunning 'Skull' formation.

The lower tier is scrappy, split half-way by a ledge with an overlap just above. The middle tier is about 200 ft (60 m) at its L end, where it turns to form a steep red wall bounding a shallow gully. The upper tier, again 200 ft (60 m), is undercut above huge terrace with 'Skull' to L.

Approach – Via path to Secretaries' and Nameless Crag. Alternatively, path from Pinnacle Ridge past Pine Wall on L and then up L through trees to base of lower tier.

Descent – Down hillside to L of The Skull.
The climbs begin from the middle tier, and are described L to R.

151 **Crag Lough Grooves**   *440 ft (137 m)*   *HVS*
FA: *T. Sullivan and I. Clough, 1959*
FFA: *A. Austin and J. Austin, 1962*
A varied climb with a hard crux, worth the struggle to find.
Start: Just L of a cave-like roof at the bottom L of the middle
tier.
1. 30 ft (9 m) Scramble up to OH.
2. 95 ft (29 m) 4c Tr. 12 ft (4 m) R across three small ribs into
    a red groove, which is climbed with decreasing difficulty to a
    ledge with small bushes.
3. 140 ft (42 m) 4a Climb a groove slightly to the R. Surmount
    a small OH and gain a small crack. This leads past a small
    pine to terrace.
4. 45 ft (14 m) 5b The most prominent break in the leaning roof
    is a hanging gangway. Pull on to its L end (crux) and follow
    it R (PR) and up groove to slab. Nut belay.
5. 60 ft (18 m) 4c Climb the groove above to slabs and ledge.
6. 100 ft (30 m) Fine open slabs lead to top.

152 **Kinloss Grooves/Autobahnausfahrt**   *435 ft (136 m)*   *VS*
FA: *I. Clough and T. Sullivan, 1959*
FA: *K. Schwartz and B. Chambers, 1969*
Varied and interesting.
Start: At tree below first break in OH R of Crag Lough
Grooves. L of a red wall.
1. 100 ft (30 m) 4c Climb to small niche below OH at 30 ft
    (9 m). Exit R and up to another niche. Continue above to
    ledge.
2. 105 ft (32 m) 4a Up slabs above anywhere to terrace.
3. 140 ft (42 m) 4b Climb steep slab at R end of OH guarding
    base of upper tier, passing heather groove at 25 ft (8 m) on
    its L. Up over bulge to slabs, then ledge.
4. 80 ft (24 m) Slabs pleasantly to top.

BUTTRESSES IN THE ALP

Above and R of Pinnacle Ridge is a flat grassy 'alp', hidden from view. The alp contains, as one approaches, South-west Buttress, Pine Wall and Styx Buttress. South-west Buttress is a small outcrop on entrance to alp, giving short routes used by instructional groups.

Pine Wall 🦋 🦋

A blatantly obvious buttress in the centre of the alp. The prominent features are a large Caledonian pine near the top, directly above a 150 ft (45 m) 'ridge'. Climbs are described L to R.

153 **Pine Wall** *220 ft (66 m)   HS*
FA: *J. Ness and A. Burgon, 1950*
A brilliant route, the best of its kind in the Glen.
Start: At the lowest point of the ridge.
1. 140 ft (42 m) 4b Up slab just L of crack of The Gutter to a platform. Up slab's edge to overlap. Move L and pull through overlap to small ledge. Slab above continually interesting, to horizontal break. Step slightly R to the deceptively blank slab above. Belay on large pine on terrace above.
2. 80 ft (24 m) Climb the wall above by a small recess just L of the crest to gain a crack in the crest.

154 **The Gutter** *150 ft (45 m)   D*
The crack R of Pine Wall to a ledge at about 100 ft (30 m). The ridge then leads to the large pine. Finish out R, or up the last pitch of Pine Wall (harder).

Styx Buttress
This lies immediately R of Pine Wall. The front face is slabby, split by an overlap. The L wall is its antithesis, forming an acutely OH prow-like roof. Routes described L to R.

155 **Black Friday**   *80 ft (24 m)   E5 6a*
FA: *K. Schwartz, B. Wright, 1969*
FFA: *M. Hamilton, J. Fantini, 1981*
Climbs wildly up through the cleft in the huge prow. Low in the grade.
Start: Directly below the prow. Gain a diag. ledge running R into the centre of the face to a niche. Pull over bulge (PR) and bridge out backwards to gain a niche in the prow. Swing crazily L to a flake leading through the cleft. Well protected, but strenuous.

156 **Resurrection**   *110 ft (33 m)   VS 4b*
FA: *I. Clough and A. Larkin, 1958*
An elegant route up the tapering slab in the crag's arete, with the crux at the narrows.
In the face to the R of Resurrection, the central line up a ramp to tiny pine, then over OH by a rib on R and direct up slab is **Damnation (VS 4b).**

157 **Itch**   *100 ft (30 m)   VS 5a*
FA: *I. Clough and T. Sullivan, 1959*
Intricate slab climbing R of Damnation.
Start: About 20 ft (6 m) R of that route at smooth slab. Climb L to just below R end of overlap. Pull through overlap (PR) to small ledge. Tricky moves up, then L, to gain a thin crack. Up this then slab to tree.

Black's Buttress 🦋 🦋
Well over on the R of Polldubh, at about the same level as High Crag, Black's lies amongst a sprawl of broken crags. Far from being black, it glows in the sun and is clearly visible from the road. Dries extremely quickly.
   Approach – From Pine Wall, passing just above the 'Block' (a 30 ft (9 m) boulder sitting in a slight depression) to reach a terrace cutting back towards the crag. A small grass terrace continues across the slabs below the main wall.

Shergar, Black's Buttress, Glen Nevis: Climber, Fiona Gunn

158 **Shergar** *90 ft(27 m)* *HVS 4c*
FA: *E. Grindley and F. Gunn, P. Long, C. Grindley, 1981*
This climbs the L edge of the cleanest section.
Start: At a small silver birch tree and climb thin R-slanting
cracks to gain a shallow L-facing corner to reach top.

159 **Land Ahoy** *90 ft (27 m)* *E3 5b*
FA: *E. Grindley and D. Gunn, 1981*
This climbs the main slab just R of Shergar. Good protection
appears after the crux, but the climbing is sustained and
brilliant.
Start: Below and slightly R of obvious crackline that begins
about 30 ft (9 m) up. Up to good foot-ledge. Step L to quartz
and up blank-looking wall on brick edges, until quartz vein
veers off R. Go L and gain crack with further thin moves. Up
crack more easily to top.

160 **Centrepiece**   *90 ft (27 m)   E6 6b*
FA: *K. Howett and G. Latter (both led), 1987*
FA: *M. Garthwaite, 1994 (after original poor PR fell out)*
Climb directly up the centre of the slab R of Land Ahoy,
gaining horizontal break with hard moves (Skyhook used on flat
hold). Then up thin crack above with further difficulty.

161 **Kaos**   *100 ft (30 m)   E2 5c*
FA: *K. Schwartz and P. T. Logan, 1972*
FFA: *E. Grindley and P. Long, 1981*
This climbs the thin vertical crack R of Centrepiece. Up first
crack and step L to tiny ledge at 35 ft (11 m). Gain crack above,
and so to top. Poorly protected and delicate.

CAR PARK AREA
There are several crags in the vicinity of the road-head car-park,
including the largest outside Polldubh. The two major ones,
Whale Rock and Car Park, offer brilliant climbing, quite
different to Polldubh.

Whale Rock   (163686) Alt. 600 ft (180 m) North-west
facing 🦋 🦋 🦋
Seen most clearly from the road just after the single track
squeezes between two massive pine trees and a large boulder. It
rests on open hillside on a small knoll across the River Nevis.
   Approach – Cross the river via a wooden bridge 100 yds
(100 m) down from the twin pines (158684).

162 **Earthstrip**   *100 ft (30 m)   E2 5c*
FA: *D. Armstrong and Andy Wright, 1983*
The obvious crack in the centre of the main face with the crux
above(!) the blank section.

Earthstrip, Whale Rock, Glen Nevis: climber, Andy Nelson

163 **Run for Home**   *100 ft (30 m)   E5 6a*
FA: *K. Howett and A. A. Moist, 1985*
This is the hairline crack R of Earthstrip, climbed on 'tinies' to
join that route at mid-height. Good gear, but sustained.

164 **Femme Fatale**   *80 ft (25 m)   E8 6c*
Very serious climbing up the scoops in the bulging nose of the
crag. Start directly below the nose. Hard pull over initial bulge
into first scoop (complicated protection includes PR low down
on ledge on L, RP's low down in crack on R and skyhook).
Move up R (small HB's in thin crack on R) into second scoop
(PR). Step R into L-diag. crack to finish. Unrepeated.

165 **Just a Little Tease**   *80 ft (24 m)   E5 6b*
FA: *D. Cuthbertson, 1984*
This climbs the twin ragged cracks in the upper half of the
prow.
Start: Above a boulder 20 ft (6 m) R of scoop in base of prow.
Place high runner 10 ft (3 m) directly above (opposition NR at
base of prow). Elongate L across a scoop to jug. Stand on it
and step L to base of cracks. Struggle up these.

Car Park Crag   (170688) Alt. 800 ft (240 m) North-west
facing 𝈙 𝈙
This is the biggest crag in the Steall area, but is disappointingly
covered in lichen. However, both the following routes are clean
and are classics at their grade.
  The crag can clearly be seen opposite the road-head car-park,
up and L of Whale Rock.
  Approach – Cross the river below the car-park via a small
weir (wet feet), and strike directly up the hillside to it.
  Topography – The most obvious feature is a clean pillar just
R of centre. Twin cracks in its L side are the only fault (Quality
Street). A series of grooves mark the central section and a clean
pillar bounds the L-hand side.

166 **Quality Street**   *220 ft (66 m)*   *E3*
FA: *K. Schwartz and B. Chambers, 1970*
FFA: *P. Whillance and M. Hamilton, 1981*
Strangely, this climb is excluded from *Extreme Rock*.
Start: Beside an inset block and a twisting tree below the wall.
1. 130 ft (39 m) 6a Up thin cracks R of block to meet curving
   crack from the L. Continue with difficulty up twin cracks
   through bulge and wall above into L-facing corner. Step R
   into another shallow corner and up to slab (nut belay).
2. 90 ft (27 m) 4c Finish up the R-facing corner above.

167 **Restless Natives**   *235 ft (70 m)*   *E5*
FA: *G. Latter, K. Howett and A. Nelson* (alt), *1988*
Climbs the clean pillar near the L end of the main crag. The
second pitch is potentially dangerous but eminently pleasurable.
Start: Below the slabby pillar where a grassy gangway slants
diag. R across the face.
1. 75 ft (23 m) 6a Up into a little niche (Skyhook). Hard moves
   out R into second niche. Up into short L-facing groove and
   crack to ledge.
2. 80 ft (24 m) 6a Up crack in slab to its finish. Go up and
   diag. R to jugs. Tr. R on to hanging glacis: poor N R. Direct
   up steep wall to lip. Pull over via flat hold in centre of slab
   above to gain tree-filled ledge. Very bold.
3. 100 ft (30 m) 5a Up slabby rib directly above to top.

STEALL AREA
The crags are scattered haphazardly. Gorge Crag can be seen
from the car-park, poking through trees just above where the
river disappears S into the entrance to gorge. On the open
hillside of Meall Cumhann above lie Wave, Spreadeagle and
Blade, amongst smaller outcrops. In the gorge itself are the
gorge walls, either side of the river. Beyond this in Steall
Valley R of the waterfall is Steall Crag, while Meadow Walls
lie on the L (on Meall Cumhann), along with Galaxy Buttress.
   Approach – A tourist path leaves the car-park and runs
through the gorge into Steall Valley, passing Gorge and Gorge

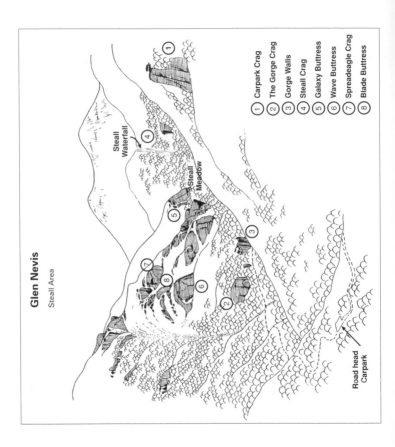

Glen Nevis

Steall Area

Steall Waterfall

Steall Meadow

Road head Carpark

1. Carpark Crag
2. The Gorge Crag
3. Gorge Walls
4. Steall Crag
5. Galaxy Buttress
6. Wave Buttress
7. Spreadeagle Crag
8. Blade Buttress

Walls. A smaller pony track branches off L from this, between the first and second streams, to cross the tourist path (before entering the gorge). It rises diag. across Meall Cumhann to base of Wave Buttress, and then zig-zags down into Steall Valley, see map on p. 128.

The Gorge Crag   (174692) Alt. 650 ft (200 m)
West-facing 🦋 🦋 🦋
Its base lies 75 ft (23 m) above the path. There is an obvious steep rib whose L wall is a slender slab and whose main R wall (seen from the car-park) is a smooth two-tiered OH-wall.

168 **Plague of Blazes**   *120 ft (36 m)*   *E2 5b*
FA: *E. Grindley, N. Williams and F. Gunn, 1982*
Climb the thin cracks up the centre of the slender slab. The crack leads up L to top of flake. Move L under bulge and up to shallow groove, which gains slab above. Finish direct up steep wall.

169 **Travellin' Man**   *150 ft (45 m)*   *E2*
FA: *D. Cuthbertson and G. Latter, 1982*
Climb the groove in the steep rib between the two faces to a ledge (5b). Then take the shallow L-hand groove above, stepping L to slabs leading R to top (5c).

170 **Cosmopolitan**   *100 ft (30 m)*   *E5*
FA: *D. Cuthbertson and G. Latter, 1982*
This climbs the centre of the OH-wall R of rib. Gain the L-facing groove from L to big ledge (6a). The cracks above are gained from the R, and succumb – usually with falls (6b). Safe but hard.

The deep crack R of Cosmopolitan is **Conscription (E1 5b)** which leads into the deep corner on R near top. The corner is **All our Yesterdays (E1 5b)** with crux of both gaining ledge on L at top.

Gorge Walls   (174691) Alt. 650 ft (200 m) 🦋 🦋 🦋
These walls lie 100 yds/metres beyond Gorge Crag, on each
side of the path, just before exiting into Steall Meadow. The
first encountered lies on the L, and is distinguished by an
OH-arete dropping nearly to path and a diag. crack running
across the face to the R. A large boulder lies on the opposite
side of the path. Just beyond this boulder the river falls between
a chaotic jumble of massive boulders, wedged against the slab
on the other side. The following two routes are on the L wall.

171   **Chimera**   *130 ft (39 m)   E4 6a*
FA: *K. Howett and A. A. Moist, 1985*
Climb the steep protectionless L arete to horizontal break, and
then the arching groove in rib above, with a hard move to finish
out L. Slabs lead up to tree. Abseil off.

172   **Easy Pickings**   *130 ft (39 m)   E4 6a*
FA: *K. Howett, A. A. Moist and C. Henderson, 1985*
This climbs the vertical crack in rib just R of Chimera to a
ledge, then swings up L (the diag. R 'wards crack is The
Gallery, E4), into ramp leading R till it is possible to grovel
over top on to slab. Teeter up L to tree. Abseil off.

173   **Aquarian Rebels**   *90 ft (27 m)   E4 6a*
FA: *D. Cuthbertson and G. Latter, 1985*
This climbs the intermittent central crackline up the slabs above
the jammed boulders across the river. Nut belay precariously on
the wedged boulders. Step down R into niche.
Pull up on quartz to base of crack leading L (Liquidator, E1
5b). Step R, then up thin cracks and groove to ledge. Cracks
above to top. Atmospheric.

Steall Crag   (177683) Alt. 800 ft (250 m) North
facing 🦋 🦋 🦋
At the far end of the flat meadow of Steall Valley, a wire

Aquarian Rebels, Gorge Walls, Glen Nevis: climber, Andy Nelson

bridge crosses the river to Steall Hut. Behind the hut is Steall Crag. The L wall is high and slabby, whilst the R wall is very steep and contains some of the best hard routes of the Glen.

174 **Lame Beaver**   *100 ft (30 m)   E7 6b*
FA: *K. Howett, 1985 (1 rest)*
FFA: *D. Cuthbertson, 1987*
A powerful route up the L side of the steep wall.
Start: 5 ft (1 m) from the L end. Gain a shield of rock and move up into a niche in the roof above. Undercling R into next niche, then pull over. Step up and L when an undercling move gains a finger-pocket, then the upper crack. Follow this to its top and escape out L. Serious.
In the centre of the wall is a shallow cave. Above it is a large niche. This is the line of **Trick of the Tail (E6 6b)**. Hard moves between the lower cave and the upper niche gains a rest. It then pulls out R into twin cracks to top. The thin crack leading into these finishing cracks, started by pulling R out of cave at the bottom, is **Arcadia (E7 6b)**, a painfully hard exercise in crack climbing.

175 **Leopold**   *80 ft (25 m)   E7 6c*
FA: *M. Hamilton, 1992 (red-pointed with protection pre-placed)*
The wider R-diagonal crack-line starting from the R side of the cave is undoubtedly one of Scotland's best hard crack climbs. Pull out of the R side of the cave and struggle all the way with a detour to good undercuts at the obvious shield of rock. Unrepeated.

Galaxy Buttress   (179687) Alt. 900 ft (270 m)
South-west facing 🦋 🦋
This smooth triangular slab guarded by a large roof is blatantly obvious half-way down Steall Meadow on the flanks of Meall Cumhann:

176 **Short Man's Walkabout**   *150 ft (45 m)*   *E4*
FA: *D. Cuthbertson and G. Latter, 1983*
A brilliant route directly through the roof and up a crack in
centre of slab.
1. 110 ft (33 m) 6b Climb the centre of the roof by a thin crack
   (PR). Pull over lip and up crack to step R to scoop. Regain
   crack and follow it to ledge. Strangely easier for midgets.
2. 40 ft (12 m) 4c Gain scoop above from R and so to top.

Wave Buttress   (177693) Alt. 1,300 ft (400 m)
South-west facing 🦋 🦋
Perched on the flanks of Meall Cumhann a few hundred feet
above the gorge. Reach it by the old pony track. Superbly
situated and relatively free of midges. It is split in two sections
by a diag. tree-infested gully. Routes are described L to R.

177 **First Wave**   *100 ft (30 m)*   *E1 5c*
FA: *E. Grindley and N. Williams, 1982*
Start at quartz blotches near R side of wall. Climb diag. R to
foot of ramp. Climb this and take direct line up steep flakes to
top.

178 **On the Beach**   *120 ft (36 m)*   *E5 6a*
FA: *M. Hamilton and R. Anderson, 1984*
The wall is split by an obvious L – R diag. crack (Crack
Attack).
Start: 20 ft (6 m) L of its base below a large flake 10 ft (3 m)
up. Climb on to flake, step R to gain a small ramp which leads
L into a faint groove. Boldly struggle up this to end of
difficulties. Up grooves above to steep upper wall and turn on L
to finish on a slab (PB).

179 **Ground Zero**   *100 ft (30 m)*   *E2 5c*
FA: *E. Grindley, N. Williams and F. Gunn and C. Grindley,
1982*
Climbs a prominent shallow hanging groove in wall just L of
obvious diagonal crack of Crackattack. Climb wall direct past

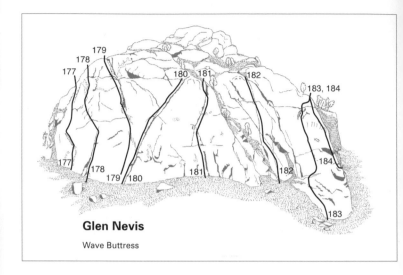

Glen Nevis

Wave Buttress

small flakes into base of groove. Up this and quartz staircase above. Bold lower wall.

180 **Crackattack**   *100 ft (30 m)   E3 5c*
FA: *E. Grindley and B. Owens, 1983*
Climb the striking diag. crackline with the crux in the final few feet. A well-protected gem.

181 **Bewsey Crack**   *100 ft (30 m)   HVS 5a*
FA: *E. Grindley and N. Williams, 1983*
Near the R edge of this L-hand section. Climb the L-hand of three short corners and the crack in the slab to gain a niche below the steep upper wall. Well protected after the start.

182 **Straight Thinking**   *100 ft (30 m)   E5 6a*
FA: *G. Latter and N. Sharpe, 1986*
Just R of tree-lined gully R of Bewsey Crack is a faint vertical

crackline starting from raised grass ledge. Climb easy at first to
bulge. Pull over direct into faint vertical crack (more prominent
diag. L crack is **The Gift, E5**) and follow it (hard) to horizontal
break (crucial runner round L arete). Teeter up R to finish.

183 **Walter Wall (Washington)**   *120 ft (36 m)   E4 6a (E5 6a)*
FA: *K. Spence, I. McKenzie, 1984*
(FA: *D. Cuthbertson, G. Latter, 1985*)
This climbs up the centre of the wall to the R of the tree-lined
gully. Follow a grass ledge that intrudes R into the wall 20 ft
(6 m) above its base. Up and R into a scoop. Up it to good
holds, then up wall without protection to horizontal crack. Hard
moves past this gains shelf. Escape R.
     (Washington starts at toe of buttress. Climb wall to NR; a
bulge forces moves L to gain scoops of Walter Wall. Up this
past horizontal crack to shelf. Shuffle L and climb faint groove
above over small bulge to finish out R – very bold.)

184 **Edgehog**   *120 ft (36 m)   E3 5c*
FA: *E. Grindley and N. Williams, 1982*
The striking R arete of the face, started from the R. NRS appear
just when most needed. Brilliant.

Spreadeagle Crag   (178691) Alt. 1,500 ft (450 m)
West facing ✗ ✗
A small indistinct path leads up the gully R of Wave Buttress, first
on the L then crossing to the R to run beneath a large crag
characterized by a slab and huge R-facing corner arching over it.

185 **Spreadeagle**   *120 ft (36 m)   E4 6a*
FA: *D. Cuthbertson and G. Latter, 1982*
On the R is a prominent corner (Slipaway, E2 5c) to the L of
which a scoop leads to a slender hanging groove bounding the R
side of the large slab. Climb the scoop below and L of the
hanging groove. Hard moves lead R into the groove, where
further hard moves are encountered just when you thought it
was all over.

186 **Chiaroscuro**   *100 ft (30 m)*   *E7 6b*
FA: *K. Howett and A. Nelson, 1988*
Takes serious and difficult line up blunt rib cutting directly
through groove of Spreadeagle. Start in short scoop between
corner of Slipaway and larger scoop of Spreadeagle. Up scoop
and three vertical slots above to projecting nose. Gain base of
hanging groove on Spreadeagle. Out L onto hanging block.
Climb directly up L side of rib above with increasing
uncertainty to flap onto sloping ledge at top.

187 **Veinity Fair**   *100 ft (30 m)*   *E3 5b*
FA: *A. Nelson and K. Howett, 1988*
Climbs slab to L. Start below small tree at L side of wall. Up
to tree and small grass ledge. Tr. 15 ft (5 m) R, then direct up
slab to quartz vein. Follow this diag. R to its end then up and R
to top. Superb but bold.

Blade Buttress   (178692) Alt. 1,550 ft (465 m)
South-facing 🦋
Directly opposite Spreadeagle Crag across the gully is a
prominent pillar with a clean cut OH-corner in the L side of
jutting blade of rock that forms the pillar.

188 **Cruisability**   *70 ft (21 m)*   *E5 6b*
FA: *G. Latter, 1986*
The impressive corner. Brilliant climbing with the crux passing
the roof at mid-height.

189 **Flight of the Snowgoose**   *90 ft (27 m)*   *E6 6b*
FA: *K. Howett, G. Latter and D. Cuthbertson, 1985*
Climbs the front of the impressive pillar R of Cruisability.
Start: In the centre of the face just L of a prominent recess.
Follow cracks to a ledge, then thin crack up centre of pillar.
Near its top tr. R across wall to R edge. Up to small foot ledge
(Skyhook runner). Thin climbing on rounded dimples gains the

Edgehog, Wave Buttress, Glen Nevis: climber, Dave Cuthbertson

top. A bold undertaking. (The thin crackline can be finished out
L at E2 5b – **Ugly Duckling**).

BEN NEVIS   (167713) Alt. 4,406 ft (1,344 m)

Introduction
As the highest hill in Britain it has always attracted attention
from tourists and climbers. Its western coast position and height
combine to produce almost unique weather conditions. This
means Ben Nevis's winter climbs are also unique, and
world-renowned, but its summer climbing is less well-known.

   The North-East Face falls abruptly from the plateau in a
complex series of buttresses, ridges and gullies extending for
almost 2 miles (3 km). Some of the faces receive an ample
supply of sun whilst others only catch a glimpse. After
prolonged rain, it takes several days of dry weather to dry the
usual weeps.

History
The Victorians were great tourists, and in the 1890s they
constructed a pony track up to a weather observatory on the
summit. One adventurous tourist recorded an ascent of the
North Face by a gully in 1880, but the first major rock ascents
came in 1892, and they were quite remarkable. The Hopkinson
family from Manchester climbed Tower Ridge and North-East
Buttress, but their ascents were unknown to the SMC regulars
who later claimed first ascents. The SMC began regular Easter
meets after the railway reached Fort William in 1894, initially
concentrating on winter projects. Then, in 1896, Edinburgh-born
Harold Raeburn began raiding the Ben's rock potential as a
guest of the SMC, often solo (Observatory Ridge and Buttress)
and often with Dr and Mrs Jane Inglis Clark. But leading at this
time was only marginally safer, with hemp rope, no runners and
nailed boots. A hut was built after the war in 1926 by the
Clarks in memory of their son, and this helped speed
development between the wars.

Alan T. Hargreaves of the Fell and Rock Climbing Club partnered George Graham MacPhee on Route 1, the chimney up the left side of Carn Dearg, but Hargreaves' best was Rubicon Wall on Observatory Buttress, wearing plimsolls. However the great James H. B. Bell and MacPhee were to dominate. MacPhee added many routes, his best being a direct to Central Trident Buttress (S); he repeated many others and later produced a guidebook. Bell meanwhile became obsessed with Orion Face. It was actually first breached by Sandy Wederburn and a Yugoslavian team, but their Slav Route was close to Zero Gully. Bell finally succeeded on a brilliant direct line in 1940, four years after his first sorties. In the same year the JMCS's leading light, Ian Ogilvie, climbed on the Ben, but his routes were not up to the standard he achieved on Rannoch Wall. He died later that year in the Cairngorms.

During the war Brian Pinder Kellet, a pacifist, volunteered to work in the forestry at Torlundy. In the evenings and weekends he repeated all the known routes and added his own, many solo. The great Route II on Carn Dearg and Left Hand Route on the Minus Face were two of his best. Carn Dearg held a particular, and ultimately fatal, attraction for him. He even attempted to gain the chimneys of Sassenach but failed to cross the slabs out of the Centurion Corner. In 1944 this outstanding climber was killed in a fall with Nancy Forsyth.

A lull until the 1950s ended with renewed attempts on Sassenach. An Aberdonian team (Tom Patey, Bill Brooker and A. Taylor) tried from the right, but ran out of steam and daylight in the first of the chimneys. Don Whillans and Joe Brown snatched it a year later.

Bob Downes and Mike O'Hara, two talented climbers from the Cambridge University club, made an initial attempt on Minus One Buttress, but were forced out left into Minus Two Gully (North-East Grooves). The next year they added three more pitches up the centre but again escaped, this time into Minus One Gully. Then in 1972 this line was added to by Ian Fulton and Ken Crocket (The Serendipity Line). The line was improved upon again in 1983 by Noel Williams and Steve Abbot when they climbed the impressive arete up the centre of the buttress, to give one of the best routes on Ben Nevis: Minus One Buttress.

In 1956 Downes teamed up with Whillans to snatch Centurion (HVS), the magnificent corner up Carn Dearg. Whillans had difficulty on the crux corner (earlier climbed by J. R. Marshall), and Downes solved the roofs at the top. The next day they climbed The Shield (also HVS).

Scottish pride was restored when Robin Smith and Dougal Haston teamed up for The Bat (E2). This and the little known Subtraction (E1) on Minus One Buttress by John McLean and Bill Smith of the Creagh Dhu continued their interest. Marshall and J. Stenhouse gave their brilliant Bullroar across Carn Dearg's front face. MacLean, Bill Smith and W. Gordon then climbed an even better route, Torro (E2). Marshall soon wrote a new guidebook, and climbed all but four of the existing routes, quite a feat considering the obstacles involved.

In 1970 the most interesting discovery was Central Trident Buttress by Creagh Dhu members. However over the next decade Carn Dearg's potential drew most of the significant developments. It started in 1977 when two teams arrived to free the crackline on the West Face. Aided by Ian Clough and Hamish MacInnes in 1959, Titan's Wall was snatched by Mick Fowler and Phil Thomas, just beating 'locals' Dave Cuthbertson and Murray Hamilton. The Big Banana Groove, an obvious feature right of Sassenach, was ascended in part by Cuthbertson, Dougie Mullin and Willy Todd, as Caligula (E3) in 1978. On sight and on lichenous rock it was a fine ascent. The continuation directly up the groove above was nabbed by Hamilton in 1983, Banana Groove (E4 6a) is one of the most stunning pitches on the buttress.

The other main event of 1983 was the ascent of the arete of Titan's Wall. Pete Whillance with Rab Anderson, pulled the stops out on a very cold windy day to give Agrippa, the Ben's hardest and most serious route.

Accommodation
Camping – Glen Nevis Campsite (125722) open March –
October tel: (01397)702 191. Wild camping in Coire Leis below
North Face cliffs.
Bunkhouses – The closest are: Ben Nevis Bunkhouse, Achintee,
Glen Nevis (125731) at the start of the pony track up Ben Nevis
tel: (01397)702 240, The Smiddy, Corpach, on the road out to
Mallaig tel: (01397)772 467, Calluna, Fort William tel:
(01397)700 451 and The Backpacker's Hostel, Fort William tel:
(01397)700 711. Further afield are Grey Corrie Lodge tel:
(01397)712 236 and Aite Cruinnichidh tel: (01397)712 315 both
in or near Roy Bridge, or slightly further along the road at
Tulloch Railway Station is Station Lodge Bunkhouse (355803).
Club Huts – There are only two climbers' huts in the immediate
vicinity. The CIC Hut (SMC) directly below the North Face
cliffs (167723) at an altitude of 2400 ft (800 m) and Steall Hut
(JMCS) in Steall Meadow, Glen Nevis (178683).
Youth Hostel – Glen Nevis Hostel (128718).

Mountain Rescue Shelters
Summit Shelter (167713); Coire Leis Shelter (174714).

Guidebooks
Ben Nevis, Rock and Ice Climbs, S. Richardson, SMC, 1994

THE NORTH FACE CLIFFS
There are rock climbs on virtually every buttress enclosed
within the coires of the North Face. Some are more suited to
ascents in their winter garb, but the following climbs are
generally solid, on clean rock and are among the finest rock
climbs in Scotland.
   Approach – 1) From Glen Nevis, starting at either Achintee
or the youth hostel, follow the pony track up Meall an t'Suidhe
(pronounced 'Mellantee', and a subsidiary summit of Ben
Nevis) to Lochan Meall an t'Suidhe. The summit track zig-zags
up R. Follow L branch over bealach, then continue under North
Face to reach CIC hut: 2 hrs 30 mins. 2) Via the Allt A

'Mhuillin. Access is also possible along a good path following stream that issues from Coire Lies, the Allt A 'Mhuillin. Start from (sign-posted) 'Allt A 'Mhuillin Car Park' (144763) at Torlundy, just off the A82 north of Fort William. From the car park in forest, follow path up R skirting golf course, to join old narrow gauge railway line. Follow this R until steep path (initially boggy) climbs up wooded hillside to reach Allt A'Mhuilinn by small dam. Follow the path up L bank to CIC hut: 2 hrs (boggy).

Topography – On the L (E) is Coire Leis at the head of the glen. It is bounded on the R by the ridge of North-East Buttress. The bay formed between this and the next ridge, Tower Ridge, contains the Orion face, Observatory Ridge and Tower Gully. The large open coire between Tower Ridge and the massive buttress of Carn Dearg to the R (W) is Coire na Ciste. This contains numerous separate buttresses including the three Trident Buttresses. The CIC hut sits below the base of Tower Ridge, see diagram on p. 169.

Descent – Normal descent off the summit is No. 3 gully into Coire na Ciste, see diagram on p. 169. See also under cliff headings for specific descents.

The Minus and Orion Faces   (169716) Alt. 2,900 ft (950 m) West facing
This huge face forms the W side of North-East Buttress which leads up to the summit of the Ben. It is split by long vertical faults into three buttresses, the Minus Buttresses. They are numbered 3 to 1 from L to R. To their R, in the back of the small bay which they enclose, is the huge Orion Face, which drops vertically from the summit itself: diagram, p. 170.

Descent – Between the tops of Minus One and Two Buttresses is an area of grass which leads diag. down L across the face beyond (Little Brenva Face of Coire Leis) as a broad terrace. This gives a possible descent. Alternatively, climb up North-East Buttress to the top and descend No. 3 Gully.

Minus Two Buttress

The central and largest of the three, characterised by a huge nose at mid-height formed by a L-facing stepped roof. Just below the nose a raised crest is bounded on the L by a slim corner heading up to the stepped roof, and on the R by a large R-facing corner.

190 **Left-Hand Route**   *800 ft (240 m)   VS*
FA: *B. P. Kellet, R. L. and C. M. Plackett, 1944*
A great little route, which climbs up the crest to beneath the stepped roof under the nose and skirts its L side.
Start: By cracks which ascend the L side of the raised crest. Low in grade.

1/2. 270 ft (66 m) 4a Up the cracks to reach ledge at foot of slab bounded on its R by the stepped roofs.

3. 30 ft (9 m) 4b From L end of ledge descend slab for 10 ft (3 m), then tr. L round rib to gain further slab. Up this on small holds to ledge below the stepped roof/corner. Alternatively, ascend diag. L up slab from belay to ledge, 4c.

4. 120 ft (36 m) 4a Continue up L edge overlooking Minus Three Gully till possible to gain rib on R (nut belay).

5. 410 ft (123 m) Easier climbing up slabs in the centre of buttress to top.

Minus One Buttress

This vertical buttress (on R-hand) is hemmed in between the deep clefts of Minus Two Gully on L and Minus One Gully on R. The gullies begin close together in the upper L-hand side of the bay below Orion Face, and move apart as they gain height, thus enlarging the buttress to form a tower-like upper half with deep grooves in the L forming an impressive crest or arete.

191 **Minus One Direct**   *860 ft (256 m)   E1*
FA: *R. Downes, M. O'Hara and M. Prestige, 1956*
FA: *K. Crocket and I. Fulton, 1972 (Serendipity)*
FA: *N. Williams and S. Abbott, 1983 (Arete Finish)*
One of the most enjoyable climbs known to mankind: sustained, on perfect rock.

Start: In the middle of the lowest rocks of Minus One Buttress.

1. 70 ft (21 m) 4b Climb up the L-facing corner above and exit R above the glacis.
2. 80 ft (24 m) 4c Ascend shallow groove in wall diag. L to detached block at about 15 ft (4 m). Pass it by crack on its R (hard). Then short walls, moving L to grassy niche.
3. 60 ft (18 m) Step R and easily to top of a huge plinth.
4. 75 ft (23 m) 5b Tr. R on to nose above OH and climb to ledge. At R end of ledge is undercut groove. Pull into this and up it (NR) until possible to climb ramp on R which leads to a belay on large platform overlooking the lower chimney of Minus One Gully.
5. 70 ft (21 m) 5a (**Serendipity**) Above is wide crack above OH (original line). Take a rising diag. line L with a hard move into a recess. Make some devious moves up this, then easier rocks lead to grassy niche.
6. 65 ft (19 m) 4c (**Arete Finish**) Step L into another recess beneath OHS in crest. Climb its slabby L wall, then steeper section above until possible to break out R on slabs to stance by stacked blocks.
7. 55 ft (17 m) 5b (**Arete Finish**) There is a prominent slab on L capped by long narrow OH. Up slab to below OH (PR), tr. L (delicate) on underclings to arete. Follow it in grand position to small very exposed stance.
8. 140 ft (42 m) 4c (**Arete Finish**) Tricky move off stance and up crack in crest leading to easier rock and the great terrace.
9. 130 ft (39 m) 4b Climb to the top of a massive flake then up the crest easily to a curiously poised pedestal.
10. 125 ft (38 m) The narrow, shattered arete above joins North-East Buttress.

Orion Face

This is the main face in the back of the bay, bounded on the L by Minus One Buttress and on the R by Observatory Ridge. Separating Orion Face from Observatory Ridge is Zero Gully. The next route climbs directly up the centre of the face:

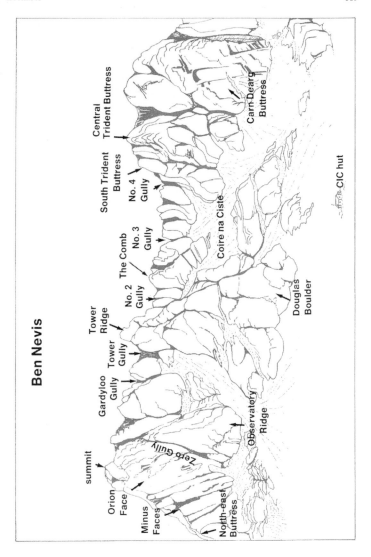

Ben Nevis

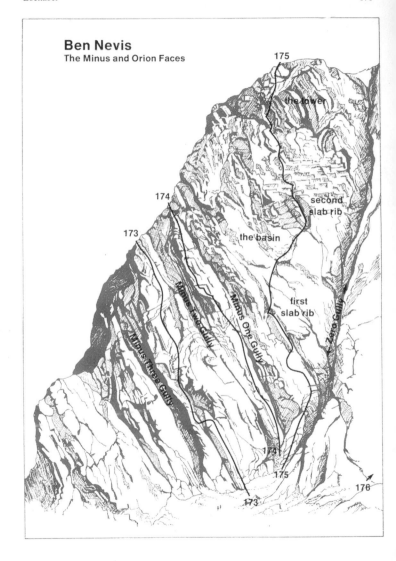

Ben Nevis
The Minus and Orion Faces

175

the tower

second
slab rib

the basin

first
slab rib

174

173

Minus Two Gully

Minus One Gully

Minus Three Gully

Zero Gully

174

175

176

173

192 **The Long Climb**   *1,430 ft (429 m)   VS*
FA: *J. H. B. Bell and J. D. B. Wilson, 1940*
Regarded by most as Bell's greatest route, this is the only truly
alpine-type route in the British Isles, as a sizeable snow patch
usually lingers below its start. It is very long and finishes on the
summit. The rock is good, and the atmosphere impressive.
Start: At an ochre-coloured rib protruding down from the face
100 ft (30 m) L of Zero Gully (the gully in the R side of the
bay).

1. 200 ft (60 m) Climb up the rib to platform.
2. 150 ft (45 m) 4a From R end of platform follow rib, steep,
   (easier further to L), to level with the first slab rib – a
   sandwiched, narrow slab on the R guarded by a lower slab
   to its L and a deep-roofed recess on its R.
3. 100 ft (30 m) Tr. R under the lower slab and OH of the rib
   itself for 10 ft (3 m) to below twin cracks cleaving the slab/
   rib. Up these with intent (think of Bell in his socks!) to
   recess.
4. 150 ft (45 m) Move out R, and up easily into the basin.
5. 150 ft (45 m) Climb up and across the basin, heading for
   the obvious second slab/rib hanging in the top R of the
   basin. This is a tapering slab, sandwiched between deep
   corners. PB below it.
6. 100 ft (30 m) 4b Climb the slab rib by its L edge on perfect
   rock. Above steeper rock is turned on L wall (poorly
   protected). Belay on crest.
7. 30 ft (9 m) The wall above is awkward and climbed on L or
   R to a stance.
8. 100 ft (30 m) Easier rock leads up and R, heading towards
   another conspicuous but larger slab in the L side of the
   final tower of the face above.
9. 150 ft (45 m) From a grassy ledge below the tower, head up
   by devious tr.s, gaining the R side of the slab.
10. 150 ft (45 m) Up rocks on its R to niche near top.
11. 50 ft (15 m) A short tricky tr. R leads to stance.
12. 100 ft (30 m) Up final rocks to crest of North-East Buttress.

Ben Nevis
The Trident Buttress

198

No. 4 Gully
(descent)

197
196
195

Great Corner

Central Trident

197

195   196

Central Gully

Jubilee Climb

South
Trident

198

193 **Observatory Ridge, Ordinary Route**   *900 ft (270 m)   VD*
FA: *H. Raeburn, 1901*
Start: At the foot of the Ridge or from the R. Tr. L above
lowest rocks to gain ridge. Reach R end of obvious terrace at
200 ft (90 m). Continue slightly L of the crest. At steep section
turn to the R flank of the buttress. Follow to narrow, easy
angled crest, overlooking Zero Gully. Ascend to plateau.

194 **Tower Ridge**   *2,700 ft (820 m)   D*
FA: *J. E. and B. Hopkinson, 1892*
FA: *W. G. McClymont and J. H. B. Bell, 1936* (Douglas
Boulder, *NW Face)*
The longest route in Britain! The following description includes
a start up the Douglas Boulder, which should not be missed.
Three chimneys in the Boulder Face as viewed from the CIC
Hut form an inverted 'N'.
Start: To R of prominent smooth slab wall of lower rocks below
the L chimney.
Climb an easy angled groove to short wall barring access to
L-hand chimney (belay). Climb wall to outer chimney (belay).
Follow chimney for a little, tr. slabs R into central chimney
(belay). Up this till 18 ft (6 m) below chockstone narrows; tr.
slabs R to rib. Up and L to chimney exit (belay). Choice of
easier lines leads to top of Boulder. Descend to gap. (This can
all be avoided by ascending easy grass slope round to E of the
Boulder to gain the gap.)
    Just L of the gap is 60 ft (18 m) chimney leading to crest of
ridge, narrow and level, leading to first step. Turn by ledge to R.
Scrambling (M) follows over several short steps and a level
section leading to base of little tower. Follow rocks on L edge
to gain awkward ledge running back R to corner, then to easy
rocks leading to base of Great Tower. A level grassy ledge
(Eastern Traverse) runs out L (exposed), crossing a groove then
to a tunnel under huge fallen block. Steep easy rocks on R gain
top of Tower. (Eastern Traverse continues L as escape route.)
Follow narrow crest to Tower Gap; negotiate this. Easier
scrambling on other side leads to final steepening. Turn on R by
ledge and groove, and collapse on the plateau.

The Trident Faces   (162720) Alt. 3,100 ft (950 m)
The large open Coire between Tower Ridge and Carn Dearg is
Coire na Ciste. Far in the back is the prominent triangular
Comb Buttress. To its R is a scree fan descending from No. 3
Gully – the easiest descent off the summit. To the R of No. 3
Gully are several buttresses running towards Carn Dearg.

Behind and L of Carn Dearg is No. 5 Gully. Between this and
No. 4 Gully are the North, Central and South Trident
Buttresses. South Trident provides the best climbs on perfect
rock, which deserve to become more popular.

South Trident Face South-east facing
This is L-hand buttress, and the most striking, separated from
Central Trident Buttress by the Central Gully. The Buttress
comprises three tiers. The lowest facing out to the CIC Hut is
steep, and cutting across the top is a broad grassy terrace rising
out R from No. 4 Gully on the L. The middle tier above this is
cut across the top by a similar smaller ledge out of No. 4 Gully.
The final tier is actually only a narrow ridge leading to the
top.
   Descent – Down either of the two ledges, or from the top it
is easiest to descend No. 4 Gully over loose scree.

The Middle Tier
The most obvious feature is a huge 'Great Corner' in the R side
of the wall. Above the L end of tier is a deep chimney groove
(Groove Climb, VD), with a prominent small pinnacle at its
exit. About 50 ft (15 m) to its R is a triple tiered corner rising
steeply L across the face (Sidewinder, VS), and to the R is an
obvious sharp arete.

195 **Strident Edge**   *335 ft (100 m)   VS*
FA: *N. Muir and D. Reagan, 1972*
This formidable-looking arete succumbs with relative ease.
Start: L of Sidewinder Corner.
1. 75 ft (23 m) Scramble up to wall 20 ft (6 m) L of
   Sidewinder.
2. 50 ft (15 m) 4b Climb up to belay in the Sidewinder Corner.
3. 120 ft (36 m) 4c Move out R and climb a steep crack to gain
   the crest of the arete.

Strident Edge, Trident Face, Ben Nevis: climber, Andy Tibbs

4. 90 ft (27 m) 4b Follow the outer L edge to the top of the middle tier.

196 **Spartacus**   *320 ft (96 m)   VS*
FA: *I. S. Clough and G. Grandison, 1962*
Continue along the big ledge past the arete of Strident Edge to the foot of a corner, 65 ft (20 m) L of the Great Corner.
1. 90 ft (28 m) 4c Climb the corner and surmount OH, tr. R to stance (PB).
2. 50 ft (15 m) 4b Follow small groove on R to flake. Descend a little across steep wall to an arete, then up this to large flake belay.
3. 80 ft (24 m) 4b Continue direct, then L above an OH to a flake crack. Follow this a short way, then tr. R to belay on arete.
4. 100 ft (30 m) Climb the groove above to top of tier.

197 **The Slab Climb**   *300 ft (91 m)   VD*
FA: *B. P. Kellet, 1944*
Good rock and situations.
Start: Mid-way between Spartacus and The Great Corner.
1. 80 ft (24 m) Climb the R of two cracks to OH. Tr. into L crack to stance.
2. 80 ft (24 m) Continue by crack to conspicuous chimney.
3. 50 ft (15 m) The chimney is strenuous.
4. 90 ft (27 m) Follow the continuation chimney to top of tier.

The chimney groove in the back of The Great Corner is **The Clanger (S)**. The following route climbs all tiers and is a combination of routes.

198 **1944 Route/Pinnacle Arete**   *917 ft (275 m)   S*
FA: *A. Raeburn, D. R. and Mrs Inglis Clark, 1902*
FA: *B. P. Kellet, 1944*
A superb route.
Start: By scrambling to base of lower tier 100 ft (30 m) R of the lowest rocks.

1. 80 ft (24 m) Climb L to steep chimney. Trend L to ledge and belay.
2. 80 ft (24 m) Climb from a large leaning block to foot of second groove from L. Tr. R under third groove to fourth groove. Stance.
3. 115 ft (34 m) Climb into groove, then using crack on R wall, reach a system of ledges which are followed to steep corner.
4. 142 ft (43 m) Finish by corner to R end of middle ledge.
5. 500 ft (150 m) Above the R end of the ledge at a point overlooking steep North Wall climb sloping ledges for 10 ft (3 m). Then awkward corner on R followed by 35 ft (10 m) of difficult rock to easier rocks. Then L on to crest and climb to foot of steep wall. Climb this direct on good holds. A further short steep section leads to narrow shattered crest of the final tier which gives scrambling to plateau.

Carn Dearg Buttress   (163723) Alt. 2,475 ft (750 m)
North-east facing
Carn Dearg (the Red Hill, pronounced Karn Jarrak) bounds the W side of Coire na Ciste. Although appearing smaller than its twin, the Douglas Boulder opposite the entrance of the Coire at the base of Tower Ridge, it is more impressive owing to its striking smoothness and amazing natural features. It is only matched by the Cairngorm's Central Gully Wall on the Dubh Loch. Dries relatively quickly (allow two days after rain), and receives sun in the early morning on the front face. Titan's Wall receives evening sunshine.

Approach – Easiest from the CIC Hut, and skirting a lower band of cliffs on the L.

Topography – There are two separate faces. The first face (NE facing) is a sweep of overlapping slabs topped by a steep wall. They are cleaved on the R by the vertical corners of Centurion, The Bat, and Sassenach, whose bases are guarded by complex roof systems. The buttress then turns an impressive vertical arete (Agrippa) to form a smaller but smooth W face (Titan's Wall). Its R side is defined by an enormous flake/

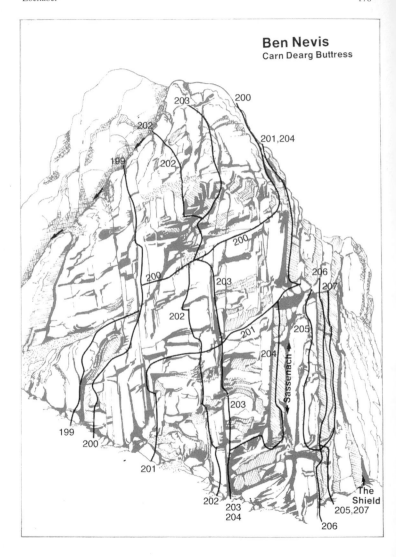

Ben Nevis
Carn Dearg Buttress

chimney (The Shield), the last route before the rocks diminish
into the recess of Waterfall Gully.

Descent – From the top of the buttress a large shelf runs
down the (L), side into No. 5 Gully. Routes from The Bat
R'wards finish by much easier rocks to top, but it is preferable
to gain ledges at top of Titan's Wall and abseil down this (old
PRS and slings in situ).

199 **Route I** *700 ft (210 m)*   *VD*
FA: *A. T. Hargreaves, G. G. MacPhee and H. G. V. Hughes 1931*
A classic outing with some good old-fashioned chimney fare.
Start: L of the lowest rocks of the minor curving buttress lying
on lower L flank of buttress.
  1. 45 ft (14 m) Climb to ledge.
  2. 60 ft (18 m) Climb the R edge to big ledge.
  3. 30 ft (9 m) Scramble by grassy cracks to big block belay.
  4. 100 ft (30 m) Tr. L and follow grooves to recess. Continue
      up R then L to platform and nut belay.
  5. 110 ft (33 m) Scrambling leads to top of minor buttress,
      walk R to foot of obvious chimney.
  6. 70 ft (21 m) Climb chimney finishing by grassy groove to
      recess.
  7. 20 ft (6 m) Climb R wall to a belay.
  8. 50 ft (15 m) Regain chimney 10 ft (3 m) higher and
      chimney to stance. Spike.
  9. 25 ft (7 m) Move out L on exposed slab to foot of final
      chimney.
  10. 40 ft (12 m) Chimney to broad ledge.
  11. 150 ft (45 m) Walk R and climb easy rock to top.

200 **Route II Direct**   *780 ft (234 m)*   *S*
FA: *B. P. Kellet and W. A. Russell, 1943*
FA: *B. W. Robertson and G. Chisholm, 1962 (direct)*
With the direct start a superb sustained route can be enjoyed
with tremendous situations for such a low-graded climb.
Immediately R of Route I is a R-facing corner. Start on grass
ledge below its slabby R wall.

1. 100 ft (30 m) Climb centre of smooth slab to small ledge, tr. R a little to wall. Then a small slanting corner and a tr. L to ledge. Follow small black crack. Flake belay.
2. 50 ft (15 m) Climb straight up to large block below a groove.
3. 30 ft (9 m) The groove then tr. R round arete to shattered ledge.
4. 80 ft (24 m) Trend up R on easy ground to reach grass ledge below chimney of Route I.
5. 50 ft (15 m) Climb chimney of Route I for 30 ft (10 m) until tr. R across slab possible to reach small stance.
6. 80 ft (24 m) Tr. R to large flake in slab below massive O H S.
7. 40 ft (12 m) Climb above flake, tr. R on vegetable garden to platform (Thread belay low) or better tr. the flake 18 ft (6 m) then ascend rock rib to thread belay.
8. 130 ft (39 m) Tr. R across buttress on obvious line to gain platform on edge of buttress (this pitch can be split if required).
9. 100 ft (30 m) Scramble up edge.
10. 110 ft (33 m) Enter a groove and follow it, mainly on R wall, to gain buttress crest.

201 **The Bullroar**   *960 ft (288 m)*   *HVS*
FA: *J. R. Marshall and J. Stenhouse, 1961*
A committing rising tr. across the centre of the face.
Start: 100 ft (30 m) R of Route II at large R-facing corner with huge boulders at the base.
1. 90 ft (27 m) 5a Up over bulge into groove (P R) easier groove to flake belay.
2. 50 ft (15 m) 4b Move up L into parallel groove to belay 15 ft (5 m) below overlap.
3. 40 ft (12 m) 4a Tr. R across the slab below overlap to crack up to P B.
4. 150 ft (45 m) 5a Descend a little and continue tr., passing a possible stance; then a descending tr. gains belay above Centurion Pitch 3.
5. 90 ft (27 m) 4c Climb crack above then tr. R under overlap to stance at end (P R).
6. 100 ft (30 m) 4b Continue tr. R under overlap then up to join

The Bat and follow easier rocks up R to terrace above Sassenach.

7. 40 ft (12 m) From L end of terrace tr. L to area of shattered rock beneath undercut groove.
8. 400 ft (120 m) 4c Up the groove and continue by a series of easy slabby grooves to the top.

202 **Torro**   *790 ft (237 m)   E2*
FA: *J. Mclean, W. Smith and W. Gordon, 1962*
FFA: *I. Nicholson and party, 1970s*
An expletive route, possibly the best E1 in Britain! Climbs the slabs L of the Centurion Corner.
Start: Just L of foot of rib of Centurion below OH-groove.

1. 100 ft (30 m) 5b Climb OH-groove (PR) to flake. Continue up groove to large flake. Climb R side. Move back L and up groove to good stance.
2. 80 ft (24 m) 5b Widening fault above, then bulge on L to edge of slab (PR). Descending tr. L across slab, round arete, then up OH-groove, through overlap, to stance on Bullroar (flake belay) below and R of twin overlaps.
3. 80 ft (24 m) 5a Diag. R round bulge to crack above: up it for 20 ft (6 m). Slightly R, then up slab to good ledge (PB).
4. 70 ft (21 m) 5c Slight crack for 20 ft (6 m) Step L on to higher slab (PR), cross this 10 ft (3 m). Pull over OH above trending L. Follow groove above to stance (PB).
5. 140 ft (42 m) 5a Up fault for 15 ft (3 m). Tr. slab R to crack. Up this to OH. Through OH L'wards, then groove to grassy stance (PB).
6. 100 ft (30 m) 4b Continues up fault to grass ledge beneath long OHS (Junction with Route II and Centurion).
7. 100 ft (30 m) 5a Centurion Pitch 6 through upper OHS.
8. 110 ft (33 m) 5b Tr. L to large black corner. Up this to grass terrace at top.

203 **Centurion**   *140 ft (189 m)   HVS*
FA: *D. D. Whillans and R. O. Downes, 1956*
Made in Scotland, driven by Englishmen. This is the huge
corner in the centre of the buttress.
Start: Directly below it.
1. 50 ft (15 m) 4c Climb L wall via cracks to platform. Under
   corner and up to ledge.
2. 120 ft (36 m) 5a The corner to stance on slab in OH-bay.
3. 80 ft (24 m) 4b Tr. L on to edge. Easy grooves till level with
   lip of big OH. Step R on to lip, and up crack to stance (PB).
4. 70 ft (21 m) 4b Back into corner. Tr. L up wall below
   OH-crack. Climb arete to stance.
5. 130 ft (39 m) 4a Slabby grooves in same line past block, then
   more easily till moves L up to junction with Route II.
6. 100 ft (30 m) 5a (common with Torro) Climb up to OH.
   Move L to steep slab. Head L up to another OH. Step from
   detached flake and tr. L (delicate) on to big slab. Easily up
   this R, to stance below 2nd tier OH (PB).
7. 80 ft (24 m) 4c Tr. R 20 ft (6 m) and up spiky arete to bulge.
   Over it. Step L to easy groove, and top.

204 **The Bat**   *900 ft (270 m)   E2*
FA: *D. Haston and R. Smith, 1959*
Subject of Smith's excellent article, and a film. The slender
hanging groove between Centurion and Sassenach provides the
main interest, gained by intricate wandering from Centurion.
Start: As for Centurion.
1. 50 ft (15 m) 4c Centurion to ledge.
2. 110 ft (33 m) 5a At 20 ft (6 m) up groove, tr. R on
   sandwiched upper pink slab to perched block. Continue R by
   shelf to block belay.
3. 90 ft (27 m) 5a Descend R for 10 ft (3 m). Enter bottomless
   groove. Up short wall to triangular slab. Follow 'V' groove
   above to gain slabs leading R into Sassenach chimneys.
   Belay below its L edge.
4. 40 ft (12 m) 5b Up steep shallow groove in Sassenach's L
   edge (The Hoodie Groove), into main corner.

The Bat, Carn
Dearg, Ben Nevis:
climber, Mick Fowler

5. 100 ft (30 m) 5b Main corner with roof and off-width crack
   in corner above (PR) to ledge on lip of wall.
6. 110 ft (37 m) 4b Groove to L end of terrace which overlooks
   top of Sassenach.
7. Either climb 400 ft (120 m) of easier (S) rock above to gain
   top of buttress, starting up undercut groove above Sassenach;
   or tr. terrace R to abseil down Titan's Wall.

Sassenach (HVS 5a) is the great chimney corner. Direct
entrance involves aid through initial roof; free at E3 6a.

205 **The Banana Groove**   *355 ft (106 m)   E4*
FA: *M. Hamilton and R. Anderson, 1983*
In the tower between Sassenach and the arete of Agrippa are
two conspicuous grooves. This climbs the L-hand one (The Big
Banana) gained from Titan's Wall.
Start: In W wall as for Titan's.
1. 120 ft (36 m) 5b Follow Titan's Wall to PB on long ledge
   near arete.

2. 35 ft (10 m) 4c Tr. L round arete and across slabs to ledge below groove.

3. 150 ft (45 m) 6a Climb directly up the corner (possible detour on L wall at one point). Where it fades, go up wall via cracks to large precarious block. Pull R across wall into small R-facing groove. Pull out wildly L to flat hold and then crack leads to ledge. Stunning.

4. 50 ft (15 m) 5c OH-groove above to terrace. Abseil down Titan's.

206 **Agrippa**   *290 ft (87 m)   E6*
FA: *P. Whillance and R. Anderson, 1983*
The OH-arete L of Titan's Wall. Very precarious.
Start: Up lower slabby rib L of Titan's.

1. 120 ft (36 m) 5c Up rib to small OH. Gain sloping ledge above, then groove to shelf below another OH. Direct over it to Titan's ledge (PB).

2. 90 ft (27 m) 6b Gain cracks in arete from L. Pull round and up to better holds leading to loose block. Stand on this (RP in crack above), swing L round arete, and up thin crack to ledge.

3. 80 ft (24 m) 5c Slight groove on R, then up L across wall to flake crack in arete. Up this to good holds and move R to terrace. Bold.

207 **Titan's Wall**   *270 ft (81 m)   E3*
FA: *I. S. Clough and H. MacInnes, 1959*
FFA: *M. Fowler and P. Thomas, 1977*
Follows crackline up centre of W wall. The free ascent was hotly competed for, Fowler beating 'locals' Cuthbertson and Hamilton by days (luckily, or it might have been renamed Laughing Pig!).

1. 120 ft (36 m) 5b Follow cracks in wall to OH at 50 ft (15 m) pull over then crackline trending R to ledge. Tr. L along ledge to PB.

Titan's Wall, Carn Dearg, Ben Nevis: climber, Kevin Howett

2. 150 ft (45 m) 6a Return along ledge and climb diag. R crack over bulges (PR). Vertical crack continues direct to top with interest sustained.

The corner line bordering the R side of Titan's Wall leading into an enormous flake chimney is **Shield Direct (HVS 5a)**.

4 SKYE

Introduction

Skye is renowned for the Black Cuillin which has attracted climbers since 1873. Its barren rocky peaks contain acres of clean rock amongst dramatic mountain scenery. The island is almost 60 miles (96 km) long, but so indented by sea lochs that one is never more than 5 miles (8 km) from salt water. This mountainous seascape creates the 'magic of Skye', although a little of that magic has recently evaporated with the completion of a road-bridge (Toll) at the Kyle of Lochalsh connecting the 'island' to civilisation. The crossing in a small ferry added intrigue and adventure and was an integral part of the attraction, now for ever lost.

There is much local variation in weather, the north of the island receiving half the rainfall of the Cuillin. Exploration of the sea-cliffs here has opened up a reliable wet-weather alternative. Neist in particular seems to miss the worst of the weather. The driest months are April, May and June.

History

During the earliest explorations it was the Skyemen Alexander Nicholson and John Mackenzie who made the biggest impact. Nicholson was a true Victorian explorer and ascended several Cuillin peaks (one now bears his name), whilst Mackenzie, the first professional guide, was a major force in Skye's early rock-climbing development. His career spanned fifty years, much of it spent in his home mountains. Until the 1894 opening of the Fort William railway, Skye was easier to get to than Ben Nevis or Glen Coe, and it became a popular venue for the Alpine Club and SMC. Most club members were actively peak-bagging, but the Inaccessible Pinnacle was conquered by the Pilkington Brothers and the Cioch of Sron na Ciche was discovered by Norman Collie in 1899.

Mackenzie partnered Collie over the turn of the century, producing numerous routes including the ascent of the Cioch

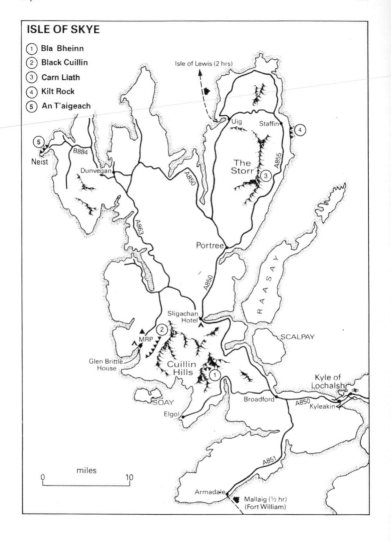

ISLE OF SKYE

1 Bla Bheinn
2 Black Cuillin
3 Carn Liath
4 Kilt Rock
5 An T'aigeach

from the L in 1906. From then on Glen Brittle House and Mary
Campbell's cottage took over from the tourist-infested and
distant Sligachan Hotel as base camp for the climbing élite. In
the following years the most dedicated duo were Guy Barlow
and E. W. Steeple, a partnership rivalling Collie and Mackenzie
for new routes. Their brilliant East Buttress Direct on Sron na
Ciche has since become a classic. Unaware of Collie's ascent a
month previously, Barlow with M. B. Buckle also made an
ascent of the Cioch by a different line. In 1907 A. P. Abraham
and H. Harland climbed directly up the lower wall of Sron na
Ciche to give Cioch Direct (S), graded originally as
'Exceptionally Severe'. Abraham's book about rock-climbing on
Skye then led to extensive development and attempts on lines
which were later to succumb at HVS.

1911 saw Archer Thomson, H. O. Jones, L. Shadbolt and A.
MacLaren snake their way up Thomson's Route(s), and
Shadbolt with D. R. Pye climbed Crack of Doom (S) in 1918,
but the most significant event was Shadbolt and MacLaren's
traverse of the ridge in 16 hrs 45 mins.

The war years saw a lull, with only one important route
added – Trap Face Route (VS) on the West Buttress of Sron na
Ciche, an isolated but significant jump in standard by J. B.
Burrel and C. N. Cross. The lull lasted until D. H. Haworth and
I. E. Hughes arrived in 1940. Their classic Crack of Double
Doom and Rib of Doom (both VS) were good hard additions
and Integrity was one of the best Severes on Skye.

The Creagh Dhu arrived in the '50s. Pat Walsh was one of
the strongest climbers in Scotland at that time, so a dramatic
rise in the island's standard was inevitable, and Trophy Crack in
1956 was the result, at E1. On the same day John Cunningham
with J. Allen and Bill Smith added Bastinado (another E1). The
other test-piece from 1956 was Ian McNaught-Davis's Cioch
Grooves (HVS). A year later Hamish MacInnes and Ian Clough
produced some superb routes, Vulcan Wall, Creagh Dhu
Grooves and Strappado in particular. Meanwhile Bill Brooker
and friends were developing the impressive Sgurr Mhic
Coinnich face of Coireachan Ruadha. This big steep wall lies

hidden away above Loch Coruisk in the heart of the Cuillin. Dawn Grooves (VS), Crack of Dawn (VS) and Fluted Buttress (S) spanned the 1950s.

The permissiveness of the '60s even affected Skye rock-climbing, with an orgy of activity on hitherto virgin rock walls. At the end of a four-week tour of the North-west, Chris Bonington and Tom Patey produced their tenth new route, adding the brilliant King Cobra to Brooker's routes in Coireachan Ruadha. The free for all saw Bla Bheinn pillaged, Clough initiating it with Sidewinder (S). Then the Great Prow fell to Wilf Tauber and friends from St Andrews, and the striking line of Jib was climbed by Martin Boysen and Dave Alcock. In Coir'a'Ghrunnda, John McLean and others from the Creagh Dhu took the two most striking lines of the cliff to give The Cleft and The Asp.

During the 1970s the most active person was Londoner Mick Fowler. He accounted for many prized lines during repeated raids into Scotland, and Skye was no exception. Here he found Dilemma, Atropos, Mongoose Direct (a line in Coireachan Ruadha by Jeff Lamb and Pete Whillance) and Stairway to Heaven. The latter was E5 and the hardest climb on the island, taking a stunning line up the big wall of the Great Prow on Bla Bheinn.

In the early 1980s a quiet Edinburgh climber, Pete Hunter, was steadily raising standards in quarries near his home. His visit to Skye gave him some stunning routes such as Spock, Acapulco Wall and Krugerrand. In 1982 Dave Cuthbertson produced Zephyr. Although not offering brilliant climbing, it was the first recorded E5. Also about this time Cuthbertson and Gary Latter had a weekend of perfect weather and added Magic, Team Machine and Chambre to Sron na Ciche, Latter being impressed by the rock's cleanness (Chambre had in fact been scrubbed clean by another aspiring first ascensionist).

Back in 1977 Noel Williams had begun attempts on a secret line in North Skye. Secrecy prevailed until Ed Grindley joined the team with his rubber dinghy. After nearly a dozen visits the team saw success, Grindley dispensing with the crux with relative ease, being fresh from a fitness session abroad. Then in 1983 he discovered Kilt Rock, and with various partners and accompanying sea-cliff addicts he accounted for most of the major lines, Hunter and Williams sharing in the spoils.

Access
Road – A new toll bridge connects Skye to the mainland at Kyle of Lochalsh.
Ferry – From the South, Mallaig to Armadale (30 mins), limited runs from May to October, not Sundays.
Air – Glasgow to Broadford (1 hr), one flight per day.
Bus – Glasgow or Edinburgh to Uig in North Skye (Citylink and Skyeways), daily all year.
Rail – Glasgow to Mallaig, via Fort William; Glasgow or Edinburgh to Kyle of Lochalsh, via Inverness.
On Skye – Numerous local bus services connect every village. These include Portree to Glen Brittle (once daily), and Dunvegan to Neist Lighthouse (intermittent Post bus). Numerous car-hire firms, such as Ewan Macrae and Beaton's (Portree); Sutherland's Garage (Broadford).

Accommodation
Camping – Sligachan site (485301) by Hotel; Clachan site (496669), just before Staffin near Kilt Rock; Glen Brittle beach (412206), official site only in Glen Brittle; Dunvegan site (295475) 9 miles (15 km) from Neist.
Rough camping – Head of Loch Slapin (564226) for Bla Bheinn; unrestricted within Cuillin Hills; Waterstein road-head (132478) at Neist (limited fresh water).
Huts – Glen Brittle Memorial Hut (412216), MCofS/BMC between campsite and youth hostel: Coruisk Memorial Hut (488196), Glasgow JMCS, shore of Loch ScavaigCoruisk.
Youth hostels - Kyleakin (750264), Skye side of Lochalsh bridge; Glen Brittle (409225), 1 mile (2 km) N of campsite.
Bunkhouses – Cuchulainn's Backpackers Hostel, Station Road, Kyle of Lochalsh. tel: (01599) 534 492; Fossil Bothy, Lower Breakish, 5 miles west of new bridge tel: (01471) 822 644;

Portree Independent Hostel, The Old Post Office, Portree tel:
(01478) 613 737; and two bunkhouses at Portnalong, north of
Glen Brittle – Skyewalker Hostel (348348), tel: (01478) 640
250 and Croft Bunkhouse and Bothies (348353), tel: (01478)
640 254. For climbers visiting the Staffin sea-cliff areas Dun
Flodigarry Hostel (464720) is close at hand, tel: (01470) 552
212 and finally Glenhinnisdale Bunkhouse, between Portree and
Uig tel: (01470) 542 293.
Hotels – The Sligachan Hotel (486299) at north end of Cuillin
Ridge, has traditional connections with climbing dating back to
the 1800's. In the 1950's and 1960's the enigmatic Tom Patey
would travel to Sligachan from Ullapool in the north west for a
night's impromptu Ceilidh. Usual Hotel accommodation and food.

Provisions
Spar shops, etc, at Broadford, Portree, Dunvegan (early closing
Wednesdays). Small shop at Torrin (580208) on A881
Broadford-Elgol road, handy for Bla Bheinn. Small shop on Glen
Brittle campsite, open evenings. Well-stocked supermarket at
Clachan (496669), near Staffin, handy for Kilt. Café, small shop
and post office, Glendale (177496) close to Neist (closed
Sundays).

Mountain Rescue
Skye Mountain Rescue Team – Post: Glen Brittle House
(411213), and Gerry Akroyd, Stac Lee, Glen Brittle.

Guidebooks
Skye and the Hebrides, Rock and Ice Climbs, Volume 1, J.
MacKenzie and N. Williams, SMC, 1996

Maps
Landranger Series: North Skye, 23; South Skye, 32. Outdoor
Leisure series; Cuillin/Torridon Hills, 8.
Harvey Maps: Super Walker Series, Cuillin

BLA BHEINN   (534218) Alt. 2,200 ft (660 m) East facing 🦋
Known and pronounced as 'Blaven' (the Hill of Bloom), it is
one of several hills joining a separate group E of the main
Cuillin backbone, separated from it by Strath na Creitheach and
Loch Coruisk.

There are three coires on the E face below Bla Bheinn and its
immediate neighbour Clach Glas, when viewed from the road at
the head of Loch Slapin. On the L is Fionna Coire, directly
below Bla Bheinn. The central coire separates Bla Bheinn from
Clach Glas, its L side forming the E ridge of Bla Bheinn and
containing the North Wall. The R-hand coire lies below the
summit of Clach Glas. The North Wall is a series of buttresses
ascending the ridge, the most impressive being 400 ft (120 m)
high and terminating in a prominent rib, The Great Prow. The
buttresses continue, more broken, as far as the 'half-crown
pinnacle' overlooking the col. Dries reasonably quickly.

Approach – From the head of Loch Slapin (56126) on the
A881 Broadford-Elgol road. Take path up N bank of Allt na
Dunaiche into Coire Uaigneich (the Central Coire). This is
scree-filled, and the easiest line lies near the stream on the R.
Alternatively, climb the E ridge itself, gaining the top of the
cliff and descending scree-filled Scupper Gully to R of Prow
(looking out): 2 hrs.

Descent – Scupper Gully.

208 **Sidewinder**   *380 ft (111 m)   S*
FA: *I. S. Clough, A. Silvers, J. Greenwood and D. J. Walker, 1968*
Climbs the L side of the main wall of the Great Prow. The
most obvious feature of the wall is a huge open corner (Jib).
Start at a short slabby groove in the wall L of this corner.
1. 100 ft (30 m) The short slabby groove leads to a crack in its
    R wall. Up the crack and its R fork to stance (PB).
2. 50 ft (15 m) Continue up grooves to ledge.
3. 130 ft (36 m) Continue in same line for 70 ft (21 m). Then
    follow a trap fault diag. R to a pedestal.
4. 100 ft (30 m) Climb the wall above to top.

Bla Bheinn
The Great Prow

Scupper Gully (descent)

208
209
210
211
212

209 **Jib**   *430 ft (128 m)   E1*
   FA: *M. Boyson and D. Alcock, 1969*
   Follows excellent line of big corner bounding upper L side of
   main face, starting from the R.
   Start: 15 ft (5 m) R of a central Chimney (Stairway to Heaven)
   at overhung gangway.
   1. 130 ft (39 m) 5b Climb L-trending gangway, then steep wall
       to ledge. Tr. L passing ledge to gain base of main corner
       line.
   2. 130 ft (39 m) 4c Climb the crack, sustained.
   3. 50 ft (15 m) 4c The corner becomes a chimney and leads to a
       stance.
   4. 120 ft (35 m) 4b The fine groove out on the R wall provides
       an excellent finish.

210 **Stairway to Heaven**   *400 ft (120 m)   E5*
   FA: *M. Fowler and P. Thomas, 1977*
   A mean meander up the great wall between Jib and Great Prow.
   Start: At foot of deep groove which narrows to a crack some
   50 ft (15 m) L of start of Jib.
   1. 100 ft (30 m) 5b Up the groove and wide crack through Jib;
       tr. L to niche.
   2. 60 ft (18 m) 4c Follow the crack above to further niche.
   3. 100 ft (30 m) 6a Move up to a small overlap above. Follow
       it L until possible to surmount OH via short crack. Tr. R
       along lip with difficulty to narrow ledge above OHS, then
       diag. up R to short crack leading to stance (PB) on slanting
       gangway below larger OH.
   4. 140 ft (42 m) 5b Follow crack under overlap up L till
       possible to climb overlap and move up via flakes to ledge.
       Finish up wall and R to top.

211 **Finger In The Dyke**   *400 ft (120 m)   E5*
   FA: *P. Thorburn, G. Farquhar and G. Latter, 1997*
   A serious but atmospheric route up the arete of the Great Prow.
   Start at L slanting dyke at L side of cave in base of arete.
   1. 100 ft (30 m) 6a Follow dyke to small R facing corner and

gain shelf above. Up this short way and swing R into
undercut groove. Follow this till it fades. Descend slightly
down and R across lip of roof to 'hole'. Continue R across
slabby niche where crack leads to hanging belay below loose
niche.

2. 100 ft (30 m) 5c Follow crack through niche and climb wall
   on hollow holds, moving R round arete below bulge. Gain
   ramp above, move L round arete and step down to belay in
   scoop.

3. 150 ft (45 m) 5c Continue direct through dyke and follow
   good holds R to arete. More easily up wide L slanting crack
   and continuation to terrace.

4. 50 ft (15 m) Scramble to top.

212 **The Great Prow**   *345 ft (105 m)   VS*
FA: *T. W. Band, P. W. F. Gribbon, N. S. Ross and W. Tauber,
1968*

A classic since its inclusion in *Hard Rock*, but there's still a
little loose rock about. The situations are impressive.

Start: Below the Prow at an OH-chimney corner.

1. 115 ft (36 m) 4c Climb the OH-crack to exit on to a slab.
   Belay at its top.

2. 130 ft (39 m) 4b Continue up the crack above to a pedestal
   ledge.

3. 40 ft (12 m) Move back down from the pedestal, level with
   an orange-coloured slab, and follow a thin diag. fault up the
   wall L to gain crest, then up to PB.

   60 ft (18 m) Continue up a ramp until a crack on R leads back
   to the crest and hence the summit.

CUILLIN 🦋 🦋 🦋

When seen from Glen Brittle the Cuillin Ridge (pronounced
Coolin) presents a series of five open coires facing W. From the
N they are Coire na Creiche, Coire a' Ghreadaidh, Coire na
Banachadich, Coire Lagan and Coir'a' Ghrunnda. They all
contain some climbing. In Coire na Creiche lies the NW face of

Sgurr a' Mhadaidh, with Thor and Megaton. These prove
disappointingly loose; indeed a rock fall has obliterated part of
Megaton. There are better climbs towards the S end of the
ridge, concentrating around Sgurr Alasdair and its neighbouring
peaks.

The showpiece is Coire Lagan with Sron na Ciche and The
Cioch. The S-most coire, Coir'a' Ghrunnda, houses the S face
of Sgurr Alasdair. Finally on the E (Coruisk) side of the ridge
directly over from Coire Lagan is the huge Coireachan Ruadha
(Red Corries) containing the impressive NE face of Sgurr Mhic
Coinnich.

All the cliffs are of very rough gabbro, a coarse-grained
igneous rock which is intruded by trap faults (dykes) of dark
basalt or dolerite.

SRON NA CICHE   (445204) Alt. 2150 ft (650 m) North-west
facing
A massive cliff dominating the S side of Coire Lagan as an
almost continuous half-mile wall. Probably the most famous
rock face in Britain, and certainly the most popular on Skye,
gaining 1,000 ft (300 m) at its highest. Its name, 'the Spur of
the Cioch', is derived from the remarkable rock protuberance in
the centre of the face. Despite gabbro's reputation as the
roughest rock in Britain, the Cioch's popularity has left many
routes exceptionally polished.

Approach – A large stony 'runway' leaves the Glen Brittle
campsite and leads into upper Coire Lagan. After a small loch
another path branches off R from it to the base of the cliff: 1 hr
15 mins.

Topography – The face is cut into three sections by deep
gullies. The scree slope on the L is the Sgumain Stone Chute
(not to be confused with the Great Stone Chute of Sgurr
Alasdair), descending from a small col between Sgurr Sgumain
and Sron na Ciche. The L-hand buttress is Eastern Buttress, and
to its R is Eastern Gully, which separates it from the main
Cioch face. The Cioch sits in the centre, just above a large
terrace running diag. L to R across entire face. Cioch Gully

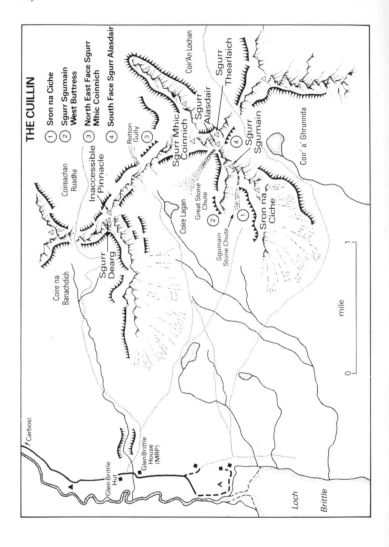

THE CUILLIN

① Sron na Ciche
② Sgurr Sgumain
   West Buttress
③ North East Face Sgurr
   Mhic Coinnich
④ South Face Sgurr Alasdair

Carbost

Glen Brittle Hut

Glen Brittle
House
(MRP)

Loch

Brittle

Coire na
Banachdich

Coireachan
Ruadha

Coir'An Lochan

Inaccessible
Pinnacle

Sgurr
Dearg

Rotten
Gully

③

Sgurr Mhic
Coinnich

Sgurr
Alasdair

Sgurr
Thearlaich

Coire Lagan

Great Stone
Chute

②

Sgurr
Sgumain

Coir' a' Ghrunnda

Sgumain
Stone Chute

①

Sron na
Ciche

④

mile

0

1

descends from the R side of the Cioch and forms part of an amphitheatre separating Cioch face from the massive sprawl of Western Buttress to the R (see the diagram on p. 200).

Descent – Normal via the Sgumain Stone Chute (SSC). But also W ridge of Sron na Ciche (from Western Buttress), or down slabby ramp down L side of Eastern Buttress into base of SSC (from Eastern Buttress).

Eastern Buttress
There are two distinct faces, the E Face, a barrel affair overlooking the Stone Chute, with a big main face; and the W Face, the L wall of Eastern Gully, overlooking the Cioch and separating the two in an almost separate ridge (Direct Route). The Eastern Buttress contains the finest climbs in the Cuillin. The main feature of the E Face is a huge vertical corner system (Creag Dhu Grooves) in the centre, whose lower half is formed by a gigantic flake.

213 **Team Machine** *555 ft (168 m)   E4*
FA: *D. Cuthbertson and G. Latter, 1982*
A scary tr. across the E Face, tackling the obvious horizontal crack out of the short gully on the L (Kinloss Gully) and finishing up the smooth main wall R of Creag Dhu Grooves. Start: In Kinloss Gully.
1. 100 ft (30 m) 4c Up gully till level with crack.
2. 75 ft (24 m) 6a Take horizontal crack across steep face to nut belay under roof on the arete.
3. 140 ft (42 m) 5b Up to R end of roof. Follow thin descending crack into Creag Dhu Grooves chimney. Up this a little to ledge.
4. 100 ft (30 m) 5a Gain ledge on arete. Up to thin break. Follow this across face to gain a trap fault (The Snake) up this to ledge (PB).
5. 140 ft (42 m) 4a Follow the trap fault to top as for Snake.

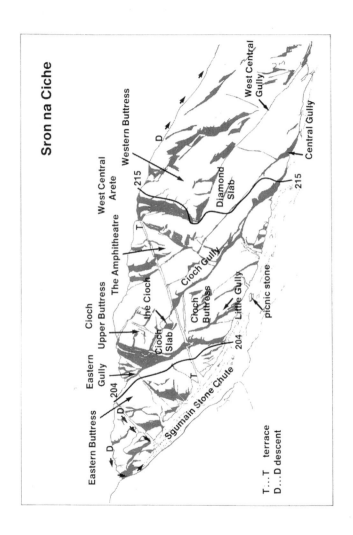

Sron na Ciche

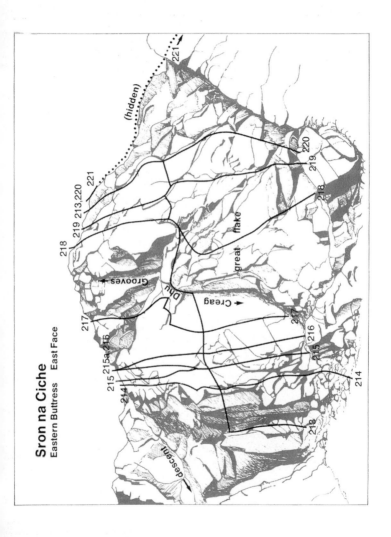

Sron na Ciche
Eastern Buttress   East Face

214 **Spock**   *230 ft (69 m)   E2*
FA: *P. Hunter and C. Lees, 1980*
Short but brilliant: climbs groove in arete to L of Creag Dhu
Grooves.
1. 130 ft (39 m) 5c Up O H -cracks in arete till they fade.
    Continue up arete via shallow groove (thin) to reach ledge
    above obvious roof (nut belay).
2. 100 ft (30 m) 5a Go diag. R to finish up steep crack just L of
    Vulcan Wall cracks.

215 **Vulcan Wall**   *220 ft (66 m)   HVS*
FA: *H. MacInnes, D. U. Temple and I. S. Clough, 1957*
This climbs the cracks up the slabby face just R of Spock. Start
on rock ledge below the slab.
1. 75 ft (23 m) 5a Climb up L -hand side of slab to ledge
    (block). Move up to ledge 15 ft (5 m) higher on L.
2. 85 ft (26 m) 5a Continue by a line of cracks to a small ledge
    on R.
3. 60 ft (18 m) 4c Rising L tr. gains better holds. Tr. L to edge
    and up to top. (**The Chambre Finish (E2 5c **)** climbs the
    thin crack directly above belay.)

216 **Uhuru**   *230 ft (70 m)   E3*
FA: *K. Howett and T. Prentice, 1990*
Excellent climbing up thin crack in silver-streaked wall R of
Vulcan Wall.
Start: At first crack R of more obvious crack of Dilemma.
1. 80 ft (25 m) 5c Climb crack to tiny overlap. Follow flake
    above to small ledge. Thin crack directly above with hard
    moves R and up to gain big ledge (shared with Vulcan
    Wall). Big block belay on L.
2. 150 ft (45 m) 5c Step R off block into thin crack and gain
    overlap. Pull over R-wards to small ledge. Move up and R
    into main crackline. Follow with hard move at mid-height to
    ledge. Gain and climb obvious crack above R end of ledge.
    Exit L past perched block at top.

217 **Dilemma**   *260 ft (78 m)   E3*
FA: *M. Fowler and P. Thomas, 1977*
Another plum line pillaged by Fowler, up thin cracks in centre
of Vulcan Slab. Start up thin crack R of Vulcan (the thin crack
just R again is **Pocks, E2, 5b 5c**).
1. 150 ft (45 m) 5c Up crack, then up to overlap on R. Tr.
   under it to faint groove. Pull over and gain descending tr.
   into small niche just L of large stance of Creag Dhu
   Grooves.
2. 110 ft (33 m) 5b Cracks diag. L up slab and continuation line
   through OHS in upper wall to top.

Creagh Dhu Grooves (E3, 4b, 5c, 5c) climbs the central corner
line, starting up the chimney which is formed by a gigantic
flake in wall R of Vulcan Slab. The upper corner is technical
but well protected.

218 **Enigma**   *450 ft (135 m)   E3*
FA: *M. Hamilton and D. Mullin, 1979*
Starts up the front face of the giant flake and finishes up
stunning vertical crack in upper wall.
Start: 30 ft (9 m) R of Creagh Dhu Grooves at R end of large
flat ledge with deep crevasse.
1. 120 ft (36 m) 5a Up wall via L-slanting groove. Then slightly
   R by cracks to nut belay on L below top of flake.
2. 80 ft (24 m) 5b Climb easily R and up, crossing the R side of
   the giant flake, to gain thin R-slanting groove leading to
   large overlap. Tr. R below it to ledge.
3. 120 ft (36 m) 5c Above and L is thin crack splitting wall; up
   it to belay.
4. 130 ft (39 m) Scramble up crack to top.

219 **Strappado Direct**   *300 ft (90 m)   E2*
FA: *P. Hunter and C. Lees, 1980 (upper half)*
FA: *G. Szuca and C. Moody, 1988 (direct start)*
The original line started up the R side of gigantic flake, then
wandered across face on R. The line is now directly up wall.

Start: Just L of the obvious vertical trap fault of Snake.
1. 90 ft (27 m) 5a Climb up to a crack just L of Snake on the
    slabby wall. Up it to a ledge, poor gear.
2. 100 ft (30 m) 5b/c Step L and climb crack.
3. 110 ft (33 m) 5a Continue up arete on L to top.

220 **The Snake**   *360 ft (111 m)   VS 4c*
     FA: *W. Sproul, J. Renny and J. Hall, 1955*
     On the wall R of Strappado is a weaving trap fault, the line of
     the route. Start 10 ft (3 m) R of R side of giant flake below the
     trap fault.
     1. 120 ft (35 m) 4c follow the fault to PB.
     2. 120 ft (35 m) 4c The fault again leading to PB in groove.
     3. 135 ft (40 m) 4a Finish up the dyke to crest of buttress.

221 **Direct Route**   *590 ft (180 m)   VD*
     FA: *E. W. Steeple, G. Barlow and H. Doughty, 1912*
     A very popular classic, now polished. It climbs the front of the
     extended rib between E and W faces of the Eastern Buttress,
     with an exhilarating crux near the top of the buttress to R of
     Snake. Start from the terrace which splits the bottom of the
     buttress and leads into Eastern Gully, then keep to the edge of
     the buttress overlooking Eastern Gully.

Cioch Face
Immediately below the Cioch is Cioch Buttress. This terminates
at the terrace. Above the L end of the terrace, and L of the
Cioch is Cioch Slab which leads to the crevasse ledge below
the upper buttress and whose top forms a horizontal knife ridge
leading out to the top of the Cioch itself (see diagram on page
201 for more detail). Routes can be combined at their respective
grades to give a sustained line up the entire face.

Cioch Buttress
In the L side is a subsidiary gully branching down R from

Strappado Direct, Sron na Ciche, Skye: climber, George Szuca

Eastern Gully (Little Gully). In base of its R wall is an obvious deep diag. crack (Bastinado). A picnic stone lies at its base.

222 **Acapulco Wall**   *400 ft (120 m)   E3*
FA: *P. Hunter, 1980*
A direct line just L of Bastinado with a poorly protected crux.
Start: Just R of Little Gully at base of ramp. 15 ft (5 m) L of Bastinado's crack.
1. 90 ft (27 m) 5b/c Climb the ramp and short wall to ledge. Gain steep crack leading to big ledge with big blocks.
2. 45 ft (34 m) 5c Swing L awkwardly and gain thin crack. Up it, and a bulge, to small ledge. (Bastinado's crux groove now lies 10 ft (3 m) R.) Up wall above to a niche with OH. Climb this to tiny spike, then R and up wide crack (block belay).
34. 195 ft (59 m) 4c Slabs and cracks more easily to terrace below Cioch.

223 **Bastinado**   *300 ft (90 m)   E1*
FA: *J. Cunningham, J Allen and W. Smith, 1956* (IPA)
An excellent entry pitch to one of the harder routes on the Upper Tier. Start below the deep diag. crack.
1. 115 ft (35 m) 4c Climb to the crack. Follow it to big grass ledge.
2. 30 ft (10 m) 5b Climb corner above direct then trend L to sloping ledge.
3. 30 ft (10 m) 5b Step L and up into OH-groove. Climb this until possible to step R to triangular corner.
4. 115 ft (35 m) 4b Climb crack behind corner to small rock ledge. Continuation crack, easier, to terrace.

224 **Cioch Grooves**   *410 ft (123 m)   HVS*
FA: *I. McNaught-Davis and G. Francis, 1957*
Varied and somewhat worrying on 2nd pitch.
Start: On small grass shelf that cuts up R on to face 30 ft (9 m) R of obvious flat picnic stone.
1. 130 ft (39 m) 4c Up the prominent corner crack till it

Sron na Ciche
Cioch Face

steepens. Step L into parallel crack which is followed to easy
slabs and ledges.

2. 80 ft (24 m) 5a Up slabs L to beneath steeper wall. Pull up
and R to gain hollow blocks (old remains of PR). Tr. R (very
thin) and pull over on to slab above. Up to below steep
corner crack.

3/4. 200 ft (60 m) 4b Up the jam crack and continuation line to
large ledge with huge block. Terrace lies just above by
scrambling.

225 **Cioch Direct**   *500 ft (150 m)   S 4a*
FA: *H. Harland and A. P. Abraham, 1907*
Polished by eighty years of traffic, making the crux a terrible
proposition if wet.
Start: Below obvious large fault line down and R of Cioch
Grooves. Climb the fault, at first an open corner, then
constricting to chimneys. The last is the crux, from which a
sloping shelf leads L to boulders. A tr. L across broken slab
gains twin cracks which lead to the terrace.

Cioch West (S) climbs up the toe of the buttress to R of Cioch
Direct just to L of Cioch Gully ('CW' scratched at base), via a
prominent chimney. 300 ft (90 m) above this is grass ledge.
Well scratched wall on R leads to a short chimney; an airy tr. L
then leads to slabs and a corner, and a further steep wall gains
the terrace.

226 **Crack of Doom**   *550 ft (165 m)   HS*
FA: *B. Ritchie and C. B. Milner, 1936 (direct start)*
FA: *D. R. Pye and L. G. Shadbolt, 1918 (the crack)*
FA: *A. S. Piggott and J. Wilding, 1921 (direct finish)*
A well-trodden direct up face just R of Cioch Gully. Scramble
up Cioch Gully passing a grass terrace and a large chockstone
to a belay 30 ft (9 m) above.

1. 130 ft (39 m) Climb square corner on R to short slab on R

Crack of Doom, Sron na Ciche, Skye: climber, Gerrie Fellows

wall of gully. This gains holds leading diag. R to open 'V'-scoop. Climb R round another slab and up steep corner to narrow ledge.

2. 70 ft (21 m) Tr. R from ledge for 8 ft (2 m) and ascend a steep shallow groove and continuation line leading to terrace.
3. 130 ft (39 m) Moderate slabs lead to foot of crackline.
4. 120 ft (36 m) Climb crack to chockstone. The crack narrows above and is climbed on small holds (crux), to finish at foot of sloping glacis.
5. 100 ft (30 m) Climb steep upper wall directly up from bottom end of glacis to plateau.

The Cioch and Cioch Slab
The following three routes climb the 'middle tier' above The Terrace. Either climb a route on the lower wall or access along The Terrace.

227 **Arrow Route**   *200 ft (60 m)   VD*
FA: *I. Allen, 1944*
A brilliant friction climb up the centre of Cioch Slab.
1. 50 ft (15 m) From the terrace take a central line trending slightly L to a diag. break.
2. 150 ft (45 m) Upper slab is almost protectionless and full of shallow pockmarks, with the crux at top.

228 **The Cioch**   *200 ft (60 m)   D*
This is the best and easiest way on to the Cioch. Start at base of the terrace on Eastern Buttress, follow it across Eastern Gully and over to below Cioch. A long pitch up the corner between Cioch and Cioch Slabs leads to the 'neck'. A startling exit is made on to the neck, and so to the top. *Descent*: From the neck either abseil down the corner to terrace, or follow ledge below upper tier and down Eastern Gully (M).

The Cioch, Sron na Ciche, Skye

229 **Overhanging Crack**   *150 ft (45 m)   E2*
FA: *M. Hamilton and G. Cohen, 1978*
Climbs a spectacular line up the Cioch itself. Start below the
long corner bounding the L side of the Cioch. Climb up for
80 ft (25 m). Tr. out R into crack in east side of Cioch. This
leads to airy position on front slab of Cioch.

Upper Buttress
This lies above the Cioch Slab. A crevasse terrace separates the
two. The neck leading out to the Cioch begins at edge of main
buttress where there is a spacious ledge and grass patch. Gain it
via the normal route up Cioch (D).

230 **Atropos**   *300 ft (90 m)   E1*
FA: *H. MacInnes and I. Clough, 1958*
FA (after rockfall): *M. Fowler and P. Thomas, 1977*
Start: At the next break L of Integrity.
1. 100 ft (30 m) 5a/b Climb steep barrier wall to slab; up this
   slightly L (PR). Diag. R tr. across slab to beneath OH just L
   of Integrity.
2. 60 ft (18 m) 4c Pass OH on L, up to beneath roof.
3. 140 ft (42 m) 5a Diag. L tr. through roofs then back R above.
   Then direct to top.

231 **Integrity**   *245 ft (74 m)   S*
FA: *D. A. Haworth and I. E. Hughes, 1949*
One of the best routes on Skye, taking a surprisingly easy line
up a formidable piece of rock.
Start: Below a recess 20 ft (8 m) L of the grass patch.
1. 110 ft (33 m) 4b Climb the recess and emerge on to slab;
   follow R crack to below roof.
2. 60 ft (18 m) 4a R into R-facing corner over small roof to
   cramped stance.
3. 75 ft (23 m) The general line becomes a chimney which ends
   on the glacis near top. Walk L up this to top.

232 **Trophy Crack**   *255 ft (76 m)   El*
FA: *P. Walsh and H. Mackay, 1956*
This climbs the crack and corner line R of Integrity, and is low in grade.
Start: Just R of the edge of the wall at a small pinnacle above the grass patch that lies behind the Cioch.
1. 120 ft (36 m) 5a/b Breach the initial steep crack above pinnacle. Follow the crack into a niche where a move L, then back R, gains big ledge.
2. 135 ft (40 m) 5a/b Follow the corner crack above and struggle over the roof (alarming but OK). Easier rocks lead to the glacis.

233 **Wallwork's Route**   *250 ft (75 m)   VD*
FA: *W. Wallwork, H. R. Kelly and J. Wilding, 1915*
From the grass patch at base of Trophy Crack tr. R along a horizontal trap fault. Where it turns vertically up wall follow an easier angled groove/ramp line leading out R under the steep wall on the edge of the massive drop, to gain a big ledge on the very limit. Climb the cracks up the short steep wall round to the R to gain the bottom end of the glacis.

Western Buttress
The massive sprawling face R of the Cioch face and Amphitheatre. Route-finding is the major problem, and the climbs are generally quite serious. The face is split diag. by two prominent rakes, Central Gully and West Central Gully. Above the latter, in the centre of the face, are several large nose-like roofs, and above the L-most roof is a prominent huge arete (West Central Arete). Between the two gullies is Diamond Slab, the cleanest area of rock: see diagram, p. 200.

234 **Mallory's Slab and Groove**   *900 ft (300 m)   VD*
FA: *G. H. L. Mallory, D. R. Pye and G. Shadbolt, 1918*
Be prepared for harder variations. It takes an almost direct line skirting the L side of Diamond Slab and finishing up West Central Arete.

Start: Mid-way between Cioch Gully and Central Gully at a prominent crack immediately R of a large OH. Climb the crack and exposed slab to gain Central Gully. Up this L for roughly 150 ft (45 m) to base of obvious crack line up to R. Up this and continuation line towards the big roof below West Central Arete. Pass the OH on L to enter defined gully (upper part of West Central Gully). Tr. R on to West Central arete, to finish in exposed position just L of crest.

SGURR SGUMAIN, WESTERN BUTTRESS   (445207) Alt. 2,000 ft (600 m) West facing

The large open bowl of Coire Lagan is split centrally by the long N ridge of Sgurr Sgumain. To the L is upper Coire Lagan and to the R is the gully containing the Sgumain Stone Chute. At the end of this ridge is a large slabby buttress clearly seen on the approach path. An easy rake crosses the lower part of the buttress from L to R and passes beneath a prominent white patch in the centre of the face.

Approach – Big path from Glen Brittle to just below Lochan Coire Lagan: 1 hr 15 mins.

Descent – Into Sgumain Stone Chute on R.

235 **The Klondyker**   *445 ft (135 m)   HVS*
FA: *A. Tibbs and D. Bearhop, 1988*
Improbable climbing running parallel and R of prominent chimney (**The Slant, D**) marking L side of front face. Start 25 ft (8 m) below and L of white patch.
1. 100 ft (30 m) 4b Diag. L up slab to corner L of chimney. Layback corner till possible to move R to cracked slab leading to belay below steep wall.
2. 100 ft (30 m) 5a Climb small corner and cracks to gain L side of large sloping ledge in steep wall. From block on L gain thin crackline leading to wider crack through OH to ledge (PB).

Trophy Crack, Sron na Ciche, Skye

3. 65 ft (20 m) 4a Groove above P until easy tr. L leads to ledge at foot of yellow groove.

4. 100 ft (30 m) 4c L round edge (exposed) and up L past OH to basalt recess. Climb to small ledge and short wall above to bigger ledge.

5. 80 ft (25 m) Move R and finish up fine arete.

236 **Sunset Slab and Yellow Groove**   *585 ft (175 m)   VS*
FA: *J. D. Foster and B. L. Blake, 1951*
FA: *I. S. Clough, D. J. Temple and party, 1958/64*
A long route on excellent rock up the centre of the buttress.
Start: Immediately below the white patch.

1. 180 ft (54 m) Easy. Follow a L-slanting slab above and parallel to the larger line of Slant to base of steep crack on R wall.

2. 75 ft (23 m) Take the crack for 45 ft (14 m), then tr. easily to the R to nut belay. (Original route escaped R on to West Trap Route.)

3. 100 ft (30 m) 4c Climb up to a corner to below OH-crack. Up wall to L of corner to ledge; continue by upper crack (crux) to grass ledge.

4. 50 ft (15 m) 4b Climb an easy slab, move round a corner and climb a steep groove. Tr. under OH to broad ledge with vertical yellow wall on L.

5. 40 ft (12 m) 4a Move R to a stance on arete.

6. 140 ft (41 m) 4a Climb the arete, avoiding steep upper section on R to gain ledge. Climb steep corner to reach easier rocks.

SOUTH FACE OF SGURR ALASDAIR   (451207) Alt. 2,500 ft (750 m) South-west facing
This steep little face lies directly below the summits of Sgurr Alasdair and Sgurr Thearlaich in the back of the upper cul-de-sac of Coir' a'Ghrunnda. Although a comparatively short cliff, this amazing coire of bare glaciated rock is well worth a visit.

Approach – Branch R off the Coire Lagan path just before it

enters a tiny ravine. A boggy path skirts Sron na Ciche. Coir'
a'Ghrunnda is guarded by glacial slabs. A cairned path leads up
immediate L flank of stream till barred by the slabs. It then
ascends 100 ft (30 m) on L to terrace, passing barrier. Easy
scrambling gains Lochan. The cliff in question lies in back of
subsidiary coire on L: 2 hrs 15 mins.

Topography – There are two walls separated by a narrow
gully (Thearlaich-Dubh Gully) which leads up to the famous
'TD' Gap on the ridge. The R wall is Thearlaich-Dubh Buttress,
the wall on L is Alasdair-Thearlaich Buttress.

Alasdair-Thearlaich Buttress
The most obvious feature is the vertical diedre (Con's Cleft),
and to its L is a shallow bay bounded on both sides by small
caves. The back of the bay contains vertical crack and chimney
lines.

Descent – Climbs finish with scrambling to top of Alasdair
Stone Chute, which gives a quick way back to Glen Brittle.
Alternatively, to gain base of cliff go down SW ridge to
Alasdair-Sgumain col avoiding Bad Step (VD) just before col
by excursion down a chimney on L (looking down). Easy slope
leads back to base of cliff.

237 **Commando Crack**   *248 ft (75 m)*   S
FA: *A. C. Cain and B. L. Dobson, 1950*
The prominent deep chimney crack immediately R of the
L-hand cave of the bay.
Start: Below crack leading into chimney.
1. 40 ft (12 m) Up the rib immediately R of crack till possible
   to enter it. Climb L-hand line to pinnacle belay high on L.
2. 60 ft (18 m) Up R wall into chimney. Awkward OH, then
   belay on L.
3. 80 ft (24 m) Up crack on R to sentry box below
   OH-chockstone. Thread it and climb nose on L to stance.
4. 80 ft (24 m) Layback the R crack and cross to L crack of
   chimney.
5. 100 ft (30 m) Scrambling leads R to top of stone chute.

The Asp (E2 5bc) climbs the prominent flared chimney R of the last route, passing through a steep band into the prominent corner leading to the top.

238 **Con's Cleft**   *220 ft (66 m)   HVS*
FA: *J. MacLean and party, 1965*
An appealing line for the connoisseur up the diedre.
1. 100 ft (30 m) 5a Up the steepening diedre and over bulge (crux), then up to ledge.
2. 120 ft (36 m) 4c The diedre, avoiding any loose rock near top, via R rib.

Thearlaich-Dubh Buttress
Like the other buttress, the most obvious feature is a vertical diedre and this gives an enjoyable companion route.
   Descent – Either go R down the ridge into the bealach R of cliff, or more conveniently, descend Thearlaich-Dubh Gully from the Gap.

239 **Grand Diedre**   *200 ft (60 m)   VS 4c*
FA: *H. MacInnes, I. S. Clough and D. Pipes, 1958*
Climb directly up corner to a stance. Continue directly up the diedre, without any impulse to wander, to the top. O H at 50 ft (15 m) is crux. Very popular.

EAST FACE OF SGURR MHIC COINNICH   (449214) Alt. 2,200 ft (660 m)
The Coireachan Ruadha is a remote group of coires on the E side of the main ridge, named after the outcrops of reddish peridotite common here. The most substantial cliff here lies on the E side of Sgurr Mhic Coinnich, its main drawback being that it catches the sun only in the morning and takes three or more days to dry. The climbing on the main cliff is, however, excellent.
   Approach – The cliff lies on the E side of the N ridge of Sgurr Mhic Coinnich. Access is a bit awkward. Take the path into upper Coire Lagan. The bealach lies to the L above scree fans. Follow the ridge R which drops to the lowest point

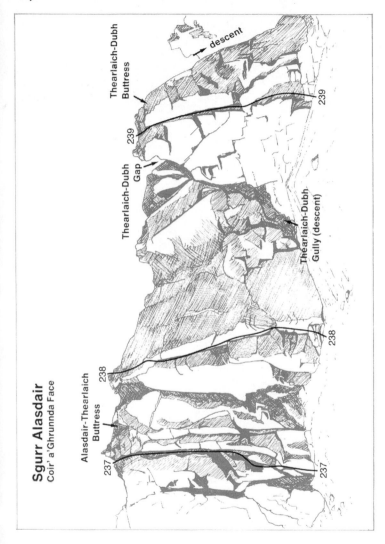

Sgurr Alasdair
Coir' a'Ghrunnda Face

Alasdair-Thearlaich Buttress

237

238

Thearlaich-Dubh Gap

Thearlaich-Dubh Buttress

239

Thearlaich-Dubh Gully (descent)

descent

(2,638 ft (790 m)). Descending the E side from here is Rotten Gully, loose scree, which requires care. 300 ft (90 m) down exit R to terrace below cliff. Alternatively, follow ridge to conspicuous nick in skyline (The Notch). Grass rake descends to R down E side above face, then tr. back L to base of crag. Very exposed.

Topography – On leaving the Rotten Gully there is first the slightly smaller NE Buttress before reaching the main Fluted Buttress. NE Gully separates the two. Fluted Buttress (almost 650 ft (210 m)) protrudes into a frontal nose. Its SE (L) face cuts back into a large bay, from the back of which is another exiguous gully. The SE face is split centrally by a prominent corner cleft (Mongoose) and the front of the face is similarly split by a large corner.

Descent – Down NW Ridge and Rotten Gully.

240 **King Cobra**   *600 ft (180 m)   E1*
FA: *C. J. S. Bonington and T. W. Patey, 1960*
A brilliant route up the prominent 100 ft (30 m) diedre just R of the exiguous gully and L of the Central Cleft. Scramble up the gully for 150 ft (45 m) until easy tr. R across to big flake at base of diedre.
1. 80 ft (24 m) 4c Up R wall of diedre (PR) to big ledge.
2. 80 ft (24 m) 5b Tr. R into another diedre. The next 20 ft (6 m) are the crux, after which easier climbing leads to ledge (PB).
3. 50 ft (15 m) 4b Easily up rib on R to comfortable shelf under OH.
4. 120 ft (36 m) 4c/5a Climb the wall 15 ft (5 m) R of the continuation groove to slab below OH. Tr. R to avoid OH and climb ramp to V-shaped groove leading to large OHS. Climb out on L wall of groove and swing across to jammed spikes on L. Up short chimney to stance.
5. 140 ft (42 m) 4c Tr. L across slab into chimney. Follow this, passing ledge to its top. Platform.

Con's Cleft, Sgurr Alasdair, Skye: climber, Matt Shaw

6. 90 ft (27 m) 4c Finish up further chimney set in narrow buttress above.

241 **Mongoose Direct**   *585 ft (195 m)   E1*
FA: *J. Lamb and P. Whillance, 1974*
FA: *M. Fowler and P. Thomas, 1977 (direct)*
Climbs a direct line up the central cleft, which unfortunately takes a long time to dry.
Start: Directly below the line of the cleft at a corner crack.
1. 80 ft (24 m) 5a Up the corner to a sloping ledge.
2. 60 ft (18 m) 5a Continue up a similar corner crack, then a slab to base of deep groove of main cleft.
3. 120 ft (36 m) 5b Climb a crack in the R wall, then the groove to where it splits in two (junction with Dawn Grooves). Up into clean-cut V-groove of L-hand branch (crux), to niche on L.
4. 120 ft (36 m) 5a The chimney groove continuation to ledge.
5/6. 240 ft (81 m) 5a Step up L across the OH in the chimney line, and continue to easy rocks. Further easy pitch to top.

242 **Dawn Grooves**   *585 ft (195 m)   VS*
FA: *R. W. Barclay and W. D. Brooker, 1958*
Well worth the effort of getting here. It takes a line up the wall R of the central cleft of Mongoose. Start up a crackline in the wall which becomes a chimney after 150 ft (45 m).
1. 150 ft (45 m) Climb the crack to a shelf crossing the face below the chimney.
2. 150 ft (45 m) The shelf steepens L'wards to form a groove line. Climb this, to join Mongoose at bifurcation.
3. 120 ft (36 m) Tr. 15 ft (5 m) R to crack on R wall of R-hand and lesser groove. Up crack and its general line up slabby edge of buttress to ledge. The 50 ft (15 m) steep wall above leads to ledge girdling upper part of buttress.
4. 120 ft (36 m) Tr. L for 40 ft (12 m) to a chimney. Up this to OH and exit L to flake. Steep slabs above lead diag. R to continuation of groove line (chimney and V-groove).

5. 45 ft (14 m) Up the chimney and 5 m V-groove and so to summit ridge.

243 **Fluted Buttress**   *640 ft (210 m)   VS*
FA: *W. D. Brooker and C. M. Dixon, 1950*
In the front of the buttress is a huge R-angled corner (Cocoa Cracks, HVS).
Start: On the terrace R of this.

1. 100 ft (30 m) Climb a little rib for 25 ft (7 m), then tr. up under OHS for about 50 ft (15 m) when they can be climbed to a ledge. Poorly protected.

2. 500 ft (150 m) Follow ledge R then up easy angled chimney. Continue up to the R to the edge of NE Gully. Exposed climbing on R wall until angle eases. A broken groove leads L back into centre of buttress to gain terrace. Climb a rib on the L heading of an OH-nose, split by crack. Climb its R wall by a hard groove crack till easy rocks lead to top.

CARN LIATH   (496559) Alt. 1,300(400 m) North-west Facing
Stretching for over 12miles (30 km) from just north of Portree, the Trotternish Ridge forms the backbone of the north east peninsula of Skye. It offers a spectacular walk along the longest ridge on the island; in impressive surroundings conjuring images of a 'Land That Time Forgot'. The most famous of its features are the tottering pinnacle, The Old Man of Storr near the southern end, and the landslip of the Quiraing hiding the amazing 'Table' of verdant grass between its brooding precipices in the north. However most of the rock is rotten basalt. The one exception is the northern tip of The Storr, where slightly hidden in a 'secret valley', lies a buttress of excellent dolerite. A jumble of massive boulders in the valley also offer great bouldering.

Approach – Park on the A855 some 4miles (13 km) north of Portree where it crosses the Rigg Burn (512561). Follow the burn then the steeper hillside diagonally up right into an obvious notch in the skyline. Contour round into the hidden valley. 50 mins.

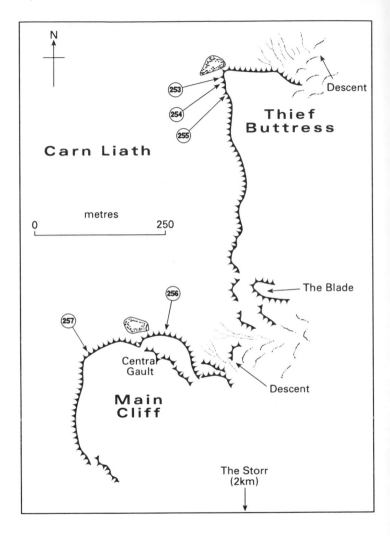

Topography – Thief Buttress is the furthest north which forms two faces (north and west) with a distinctive arete between and a huge boulder at its base. Further up the valley (south) the crag continues past a feature known as The Blade to reach the bigger Main Cliff. This forms a large buttress facing north and west. Protection is sometimes lacking and the northern outlook can make it all feel imposing – all added pleasures.

Thief Buttress
The huge boulder's south face holds a good crack (**KIP 25 ft (8 m) VS**). Descent is either side of the buttress. Routes described start at the arete then round onto the west wall.

244 **Bengal Lancer**   *135 ft (40 m)   E2*
FA: *M. Hudson and A. Holden, 1994*
1. 80 ft (25 m) 5b The excellent arete. Follow grooves and cracks immediately R of toe of buttress to gain true arete at 30 ft (10 m). Hard moves gain ledge. Swing R into bottomless groove and follow crack to ledge below OH.
2. 50 ft (15 m) 5b Step up to arete and shelf on R side (PR). Committing moves up arete to top.

245 **The Judge**   *100 ft (30 m)   HVS 5a*
FA: *D. Brown and R. Brown, 1993*
Climbs the vertical crack to the R of arete leading into hanging groove. Steep but well protected.

246 **Arbocranker**   *100 ft (30 m)   E2 5b*
FA: *A. Holden and M. Hudson, 1993*
The L-facing corner and crack direct to R of The Judge. Climb either the corner or its R arete to ledge. Follow sustained crack with crux at top.

The Main Cliff
Further south up the valley, the west-facing wall continues as a series of short buttresses leading to the Main Cliff. Just before a

descent in the north east corner of the cliff lies a pinnacle called The Blade. An ascent of this offers a fine though poorly protected line called **The Blade, 80 ft (25 m) HVS 4c**. This climbs the western arete starting up the gully below its R side and climbing L to gain ledges, then the wild arete above.

Topography – There is a small east face just R of gully descent. This turns an arete to a north face which is split centrally by a dirty corner fault-line below which sits a huge boulder. Further R the wall turns another blunter arete and begins to diminish in height. The two routes described are situated one either side of the fault-line.

247 **Heart's Highway**   *200 ft (60 m)*   *E1*
FA: *M. Hudson and A. Holden, 1992*
Starts up grooves in the arete between the east and north faces. Start on pedestal at toe of arete.
1. 100 ft (30 m) 5b Climb grooves until step L possible to small shelf. Step L and up shattered chimney then back R. Diag. R to OH, Over OH on R end and follow groove to small ledge.
2. 100 ft (30 m) 5b Diag. R with hard moves to gain slight bulging nose. Climb crack above to top.

248 **Prospect of Rona**   *215 ft (65 m)*   *E1*
FA: *M. Hudson and R. Brown, 1991*
Climbs the line of least resistance up the wall R of the central fault. Start at the base of a vertical crack some 30 ft (10 m) R of a subsidiary buttress up R of huge boulder.
1. 80 ft (25 m) 5a Climb crack and precarious layaway to gain ledge.
2. 135 ft (40 m) 5b Move L up wall to weakness in OH. Pull over into niche (crux). Tr. L onto pocketed wall then up to foot ledges. Tr. L to reach edge and climb corner over OH to final steep crack. Exposed.

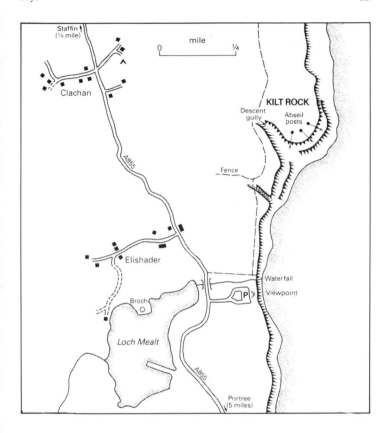

KILT ROCK, STAFFIN   (507666) Alt. 200 ft (60 m) South-east facing 🦋

There are more or less continuous cliffs along the NE coast of Skye around the village of Staffin, giving the peculiar style of jamming and laybacking that is rare in Scotland. Kilt Rock was the first to be developed. It consists of a columnar dolerite sill sitting on a lower band of loose shale and grass.

Many of the routes are a full rope length with no belay at the top, so a back-up rope must be left in place. As some routes start above unclimbable shale and grass, they must be approached by abseil. There are stakes in place, but do not rely on them singly.

Approach – Follow A855 from Portree towards Staffin. Two miles S of Staffin is a car-park and viewpoint for Kilt Rock by the outflow of Loch Mealt, an impressive waterfall (509655). Follow cliff-top fence for ¼ mile (400 m) to the rock. An easy gully descends S side of the rock. Routes are described from the gully wall round to the front face. Non-tidal.

249   **The Electric Bagpipe**   *110 ft (33 m)   HVS 5a*
FA: *N. Williams and P. Hunter, 1983*
Start below a giant flake at a short corner R of Sporran. Up the corner and then the front of the huge flake until forced into the crack on its L. From the top of flake layback up crack on R. Step L on to wall and so to ledge. Up R to finish.

250   **Clandestine**   *140 ft (42 m)   VS*
Slanting line R across wall of gully. Climb short corner of The Electric Bagpipe, then move R and up to triangular recess. Step R into further recess then L-hand of parallel cracks. Finish up L side of pedestal.

R. of Clandestine is a prominent slab near the top of the wall. The following routes finish on this slab.

251 **Tartan Terror**   *140 ft (42 m)   E1 5b*
FA: *P. Hunter and N. Williams, 1983*
Climb a broken groove just R of base of gully wall around t
he corner, to reach a slab. Step R and climb steep crack to
slab.

252 **Skyeman**   *140 ft (42 m)   E2 5b*
FA: *P. Hunter and N. Williams, 1983*
Follow the crack immediately R of Tartan Terror, finishing in
centre of slab. Sustained.

253 **Wide Eyed**   *140 ft (42 m)   E2 5b*
FA: *E. and C. Grindley, 1983*
The chimney crack in the corner R of Skyeman.

The following routes have hanging or semi-hanging belays to
start, and are best approached by abseil. Difficult to identify
them from above.

254 **Edge of Beyond**   *150 ft (45 m)   E2 5b/c*
FA: *P. Hunter and W. Jeffrey, 1983*
There is a large boulder at the top. Climbs the next groove R of
Wide Eyed, with a short excursion on to L-bounding arete at
half-height.

255 **Grey Panther**   *150 ft (45 m)   E1 5b*
FA: *E. Grindley, N. Williams, P. Hunter and W. Jeffrey,
1983*
The groove-cum-recess R of Edge of Beyond. Sustained.

256 **Internationale**   *150 ft (45 m)   E3 5c*
FA: *R. Swindon and E. Grindley, 1983*
The conspicuous jamming crack R of Grey Panther, moving R
to finish.

NEIST   (29475) Alt. sea-level West facing
On the W-most tip of Skye, overlooking the Outer Hebrides and
Rhum, is Neist (a Norse name meaning 'point'). The area has
an abundance of huge dolerite cliffs, but they are only of good
quality in the vicinity of the lighthouse.

The most impressive feature is An T'aigeach, the Stallion's
Head, a 350 ft (105 m) prow rising directly from the sea to the
summit of Neist: the classic Supercharger climbs its centre.
Beyond An T'aigeach are five bays containing many one-pitch
routes on good rock. All tidal. The extensive cliff just below the
car park (known as The Upper Crag) has also now been
developed. Refer to definitive guide if interested in a longer
stays' climbing here.

Approach – About 1 mile (1.6 km) S of the centre of
Dunvegan a single-track road (B884) goes W to Glendale and
Milovaig. A minor road branches off at Upper Milovaig and
descends to Loch Mor and the hamlet of Waterstein, finishing at
a car-park overlooking Neist.

An T'aigeach
Descent – 1) Abseil down line of route to platform. 2) Abseil
into bay due N (or descend slopes further N), and tr. round at
low tide. A short wade is necessary in final section, unless there
are spring tides and calm seas.

257 **Supercharger**   *380 ft (115 m)   E2*
FA: *E. and C. Grindley, W. Jeffrey and N. Williams, 1981*
This forges directly up the centre by the easiest line; it only
succumbed after numerous visits and much gardening. There is
still some loose rock. From L end of platform (clear of water at
all tides) two vertical parallel crack/grooves lead to steeper
rock. Climb L-hand one.
1. 90 ft (27 m) 5b Up crack and into groove above. Follow this
   over small overlap and step L at its top on to ledges (PB).
2. 90 ft (27 m) 5a Up L on to higher ledge. Pull R into steep

Grey panther, Kilt Rock, Skye: climber, Ed Grindley

corner. Pull out at top into easy chossy gully. Scramble up and R over huge blocks on to large platform (block belay).

3. 120 ft (36 m) 5c In wall above is huge flake. Gain from R and up it L to corner below stepped roofs. From top of flake, fingery moves lead up and R on to face. Up its R edge to R end of large roof. Cracks up leaning wall past roof. Pull strenuously L to gain sloping groove, and thus to ledge. Poorly protected initially.

4. 80 ft (24 m) 5a from L end of ledge an awkward crack leads to grass ledges. Scramble up to summit.

Supercharger, Neist, Skye: climber, Paul Proctor

5 TORRIDON

Introduction

Although it takes its name from the area between Loch Carron and Loch Maree, the strikingly beautiful belt of Torridonian sandstone stretches intermittently from the Kyle of Lochalsh to Cape Wrath. Regular, gently inclined parallel beds of rock produce remarkable terraced cliffs which at times completely encircle the mountains. Often they result in the worst features of sandstone, which have been described as: 'wet, occasionally overhanging bands of cliff separated by steep grass ledges girdling the crag – all rock when seen from below and all grass from above.'

The exceptions are described in this chapter, and offer climbs of great quality. Also included are the superb low-altitude gneiss crags by the sea at Lower Diabaig, a reliable bad-weather alternative on alternative rock, and the quartz ramparts of Beinn Eighe.

History

Torridonian exploration remained largely undocumented until the modern SMC Guide of 1993. The pace of development was never hectic, nor did it see many visits from the major activists of each era (Tom Patey being the exception). This is not to say, however, that there was no potential; it simply appears that few realized it.

Its history started when Messrs H. G. S. Lawson, Willie Ling and George Terlius Glover recorded a visit into Coire Mhic Fhearchair on Beinn Eighe, and climbed a scree-filled gully on Sail Mhor in 1899. At the turn of the century, Norman Collie and party attempted West Central Gully, to be stopped by the overhanging head-wall. They traversed left on to Central Buttress but ran out of time and retreated. Returning the next day they descended from the top to their high point, and climbed back out – a strange first ascent! Collie also made the first climb on the Applecross Cioch, via a chimney on the south

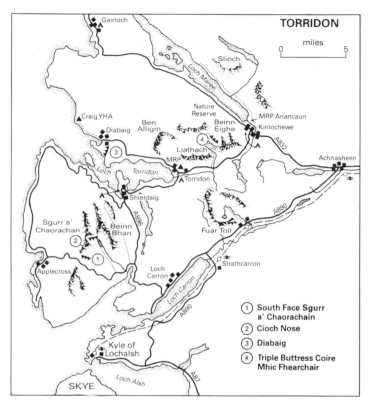

TORRIDON

miles
0   5

Gairloch

Slioch

Loch Maree

Nature
Reserve

MRP Anancaun

Craig YHA

Ben
Alligin

Beinn
Eighe

Kinlochewe

Diabaig

③

Liathach

Achnasheen

A832

MRP

Loch   Torridon

Torridon

A890

Shieldaig

Sgurr a'
Chaorachan

②

Beinn
Bhan

A896

Fuar Toll

①

Applecross

Loch
Carron

Strathcarron

Loch Carron

A890

① South Face Sgurr
  a' Chaorachain

② Cioch Nose

③ Diabaig

④ Triple Buttress Coire
  Mhic Fhearchair

Kyle of
Lochalsh

A87

SKYE

Loch Alsh

face in 1906, but this and Glover's ascent two years later were
more suited to entomologists and botanists.

In 1922, A. S. Piggot and Morley Wood made the first true
ascent of Central Buttress, and several years later Hamish
Hamilton and W. Kerr made another ascent by a better line.
Little then seems to have been done until the 1950s. RAF
teams climbed here but left no record of their ascents. Then

Tom Patey arrived with his Aberdonian accomplices. His first route, on the Cioch in 1952, was The North Wall.

In 1954 L. S. Lovat and Tom Weir climbed several routes on the triple buttresses of Beinn Eighe. One was lost to a scant description, whilst one was an attempted line up the left face of East Buttress. After six hours of 'very severe' climbing, they were forced to give up, only 99 ft (30 m) below a prominent gargoyle on the upper crest. Patey finished past this when he climbed Gnome Wall five years later. He did many of his routes solo whilst living at Ullapool as the local GP, but the summer of 1960 was spent climbing with Chris Bonington. On The Cioch they attacked the nose, but after two pitches found themselves hemmed into a balcony on the steepest section, the way barred by a formidable wall and roof. It was pouring with rain and the situation looked 'unpromising', but Bonington's lead found jugs and a 'glorious Diff'.

The biggest breakthrough in standards occurred in 1961 when Robin Smith and W. Whightman climbed Boggle (E1 5b), on the Eastern ramparts of Coire Mhic Fhearchair. Back on Applecross, Patey climbed Sword of Gideon (VS) on the South Face of Sgurr a' Chaorachain which was later peppered with so many routes that the SMC refused to report any more. The late 1960s saw a mixed bunch visiting Coire Mhic Fhearchair's Eastern Wing, including that roving Yorkshireman Alan Austin who did Rampart Wall (HVS). Meanwhile R. A. Hobbs and C. W. Dracup were the most active partnership on the Cioch, with Maxilla and Cleavage, both VS.

The 1970s saw the Eastern Wing of Coire Mhic Fhearchair at last recognized as a series of fine cliffs by a handful of West Highland devotees, among them Rob Archibald and Geoff Cohen. Birth of the Cool (E1), Colgora (HVS), Sundance (E1) and Groovin High (E1) date from this period. Meanwhile down by the beach Ed Grindley and Austin were quietly developing Diabaig slabs with Route I, Route II and the brilliant The Black Streak (E1).

A five-year lull was broken in the early 1980s when Brian Sprunt and Greg Strange caught some good weather and

climbed Pale Dièdre and The Reaper in Coire Mhic Fhearchair.
In 1982 Andy Nisbet and Richard McHardy climbed an
excellent line at Diabaig, only to be told a mystical
Northumbrian team had beaten them to it – or had they? In
1987 Torridon's hardest route fell to Graeme Livingston and
Nisbet with Ling Dynasty (E5) on the Eastern Wing, which
tackles two big roof cracks. At Diabaig, the prominent pillar
(E2) was ascended by Gary Latter only to discover that Murray
Hamilton had done so some years previously. Northumbrian
Kevin Howett then climbed three lines on the nearby Little Big
Crag, including the very bold Local Hero (E6), and plugged a
gap on the slabs with Wall of Flame (E4).

Finally in 1988 Nisbet made maximum use of a good June
and climbed a dozen routes in Coire Mhic Fhearchair with
several different partners, producing many of its best. Howett
and Latter's offering that year from Diabaig was Afterglow
(E4), another route with immaculate slab climbing.

Access
Rail – Inverness to Kyle of Lochalsh, via Achnasheen and
Strathcarron.
Bus – Post bus daily. Interconnecting services meet trains and
link every village.

Accommodation
Camping – Torridon campsite (905558), SYHA, cheap with
good facilities at public toilets nearby; Shieldaig site (815542),
private, on beach in village; Applecross (714444), site with all
facilities behind village.
Rough camping – Unrestricted in most areas except within the
bounds of the two nature reserves, Beinn Eighe and Beinn
Damph. Thus restricted to S side of road up Glen Torridon.
Most popular is (916555) amongst trees 1 mile (2 km) W of
Information Centre. There are no available sites at Diabaig,
official or free.
Bunkhouse – Gerry's Achnashellach Hostel (037493), 1 mile
(2 km) N of Achnashellach railway station on A890, apply Craig,

Strathcarron, Ross-shire, tel: (01520) 766 232; Kinlochewe
bunkhouse (028619), next to hotel, tel: (01445) 760 253.
Club Huts – Ling Hut (957563), SMC, 300 yds/metres down
track opposite NTS Car-park for Coire Dubh Mhor path in Glen
Torridon; Inver Cottage (150559), Jacobites MC, near
Achnasheen.
Youth hostel – Torridon (904559), modern hostel, always full.
Hotels/Self-catering – Loch Torridon Hotel (889543) also has
chalets, and the only public bar, 'The Ben Damph', which is
warm, with good ale and good food. B & B in all villages.
Cromasaig B & B, Torridon Road, Kinlochewe, owned by
climbers (tel: 01445 760 234).

Provisions
All the main villages have garages and post office/shops. Loch
Carron is the biggest. Most garages closed Sundays. Kinlochewe
has café shop and garage as well as a small outdoor shop
specialising in climbing hardware and clothing – Moru Outdoor
tel: (01445) 760 322, open summer and winter.

Mountain Rescue
Torridon Mountain Rescue Team – Posts: Torridon youth hostel
(904559), Rescue Post with facilities; Anancaun (025629), 1
mile (2 km) NW of Kinlochewe.

Guidebooks
Northern Highlands, Rock and Ice Climbs, Vol. 1, G. Cohen,
SMC, 1993

Maps
Landranger Series: for Applecross & Diabaig – Raasay and
Loch Torridon, 24; for Beinn Eighe and Glen Torridon –
Gairloch and Ullapool, 19, and Glen Carron, 25. Outdoor
Leisure: Cuillin/Torridon Hills, 8.
Harvey Map: Super Walker, Torridon

Applecross Peninsula

From the main road the Applecross hills appear as a succession of huge bastions. The majority epitomize the worst of Torridonian sandstone, but the flanks of Sgurr a' Chaorachain (pronounced Skoora-kooraken) contain compelling exceptions, with superb climbing.

SGURR A'CHAORACHAIN, SOUTH FACE   (789413) Alt. 1,300 ft (390 m) 🦋 🦋

This cliff is composed of six tall narrow buttresses of immaculately clean red rock, which appear to have been sandblasted. Their bases lie only minutes' walk above the road half-way up towards the Bealach-na-Ba on the Tornapass to Applecross road. They give almost guaranteed climbing during inclement weather.

Topography – The buttresses are numbered 1 to 6 from L to R. Buttresses 1 and 5 are the highest, both reaching lower down the hillside. Separating each buttress are deep gullies and chimneys.

Descent – Down hillside to L.

Buttress One
The lower tier is a clean narrow buttress. The main second tier is a barrel-type wall. On the L is a steep section. A prominent vertical crack then bounds the L edge of main face. Just to its R is a thin crackline starting near a grey 'splodge' leading to a triangular roofed niche (Gideon's Wrath). On R edge of the face is groove line (Sword of Gideon).

258 **Gideon's Wrath**   *300 ft (90 m)   HVS*
FA: *K. Crocket and C. Stead, 1971*
Start: At second tier at the thin crack below obvious triangular niche.
1. 60 ft (18 m) 4c Thin crack to niche. Tr. L for 10 ft (3 m) to below OH (PB).
2. 100 ft (30 m) 5b Pull over OH above and take obvious line

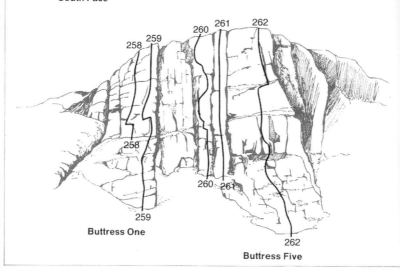

Sgurr a'Chaorachain
South Face

trending R (NR) to short wide crack. Continue up and R to
pass just R of biggest bulge.
3. 140 ft (42 m) Short walls and corners to top. (It is possible to
exit R from triangular niche and continue directly up cracks
above in two pitches, HVS 5a 5a.)

259 **Sword of Gideon**   *350 ft (104 m)   VS*
FA: *T. W. Patey, 1961*
The original route on this crag.
Start: At lowest point of buttress.
1. 150 ft (45 m) 4a Easy climbing up the lower tier on perfect
rock.
2. 120 ft (35 m) 4c Climb the groove in R edge till holds run
out. (NR). Tr. 12 ft (4 m) L and step down and tread

delicately across to a niche (crux) with small ledge in centre of face (possible belay). Climb prominent crack above to ledge. Continue up corner (awkward start), difficulties easing after 20 ft (6 m).
3. 80 ft (24 m) Continue more easily on R side of upper tier.

Buttress Three
The next route climbs the centre of No. 3 Buttress:

260 **Bumbly Two**   *440 ft (132 m)*   S
FA: *D. Beattie, K. Hiles and E. Gautier, 1970*
Start: At its foot.
1. 140 ft (42 m) Climb just R of centre of lower section.
2. 90 ft (27 m) Up wall above to gain ramp heading L to avoid vertical section to gain ledge.
3. 90 ft (27 m) Tr. ledge R to crack near R side of wall. Up this, then back L into centre of buttress. Up to belay.
4. 120 ft (36 m) Turn wall above on L, then up cracked slab. A groove, then easy rocks.

Buttress Four
261 **Bumbly One**   *420 ft (126 m)*   S
FA: *T. Cardwell, B. Beattie and C. Brooke, 1970*
Climbs the centre of No. 4 Buttress, starting at an obvious crack in the toe, in four pitches on good rock.

Buttress Five
262 **Swordstick**   *500 ft (150 m)*   HS
FA: *T. Patey and J. S. Cleare, 1968*
Takes a central line on the buttress – a prominent groove lying to L of a prominent OH-prow in centre. On R of prow is a black wet area.
Start: At the bottom!
1. 150 ft (45 m) Scramble up past obvious rounded boss to base of prow.
2. 100 ft (30 m) Up to L of prow, to OH. Step L and gain groove. Up its steep L wall until easier ledges trend L to nut belay on edge of grassy groove.

3. 60 ft (18 m) Up wall beside main groove to terrace.
4. 130 ft (36 m) Go R along it for 30 ft (9 m) to chimney.
5. 60 ft (18 m) Easily up this to top.

SGURR A'CHAORACHAIN, THE CLOCH   (795426) Alt.
1,300 ft (400 m) South-east facing ✖
From the summit of the mountain a fine spur runs NE into
Coire nan Arr to terminate in its most prominent feature – The
Cioch. Its outer face is almost 1,000 ft (300 m) high and it is
separated from the main ridge by a distinct neck.
   Approach – Most easily reached from the mouth of the glen
where the Applecross road crosses the Russel burn issuing from
Loch Coire nan Arr. Alternatively leave the summit of the
Bealach-na-Ba and head up to the summit of Sgurr
a'Chaorachain. Descend an open gully 330 ft (100 m) E of the
top into Coire S of Cioch.
   Topography – Seen from the front, the nose is split into two
tiers by a middle ledge. This runs horizontally L on to the SE
Face where it broadens from a thin rocky ledge into a wide
heathery terrace. The original route starts from the ledge
and climbs the front of the nose. Gain the ledge easily from
the L.
   Descent – Follow ridge to back of coire, and descend here.

263 **Cioch Nose**   *450 ft (135 m)*   *VD*
FA: *T. W. Patey and C. J. S. Bonington, 1960*
'The Diff to end all Diffs' – to quote the first ascensionist. The
middle ledge passes two grassy bays, becomes narrower and is
OH by a low roof. 50 ft (15 m) beyond this it narrows and
becomes rocky. Above where the path goes round a projecting
rock lies the original start up broken rocks.
Start: To R of projecting rock at short crack where ledge
becomes deeper.
1. 90 ft (27 m) Climb the crack for a few feet, then go L on to
   ledge. Up to spike. Easier rocks up side of block above, and
   to the L to upper ledge. Go R along ledge to below open
   chimney capped by roof.

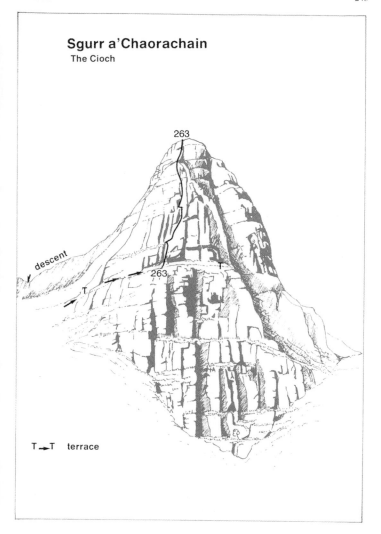

Sgurr a'Chaorachain
The Cioch

263

descent

263

T

T → T   terrace

2. 70 ft (21 m) Up chimney (strenuous) and exit R on to easy but exposed rock leading to niche under OH.
3. 60 ft (18 m) Tr. few feet R and up vertical wall (very exposed), bearing L to ledge.
4. 80 ft (24 m) Leave the ledge by an awkward mantel. Up L of OH above then R above it. Finish direct to grass ledges.
5. 150 ft (45 m) Easily up ridge on R to Cioch summit. Finish by descending into neck then scrambling up ridge to girdling wall. Climb this direct (S) or by groove at extreme L end (D).

Torridon
DIABAIG   (801595) Alt. 330 ft (100 m) 𝄂𝄂

From Torridon village a single-track road runs 9 miles (14 km) W to the beautiful village of Lower Diabaig and one of the best-kept climbing secrets of the 1970s. There are many cliffs on the W flank of Meall Ceann na Creighe, the hill SE of the village. The main cliff, hidden from view, is a huge undulating slab of immaculate gneiss, seemingly almost entirely composed of tiny rough crystals. Also described here are shorter climbs on the lower walls just beyond the village.

Approach – Take the road to the very end at Lower Diabaig, where there is a car-park at the jetty. From the last house at the far end of the road, a path to its L branches R by a stone barn, then on past some boulders and over a tiny outcrop to reach a fence and iron gate. Diabaig Pillar and Little Big Crag lie down to the R. The main slabs lie ½ mile (1 km) along the path through the gate: 15 mins.

Diabaig Pillar and The Little Big Crag West facing
The Pillar is obvious from the village presenting a slim blank-looking wall of bright red rock, approx. 150 ft (45 m) high with an inset slab in its top L corner above a horizontal roof. The Little Big Crag starts below the Pillar and gains height to the R. It is split by a deep-set corner/gully. The steep wall on its R with a severely undercut R side contains the best routes to date.

Descent – From Little Big Crag this involves scrambling up and R from tree-lined ledge.

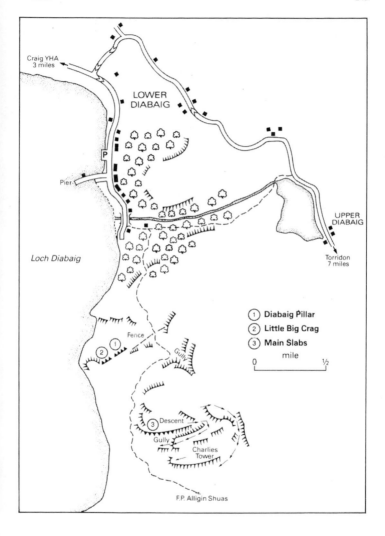

Craig YHA
3 miles

LOWER DIABAIG

P

Pier

UPPER DIABAIG

Torridon
7 miles

Loch Diabaig

Fence

Gully

① Diabaig Pillar
② Little Big Crag
③ Main Slabs

mile
0   ½

② ①

③ Descent

Gully

Charlies Tower

F.P. Alligin Shuas

Diabaig Pillar, Diabaig: climber, Andy Nelson

264 **The Pillar** *155 ft (48 m)* *E2 5b*
FA: *M. Hamilton, 1983*
A brilliant route up a hairline crack in the centre of the Pillar.
Comparable to Wales's Left Wall, but better!
Start: Just R of fault running down from roof. Up wall on large
holds. Step L into crack above roof. Directly up wall above,
moving slightly R on small hidden holds to gain horizontal
crack. Pull up, then follow hairline crack to top. An outstanding
excursion. **Dire Wall (E2 5b)** is a variation branching out L
above the roof to gain and climb the soaring arete in the upper
half.

The following climbs ascend the severely O H-R-hand section of
Little Big Crag. It is split through the centre by a vertical fault
of cracks and small corners leading to a roof. This is the line of
Rubblesplitskin (E2 5c). The twin lower cracks prove stretchy
and the upper roof is wild. The fault up the L-hand side is
Final Demands (E3 6a) and is strenuous, but well protected.

265 **Local Hero**   *130 ft (39 m)   E6 6a*
FA: *K. Howett, 1987*
Sustained and quite serious climbing up the blank-looking wall
L of Rubblesplitskin. Numerous RP1s required for upper wall.
Start: Just L of Rubblesplitskin. Up L of large blocky shield to
small ledge on its top. Pull up to roof R'wards via twin pockets.
Reach through L to small jug, then hard moves to pull over R
to semi-rest position. Up ochre wall above slightly L to easy
ground, and tree belay up R.

266 **Edgewood Whymper**   *130 ft (39 m)   E3 5c*
FA: *K. Howett and D. Cuthbertson, 1987*
This climbs the R edge of the buttress starting 5 ft (1 m) R of
Rubblesplitskin below the undercut edge. Pull over on to wall
and ascend R into corner. Up this to large flake, then through
overlap R on to large front ledge. Diag. up R following edge on
to slab; up this to tree.

Main Wall South facing
A huge undulating slab split by prominent cracklines. The rock,
which dries very quickly, streaked by dark black seepage stains,
is clean and free of vegetation, and the climbing is indescribable.
The wall degenerates into a deep gully on the R. 30 ft (9 m) L
of this gully is a R-facing corner, containing a holly tree, which
curves to form an O H running back R to the gully. The first
route starts midway between this corner and the gully.
    Descent – Follow the top of the slabs R up hillside until
possible to cut across the upper part of the gully that bounds the
R side of slabs, and take a line down the spur, keeping more to
its L side (looking down), with scrambling for last few feet.

267 **Route I**   *220 ft (66 m)   VS*
FA: *E. Grindley and A. Austin, 1975*
Start: Below the centre of the O H, between R-facing corner and gully.
1. 105 ft (32 m) 4c Up the wall until possible to tr. L to holly
    tree. Pull L over overlap and continue L and up more easily
    to grass ledge. Block and tree belay.

2. 115 ft (34 m) 4c Easily up R above ledge to gain awkward scoop capped by a small OH. Over this, then up L into deep crack leading to top. Crack can be climbed direct from belay (a little harder).

268 **The Black Streak**   *220 ft (66 m)   E1*
FA: *A. Austin and R. Valentine, 1976*
A brilliant climb up cracks in the biggest seepage line. Generally reasonable climbing, with only very short cruxes.
Start: Just L of the holly corner of Route I.
1. 100 ft (30 m) 5c Climb the thin crack up slab just L of corner. At 60 ft (18 m) it veers R and thins (crux). Continue up to grass ledge, block and tree belay.
2. 120 ft (33 m) 5b Climb up thinly via black streak on slab to gain base of deep crack in streak. This leads pleasantly to top.

269 **Wall of Flame**   *230 ft (69 m)   E4*
FA: *K. Howett and C. Thomson, 1987*
Climbs the centre of the slab between The Black Streak and the next crackline L (Northumberland Wall). Superb climbing. Named after the effects of a shimmering sunset as the final moves were completed. L of The Black Streak a L-facing corner is capped by a roof.
Start: Immediately R of its arete.
1. 110 ft (33 m) 6a Up R of the arete via slimmer corner. Gain and climb faint diag. line R across slab to its end. Follow thin crack with help from holds on its L to small overlap. Pull over and step R to reach large flat hold (just L of crux of The Black Streak). Direct up blank slab to impasse below isolated overlap. Diag. L to gain base of thin crack in bald slab above (thin); up to belay of The Black Streak.
2. 120 ft (36 m) 5c Move L from ledge along quartz line for 10 ft (3 m) to reach tiny flake. Up with some trepidation to OH. Pull round L on to ledge. Then thin crack on L and obvious direct line to top.

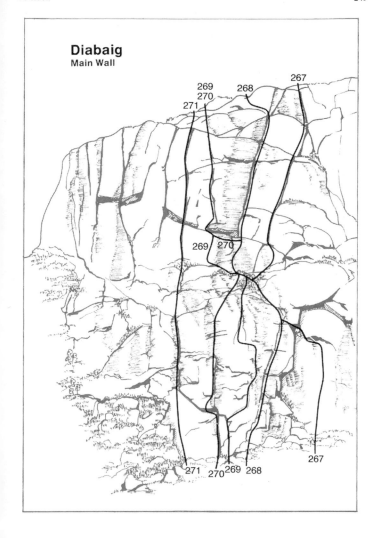

Diabaig
Main Wall

270 **Northumberland Wall**   *220 ft (66 m)*   *E2*
FA: *A. Nisbet and R. McHardy, 1984*
Climbs the intermittent cracks up the next black streak to L.
Start: At short L-facing corner L of The Black Streak and Wall
of Flame.
1. 100 ft (30 m) 5c Up corner to overlap; step L and pull over,
   then back R to base of crackline. Follow this with good
   protection over bulge (crux) to easy slabs. Follow R diag. to
   line grass ledge of Black Streak.
2. 120 ft (36 m) 5c Follow the Black Streak to horizontal break.
   Tr. L under OH to join Wall of Flame and follow its crack
   on L of OH to top.

271 **Route II**   *220 ft (66 m)*   *HVS*
FA: *A. Austin and E. Grindley, 1975*
This climbs the smaller streak just L of Northumberland Wall
and the deep crack above.
Start: 10 ft (3 m) L of corner of Northumberland Wall.
1. 100 ft (30 m) 5a Climb direct to L end of overlap and gain
   crack through it which continues up streak to easy slabs to
   grass ledge.
2. 120 ft (36 m) 5a Up crack above with continual interest,
   especially for those who deplore jamming.

BEINN EIGHE, COIRE MHIC FHEARCHAIR   (945603) Alt.
2,150 ft (650 m) North-west facing 🦋 🦋
On the N side of Beinn Eighe (pronounced 'Ben Ae') are three
main corries. The most westerly, formed by the projecting
ridges of Sail Mhor and Ruadha-Stac Mor, contains the
beautiful Loch Coire Mhic Fhearchair (pronounced
Corryvikerker) backed by the Triple Buttresses which make this
one of the most impressive corries in the area. The rock is a
lower tier of sandstone and an upper tier of Cambrian quartzite.
The sandstone is rounded, lacks protection and is generally
harder than it looks. In contrast the quartzite is easier than it

Route II, Main Slabs, Diabaig: climber, Billy Hood

appears, being covered in numerous in-cut holds and thin cracks.

The cliff is slow to dry, requiring about a week after prolonged rain. Far East Wall receives most sun, from mid-afternoon in summer, and dries more quickly.

Approach – From the NTS car-park in Glen Torridon (959569) a good path ascends Coire Dubh Mor between Beinn Eighe and Liathach. A smaller path branches off R and skirts Sail Mhor into the Coire. 5.5 miles (8 km): 2 hrs 15 mins.

Topography – The Triple Buttresses are 1,000 ft (300 m) high and point due N. Their lower tier of sandstone forms plinths for the quartzite crests above. These slim into prominent ridges inclined to the W so that they have large L walls and narrow R walls hidden in the flanking gullies. Running L'wards from the top half of the East Buttress, its quartzite L wall extends as an impressive face, the Eastern Ramparts. Further L and at the same level is a further quartzite cliff, the Far East Wall. The best of the modern routes lie on these two walls, whilst the buttresses give classic big mountain excursions: see diagram, p. 248.

Descent – Down a ridge between Far East Wall and a prominent red stone chute in the SE corner of the coire. Quickest descent from the Eastern Ramparts is down steep, unpleasant ground between the two walls (D).

West Buttress

Central and West Buttresses are separated by the deep and gloomy West Central Gully. To its R the West Buttress presents an impressive sandstone lower tier leading to the crest and a broad terrace. Above this the crest is broken but to the L the upper tiers of quartzite overlooking the gully are steep and imposing. The following two routes can be combined to give one of the best outings on the mountain experiencing both types of rock.

272 **Cyclonic Westerly**   *300 ft (90 m)   E3*
FA: *A Nisbet and G. Ollerhead, 1992*
Climbs front of sandstone buttress on perfect rock. Start just R
of edge of buttress below slim vertical corner.
1. 30 ft (10 m) 4c Climb lower rocks to base of corner.
2. 80 ft (25 m) 5c Move out L to base of shallow groove in L
   arete of main corner. Step L and up wall direct to steep
   flakes leading to good ledge.
3. 135 ft (40 m) 5b Climb L under OH onto slabier face. Trend
   R and follow L-slanting groove to OH. Climb this direct then
   easy grooves to big ledge.
4. 50 ft (15 m) 4c Continue to the broad terrace above
   sandstone tier.

The crest of Western Buttress is easily scrambled up until it
gets steeper. Tr. L onto gully face and climb a short loose pitch
(VD) to gain a second higher terrace leading L under the steep
wall. The most prominent feature is a huge groove just L of
centre taken by **Chop Suey 330 ft (100 m) E1** (unfortunately
loose in places).

273 **Force Ten**   *315 ft (95 m)   E2*
FA: *A Nisbet and G. Ollerhead, 1992*
Sustained and spectacular climbing just R of Chop Suey and
taking prominent white-streaked ramp in upper wall. Start below
huge groove of Chop Suey.
1. 100 ft (30 m) 5b Climb sharp R arete of groove to ledge.
2. 70 ft (20 m) 5c Continue R of arete to gain upper girdle
   ledge. Pull through capping OH and gain ramp. Follow ramp
   L to belay near its top.
3. 100 ft (30 m) 5b Tr. L round arete and climb steep cracks of
   continuation grooves of line of Chop Suey to easy ground.
4. 50 ft (15 m) 5a Climb directly above to top.

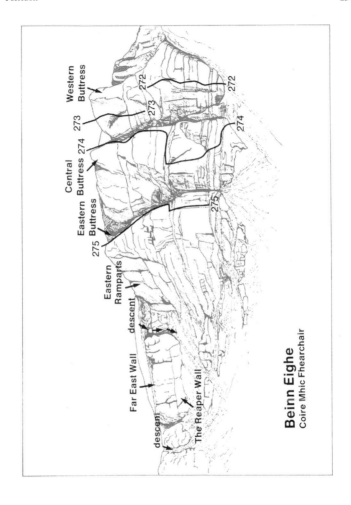

Beinn Eighe
Coire Mhic Fhearchair

274 **Central Buttress**   *920 ft (276 m)*   *S*
FA: *J. R. Sutcliff and M. Green, 1968 (sandstone tier)*
FA: *J. F. Hamilton and W. Kerr, 1926 (quartzite tier)*
The most sustained and enjoyable way up the buttress.
Magnificent situations. A grass shelf rings the base of the
buttress gained easily from the R. A prominent feature in wall is
a diag. R-to-L rake (Piggot's Route). This climbs wall to L
finishing near top of rake.
Start: 50 ft (15 m) L of conspicuous pinnacle leaning against
face.
1. 90 ft (27 m) climb to top of 15 ft (5 m) projecting rib. Up L
   to small slab, then to foot of groove. Up this to second ledge
   (thread belay).
2. 80 ft (24 m) Avoid bulge by tr. R then L into groove. Then
   trend L to gain ledge, and continue up and L to better ledge.
3. 150 ft (45 m) Continue up L via short wall, then turn pillar
   of blocks and up it. Further steep wall to easy rock and
   broad terrace. Walk along terrace to near R end 100 ft (30 m)
   R of terrace's highest point.
4–6. 300 ft (90 m) Follow steep rocks overlooking the gully
   trending up R till possible to break back L towards crest. Up
   to ledge below tower. Frequent stances.
7. 80 ft (24 m) Attack final tower first R of centre at detached
   flake. From its top climb slab up R on small holds till
   possible to go direct to stance.
8. 220 ft (66 m) Continue up open chimneys finishing abruptly
   on top.

275 **Eastern Buttress**   *950 ft (285 m)*   *VD*
FA: *G. B. Gibbs, E. Backhouse and W. A. Mounsey, 1907*
The lower sandstone tier is surprisingly difficult, whilst the
upper tier is easy. The climb overall gives a great route on good
but ledge-ridden rock. Start below the conspicuous chimney
near the R end of lower tier.
   Climb the chimney, usually wet, starting up the R wall. It
becomes easy after 70 ft (21 m) and leads to broad terrace.
About 30 ft (9 m) L of extreme R end of face above, climb up

steep wall on good holds to large ledge at 100 ft (30 m). Follow the crest of the buttress to the top, brilliantly exposed.

Eastern Ramparts

Prominent features of the face are: the horizontal girdle starting on L and cutting face in half as it increases in height to R; a pale shallow corner above girdle in centre of face (The Pale Diedre); a white wall at R end of face above girdle, bounded on its L by a grey tower and on its R by a big corner (Fairytale Groove). At the L end, just before the cliff reduces towards Far East Gully, is a slim V-groove with an OH at 100 ft (30 m). This is **Cornice Groove. (50 m (165 ft), VS 5a)** which turns the OH on L. To its R is an imposing wall bounded on its R by a large r-facing corner. The wall is climbed centrally by **Olympus (HVS 230 ft (70 m), 4c, 4b)** skirting initial OH on R, moving back L then pale rock to ledge. The steep second pitch climbs directly above via shallow corner and flake crack. The large corner R of Olympus is **Claustrophobic Corner (E1 5a, 5b)**. From a ledge after the corner it breaks through OHS on R via jutting block. Just R of this is a wet recess capped by a roof.

276 **Turkish Delight**   *320 ft (95 m)   E3*
FA: *A. Cunningham and A. Nisbet, 1987*
Takes a crackline between the recess and big L-facing roofed corner system on R. Sustained but well protected.
Start: Below R end of short ledge below girdle.
1. 120 ft (35 m) 4c Up shallow corner to ledge. Up R to girdle. Stand on big blocks under roofed fault. Tr. L on to block below first crackline to L.
2. 80 ft (24 m) 5b Up crackline bending R over bulge. Move L up wall away from fault, and up to block belay below thin crack.
3. 120 ft (35 m) 5c Crack into red corner. OH-crack above, then straight up finishing at L end of the fault.

277 **The Pale Diedre**   *330 ft (100 m)   E2*
FA: *B. Sprunt and G. Strange, 1980*
The prominent feature in middle of upper cliff. A particularly great route.
Start: Below the diedre at foot of vertical crack (cairn).
1. 130 ft (40 m) 5b Crack direct to OHS. Move L and up to below diedre.
2. 110 ft (33 m) 5c Diedre. Magnificent.
3. 90 ft (27 m) Finish up easy groove on R.

278 **Fear of the Dark**   *330 ft (100 m)   E1*
FA: *A. Nisbet and S. Blagborough, 1988*
Climbs a discontinuous corner line bounding the L side of the white wall.
Start: Below a prominent chimney line (Shang-High, HVS).
1. 130 ft (40 m) 5a Up R side of chimney and wide crack by R side of roof to girdle. Walk R 30 ft (10 m). Belay below white wall.
2. 70 ft (21 m) 4c Climb reddish corner L of white areas and move L to ledge.
3. 130 ft (40 m) 5b Tr. R round arete. Up it for few feet then R into main corner. Corner to roof. Tr. R and up wall over bulge into final groove, just R of huge roof.

279 **Fairytale Groove**   *330 ft (110 m)   HVS*
FA: *A. Nisbet and C. Forrest, 1988*
An exposed route up big corner bounding R side of white wall.
Start: Below a narrow chimney R of chimney of Fear of the Dark (old cairn).
1. 150 ft (45 m) 4b Climb immediately R of chimney to reach girdle.
2. 150 ft (45 m) 5a Tr. R and up to roofed recess. Pull out L into main corner leading to easier rocks.
3. 30 ft (10 m) Λ short wall to easy crest of East Buttress.

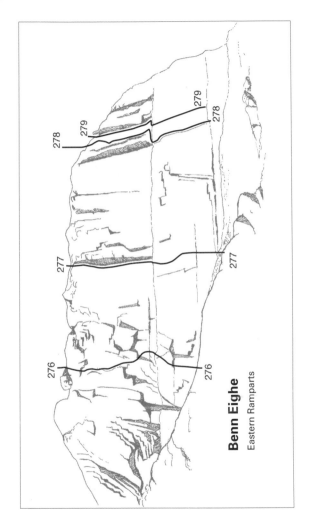

Benn Eighe
Eastern Ramparts

Far East Wall
The cliff gains height from the L, first as broken quartzite, then to form a compact steep grey wall with a white-streaked bulging nose on its L side and a big corner bounding its R (The Reaper Wall). The central section of the cliff is mossy and broken and slow to dry. On the R side of cliff is a big grey pillar of excellent rock. A horizontal fault splits the face at one-third height.

The Reaper Wall
The next two routes climb the main Reaper Wall face with a common start up to horizontal fault. Angel Face then goes diag. L above bulging nose, Seeds of Destruction goes directly up.

280 **Moonshine**   *320 ft (95 m)   E4*
FA: *C. Forrest and A. Nisbet, 1988*
Stunning sustained route up OH-groove L of bulging nose. Start on long grass ledge below buttress, 30 ft (10 m) from L end.
1. 80 ft (25 m) 5b Direct up wall past small rock scar. Move R to flake-line leading to horizontal break.
2. 120 ft (35 m) 6a Diag. L into OH-groove. Follow it (hard) to foothold on L arete. Direct above till level with huge OH on L. Up R to ledge.
3. 120 ft (35 m) 5b Short corner then L up easy wall to top.

281 **Angel Face**   *320 ft (95 m)   E2*
FA: *A. Nisbet and C. Forrest, 1988*
Sensational and improbable line.
Start: At L end of long flake embedded against R side of lower wall on long grass terrace.
1. 50 ft (15 m) 5a Climb a narrow ramp L. Move R into shallow groove leading to grass ledge below bigger groove on R.
2. 120 ft (35 m) 5c L-leaning groove to horizontal fault (hard). Tr. 15 ft (5 m) L along fault to pedestal. Wall above and L to gain tiny ramp (bold). Up ramp to crack where long step leads to thinner crack. Up this to roof. Tr. L under it to the edge (airy), then back R to ledge.

3. 150 ft (45 m) 5b Crack above R end of ledge. When it turns nasty go out R and up to flake/ledge. Up wall to smaller flake/ledge. Tr. L to large block. Trend R across slabby rock to steep blocky finish.

282 Seeds of Destruction   *320 ft (95 m)   E3*
FA: *A. Nisbet and W. Todd, 1988*
Another amazing line.
Start: As for Angel Face
1. 50 ft (15 m) 5a Angel Face.
2. 70 ft (21 m) 5c L-leading groove to horizontal fault. Then L to pedestal (Angel Face). Move R (poor PR), pull over bulge to shallow corner. Belay on R under smooth groove.
3. 100 ft (30 m) 5c Groove to big ledge on R. Back down and tr. L into L-facing corner. Up this to R end of large flake ledge of Angel Face. Nut belay on higher one.
4. 100 ft (30 m) 5c Up to small rock scar. Steeply up and L to horizontal break. Tr. R and gain curving groove on R. Above this, steep blocky ground direct to finish.

283 Colgarra   *330 ft (100 m)   E2*
FA: *R. Archibald and G. Cohen, 1976*
FFA: *A. Nisbet and S. Blagborough, 1988*
Very steep route up centre of cliff.
Start: At a deep slit cave and finish up hanging chimney near top immediately R of big L-curving groove.
1. 35 ft (12 m) 4c L side of cave, then diag. L to grass ledge.
2. 75 ft (23 m) 5b Tr. R to gain groove. This passes horizontal fault to jammed flakes on R.
3. 100 ft (30 m) 5c From just above belay, gain rib on R and up flakes to large flake. Climb groove above, and hanging chimney to grass ledge.
4. 120 ft (35 m) 5b Up and slightly L to small OH. Over this and crack to easy ground.

The next routes are on the big grey buttress forming R side of cliff. **Kami Kaze (MVS)** follows the big chimney line on the L

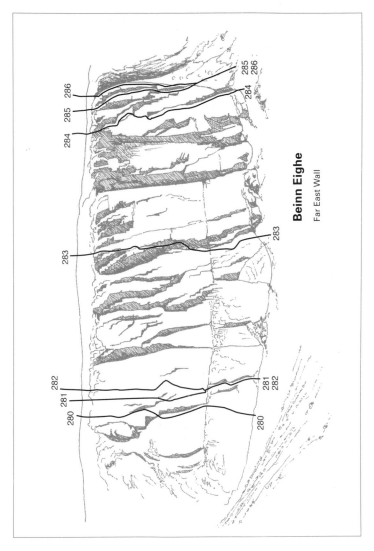

Beinn Eighe
Far East Wall

of the buttress, starting from a damp OH-recess, and then tr. R
into a groove. This, then another tr., gains the fault line. The
final tr. L out of a cave is exciting, but the line generally is a
little vegetated. In the centre of the buttress is a chimney line in
the lower part and to its R is a big groove line taken by
Grooving High.

284 **Ling Dynasty**   *360 ft (110 m)   E5*
FA: *G. Livingston and A. Nisbet, 1987*
Climbs a powerful line up the superb crack through the OH's
above the initial pitches of the prominent chimney. Start at a
wet cave at base of chimney.
1. 80 ft (25 m) 4c Climb L side of cave (loose).
2. 100 ft (30 m) 5b Climb chimney and continuation steep crack
   on R wall to gain good ledge.
3. 80 ft (25 m) 6b Step L into crack. Climb it to OH. Pull out R
   into continuation crack and up this to big OH. Tr. R to R end
   of OH and belay.
4. 50 ft (15 m) 6a Return L. Climb wide crack in OH. Go L up
   ramp to belay.
5. 50 ft (15 m) 4c Move R and follow corner to top.

285 **Grooving High**   *300 ft (90 m)   E1*
FA: *R. Archibald, J. Ingram and G. S. Strange, 1973*
Start: Up and R of the slit chimney.
1. 100 ft (30 m) 4c A short corner, then go L over blocks into
   successive corners and a short bulging wall leading to a large
   ledge.
2. 100 ft (30 m) 5b Climb two very steep corners above.
3. 100 ft (30 m) 4c Move R and continue in steep grooves to
   top.

286 **Sumo**   *280 ft (85 m)   E3*
FA: *A. Cunningham and A. Nisbet, 1987*
Takes vertical crackline in wall R of Grooving High. Start 6 ft
(2 m) R of that route.

1. 100 ft (30 m) 4b Corners and short walls to large ledge.
    Crawl R to belay.
2. 100 ft (30 m) 6a Climb steep corner and crackline to enter
    groove below OH. Step L then up to OH and re-enter groove.
    Bulge to a belay.
3. 80 ft (25 m) 5b Shallow groove above to horizontal cracks.
    Tr. R into corner up this then diag. L to small OH. Finnish R
    up small ramp and back L to top.

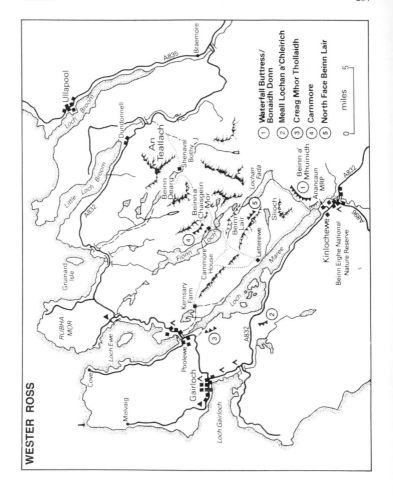

6 WESTER ROSS

Introduction

The last great wilderness of Scotland is a vast expanse of complex ridges, mountains and long, remote lochs. Thankfully, past owners of the estate wished to maintain this remoteness, preferring to use the traditional method of stalking with ponies. As a result the area is criss-crossed by well-maintained paths, making walking easier and compensating a little for the massive distances involved. Described here is Carnmore Crag, the showcase of the North, three easily accessible crags just outside Poolewe, the recently developed Stone Valley Crags on Meall Lochan a'Chleirich to the south of Gairloch and the cliffs of Beinn a'Mhuinidh above Kinlochewe.

History

The first recorded climbs in this area are from 1899. The aficionados of nearby Torridon, Willie Ling and George Glover, accompanied by Charles Inglis Clark, investigated the Beinn a'Mhuinidh waterfall and after a long struggle with vegetation completed The West Climb (Severe). The Ling/Glover team continued some exploration but little else of note was completed.

The real development of the area started in earnest in the 1950's by several University Climbing Clubs, having been alerted to the potential by a 'Summary of Rock Climbing in the Northern Highlands' by Frank Cunningham (published in the 1951 SMC Journal). Students from Glasgow, Edinburgh, Leeds and Cambridge all participated. Wrangham and Clegg (Cambridge) made tentative explorations of Beinn Airigh Charr, A'Mhaighdean and Torr na h'Iolaire in 1951 and produced the first climb on Carnmore in 1952 (Diagonal Route, Severe). It was mainly Cambridge University climbers that capitalised on this knowledge with Mike O'Hara, George Fraser, Bob Kendal and friends at the forefront. Fionn Buttress (VS) and Dragon (HVS) came in 1957. This team in particular spent several years quietly at work having Carnmore virtually to themselves.

Word of the quality and scale of the cliffs (especially Carnmore) spread and the main activists of the time started to pay visits. Dougal Haston and Robin Smith climbed the impressive Gob (HVS) in 1960; Balaton (E1) was climbed by Con Higgins and W. Gorman; John McLean, John Cunningham and A. Currey established Abomination (HVS) in 1966 and Geoff Cram established St George in 1967 at E1, followed by Sword by Dick Isherwood using 3 aid points in 1967. This latter route took some years to become recognised as a major advance for the area at E2 and was climbed free by G. Duckworth in 1980. Rab Carrington visited with John Jones and explored Ghost Slabs and later plucked Carnmore Corner, another E2.

Meanwhile the first routes were being done at Creag Mhor Thollaidh by Tom Patey and the Squirrels from Edinburgh. Of particular note was Chris Jackson and Brian Andrews' ascent of Catastasis (E2) in 1968. There were also visitors from afar with additions by Peak district based Paul Nun and Tom Proctor, and Lakeland climbers Pete Botterill and Jeff Lamb (The Bug, E2). Cunningham and Bill March visited the Bhonaidh Donn and established the excellent Vertigo (HVS, 1971) admirably summing up the exposure from the base of the crag.

A lull followed until the next resurgence of interest in the 1980's. This proved to be a rude awakening for Carnmore whose potential had been largely overlooked in preference to outcrop development in the central highlands. Dougie Mullin on-sight climbed Wilderness at E4, and Dougie Dinwoodie produced the excellent Orange Bow (E5) in 1985. He returned with fellow Aberdonian Graeme Livingston the following year and they climbed Lion Rampant and Ride of the Valkyrie (both E5) and the hard Death Wolf (E6).

Renewed interest in Creag Mhor Thollaidh came in the early 1980's principally from Rab Anderson accompanied by Murray Hamilton and Graham Nicoll. They climbed Decadent Days (E2), Murrays Arete (E3), Loctite (E3) and others. Coincidentally, Kevin Howett and Andy Nelson started visiting and developed nearby Loch Maree Crag, producing the excellent Spirit Air (E4) and Jarldom Reach (E5). Further developments here came from these two separate teams right through to the early 1990's producing many of the best and hardest climbs on the 'Tollie' crags.

The potential of the small outcrops all around this area had been looked at by local resident Steve Chadwick but it was fully developed by others raiding from afar. The exact relationship between Chadwick's explorations and the recorded routes here has yet to be fully sorted out. Rab and Chris Anderson spent most summer weekends of 1995 and 1996 secretly developing Loch Thollaidh Crags with a range of routes from Severe to E6. Dave Cuthbertson also played a part and typically produced the hardest route of the area, Conquistador E7 7a, using a pre-clipped peg to protect the hard lower wall.

After spotting the crags of Meall Lochan a'Chleirich, Bob Brown and the 'Indomitable Lord', John 'Thug' Mackenzie began an Anderson-style pillage of all the lines in this area starting with Stone Valley Crag, producing some classics of all grades in the process such as Rum Doodle Arete (S), Bald Eagle (HVS), Melting Pot (E3) and Blood Feud (E2). The stunning central face of the Bhonaidh Donn finally saw more additions in 1996 from Tom Prentice and Chris French with Dream Ticket (E3) and Balances of Fate (E2) whilst Brown and Mackenzie were joined by Blyth Wright, Graham Ettle and Ian Taylor at Meall Lochan a'Chleirich and gave Golden Eagle (E3) and Cat Burglar (E4). Between them they produced nearly 50 routes on some of the best Lewisian Gneiss on offer. Finally, Paul Thorburn and Rick Campbell added North By North West (E7) to the Bhonaidh Donn in 1997.

Access

Rail/bus – Inverness to Kyle of Lochalsh, change at Dingwall or Achnasheen for bus connections to Kinlochewe. Carnmore and Tollie are best approached from Poolewe. Beinn Lair can be approached from Kinlochewe.

Accommodation

Camping – Poolewe (862811), NTS site, expensive, all facilities; Gairloch (797774) sites in village centre and on B8021, the Melvaig Road, 4 m (6.5 km) distant; Kinlochewe (025619) campsite, all facilities. Badralloch Campsite (065915) on the north shore of Little Loch Broom, near Dundonnell, tel: (01854) 633 281.

Rough camping – Poolewe Bay (850810) by B8057 to Inverasdale. Camping is no longer permitted at Tollie Bay below Tollie Crag because of litter problems. Letterewe Estate – the owners prefer climbers to use the barn beside Carnmore House.

Bothy – Carnmore House (980769) at base of cliff, has wooden stable freely available, and basic but dry.

Bunkhouses – Kinlochewe Bunkhouse (028619), Kinlochewe Hotel, Kinlochewe, Wester Ross (tel. 01445 760253). Badachro Bunkhouse (778737), Badachro Village, on the B8056 road to Red Point. Auchtercairn Hostel, near the Gairloch village junction tel: (01445) 721 131. Rua Reidh Lighthouse (740919), on the headland north of Gairloch tel: (01445) 771 263. Badralloch Bothy (065915) see camping above. Sail Mhor Croft (064893) Camusnagaul, near Dundonnell (tel. 01854 633 224). Cromasaig B&B, Torridon Road, Kinlochewe, owned by climbers tel: (01445) 760 234.

Youth hostel – Carn Dearg (763776) near Little Sand Farm campsite, 3 m (4.8 km) from Gairloch on B8021.

Provisions

Gairloch and Poolewe have shops, garages, cafés and chip shops. The Mountain Shop (with café) in Gairloch is a particular treat whilst Slioch Mountain Clothing factory has a shop in Poolewe. Kinlochewe has café shop and garage as well as a small outdoor shop specialising in climbing hardware and clothing – Moru Outdoor tel: (01445) 760 322, open summer and winter. Early closing in the area is Wednesdays.

Mountain Rescue
Dundonnell Rescue Team, dial 999.
Torridon Rescue Team – Post: Anancaun (024630) 1 mile
(2 km) W of Kinlochewe.

Guidebooks
Northern Highlands, Rock and Ice Climbs, Volume I, G. Cohen,
SMC, 1993

Conservation Information
Letterewe and Fisherfield and Heights of Kinlochewe are all one
estate. The present owner helped formulate an access agreement
called the "Letterewe Accord", accepting wild camping and
walking and climbing access as a right (a catalyst for the
"Access Concordat"). The estates prime period for stalking
deer is September to November. Please contact during this time
for advice on stalking locations. Please use mountain bikes only
on tracks, the ancient stalkers' paths are susceptible to erosion.

Map
Landranger Series: Gairloch and Ullapool, 19.

BEINN A'MHUINIDH   (034658)
This is the hill just N of Kinlochewe which has an almost
continuous band of quartzite cliff running diag. up the hillside
to encircle its plateau-like top. The largest and cleanest section
is the Bonaidh Donn, just after the cliff turns the corner into
Glean Bianisdail, the small glen to its W. As the cliffs run back
towards Kinlochewe they terminate at a 300 ft (90 m) wall
containing a huge waterfall. All the routes have a serious feel.

Approach – From the hamlet of Incheril just E of Kinlochewe
there is a small car-park by a farm (033624). A track through
the farm passes a small cemetery and a path runs L along bank
of River Kinlochewe to beneath waterfall. Cross ravine below
waterfall, directly under it.

Waterfall Wall   (024648) Alt. 1,700 ft (360 m) South facing 🦋 🦋

The main feature in the L wall is a cornerline with large roofs. The best route climbs up the wall just to L of this.

Descent – Down steep grass to R of waterfall.

287 **The Alley**   *300 ft (90 m)   S*

FA: *I. G. Rowe and A. J. Trees, 1967*

Start: At foot of square pillar up and L of waterfall.

1. 100 ft (30 m) Climb front of pillar to big tree. Two short walls above gain triangular ledge with smaller trees.
2. 100 ft (30 m) The large corner lies up and R. Tr. R on to wall on its L, then up this slightly L and gain short chimney. Exit L to ledges.
3. 100 ft (30 m) Finish up the steep groove in wall above.

The Bonaidh Donn   (022656) Alt. 1,860 ft (550 m) West facing 🦋 🦋

The line of broken cliffs continues up and L from the waterfall. The ground below them becomes a terrace with a lower tier of broken rocks as it turns the corner into Glean Bianisdail. A good path develops just past a compact 'Little Buttress', and continues along the now very exposed and shrinking terrace. The first feature is a vertical rib with a prominent beak (**Route II, D, climbs wall just on its** L). 165 ft (50 m) beyond this is the most compact and impressive section, a red concave wall. Down the R side is a chimney/corner line (**Safari, VS**). The red wall merges into grey slabs on the L which are flanked by a big open corner (unclimbed) with a prominent crest. The lower wall is heather infested.

Descent – Walk back towards Kinlochewe past corner of hill. When broken rocks above cliff diminish a small deer-path cuts back R (looking out) above 'Little Buttress' to descend to start of path on terrace (difficult to locate).

288 **Vertigo**   *290 ft (86 m)*   *HVS*
FA: *J. Cunningham and W. March, 1971*
An impressive route climbing a flake up the centre of the
concave wall. Start at a large block at the base of the wall.
1. 120 ft (36 m) 4c Climb easily up L to foot of flake and
   follow it to small ledge (PB).
2. 70 ft (20 m) 5a Tr. L and step onto grey wall. Up and L to
   pull onto even steeper wall above. Climb this to hard move
   L into obvious groove 15 ft (5 m) above. Climb groove to
   belay.
3. 100 ft (30 m) 4b Climb over OH above. Move up and R
   towards easy corner but climb slab on its L to top.

289 **Dream Ticket**   *235 ft (70 m)*   *E3*
FA: *T. Prentice and C. French, 1996*
Climbs the stunning wall R of Vertigo. Start as for Vertigo at
large block.
1. 165 ft (50 m) 5c Climb ledges to prominent twin thin cracks.
   Move up R to L end of OH. Back L into centre of wall and
   continue to small OH level with top of Vertigo flake. Pull
   over and climb crack above. Follow scoop R to belay on
   edge of wall.
2. 70 ft (20 m) 5b Move back L and follow R edge of wall to
   easier ground.

290 **A Walk on the Wild Side**   *420 ft (126 m)*   *S*
FA: *A. J. Trees and I. G. Rowe, 1967*
Good steep route with ridiculous exposure. It climbs the crest of
the big corner L of grey slabs.
Start: Directly below it to R of tall square-cut recess.
1/2. 200 ft (60 m) Up the steep wall on good holds, then
     scramble to base of crest.
3/4. 220 ft (66 m) Climb the crest by cracks and grooves,
     finishing by an exposed short wall on the very crest.

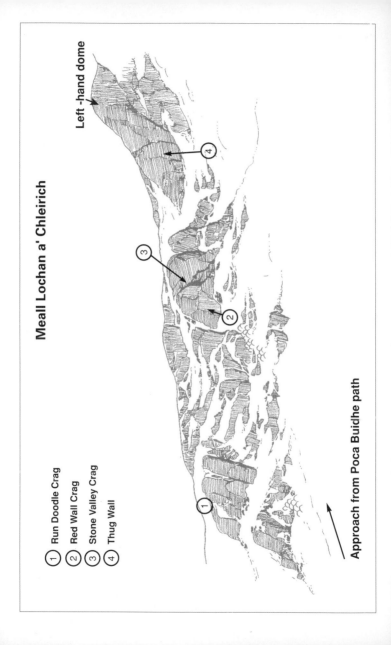

Meall Lochan a' Chleirich

① Run Doodle Crag
② Red Wall Crag
③ Stone Valley Crag
④ Thug Wall

Left-hand dome

Approach from Poca Buidhe path

MEALL LOCHAN A'CHLEIRICH (870716) Alt. 1,300 ft
(300 m) South Facing

This small craggy hill lies just west of Slattadale, a small hamlet on the south shore of Loch Maree at the point where the A832 leaves Loch Maree to cross over the pass towards Gairloch. As Loch Bad an Sgalaig comes into view at head of pass the crags can be seen on hillside to L. The rock is clean gneiss similar to Diabaig but rougher. The area is a veritable sun-trap and crags dry fast after rain. Recent planting of native trees is part of Caledonian Forest Millennium Project and should in time transform this open moorland into magnificent forest.

Approach – Limited parking at white barn on R side of road just before Loch Bad an Sgalaig (856721). A track on opposite side of road is start of path to Poca Buidhe deep in Flowerdale Forest. Follow track through a gate for 1 km and crags lie on hill above.

Layout – Refer to crag layout diagram. Very prominent from path are two domes of rock near summit. Under L side of L dome is steep wall named Thug Wall. The biggest crag is Stone Valley Crag, a large slab about 300 ft (100 m) directly below these domes and easily recognised by silvery R arete. Its true size is hidden until close-up. Immediately to L is steep red coloured wall (Red Wall Crag). L again are several small crags leading across hillside for several hundred metres to next big crag – Rum Doodle Crag – with prominent arete about 130 ft (40 m) high. Below this is Red Barn Crag, almost lower tier to Rum Doodle Crag and lowest climbed-on crag in area.

Climbs described from lower crags to upper ones, L to R.

Rum Doodle Crag South Facing

291 Rum Doodle Arete   *130 ft (40 m)   HS 4a*
FA: *R. J. F. Brown and J. R. Mackenzie, 1995*
Start below arete forming L side of crag, at small groove on L.
Gain arete. Follow edge direct, bold and exposed.

Red Wall Crag South Facing
About 300 ft (100 m) R of Rum Doodle Crag forms the steep
wall immediately to L of Stone Valley Crag; predictably red. It
is separated from its neighbour by the steep grassy descent
gully. Routes described L to R.

292 Bold As Brass   *80 ft (24 m)   E3 5c*
FA: *J. R. Mackenzie and R. J. F. Brown, 1996*
Climbs red coloured L-bounding pillar of wall. Gain small
ledge, step up R to below a cracked 'flange'. Climb it then step
L to thin curving crack. Continue up wall just R of crack (crux)
then crack itself to top.

293 Flaming June   *120 ft (35 m)   VS 5a*
FA: *R. J. F. Brown and J. R. Mackenzie, 1995*
A steep route up groove line on R side of red pillar. Start R of
Bold As Brass below R end of small ledge. Climb up to ledge.
Reach 'flange' then tr. R to ledge with small trees. Climb flake
above, step L into niche below small OH then step back R
towards heather. Climb up and L into open corner which is
followed to ledge. Short rib above to top.

294 Lucky Strike   *80 ft (24 m)   HVS 5a*
FA: *R. J. F. Brown and J. R. Mackenzie, 1996*
Sustained and varied climbing up the centre of the wall to the R.
Start at pronounced groove R of Flaming June. Climb groove on
smooth rock to large spike. Stand on this and climb
blank-looking wall up R on hidden holds.

Stone Valley Crag South Facing   🦋 🦋 🦋

Formed by a lower tier leading to grass ledge. Above this the
crag is an undulating slab with prominent water-washed groove
R of centre. The most prominent feature is silvery L arete
(Open Secret). The short steep lower wall contains a central
'gully' with chockstones. Routes are described L to R.

Descent – The open grassy gully on L of crag.

295 Open Secret   *150 ft (45 m)*   *HS*
FA: *J. R. Mackenzie and R. J. F. Brown, 1995*
1. 50 ft (15 m) Climb short crack on L of lower wall, trend L
   to below arete.
2. 80 ft (25 m) 4b Climb crack in arete to where it bends R.
   Continue up thinner snaking crack trending L up slab.

296 Bald Eagle   *165 ft (50 m)*   *HVS*
FA: *R. J. F. Brown and J. R. Mackenzie, 1995*
Start as for Open Secret.
1. 50 ft (15 m) Climb short crack on L of lower wall, trend R to
   base of a corner.
2. 120 ft (35 m) 5a Climb corner and step L at its top to climb
   thin crack. Where it ends climb direct over two bulges with
   surprising ease to below thin crack. Climb this then boldly
   up red slab centrally and direct over wall at top.

297 Blood Feud   *180 ft (54 m)*   *E2*
FA: *J. R. Mackenzie and B. Wright, 1997*
To R of initial crack of Open Secret is small ledge with small
tree. Start just L.
1. 90 ft (27 m) 5b Up wall L of tree to recess. Bald wall behind
   tree via crack and go direct where crack veers R. Step L and
   follow fine slab to grass ledge.
2. 90 ft (27 m) 5a Above are twin black streaks. From the L of
   these tr. R and up into them. Finish up crack above through
   the headwall to top.

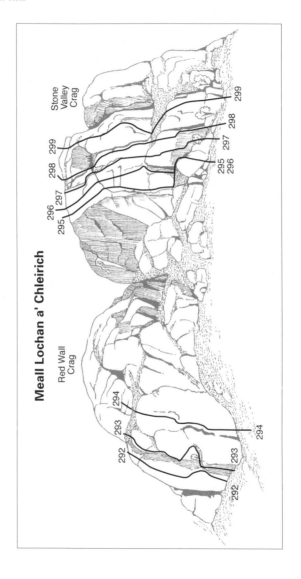

298 **Stone Diary / Inside Information**   *165 ft (50 m)*   *HVS*
FA: *(Both routes) R. J. F. Brown and J. R. Mackenzie, 1995*
This combination of two routes gives excellent sustained
climbing. Start just L of central chockstone gully.

1. 70 ft (20 m) 5a Gain a plinth and climb steep rib between
   gully and smooth pod to L. Step L and friction up bald slab
   to grass ledge. Step R to flake belay below fine water-worn
   groove.
2. 100 ft (30 m) 4c The excellent groove to a ledge. Step L and
   climb flake to awkward exit by small corner.

299 **Melting Pot**   *165 ft (50 m)*   *E3*
FA: *J. R. Mackenzie, R. J. F. Brown and G. Cullen, 1995*
Climbs main upper buttress to R of Inside Information
beginning R of the Gully in lower tier. Start at rib R of tree.

1. 70 ft (20 m) 4c Climb wall then up to step R to ledge. Up
   short wall above and scramble to flake belay below
   water-worn groove of Inside Information.
2. 100 ft (30 m) 6a Step onto ramp and climb L-hand crack to
   sloping hold. Step R and climb R-hand crack to distinctive
   'shield'. More easily to top.

Variation: **Golden Eagle, 100 ft (30 m) E3 6a.** Climbs the
L-hand crack directly to the top. The best crack climb on the
best rock on the hill.

Thug Wall   South Facing   🦋 🦋 🦋
Almost 300 ft (100 m) above Secret Valley Crag are two domes
(separated by a gully) near the summit of the hill. Near the L
base of the L-hand dome is an OH-wall containing series of
excellent steep routes. A prominent feature is the slim slanting
red slab (The Thin Red Line, HVS 4c but on poor rock)
bounding the L side of the Thug Wall. To the R the crag turns
a right-angle and contains a vertical chimney, This is **The Lum
230 ft (70 m) VD**. It climbs chimney and OH-crack L of red
corner and crack round front face followed by easy slabs.
Routes described L to R.

300 **Cat Burglar**   *100 ft (30 m)   E4 6a*
FA: *I. Taylor, G. Ettle and R. J. F. Brown, 1997*
The L-slanting thin crack R of the slim slab is **The Flashing Blade (E3 6a)**. This route climbs the formidable wall to the R. Start up curving groove further R (The Thug). Step onto wall to follow thin OH-crack.

301 **The Thug**   *120 ft (35 m)   E2*
FA: *R. J. F. Brown and J. R. Mackenzie, 1996*
1. 50 ft (15 m) 4c The fine OH-crack on R side of wall. Start L of crack at curving groove. Up groove then R to small ledge below crack.
2. 70 ft (20 m) 5b The crack must be attacked forcefully to reach the ledge above. Finish up easy arete.

CREAG MHOR THOLLAIDH   (865775)
Creag Mhor Thollaidh, (pronounced 'Tollie') is an extensive hill of rugged outcrops of Lewisian gneiss at the W end of Loch Maree. The two main crags, Upper and Lower Tollie, lie hidden from the road above Tollie Bay. They receive the sun well into the evening in summer. Both crags offer just off-vertical routes following numerous cracklines. There is little seepage, and they dry quickly after rain. When nearby crags are being drowned out, Tollie often remains dry.

Loch Maree Crag lies one mile further along the shore and is a different proposition, very steep and receiving the sun only in the early morning. It does, however, remain dry even in quite heavy rain, and gives strenuous and sparsely protected climbs of high quality.

Approach – The small road to Tollie Farm is followed to a car-park in Tollie Bay. In the bay is an old jetty and above lies Lower Tollie Crag. The Upper Crag is above and L. To reach them requires a taxing two-minute trudge.

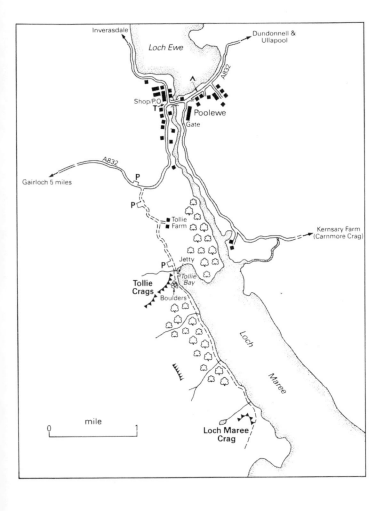

Inverasdale

Loch Ewe

Dundonnell &
Ullapool

A832

Shop/P.O.

T

Poolewe

Gate

A832

Gairloch 5 miles

P

P

Tollie
Farm

Kernsary Farm
(Carnmore Crag)

P

Jetty

Tollie
Bay

Tollie
Crags

Boulders

Loch

Maree

mile

0   1

Loch Maree
Crag

Lower Tollie Crag   (869779) Alt. 150 ft (45 m) South-east facing ✖ ✖ ✖
There are two faces to the crag. The East Face is smooth and OH, and turns a corner to rear up to the 300 ft (90 m) South Face. A large R-facing arching corner capped by a roof (**Friday the 13th 220 ft (66 m) HVS 5a**) separates the two faces. Routes are described R to L.

Descent – A small steep gully runs down the R side of the R end of the East Face, and can be descended from all routes. Abseil descent possible for some routes.

The East Face
The R end is defined by a steep arete (**Hamilton's Groove and Arete, E3 6a**). To the L the smooth OH-hall is cut horizontally by a roof. A crack strikes through this and is the next climb:

302 **Cloud Cuckoo Land**   *90 ft (27 m)   HVS 5b*
FA: *R. Anderson and G. Nicholl, 1987*
Climb up under the roof. Pull through with surprising ease and follow continuation line, finishing at a groove, tree belay. Abseil off.

303 **Loctite**   *100 ft (30 m)   E3*
FA: *R. Anderson and G. Nicholl, 1987*
Start just below the tree-lined ledge slanting L into Friday the 13th.
1. 30 ft (9 m) 5c Gain a thin crack and climb it to the ledge.
2. 70 ft (21 m) 6a Take the R-slanting flake crack in wall above. Pull L and follow a thin crack over a bulge to gain a short ramp. Step L then up to gain heathery ledge.

The South Face
The large R-hand side is split just L of centre by a chossy broken fault (The Trip, VS). The two most prominent features to the R are a thin vertical disjointed crack (Decadent Days) and a large curving crack in upper part (Catastasis E1). L of The Trip is a big open corner, its lower half herbaceous and

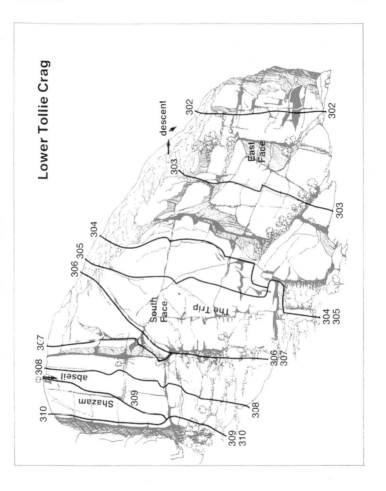

Lower Tollie Crag

tree-infested. Breaking out R across the upper face is a big flake fault (The Handrail). The upper corner becomes clean and square-cut. The slabby face to its L then finishes as a pronounced arete.

304 **Gudgeon**   *230 ft (69 m)   E2*
FA: *C. Jackson and T. Proctor, 1971*
FFA: *R. Anderson and C. Grieves, 1988*
A lovely route up the R side of the upper half of the face above the arching corner of Friday the 13th.
Start: Below the fault of The Trip.
1. 70 ft (21 m) 5b Climb a clean rib to heathery break under OH. Descend R to corner. Up corner, move L and up further groove to OH. Tr. R to end of grass ramp on Friday the 13th.
2. 90 ft (27 m) 5c Above and L is arching crack of Catastatis. To its R is a small groove. Climb the groove to horizontal break. Step R on sloping ledge to gain twin thin cracks, follow to big flake (PB).
3. 70 ft (21 m) 5a Follow flake and cracks above to shoulder of crag.

305 **Decadent Days**   *300 ft (90 m)   E2*
FA: *R. Anderson and M. Hamilton, 1983*
Forceful direct line up thin crackline in centre of face.
Start: Below The Trip as for Gudgeon.
1. 150 ft (45 m) 5c Up the rib to the heather break. Follow down R to corner of Gudgeon. From its top step L on to lip of small roof. Follow thin crack up wall to big diag. crack (nut belay).
2. 150 ft (45 m) 5c Step L in diag. crack. Move back R for 10 ft (3 m) to gain almost direct line of thin cracks to top.

306 **The Handrail**   *250 ft (75 m)   S*
FA: *T. W. Patey and M. Galbraith, 1966*
Below the big R-angled corner on L side of face is a tree-lined depression. Scramble up this to tree belay near its top. The deep fault line shoots out R across the face and contains the

occasional small tree. Climb it in two pitches with incredible exposure.

The clean-cut corner is **Stoney Broke (HVS 5a)**, with pleasant wide bridging by-passing any greenery in the back. The R arete gives a hard route with an odd name:

307 **Rain in the Face**   *120 ft (36 m)*   *E3 6a*
FA: *D. Dinwoodie and A. Ross, 1987*
Gain the base of Stoney Broke and its arete by the fault of Handrail, and a short hand tr. L along flake. On L side of arete above is slim groove, gain this (PR), climb it to roofs. Pull round R side of roof to climb foxy crack just R of arete to top. Abseil off tree at top of Stoney Broke to get down.

The obvious crackline up centre of wall on L is **Shazam (E1 5b)**. The next route climbs the wall and thin crack between Stoney Broke and Shazam:

308 **Each Uisage/Across the Lines**   *160 ft (48 m)*   *E4*
FA: *R. Anderson and C. Grieves, 1988 (pitch 1)*
FA: *D. Dinwoodie and A. Ross, 1987 (pitch 2)*
Start on ledge below obvious crack of Shazam. Tree belay.
1. 80 ft (24 m) 6a Above is short very thin crack. Gain crack. Step R and up to horizontal break. Up to next break, then up to OH. Step L up and R to good holds. Easier R to ledge (PR).
2. 80 ft (24 m) 6a Step L and up to break (PR); gain crack leading to tree at top.

309 **The Angry Magician**   *170 ft (52 m)*   *E1*
FA: *K. Howett and H. Harris, 1994 (alt)*
A natural diagonal line from L arete of crag crossing Shazam and finishing at top of Across The Lines. Start by scrambling up into oak tree at base of arete.
1. 90 ft (27 m) 5a Pull through OHs on hollow sounding blocks heading slightly L onto wall. Climb diag. line R up centre of wall to belay at small tree in vegetated crack-line of Shazam.

2. 80 ft (25 m) 5b Climb up and R to ledge in deep diag. crack. Continue up to horizontal crack then follow obvious R-diag. scoop with continual interest and little protection to top. Excellent pitch.

310 **Murray's Arete**   *150 ft (45 m)   E3 5c*
FA: *M. Hamilton, 1983*
Climbs conspicuous sharp L arete of crag giving serious climbing in middle section.

Upper Tollie Crag   Alt. 500 ft (150 m) South
facing 🦋 🦋 🦋
The main face is a pyramid shape banded on R by broken ground. Two huge faults run full length of face. **Cocaine (HVS 5a)** is R fault, dirty and disjointed; **Knickerbockerglory (E1 5b)**, the L fault, proves to be an arboreal struggle up a chimney festooned with chockstones and trees, the crux an excursion on L wall past a man-eating holly bush.

311 **The Bug**   *165 ft (57 m)   E2 5b*
FA: *L. G. Brown and R. G. Wilson, 1975*
FFA: *C. Maclean and A. Ross, 1983*
L of Knickerbockerglory a R-slanting groove runs up to join it at third height. Thin crack climbs undulating wall above its start. Gain crack from L, follow over bulge and gain ramp leading up R. Crack though bulge above ramp. Follow it R then back L to further bulge. Direct over this via thin continuation crack to easy slab. Belay. Scramble easier up for 30 ft (9 m) to escape.

312 **The Heretic**   *170 ft (51 m)   E3 5b*
FA: *R. Anderson and G. Nicoll, 1987*
Fingery climbing up blank wall L of The Bug. Start 10 ft (3 m) L below some blocks. Stand on the blocks. Step R and follow shallow slabby groove to gain L end of Bug ramp. Good hold on wall above helps gain short diag. crack. Up this past shallow scoop. Stand in horizontal crack. Continue R and then L to

further diag. crack; up to yet another, then direct over on to slab. Scramble off L easily.

Loch Maree Crag   (879769) Alt. 150 ft (45 m) North-east facing 🦋 🦋 🦋
From the jetty in Tollie Bay take tiny path through huge boulders, then along the loch shore. The first sighting of the crag is when one emerges from the trees into a flat rocky bay.

   Topography – The crag is formed by two walls at 90° to each other, forming a distinctive nose pointing N. The path continues up to the immediate L of the crag and over the hill. The rock in the nose itself is broken and vegetated, whilst the R wall rises up to form a gully and is acutely OH. The L wall is smooth and gently impending. It is bounded on the R (as it turns into the nose of the crag) by a stunning OH-arete, and a distinctive L to R diag. central fault splits it in two.

   Descent – By abseil (in-situ gear), or horrible scramble up L.

313   **Spirit Air**   *160 ft (48 m)*   *E4 6a*
      FA: *K. Howett, 1987*
      A gob-smacking line taking a thin crack in L side of the arete. From toe of crag, climb thin groove up the edge. From its top make committing moves up and R into crack. Follow this with sustained interest in a mind-blowing position until it fades. Above, a horizontal crack leads L and up to a grey 'shield' of rock in middle of face. Climb its R side, then go R again past another horizontal crack, until moves diag. L lead to the huge central fault. Up this to tree.

314   **Arial**   *160 ft (48 m)*   *E3 5c*
      FA: *K. Howett, G. Ridge and J. Horrocks, 1992*
      Probably the 'easy' classic of crag following stunning flake-crack up centre of wall below abseil tree at top of Spirit Air. Start below obvious thin crack in centre of wall with sapling at 15 ft (5 m). Follow crack through bulge then bigger crack direct with continuous interest past bend R to form flake. Direct up shallow groove to holly tree.

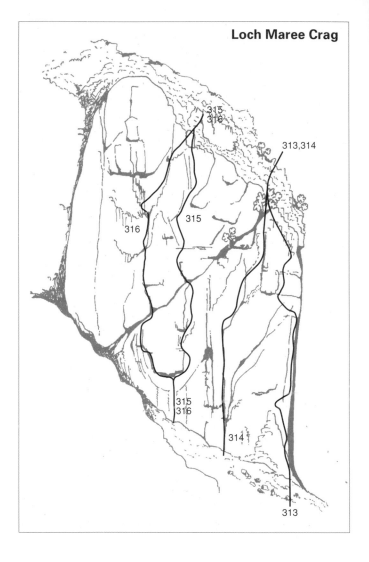

Loch Maree Crag

315 **Blasad den Iar**   *160 ft (48 m)   E3 5c*
FA: *K. Howett, 1987*
This takes a direct line through the central fault.
Start: 50 ft (15 m) L of the arete in the constriction of the gully.
Climb up a white seepage of calcite just L of a continuous
greasy seep. Gain shallow ramp and follow it R to its end.
Climb L over the roof L of a small hanging corner on jugs. Up
to corner top. Go diag. R (loose block) to gain thin hanging
crack, and so to central fault. Pull through directly via L-facing
flake. Directly up on good holds to horizontal crack. Thinner
climbing follows thin intermittent diag. crack to good holds
(NRS above). Climb diag. R into slim R-leading scoop. Follow
until just below top. Take wall direct to L of large precarious
block. Belay on R.

316 **Jarldom Reach**   *170 ft (51 m)   E5 6b*
FA: *K. Howett and A. Nelson, 1987*
Follows wall to L of Blasad den Iar via series of scoops.
Serious climbing with crux near top.
Start: As for last route. Up the calcite to the ramp. Exit this
immediately L into cracks leading up to base of central fault.
Follow this R to just beyond a large wedged block (possible
stance), pull out of break via flake, follow to another flake. Step
L and pull into the scoop. Follow a thin diag. groove exiting R
from scoop to a jug at its top. Pull up and L through white
bulge by thin moves into second scoop. Tr. horizontally R and
follow slim leaning groove with increasing difficulty until a
hard move R gains jugs. Finish past large perched block. Belay
on R.

CARNMORE CRAG   (980774) Alt. 1,400 ft (450 m) South
facing ✄
Carnmore, a massive sweeping cliff of clean rough gneiss, and its
twin neighbour, Torr na h'Ioliare, lie on the S spurs of Beinn
a'Chaisgein Mor, overlooking the S end of the Fionn Loch. Tor na
h'Ioliare, visible from Poolewe, appears the more impressive, but
from Carnmore House the continuous steep clean rock of Carnmore

dominates. Its remote setting, sunny aspect, and excellent rock combine to give climbing comparable with the best in Britain.

Approach – From Poolewe a single-track road runs by River Ewe to Kernsary Farm (locked gate half way), 11 miles (17.5 km). Permission to drive to the Kernsary/Scatwell Estates boundary may be given: contact the factor at Scatwell and Inverin Estates.

Topography – Nearly 900 ft (270 m) high, the face is split in the centre by a large grassy central bay. The L side of the face is a continuous nose of rock (Fionn Buttress), the full height of the face. The lower wall below the central bay is characterized by a curving red scar on L bounding Fionn Buttress and an area of huge corners in the centre. Above the central bay is the upper wall containing the classic Dragon and Gob, and a huge corner on R (Carnmore Corner). An easy ramp of slabs runs up R of Carnmore Corner to top. Below this is the grey wall. The central bay can be reached from The Gangway (M), running L out of minor gully on R directly below the grey wall.

Descent – Down steep grass scoop to L of upper slabs of Diagonal Route (S) on to Baisin, or down hillside to L of buttress: see diagram, p. 291.

317 **Fionn Buttress**   *800 ft (240 m)*   *VS*
FA: *M. J. O'Hara and W. D. Blackwood, 1957*
Steep and exposed on perfect rock. One of the finest outings in Scotland.
Start: From a turf ledge at the front of a large O H -chimney running up the lower wall at a prominent pale patch.
1. 100 ft (30 m) Climb up a slab and R into corner. Pass loose block on R wall of corner, and go round to a ledge. Climb crack in wall on R for 10 ft (3 m), then step on to a slab. Cross this and belay at chockstone in chimney beyond.
2. 80 ft (24 m) Up the R wall and then follow turf trending R. Up flake leaning against grey slabs and belay at their top.
3. 50 ft (15 m) 4c Go straight up slab, then L to a ledge. Head

Spirit Air, Loch Maree Crag: climber, Kevin Howett

back keeping high as possible for 10 ft (3 m), then go up to an OH-ledge.

4. 80 ft (24 m) Cross L to wet recess (loose blocks), up the corner above (usually wet) to turf recess.

5. 80 ft (24 m) 4c Up corners or walls above to gain the OH. Surmount this by sensational moves 10 ft (3 m) from its R-hand end. Move R to stance.

6. 80 ft (24 m) Tr. R across the face to a stance and belay on the true nose of the buttress.

7. 150 ft (45 m) 4b Gain a flake up on L by a steep groove above the belay (strenuous). Above it, move L few feet then up R to ledge.

8. 120 ft (36 m) 4b Up the crest to a heather ledge and perched blocks below an OH-slab. Over the blocks, and up slab to shelf. Move R to its top R corner.

9. 60 ft (18 m) Finish up the wall above, trending L.

Lower Walls

To the R of Fionn Buttress are two prominent ribs containing a heathery bay. The first rib contains a curving red scar. R of the second rib is a conspicuous tall recess (climbed by Balaton) and then an area of vegetated slabs (Botanist's Boulevard).

318 **Black Mischief**   *400 ft (120 m)   VS*
FA: *D. E. H. Maden and R. D. Sykes, 1966*
Starts in the back R-hand corner of the heathery bay between the two ribs. A good entry pitch to Gob. Start at foot of obvious black groove capped on R by square-cut OH.

1. 90 ft (27 m) 4b Easily to first bulge in groove, turn on R. Up groove to another bulge (TR). Exit L to stance.

2. 80 ft (24 m) 4c Up to R where groove steepens (spike). Move delicately R under bulge on to slab. Tr. diag. across slab to ledge on skyline. Crack above and exit R (hard) to grass ledge level, but R of square-cut OH (thread belay).

3. 60 ft (18 m) 4c Cracked wall above with hard move above a ledge (PR). Then move easily to large ledges.

4/5. 200 ft (60 m) Easier to central bay.

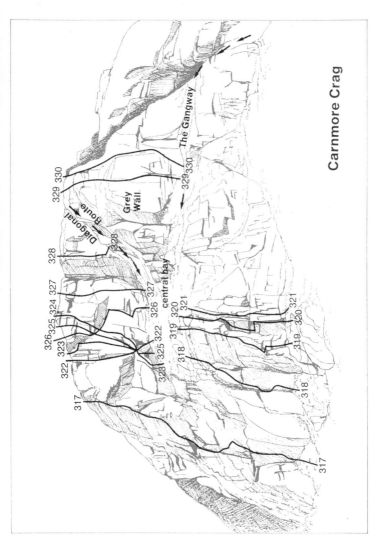

Carnmore Crag

The next route climbs the wall just L of the conspicuous tall recess in the centre of the lower wall taken by Balaton:

319 **999**   *370 ft (111 m)   E1*
FA: *A. Tibbs and A. Winton, 1984*
L of the Balaton Recess is a corner immediately R of two large red flakes.
1. 100 ft (30 m) 5b/c Corner to roof, turn roof on L, Climb crack above till easier rock in same line leads to belay.
2. 120 ft (36 m) 4c Tr. R to rib overlooking Balaton recess. Climb rib to finish up conspicuous curving groove.
3. 150 ft (45 m) Easily to central bay.

320 **Balaton**   *380 ft (114 m)   E1*
FA: *W. Gorman and C. Higgens, 1966*
A great route on excellent rock. Start below R-hand corner of recess.
1. 80 ft (24 m) 5a Up the OH-corner crack to a belay.
2. 30 ft (9 m) 5b Descend to gain a sandwiched slab in back of recess. Tr. L across it between roofs into foot of L corner (PB).
3. 120 ft (36 m) 5a Climb the corner to slab. Tr. R, turn OH, then up L to below big OH. Break R and up to stance (PB).
4. 150 ft (45 m) 4c Up and L of a rib on skyline, then slabs to bay.

321 **Running Bear**   *320 ft (96 m)   E3*
FA: *D. Dinwoodie and J. Wyness, 1987*
FA: *D. Dinwoodie and A. Nisbet, 1988 (direct)*
Climbs the R rib of Batalon.
Start: Below it.
1. 110 ft (33 m) 6a Climb up on to tall block. Move L over bulge. Direct up rib with difficulty, ignoring possible escapes off to the R, to a crevasse at top of rib (nut belay).
2. 80 ft (24 m) 5a Climb bulge above and up L into groove. Up this to slabs and belay.
3. 150 ft (45 m) More slabs to central bay.

Upper Wall

The L side of the upper wall contains a huge grey slab capped by roof and leaning wall above. The wall is split by a long corner (**Abomination, HVS 5a**) separating the leaning wall from central section. A roof splits this latter section diag. down R, diminishing as it does so. R again is a huge corner (a prominent feature), before the slabs of Diagonal Route runs up to top. Routes are described L to R.

The leaning wall above the slab at L end of the wall contains **Death Wolf (E6 6b 6a 5c)**, climbing the flake gangway through the guarding roof and small scoop and wall above, heading towards the arete on R. Then L up wall to knobbles, then up to large ledge. Short wall leads to top.

322 **Abomination**   *320 ft (96 m)*   *HVS*
FA: *J. McLean, A. Curry and J. Cunningham, 1966*
Climbs the long corner bounding the R side of the leaning wall. There is a further corner just to the R (Death Master, E4 6a). Start at easy vegetated crack in corner of steep wall under the grey slab.
1. 100 ft (30 m) 4b The 'vegan' crack to grass ledge on top of grey slab (PB).
2. 110 ft (33 m) 5a Off L end of ledge is the corner. Near the L edge is crack; up this crack to ledge. Awkward near top.
3. 100 ft (30 m) 5a Continue up corner to OH, move R and up wall on flakes to top of buttress.

323 **Dragon**   *340 ft (102 m)*   *HVS*
FA: *G. J. Fraser and M. J. O'Hara, 1957*
Well protected in scary position.
Start: At lower R corner of easy grey slab.
1. 110 ft (33 m) Climb out L on to slab, and up its edge to narrow heather ledge.
2. 110 ft (33 m) 4c Abomination corner is on L: above is shallow groove up to prominent OH. Pass OH on R, tr. L by cracks and gain easier groove to spike R. Go up R to huge pedestal belay.

Dragon, 'the droopy
flake', Carnmore Crag:
climber, Alan Winton

3. 70 ft (23 m) 5a Up and slightly L into deep crack in yellow
   rock (the droopy flake) leading beneath huge roof. Escape L
   at top onto tiny rib (PR), tr. L across steep slab (crux) into
   corner.
4. 30 ft (9 m) 4a Tr. out L on to rib and up this to top.

324 **Lion Rampant**   *250 ft (85 m)*   *E5*
FA: *G. Livingston and D. Dinwoodie, 1986*
Main pitch takes wall R of Dragon, then breaks through roof in
a break just R of Gob break.
Start: at steep crack in R-bounding wall of Dragon slab.
1. 60 ft (18 m) 6b The crack to ledge on Dragon slab.
2. 100 ft (30 m) 6a Climb up wall to R of Dragon, past spike to
   expanding block. Direct over bulge. Move R to small ledges at
   foot of great shallow scoop. Up L, then out R and up to
   expanding flake. Move out L to another flake and gain
   L-slanting ledge above. Continue direct up unprotected wall

above, just beside arete overlooking Sword groove (poor PR),
to gain ledge. L along this to R side of huge detached blocks.
3. 75 ft (14 m) 6a Wall on R to join Gob, under roof. Up into
   small corner, pull out R on layaways to slabs above.
4. 45 ft (14 m) 5c Direct to OH above. Tr. L to pull over on jug
   and swing up R to blocks. Veer L up steep wall to big
   OH-flakes to top.

325 **Sword**   *340 ft (102 m)   E2*
FA: *R. Isherwood and E. Birch, 1967*
FFA: *G. Duckworth and party, 1980s*
A fine natural line up big groove cutting through centre of
upper wall.
Start: Below a dirty groove exiting L from a shallow cave R of
the Dragon slab.
1. 50 ft (15 m) 4c Up the groove to gain R end of ledge at top
   of Dragon slab.
2. 150 ft (45 m) 5c Tr. R for about 10 ft (3 m) on lip of OH,
   then climb up and R below stepped corner to gain the main
   groove line. Climb the main groove to gain the tr. line of
   Gob below the big roof. Small stance.
3. 60 ft (18 m) 5c Up and R into the main breach in leaning
   roof above (PR) with a hard move for short-legged varieties.
   Move R to rib and on up to stance.
4. 80 ft (24 m) 5a Shallow groove to top.

326 **Gob**   *420 ft (126 m)   HVS*
FA: *D. Haston and R. Smith, 1960*
A brilliant trip up this impressive wall by line of least resistance
up and L under capping roofs.
Start: Below OH low down and R of Sword.
1. 150 ft (45 m) 4c Tr. L along ledge below OHS to their L
   end. The wall above is climbed via cracks R to shallow
   corner. Up this to beneath big roof.
2. 150 ft (45 m) 4b Tr. L below roof (hard passing a shield
   mid-way) to pulpit stance beside obvious large R-leading
   fault through roof.

    3. 120 ft (36 m) 4c Through break R to slabs. Climb shallow
       groove directly above to top.

327 **Wilderness**   *260 ft (78 m)*   *E4*
FA: *D. Mullin and M. Lawrence, 1980*
This climbs up the L wall of the massive open book corner at R
side of upper wall, utilizing part of obvious crack.
Start: 30 ft (9 m) L of crack on small ledge.
    1. 60 ft (18 m) 5b Into groove on L, tr. steeply L across face to
       base of crack.
    2. 120 ft (36 m) 6a Crack diag. for 6 ft (2 m) then L onto face
       and L up to recess. Thin crack R to join slight groove line
       going up and L. Follow to scoop, then wall above and twin
       cracks to base of corner.
    3. 80 ft (24 m) 5b Climb corner, then thin crack.

The crack followed in its entirety is **Jivaro Crack (E4 6b)**. The
massive corner is **Carnmore Corner (E1 5b)**, usually wet. The
incredible R arete gives the next route:

328 **The Orange Bow**   *120 ft (36 m)*   *E5 6a*
FA: *D. Dinwoodie and D. Hawthorn, 1985*
Start on ledges on R 30 ft (9 m) from top of last slab of
Diagonal Route. Tr. L along slabby shelf. Over tricky bulge and
up L to big footholds, then swing out L on flakes and follow
vague intermittent crack up OH-wall. When it fades tr. R and up
to ledge. Up edge to finish up L-slanting crack on L side.

The Grey Wall
Gain the wall via the gangway. Its L side has a break running
into a hanging corner capped by an OH. Just R is a very
prominent diedre with cracks in its R side. The corner is (**It
Was Twenty Years Ago Today, E1 4c 5a**), whilst the cracks
are (**The Cracks, VS 4c**).

329 **Crackers**   *255 ft (77 m)*   *E3*
FA: *D. Hawthorn and C. MacLean, 1985*
Climbs the central cracks in the Grey Wall main face.
Start: 50 ft (15 m) R of the steep groove which lies between the
main wall and the hanging corner on the L.
1. 75 ft (23 m) 5c Climb the steep crack.
2. 150 ft (45 m) 5a Continuation cracks to ledges, easy
    scrambling to top.

330 **Trampoline**   *200 ft (60 m)*   *HVS*
FA: *R. Isherwood and E. Birch, 1967*
In the wall R of Crackers is a diag. tr. line with a niche.
Start: Below this.
1. 85 ft (26 m) 5a Climb into the niche. Tr. R until angle eases.
    Wall above by twin cracks and slab to stance.
2. 115 ft (35 m) 5a Climb slabs on L to below crack. Move R
    to short corner. Then R to wall. Steeply up crack above and
    easy slab (block belay). Easy slabs to top.

BEINN LAIR   (982733) Alt. 1,400 ft (450 m) North
facing 🦋 🦋
The long ridge of mountains on the N side of Loch Maree
(Beinn Airigh Charr in W, Meall Mheinnidh and Beinn Lair to
Slioch in E) all have great escarpments of hornblend schist on
their N flanks. They are at their most impressive on the North
Face of Beinn Lair overlooking the Alt Gleann Tulacha which
runs into the head of Lochan Fada. There are more than 20
separate buttresses or ridges divided by deep-cut gullies and
varying in height between 500 ft (120 m) and 1,500 ft (450 m).
   The compact schist has been weathered into a profusion of
incut holds, generally sound and relatively free of vegetation but
often greasy. Belays and runners are singularly lacking.
   Approach – 1) From Kinlochewe via a path up Glean
Bianisdail past Slioch to Lochan Fada and the S shore (boggy),
to below the cliff (10 miles (16 km)). 2) From Poolewe, via
Kernsary, path to Carnmore (14 miles (23 km)).

Accommodation – Carnmore House, 4 m (6 km) from the crag, and camping below the face.

Topography – Directly below the N summit of Beinn Lair are four buttresses forming a butterfly shape on the hillside. To the W (R) is the main face, separated from those buttresses by a huge amphitheatre. This main face consists of four big buttresses, Molar on the L, Angel and Wisdom in the centre, split apart by the thin Bat's Gash, and Wisdom being the unmistakable slender cigar shape on the R. R again is the Tooth, which ends the main face. Further R still are two more buttresses which are the furthest W on Beinn Lair.

Descent – The amphitheatre between Butterfly and Molar Buttresses.

331 **Wisdom Buttress**   *700 ft (210 m)*   *VD*
FA: *J. Smith, A. Hood and J. S. Orr, 1951*
A magnificent climb, exposed, sustained and the best of its grade in the area.
Start: At bottom R corner of buttress, which is a conspicuous slender cigar shape.

1/2. 250 ft (75 m) Climb diag. L above a lower OH, then up slightly R to a small platform and an obvious line of weakness, until it ends at a diminutive stance beneath a small OH.

3. 75 ft (23 m) Tr. L and evade the OH by a slab.

4. 100 ft (30 m) Continue direct up slabs on L, then tr. back by ledge to centre of buttress.

5. 100 ft (30 m) Climb the nose by an excursion on the R wall (steep on sloping holds), before returning to the crest to belay.

6. 175 ft (58 m) Continue up steep nose above and crest of buttress to top.

7   COIGACH AND ASSYNT

Introduction

North of Ullapool, isolated mountains in flat, loch-studded surroundings dominate the landscape. They form the central section of the coastal band of Torridonian sandstone that stretches from the Kyle of Lochalsh to Cape Wrath. In the heart of the Coigach hills, just N of Ullapool, the tooth-shaped peak of Sgurr an Fhidhleir presents an Alpine-scale face, whilst facing it from the N is the tourist magnet, Stac Pollaidh (Stack Polly). Close to the road and much smaller than the other Coigach hills, Stac Pollaidh is nonetheless a mountain in miniature, with an impressive cliff-studded summit ridge.

Further N on the point of Stoer in the crofting region of Assynt is a sporting little sea-stack which will attract connoisseurs of such inaccessible summits.

History

For such a remote area which even today retains many single track roads, it is surprising that initial exploration was in the early 1900's when the Inglis Clark family climbed Western Buttress on Stac Pollaidh. Just after this Willie Ling attempted the nose of Sgurr an Fhidhleir but was defeated by protection-less slabs. Further development came in the 1950's with Ian Clough and RAF Kinloss teams climbing various lines at Stac Pollaidh including November Grooves (VS). Then in the 1960's Tom Patey started making additions all over the area while resident in Ullapool as the local Doctor. The Nose of the Fhidhleir saw its first ascent by Neville Drasdo accompanied by Mike Dixon in 1962. This spurred many into action, Patey in particular producing Enigma Grooves (HVS); Rab Carrington and John MacLean climbing Felo de Se (E2); Anderson and Mair completing Jack The Ripper (HVS); all on Stac Pollaidh. John Mackenzie and D Gilbert had an exciting day out in 1979 producing the superbly situated Tower Finish to the Fhidhleir – a long and committing climb.

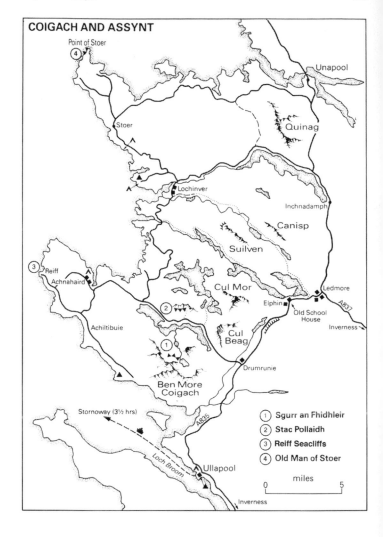

COIGACH AND ASSYNT

Point of Stoer
④

Unapool

Stoer

Quinag

Lochinver

Inchnadamph

Canisp

Suilven

Reiff
③
Achnahaird

Cul Mor

Ledmore

Elphin

Old School
House

Inverness

Achiltibuie

Cul
Beag

②

Ben More
Coigach
①

Drumrunie

Stornoway (3½ hrs)

① Sgurr an Fhidhleir

② Stac Pollaidh

③ Reiff Seacliffs

④ Old Man of Stoer

Loch Broom

Ullapool

miles

0   5

Inverness

The beginning of the extensive development of the sea cliffs at Reiff started in the late 1970's. Initially this was purely at the hands of Aberdonian Brian Lawrie who spent 10 years soloing many 5c and 6a graded climbs (and even up to E3 6b). By 1987 Lawrie had done over 100 routes here. Thereafter other Aberdonian teams (including Andy Tibbs) started adding numerous routes as well, but soon they did not have it all to themselves. Andy Cunningham, instructing at Glenmore Lodge, with Jenny Pickering and Keith Geddes developed whole new areas including some of the bigger crags. Cunningham produced a guide in 1990 which contained over 350 climbs.

During visits to Reiff, Tibbs obviously noticed the potential of Stac Pollaidh. He completed several routes here but news of his on-sight attempts on the impressive central line on the main western buttress spurred Tom Prentice to visit. Prentice then found himself at the forefront of modern development at Stac Pollaidh accompanied by Simon Richardson and Tibbs. Prentice completed the central line as Expecting to Fly with a mossy E4 crux. He went on to dominate development of this wall with Rab Anderson, producing a superb clutch of routes such as Walking on Air (E4) and Mid-flight Crisis (E4).

Recent explorations in the area have led to E6 and E7 being a reality at Reiff and the development of Camus Mor on Ben More Coigach by activists of old making a welcome return

Access
Bus – Inverness to Ullapool, Local Express, Citylink, twice daily; Ullapool to Drumrunie and Achiltibuie, minibus daily; Lochinver to Raffin (Point of Stoer), post bus twice daily.

Accommodation
Camping – Clachtoll (040274) on B869 to Stoer; Achmelvich site (054248) N of Lochinver near youth hostel, all facilities; Brae of Achnahaird (019137) by sandy bay on W coast road to Achiltibuie.
Rough camping – Unhindered if inconspicuous.
Bivvy site – Boulder howff beside Lochan Tuath at top end of

boulder field on NE side of Lochan (107056), below Sgurr an Fhidhleir.

Bunkhouses – West House Tourist Hostel in centre of Ullapool, tel: (01854) 613 216; Ceilidh Place Bunkhouse in centre of Ullapool, tel: (01854) 612 103; Assynt Field Centre, Inchnadamph, 25 miles (57.5 km) N of Ullapool, tel: (01571) 822 218.

Youth hostels – Ullapool village centre (130940); Achinver (043056) near S end of Achiltibuie; Achmelvich (059248) near Lochinver.

Provisions
Usual facilities at Lochinver, Stoer and Ullapool. Cafés in Ullapool. Lochinver early closing Tuesdays, Ullapool Wednesdays. Mountain Man Supplies shop for all climbing equipment, Shore Road, Ullapool. Also has excellent climbers' café.

Mountain Rescue
Dundonnel Rescue Team, Assynt Rescue Team – Posts: police station, Ullapool (128942); Inchnadamph Hotel (252216) by Lairg on A837, 25 miles (57.5 km) N of Ullapool. Nearest telephone to crags: Dumrunie junction (166054).

Guidebooks
Northern Highland, Rock and Ice Climbs, Vol. 2., G. Cohen, SMC, 1993

Maps
Landranger Series: Loch Assynt, 15; Gairloch and Ullapool, 19.

Conservation Information
Stac Pollaidh lies within the Inverpolly National Nature Reserve – camping is discouraged, but free access. Sgurr an Fhidhleir lies within the Ben More Coigach Estates, the Scottish Wildlife Trust being owners.

SGURR AN FHIDHLEIR (095055) Alt. 1,480 ft (450 m) North facing 🦋 🦋

The N slopes of the Ben More Coigach massiff are very precipitous with those on the satellite peak of Sgurr an Fhidhleir (pronounced 'fiddler') being the most impressive. Here they form a steep tooth-shaped peak whose main face is a massive triangular wall, whilst the E face confronting Loch an Tuath is a formidable sweep of steep slabs with a prominent huge corner. The following route climbs the massive triangular N face.

Approach – Off the Drumrunie to Achiltibuie road. Park at Feur Loch (138068), a small loch at E end of Loch Lurgainn. Cross river, follow stream from Feur Loch (Alt. Claonaidh) leading steadily upwards to Lochan Tuath below face, 4½ miles (6.5 km): 1 hr 45 mins.

Topography – Lower half of face is unpleasantly vegetated, split by twisting grassy groove in centre. At about mid-height are the Pale Slabs (a key feature), which are split by two grass terraces. Above, a steep buttress continues to upper shoulder.

Descent – From summit cairn go S along cliff-top to head of bealach with prominent earth gully (095050). Down this.

332 **The Fiddler Nose Direct (Tower Finish)** *1,000 ft (300 m) HVS (E1)*
FA: *N. Drasdo and C. M. Dixon, 1962 (Nose Direct)*
D. Gilbert and J. Mackenzie, 1979 (Tower Finish)
No ordinary route, its ascent was the climax of numerous attempts over the last century.
1. 400 ft (120 m) 4b Start below long grassy groove. Climb cracks and corners by any line to gain and then climb groove, to cave. Step right and follow groove to grass bay below Pale Slabs.
2. 80 ft (24 m) 4a First slab centrally to its upper L corner (PB).
3. 80 ft (24 m) 4c Second slab by steep R-angled grassy groove on L, with hard finish on to good ledge below largest slab.
4. 140 ft (36 m) 5a Climb third slab by its L edge. Step on to undercut slab R of edge. Up, then L a few feet to nasty step

in to groove (hard). Up groove to good ledge (possible belay). Step right and surmount overlap (PR). Follow slab or corner to ledge overlooking L edge.

5. 150 ft (45 m) 5a Move up steep corner above, then L and up thin crack up steep wall (PR) to L of OH-prow to shoulder. Easier rocks lead up shoulder to top of peak.

Tower Finish climbs the OH prow above Pale Slabs.

4a. 50 ft (15 m) 4a Start from good ledge halfway up pitch 4. Tr. across bald slab (fourth Pale Slab) up, and R via thin grass steps, to exposed central nook (poor belay).

5. 150 ft (45 m) 5b Up OH-wall and R (NR) to OH. Pull over on R. Wall above to groove, with steep slab on R. Up crack in slab (PR), step R and mantel into groove (crux). Step R into niche.

6. 100 ft (30 m) 4c Crack above to ledge. Tr. L to groove. Up this to chimney, stance behind detached tower.

7. 50 ft (15 m) 4a Chimney on to tower then groove above to belay. Easier to top.

STAC POLLAIDH

This is the lowest of the mountains in this area, but is weathered to show the typical sandstone structure of narrow ridges and pinnacles. It rises directly above the road to Achiltibuie on the N side of Loch Lurgainn. In appearance it is like a mini-volcano, but with an extended jagged ridge. The summit is above the Western Buttress, which is also the most impressive piece of rock on the hill. The rock is clean, sound, and dries quickly. Friends are useful.

Western Buttress (106106) Alt. 1,800 ft (515 m) South-east facing ⚡⚡

Lying directly below the summit, it forms an impressive nose of sandstone facing S whose R wall tapers up the hillside towards the ridge and faces SE. In the nose are two long parallel corner lines, whilst the main wall is smooth and capped by a large roof.

Approach – There is a large car-park (018095) on S side of road. A huge path runs up towards the small bealach near the E

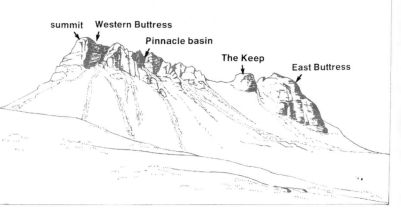

Stac Pollaidh

summit   Western Buttress
                    Pinnacle basin
                                        The Keep
                                                    East Buttress

top. From half-way along this track, branch off L and up to the prominent Western Buttress: 1 hr 30 mins.

  Descent – From summit head back E along ridge and descend by scrambling into bay below Main Wall.

333 **Western Buttress Route**   *300 ft (90 m)   D*
FA: *C. W. Walker and Inglis Clarke family, 1906*
This follows the S-most corner of the Western Buttress and was the first climb here. L of the obvious corners of November and Enigma Grooves a rectangular pinnacle sits at the base of the wall (Baird's Pinnacle). The route climbs a direct line up the SW corner, 50 ft (15 m) L of Baird's Pinnacle on fine rock. (Useful descent for the experienced.)

The twin big corner lines in the nose originate from a grassy bay at 80 ft (25 m).

334 Enigma Grooves   *240 ft (75 m)*   *HVS*
FA: *T. W. Patey and J. Mackenzie, 1962*
FA: *P. Goodwin and J. Mackenzie, 1979 (Pitch 4)*
This climbs the L-hand corner. Directly below the bay is an inset corner.
Start: On wall L of this.
1. 80 ft (25 m) 4a Climb rocks L of the corner to gain the grass bay.
2. 80 ft (25 m) 5a Climb the main corner crack and chimney above to gain a platform.
3. 30 ft (9 m) 4a Follow easy wide chimney to smaller platform on L below a narrow chimney bordering a slab.
4. 50 ft (15 m) 5b Climb the strenuous narrow chimney past chockstone (old PR) climb crux crack to top.

335 November Grooves   *290 ft (88 m)*   *VS*
FA: *D. Stewart and G. Cairns, 1954*
This excellent route climbs the R-hand corner in the nose.
Start: At the inset corner below the bay.
1. 80 ft (25 m) 4b Climb R wall of corner to gain flake. This leads to wider crack on R. Continue up this and then up L on broken ground to bay below corner.
2. 120 ft (36 m) 4b Climb the corner to the terrace ledge (grassy at first); and continue up groove line and turn OH on R to belay.
3. 90 ft (27 m) 4b Climb groove till possible to tr. R (not obvious) into chimney leading to the top.

336 Jack the Ripper   *310 ft (94 m)*   *HVS (E1)*
FA: *M. G. Anderson and G. Mair, 1964*
FA: *(Direct Finish) unknown.*
This follows a rounded rib between the nose and the SE face in a general line just R of November Grooves.

Start: As for November Grooves at the foot of the rib beneath obvious layback crack.

1. 80 ft (25 m) 4b November Grooves pitch 1.
2. 120 ft (36 m) 5a Tr. R to a slab rib. Climb this following thin cracks (crux), with sensational move R to small ledge on arete overlooking the SE wall. A shallow corner above (loose block) and crack to stance.
3. 110 ft (33 m) 4c An obvious upward tr. L into November Grooves to finish.
4a. 110 ft (33 m) 5b (**Direct Finish**) Follow L-leaning crack to ledge. From R end of ledge climb steep corner until awkward move L gains ledge. Finish up crack.

South East Face
Immediately R of the rib of Jack The Ripper the buttress forms an impressive wall of compact sandstone offering the best routes of their kind in the area. The L side of the wall is more continuous with small horizontal terrace at about mid-height. The upper section contains a distinctive OH across its entire length. The next route starts from ledge system above lower scrappy rocks accessed from L.

337 **Walking On Air**   *200 ft (60 m)   E4*
FA: *T. Prentice and R. Anderson, 1989*
Climbs crackline and corner splitting main OH. Start just R of block on ledge below twin cracks on red coloured wall.
1. 100 ft (30 m) 6a Climb cracks (hard) then easier till possible to tr. L into crack and corner. A scoop and rib lead to terrace.
2. 100 ft (30 m) 6b Step onto large block. Climb to triangular niche. Follow crack above, crux (PR), into further niche. Follow stepped corner until possible to step L into wide crack to finish.

338 **Expecting to Fly**   *135 ft (40 m)   E3 6a*
FA: *T. Prentice, 1988*
Sustained route up diag. crack and grey groove through OHS on the main SE face R of a mossy recess. Well protected.

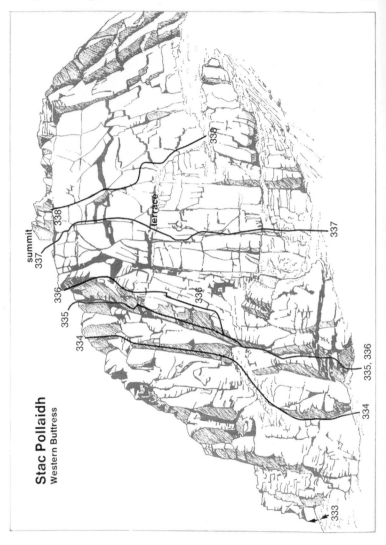

Stac Pollaidh
Western Buttress

Start: Near R end of lower wall, just R of small rocky buttress.
Up easy rock to R end of terrace (old PB). Climb flake on R
into short groove. TR L along horizontal flake and up crack
to hanging grey groove in OH; use flake crack in L arete to
move up groove. Steep move gains layaways, up (hard) to
rest. Continue up crack. (Friends 2, 2½, 3 and large rocks
useful.)

REIFF SEA CLIFFS

The single-track road leading under Stac Pollaidh continues
west to the peninsular of Rubha Mor, passing the superb
campsite in the dunes of Achnahaird and reaching the village of
Altandhu. The road continues a little further to end at Reiff, a
small collection of crofts. There are climbs along the entire
coast from Reiff, round the headland of Rubha Coigach onto the
north coast of the peninsula.

   The rock is granite and although the climbs are small (from
bouldering height to 25 m) the quality and setting make them
well worth a visit, especially as they miss the worst of any bad
weather.

   There is not enough room to outline many of the crags here
(there are nearly 450 recorded routes) so a selection of three
cliffs that are close to Reiff have been chosen as an indication
of what's on offer. On further visits one may wish to buy the
definitive guide and explore the less frequented cliffs around the
headland of Rubha Coigach itself.

ROINN A'MHILL   (151964)   West Facing ⚲
This is the small headland just north of the village, almost
formed into an island by the Loch of Reiff. The routes are
around the north west tip and are described in distinct separate
sections as approaching from Reiff.

The Pinnacle Area

Essentially this is the area around the small bay in the west side
of the headland just south of the north west tip. It comprises
two geos. The small First Geo to the east has a through cave in

the back leading to a huge hole some 80 ft (25 m) inland. Its west wall is a slab climbable anywhere at D standard.

Immediately west is the bigger Second Geo and at its seaward end is the Pinnacle. The routes described are on the headwall of the Second Geo and the wall facing The Pinnacle, the Pinnacle Walls.

Second Geo

The back of the geo has a jumble of non-tidal boulders at its base. This 'headwall' is undercut. The east side terminates as a sea-washed promontory with a distinctive fin of rock. The west side comprises a slab.

Access – For access to the headwall descend a ramp at the junction between the headwall and the east wall, or descend the corner between the slab and the west side of the headwall (D).

The next few routes are on the headwall.

339 **A Walk Across the Rooftops**   *60 ft (20 m)   E3 5c*
FA: *A. Cunningham and K. Geddes, 1988*
Follows obvious tr. line across wall. Start: down ramp descent are two cracks. Climb L hand crack to tr. line leading L to finish up vague cracks. Big Friends useful. **Absent Friends (E5 6b)** is a direct variation up centre of headwall. Follow tr. to curious 'hole'. Move R past undercut and two horizontal breaks finishing slightly L.

340 **Immaculate Deception**   *35 ft (12 m)   E1 5b*
FA: *A. Cunningham and K. Geddes, 1988*
Start at L hand side of wall by protruding block. Climb over small OH into L-trending crack leading to top. Crux near bottom.

The slab on west wall can be climbed up centre (**Jellyfish Slab, 60 ft (20 m) D**) and up its L side (**Edge of the Sea, 60 ft (20 m) VD**).

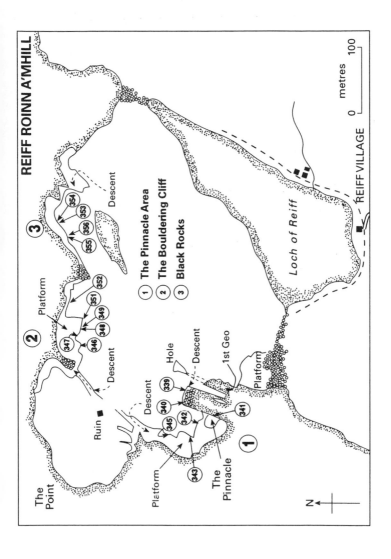

REIFF ROINN A'MHILL

① The Pinnacle Area
② The Bouldering Cliff
③ Black Rocks

REIFF VILLAGE

Loch of Reiff

The Point

Ruin

0   metres   100

The Pinnacle and Pinnacle Walls
To west of Second Geo lies The Pinnacle. It rests on large rock platform that is above high tide level. The platform runs under the Pinnacle Walls that face The Pinnacle and round corner to west.

  Access – By easy descent down gully to north of Second Geo onto platform.

341 **Moonjelly**   *30 ft (10 m)   VD*
FA: *B. Lawrie, 1970s*
Climbs central scoop in slab on east face of The Pinnacle.

342 **Channering Worm**   *30 ft (10 m)   E3 5c*
FA: *B. Lawrie, N. Morrison and M. Forsyth, 1980s*
To L is large OH at mid-height with L diag. crack running to its L end **(Totally Tropical, E4 6b)**. Start at middle of undercut wall L again. Pull over OH and grab 'crazy spike'. Make hard moves up and R to finish in L-diag. crack.

The next routes climb around the L arete of wall.

343 **Hy Brasil**   *30 ft (10 m)   VS 4c*
FA: *B. Lawrie, 1970s*
Excellent climbing starting round to L of arete and following first line out R to arete, finishing direct.

344 **Westering Home**   *30 ft (10 m)   E1 5b*
FA: *B. Lawrie, N. Morrison and M. Forsyth, 1980s*
The best route on these walls. Climb crack just L of arete.

345 **Earth Shaker**   *30 ft (10 m)   E2 6a*
FA: *B. Lawrie, 1970s*
Climbs short corner in leaning wall above the permanent pool on platform further L. Gain corner from L or R.

The Bouldering Cliff

Over the hillside directly opposite the gully descent into the platform of the Pinnacle Area is a ruin. Beyond this a grotty gully gives access to the cliffs on the north side of the headland onto a raised platform running eastwards under the Bouldering Cliff. On the L of the base of the gully is a low angled slab. The wall above the large platform is a series of walls, corners and aretes. Routes are described R to L

The first, small, groove L is **Hors D'Oeuvre, VS 4c**. The second groove is **In The Land of Dreamy Dreamers, HVS 5a**. The large open-book corner L again is **The Corner VS 4c**.

The wall then forms a right-angled arete which is **White Horses, E2 6a** giving a dynamic lower crux and a bold finish. The R-diag. ramp is **Black Zone HVS 5b**. The next routes are to L.

346 **Golden Eyes** *30 ft (10 m)   E1 5c*
FA: *B. Lawrie, 1970s*
Climb corner L of Black Zone.

347 **Romancing The Stone** *30 ft (10 m)   E4 6b*
FA: *B. Lawrie, 1970s*
Very hard start up thin crack just L of next arete. Finish direct. Repulses many people.

348 **The Hand Traverse** *50 ft (15 m)   HVS 5a*
FA: *B. Lawrie, 1970s*
Start at obvious ramp in wall L of arete. Gain and tr. break R across Romancing The Stone to finish up arete.

349 **The Ramp** *50 ft (15 m)   S*
FA: Unknown
Climb R-slanting ramp.

350 **Hole in the Wall**   *30 ft (10 m)*   *E2 6a*
FA: *B. Lawrie, 1970s*
Climb middle of wall L of The Ramp (above rock pools) to
gain 'hole'. Move L to flake. From its top gain break above and
tr. R to finish. A more direct version (**Toad in the Hole, E5 6a**)
climbs direct above first break up narrow wall.

To L wall turns 90 degrees and is grossly-OH.

351 **Wyatt Earp**   *60 ft (20 m)*   *E3 6a*
FA: *M. Hamilton and R. Anderson, 1985*
Big corner between Hole in the Wall and steep wall.

352 **Crack of Desire Direct**   *60 ft (20 m)*   *E4 6a*
FA: *B. Lawrie and N. Morrison, 1985 (original route)*
FA Direct: *A. Cunningham, 1990*
Round arete from steep wall is R-slanting crack and large break
across wall at half height. Gain break via lower corner crack.
Continue over bulge and along crack to its end. Normal Finish
(E3 6a) After bulge pull out L and finish direct.

The platform can be followed L past a tricky step into a bay
full of rock-fall boulders. This can be traversed at low tide to
reach another platform below the next section, Black Rocks.
Alternatively access is from the far east side of the wall.

Black Rocks
Further along the coast lies a small lochan. The cliffs parallel
the lochan and form a series of slabby buttresses and steep
walls above a sea level platform, before turning a slight
headland to form a series of leaning aretes and wide grooves
which drop direct into the sea. The routes described are on the
walls above the platform.
  Access – either down an obvious low-angled slab east of the
lochan and tr. L (looking out to sea) across two inlets to reach
the platforms beyond (low tide only, 4c). Alternatively abseil

from a block east of the descent slab directly down a groove
(**The Grooves, S**) to near the end of platform to the west of the
second inlet. Round the headland to the R is a slab. Routes
described L to R from here.

353 **Black Donald**   *80 ft (25 m)   S*
FA: Unknown
Good route up corner in L side of slab finishing up the narrow
slab above.

354 **Tystie Slab**   *100 ft (30 m)   VD*
FA: *B. Lawrie and N. Morrison, 1985*
Excellent route up slab. Start near L edge and climb on pockets
and horizontal breaks finishing up L on narrowing slab.

Wild hanging groove in headwall above slab is **Batman (HVS
5a)**. Bounding R side of slabs is black corner **Poll Dubh (VS
5a)**. R again is further black corner taken by Black Pig. Beyond
this platform drops down as sea-washed ledges below slabby
buttress (Black Gold).

355 **Black Pig**   *80 ft (25 m)   VS 4c*
FA: *A. Cunningham and J. Pickering, 1989*
Best route on the wall. The corner cuts into L edge of further
slab to R. Climb from L and surmount OH to gain corner.
Follow this then exit L under final OH.

356 **Black Gold**   *80 ft (25 m)   VS 4c*
FA: *B. Lawrie and N. Morrison, 1985*
Climb the centre of the black slabby buttress to R, starting by
short groove

OLD MAN OF STOER   (017352) ✗
N of Lochinver, the Rubh a Stoer peninsula culminates in the
Point of Stoer jutting out into The Minch. The Old Man sits on
a plinth ½ mile (800 m) S of the point. A deep 25 ft (7 m)

channel separates it from the mainland. It bulges like the paunch of an old monk and was thought to be unclimbable. Patey dispelled that myth. Pecking fulmars add to the difficulties in summer.

Approach – Take motorable road towards lighthouse through Raffin, and a rough track leads N to peat cuttings. Walk over the moorland 1 mile (1.6 km). Gain plinth by swimming 30 ft (9 m) (ladder handy) to gain L end of landward face. During calm seas at spring tides one can walk over without an aqualung.

Descent – 150 ft (45 m) abseil down SE corner to first platform. Move R along slim ledge on landward face (PB). Abseil to base.

357 **The Old Man**   *220 ft (66 m)*   *VS*
FA: *T. Patey, B. Robertson, B. Henderson and P. Nunn, 1966*
1. 60 ft (18 m) 4a From the obvious ledge step L along ledge for 2m and climb steep slab trending slightly R to belay on ledge at centre.
2. 70 ft (21 m) 4c Climb direct up steep wall via obvious L to R diag. crack to OH-niche. Exit from this to ledges. Continue direct (thread) to cave.
3. 40 ft (12 m) 4c Tr. R round airy arete to landward face. Fault up and R, avoiding first upward break to gain ledge.
4. 50 ft (15 m) Prominent 'V' chimney to easy rock, then a L-trending ramp to top.

358 **North West Corner**   *200 ft (60 m)*   *E2*
FA: *M. Fowler and C. Newcombe, 1987*
Takes the R arete of landward face. Double set of Friends essential. Start below arete.
1. 50 ft (15 m) 5c Climb L side of arete (bold) to reach ledge (Friend 3 belay).
2. 70 ft (20 m) 5b Flake just L of arete, then up R onto arete (rest). Move round to R-hand side and follow L-slanting crack back to edge of arete. L to belay.

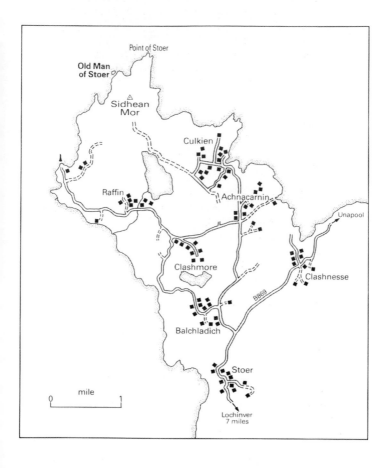

Point of Stoer

Old Man
of Stoer

Sidhean
Mor

Culkien

Raffin

Achnacarnin

Unapool

Clashmore

Clashnesse

B869

Balchladich

Stoer

Lochinver
7 miles

mile
0   1

3. 80 ft (25 m) 6a Climb L-trending ramp with difficulty (2PR)
    to ledge and junction with Original Route. Move R to large
    ledge L of arete and follow arete to top.

Old man of Stoer. Climbers on North West Corner (E2).

8   SUTHERLAND

Introduction

Just S of Cape Wrath on the NW tip of the mainland lies the huge barren expanse of the Reay Forest, once the traditional hunting-grounds of the Lords of Reay, the chiefs of the Clan MacKay. Skirting its W seaboard is the A838 to Durness. When viewed from the road, the area is dominated by three impressive hills: Ben Stack, Ben Arkle and the massive Fionaven.

Fionaven's E flank overlooks Strath Dionard, the 'oldest' valley in Britain, and contains a series of large-scale cliffs along its entire length. The area is very remote and the cliffs receive little sunshine. Few will make the effort to visit but those who do will be guaranteed a lonely, rewarding trip.

On the W coast just N of Sheigra and Kinlochbervie is another sea stack, not far from the perfect, unmolested beach of Sandwood Bay, for collectors of such things. For further interest there are now numerous climbs on the Lewisian gneiss cliffs beside Sheigra campsite which give some interesting exploration when the hills are shrouded in cloud.

History

As with other north west areas it was Ling and Glover who first recorded climbs here (South Ridge on Foinaven and a route on Ben Hope). J. H. Bell also visited albeit very briefly. Into the 1950's and Tom Weir visited Foinaven and climbed three routes. Then in 1959 prolific RAF Rescue Team member Terry Sullivan climbed Gargantua and Pantagruel on Creag Urbhard. 1962 was an active year with Neville Drasdo and Mike Dixon climbing Zig Zag on Creag Urbhard (the same year they completed the first ascent of Coigach's Fhidhleir) and Tom Patey boldly soloed Fingal (990 ft (300 m) S). Members of the Caithness Mountaineering Club also climbed at Creag Shomhairle adding The Roost (HS). Creag Urbhard saw many additions from this period; Corriemulzie Mountaineering Club members Ian Rowe and Philip Tranter climbed Chicken Run in

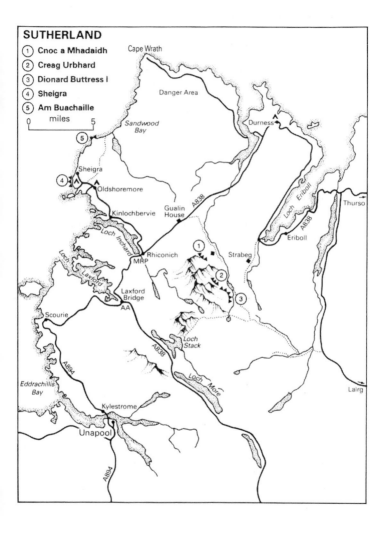

SUTHERLAND

1. Cnoc a Mhadaidh
2. Creag Urbhard
3. Dionard Buttress I
4. Sheigra
5. Am Buachaille

1965, Squirrels Bugs McKeith and Mike Galbraith made an impression with Kilroy Was Here, and Inverness Mountaineering Club also made explorations here.

On Dionard Buttress One, the Sheffield team of Clive Rowland and Tony Howard established Cengalo (VS) in 1969, and Rowland, with Paul Nunn and Bob Toogood, gave the hard Dialectic (E2 with aid) – a major advance. These Sheffield lads (joined by Martin Boysen) continued to visit for many years after, making tentative attempts on Cape Wrath's Clo Mor, developing Cnoc a Mhadaidh with Familiar and Queergang (E1), Wrath (E1) and Pilastra (HVS) as well as Land of the Dancing Dead (E1) from Tom Proctor and Chris Jackson on Creag Shomhairle. Nunn, Toogood and friends also found and started the development of the Sheigra Sea-cliffs in 1971.

By the 1980's various other teams were visiting but Nunn and A Livesey's Millennium (E2) stands out as one of the finest, completed over 2 days. In 1986 Murray Hamilton and Rab Anderson dramatically increased the standards (if not the quality of the names) with Tank Top (E6) at Creag Shomhairle. At Sheigra Boysen and Rab Carrington climbed the hideous off-width of North-west Eliminate (E6) and a couple of years later Mick Fowler and Chris Watts finally succeeded at Cape Wrath to produce Clo Mor Crack (E1).

Attention then definitely turned to the outcrops. Anderson returned to make additions to Sheigra along with Glenmore Lodge Instructors Andy Cunningham, Allen Fyffe, Andy Nisbet and Steve Blagborough, but it was in the 1990's with visits from Gary Latter, Rick Campbell and Paul Thorburn that grades attained E7 (Something Worth Waiting For by Campbell). Creag Shomhairle also saw new development from this latter team and no doubt much more will be uncovered soon.

Access

Bus – Brora (on E coast, A9 to Wick) to Kinlochbervie (local bus) via Lairg, Scourie and Rhiconich (BR connection at Lairg); Lairg station to Durness post office via Rhiconich, once

daily (BR connection). Local bus services and post buses
interconnect on small runs, but are time-consuming.

Accommodation
Camping – Sheigra site (182601), end of Kinlochbervie Road;
Oldshoremore (210587), 2 m (3.2 km) beyond Kinlochbervie;
Scourie (153446), on beach in centre of village; Durness
(404685).
Rough camping – Unrestricted.
Hotels – Rhiconich (255523); Scourie (157447); Kinlochbervie
(222567); and Durness (various).

Provisions
Usual amenities at Scourie (which also has a café) and Durness.
AA phone at Laxford Bridge, but nothing else! Petrol from
Durness, Scourie and Kinlochbervie. Early closing Wednesdays.

Mountain Rescue
Assynt Rescue Team – Post: police station, Rhiconich (255523).
Nearest telephone to Fionaven: Gaulin House (305564) near
entrance track.

Guidebooks
Northern Highlands, Rock and Ice Climbs, Vol. 2, G. Cohen,
SMC 1993.

Map
Landranger Series: Cape Wrath, 9.

FIONAVEN   (317507)
A four-mile (6.4 km) long mountain running N to S, whose
summit ridge shines white with screes of quartz. Its E side is a
series of projecting satellite summits, each one terminating in a
rock face. These are described in order as one approaches down
Strath Dionard. Many of these routes are unrepeated, and PRS,
etc, may not be in place, so let's be cautious out there!

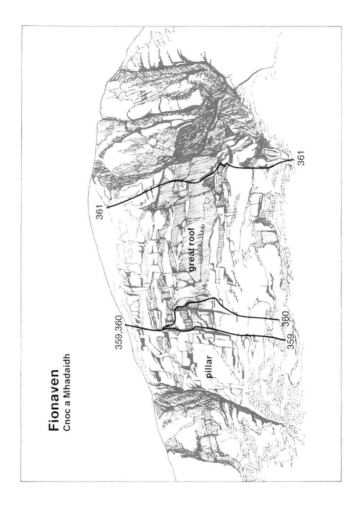

Approach – 1) Easiest down Strath Dionard. Leave A838 at small bridge just N of Gaulin House (310570), and follow track. 2) Approach from Strath Beag at head of Loch Eriboll (393539), passing Strabeg Cottage and Creag Shomhairle. Indefinite path crosses bealach Nan h'Imrich to gain upper end of Strath Dionard. Shorter to Creag Urbhard and Dionard, and less boggy.

Cnoc a Mhadaidh   (330526) Alt. 450 ft (135 m) North facing 🦋 🦋

Pronounced Crok-a-Vattee, this lies on the N-most satellite of Fionaven (Ceann Garbh), sitting above the first hut encountered on the path (home of ornithologists) – 4 miles (6.4 km), 1 hr 30 mins; boggy.

  Topography – The rock is a hybrid of quartz and gneiss, generally sound and rough. Grass fills some cracks but does not hamper the climbing. Lower slabs lead up to formidable leaning roofs only breached at their L side by a big pillar. The slabs are slow to dry. Routes are described L to R.

359 **Pilastra**   *585 ft (176 m)   HVS*
FA: *M. Boyson and P. Nunn, 1973*
The climb takes a line of R-facing corners in the R side of the pillar bounding the L side of the big roofs. Gain base of pillar by scramble up vegetated slabs to a thin crack directly beneath the series of corners 30 ft (10 m) R of large block.
1   60 ft (18 m) 4c Climb crack in steep slabs and bulge to L to grass stance.
2. 100 ft (30 m) 5a Up, then tr. L below corner. Enter corner via jammed flake and climb it. Exit L at top. Step R into upper corner.
3. 110 ft (33 m) 4c Climb corner to OH. Tr. L to crest. Up past cracked blocks, then shallow cracks in the red wall above. Up to grass terrace.
4. 50 ft (15 m) 5a Big grassy corner to OH. Tr. L, slightly down to edge. Up L to grass ledge with trees.
5/6. 265 ft (80 m) Chimney above, then scrambling up and R to finish.

360 **Familiar/Queergang**   *800 ft (241 m)   E1*
FA: *P. Nunn and B. Toogood, 1971*
The original route employed some aid through the roof and an
abseil. Familiar cuts out some of this 'Queergang' to give an
entirely free line.
Start: At slabs approx. 30 ft (10 m) R of Pilastra.
1. 150 ft (45 m) 4c Climb the slabs more or less direct to
   stance.
2. 150 ft (45 m) 5a Continue up slabs with the final section
   being a diag. ascent R towards the junction of the main roof
   and the steep pillar. Take a nut belay at black wet ledge
   some 30 ft (15 m) below the main roof, directly below an
   obvious 'fisheye' corner – a peculiar OH-crack cutting L
   through the roof (the original Queergang).
3. 75 ft (23 m) 5b A steep wall bars entry to a groove on the L.
   Climb the wall then the groove to a stance (PB). (Queergang
   abseiled down to this stance from end of fisheye corner.)
4. 40 ft (12 m) 5a Up loose corner to ledge.
5. 120 ft (36 m) 5a Tr. slabs L below steep walls into recess
   (junction with Pilastra) pitch 4. Follow Pilastra down to and
   round edge on L. Step L and move up to ledge.
6/7. 256 ft (80 m) Steep chimney of Pilastra to top.

361 **Wrath**   *500 ft (150 m)   E1*
FA: *C. Boulton, T. Lewis and P. Nunn, 1978*
This climb is on the extreme R end of the slabs with a brilliant
pitch through the roof.
Start: Under the R extremity of the great roof.
1. 100 ft (30 m) 4a Climb easily up the R edge of the slabs out
   of the gully. Head L a little near the top to nut belay under
   roof.
2. 120 ft (36 m) 5c The steep groove on the L leads to a break.
   Move R and climb a 'flying ramp' through the roof (PR) on
   to the slabs above.
3/4. 280 ft (85 m) 4c Continue up slabs and grooves in a direct
   line to the top in two pitches.

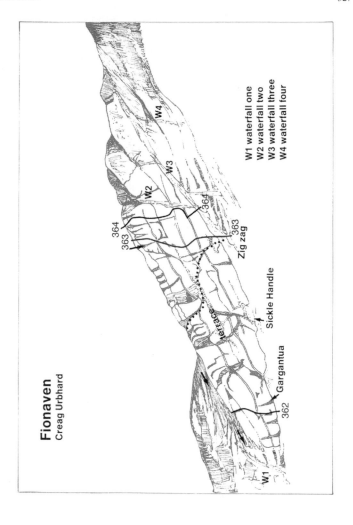

Fionaven
Creag Urbhard

W1 waterfall one
W2 waterfall two
W3 waterfall three
W4 waterfall four

W4

W3

W2

364

364

363

363

Zig zag

Terrace

Sickle Handle

Gargantua

362

W1

Creag Urbhard   (354487) Alt. 500 ft (150 m) East
facing 🦋🦋

Pronounced 'Kreg Urvard', 'the crag of the Devils-Bit Herb'
lies near the head of the desolate Strath Dionard. It is a
complex mass of quartzite which, together with the five Dionard
Buttresses and Creag Alasdair further up the glen, forms the E
face of Creag Dionard (the S top of Fionaven). Though it offers
rambling lines and variable rock, its size dominates the area and
it has become known as Fionaven's 'Big Wall'. The climbs are
noted for their scale, atmosphere and route-finding interest.

Topography – Creag Urbhard forms a diag. face running up
the hillside, split by four large waterfalls. These help identify
some of the features but their size and number vary according
to conditions. The first waterfall defines the end of Creag
Urbhard, separating it from the loaf-shaped Dionard Buttress
One to the L. The slightly concave face continues R to meet the
second waterfall which drains a small hanging coire high up at
the back. The main climbing interest lies between these two
waterfalls. The top of the face is formed by the South Ridge
which begins above the first waterfall and runs up to the top of
Creag Dionard. The face is split by a terrace at mid-height with
few features in its lower half but a series of fine slanting
diedres above. In the centre of the face is a curving fault
through the lower tier, linking the terrace with the ground and
known as the Sickle Handle. The routes are described L to R
(see diagram on p. 327).

Descent – The line of the South Ridge (M), or keeping
further R to descend a depression to gain the top of the first
waterfall (less frightening). Alternatively, a long walk to the E.

The L end of the main face is a clean white wall. The only
conspicuous feature here is a short corner in the base of the
lower tier L of two coloured streaks. This is the start of
Gargantua (HS). Directly above this in the top of the upper
tier is an obvious large corner:

362 **Whitewash**   *550 ft (165 m)   HVS*
FA: *A. Paul and B. Dunn, 1976*
Takes a R-trending line across the wall to L of Gargantua to
finish up the long groove and conspicuous steep corner at the
top.
Start: At easy angled slabs 60 ft (18 m) L of the bottom corner
of Gargantua.
1. 110 ft (33 m) 4a Climb slabs to R end of prominent OH.
   Climb bulge using a crack which is followed to a PB.
2. 120 ft (36 m) 4c Above is a vague groove: climb this direct
   for 70 ft (21 m) and tr. hard R to belay below large OH (PB).
3. 100 ft (30 m) 4c Climb R end of OH using a rib to reach the
   foot of small but distinctive L-facing, grey wall. Turn wall
   on its L by OH-groove, then climb R to PB at foot of
   prominent long groove.
4. 90 ft (27 m) 4b Ascend groove to belay at point of
   steepening.
5. 70 ft (21 m) 4b Continue up groove to horizontal break
   below final corner, or if wet climb cracked wall on R, then R
   arete (5a).
6. 60 ft (18 m) 5b Climb corner with steep and technical
   finishing moves.

363 **Masha (Direct)**   *1,000 ft (330 m)   VS*
FA: *C. Rowland and D. Marshall, 1972*
FA: *E. Jackson and S. N. Smith, 1983 (Direct Finish)*
Start at foot of Second Waterfall, just R of ZigZag (arrow
etched in rock).
1–5. 635 ft (190 m) 4b Climb lower walls direct up series of
   groove-lines heading towards the open-book corner taking
   belays where necessary. (The Corner can be wet. If dry it
   and shallow gully above gives 365 ft (120 m) 5a). From
   base of corner tr. 30 ft (10 m) R to below short steep
   wall.
6. 80 ft (25 m) 4c Climb steep wall, and small corner to slabs.
   Up and R round nose to small slab above pinnacle.
7. 135 ft (40 m) 4c Climb OH above at R end by crack to slab.

Steep groove to slabby terrace. Crack in L side of steep wall
above to easy rocks.
8. 150 ft (45 m) Scramble to top.

The next route climbs the wall R of Masha to finish up the 'V'
depression:

364 **Fingal**   *900 ft (270 m)*   S
FA: *T. W. Patey, 1962*
A great mountaineering route, taking a line up the face L of the
second waterfall to finish up the R side of the large 'V'
depression.
Start: At small amphitheatre at base of the second waterfall
climb diag. L to terrace. Tr. it R to twin cracks which form a
shallow fault, immediately L of waterfall. Follow these cracks
for 250 ft (75 m) to first true terrace. Take the line of least
resistance leading diag. L towards a shallow vegetated gully. Up
this for 250 ft (75 m) to base of depression. Climb R wall past a
flake at 40 ft (12 m) and a huge rock-fang at 120 ft (36 m). Exit
R by tr. round exposed edge to gain inset slab in corner (crux).
Slab leads to easier rocks in slabby wall on R. Take obvious
chimney in R corner narrowing above an OH-cleft. Tr. L over
slabs to gain top of depression.

Dionard Buttress One   (357486) Alt. 500 ft (150 m) East
facing 𝕏 𝕏
This is the loaf-shaped buttress lying immediately to L of the
first waterfall and provides high-grade adventurous climbs on a
big face. There is however some loose rock and occasional poor
belays.
  Topography – It is approximately 900 ft (270 m) high and
consists of an OH-lower wall leading to a diag. central break
(slabs) capped by a great roof. Above this further slabs lead to
the top. An important feature is a large OH-groove in the centre

Whitewash, Creag Urbhard: climber, Simon Richardson

of the lower wall. On the R of the roofed section a secondary
R-hand face leads up to a capping leaning wall.

Descent – Scramble down the gully to the R to gain the line
of the first waterfall and follow this to the bottom.

365 **Millennium**   *985 ft (295 m)   E2*
FA: *A Livesey, P. Nunn, 1982 (over 2 days)*
     2nd ascent took 11 hrs
This takes the OH-wall just R of centre of crag to central slabs.
Then a L-to-R-slanting fault through the great roof.
Start: R of OH-central groove.
1. 120 ft (36 m) 5a Climb a short wall to a R-trending break.
    Follow to stance (PB).
2. 130 ft (39 m) 5b Climb a wet scoop on L and up through
    steep walls to a groove. Go R to a stance under an OH (PB).
3. 150 ft (45 m) 5a Climb OH above moving R (or direct), then
    more easily to the slabs.
4. 135 ft (40 m) 5c Go L and up to a steep groove leading R.
    Climb it with difficulty to a stance.
5. 150 ft (45 m) 5b Follow the undercut ramp through the roofs
    and exit on to grey slabs.
6/7. 300 ft (90 m) 4b Shallow grooves and slabs to finish.

366 **Cengalo**   *920 ft (276 m)   VS*
FA: *E. Howard and C. Rowland, 1969*
Takes a line up the large slabby corner system bounding the R
side of the main roofs. Poorly protected. From a gully R of the
OH-lower wall it climbs a prominent wall below the roofs, then
a big slab leading L under the stepped OH on the R of the main
roof. It then moves back R above it before climbing slabs to top.
Start: From the gully at R of main face, directly below stepped OHS.
1. 140 ft (42 m) Easy slabs on L lead to ledge (PB).
2. 120 ft (36 m) 4a Move diag. L across slabs and grass patches
    to below short corner. Climb this then move back R. (PB by
    large detached block under R end of stepped OHS).
3. 70 ft (21 m) 4c Up steep slab to obvious tr. L for 40 ft

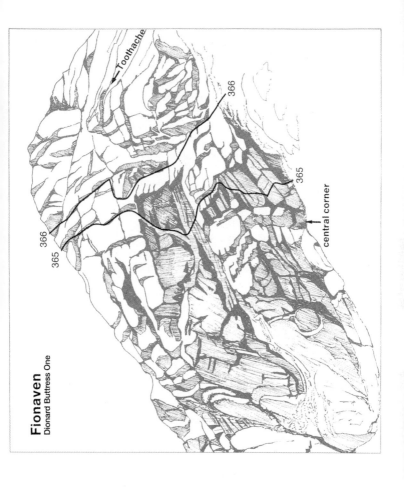

Fionaven
Dionard Buttress One

(12 m) under stepped roof. Move L on to arete and up 15 ft (5 m) to niche (PB).

4. 90 ft (27 m) 4b Climb bulge on good holds to gain slabby groove. Up this to easy ramp and follow it for 50 ft (15 m) to PB.

5. 50 ft (15 m) 4b Tr. R horizontally round corner into deep chimney (clearly seen from below).

6. 130 ft (39 m) 4b Up the chimney, and step across and up short slab. Straight up slabs and grass to below 30 ft (9 m) crack with OH.

7. 130 ft (39 m) 4b Slab R of crack to OH, turn it on L. Move diag. R to stance.

8. 120 ft (36 m) Straight up easy ground R of yellow OH to large terrace and spike belay below obvious arete.

9. 70 ft (21 m) 4b Arete to top. Scramble to summit ridge.

SHEIGRA SEA CLIFFS South Facing ✗

At the end of the road beyond Kinlochbervie is the tiny hamlet of Sheigra lying next to a beautiful sandy bay. The north side of the bay is defined by a small hill which drops into the sea as a series of geos terminating at the small headland of Na Stacain. The rock is of the finest gneiss, dries quickly and there are enough routes to warrant a longer stay, away from the mountains.

Approach – Follow road virtually to the hamlet of Sheigra and take small tarmaced road left to an imposing walled cemetery. A track leads L of cemetery to gate with excellent 'campsite' beside the beach just beyond. Go through gate and follow fence to its second corner. The First Geo lies directly ahead. The Second Geo can be reached quickly by following fence which contours the small hill. See map opposite for detail.

First Geo

This is a narrow slot with an impressive South Face which is naturally divided into two, the Inner Wall within the slot and the Outer Wall where the geo opens out and drops into the sea. The North Face of the geo, facing the inner wall, is smaller but also has some climbs recorded.

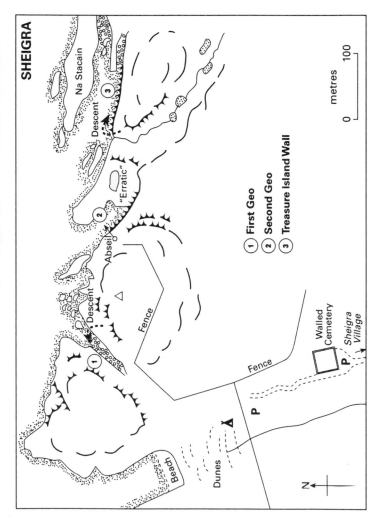

SHEIGRA

Na Stacain

③ Descent

② "Erratic"

Abseil

① Descent

Fence

Fence

Walled Cemetery

Sheigra Village

P

P

Beach

Dunes

P

① First Geo
② Second Geo
③ Treasure Island Wall

0   100
metres

N

Access – Either by abseil down the gully in the back or descending the north side by a scramble and slippery boulders at low tide. The Outer Wall of the South Face has a ledge along its base and can be reached from the end of the promontory down a slab and tr. L.

South Face, Inner Wall
The best routes are concentrated on the middle to R compact steep section. The most prominent feature is a capping OH above the highest section and above the biggest high-tide boulders. Immediately to L of OH is a large ledge near top with L-facing corner. Cracks lead up to it (**Road to Reform E3 5c).**

367   **Dying in Vein**   *80 ft (25 m)*   *E4 5c*
FA: *G. Farquhar and C. Carolan, 1995*
Takes direct line up centre of wall below OH. Start up grey ramp then wall to horizontal quartz seam. Pull R and up to R end of OH. Crack to top.

368   **Blind Faith**   *80 ft (25 m)*   *E2 5b*
FA: *A. Fyffe and A. Cunningham, 1989*
Start beside largest boulder. Gain R-curving crackline from R. Follow continuation crack up L to ledges in pink groove. Move R into alcove then R again up black crack.
Blind Faith Direct (E2 5c) climbs wall direct into and up pink groove.

369   **Monkey Man**   *80 ft (25 m)*   *E3 5c*
FA: *A. Cunningham and A. Fyffe, 1993*
The superb steep crackline to R.

370   **Here and Now**   *80 ft (25 m)*   *E6 6b*
FA: *G. Latter and R. Campbell, 1995*
Climbs up the centre of the orange wall. Start up R-diag. crack just R of Monkey Man. Follow diag. crack then R to undercuts and flake. Gain good hold above. Climb flared crack slightly on

L (hard) to flat holds. L again to further flared crack to good holds then R and up to finishing shallow orange groove.

South Face, Outer Wall
This is separated from the Inner Wall by an inset corner. The main features of the wall R of corner are three black streaks.

371 **The Sound of the Surf**   *80 ft (25 m)   E4 6a*
FA: *G. Latter and R. Campbell, 1995*
This climbs thin crackline up L streak leading through capping overlap.

372 **Looking for Atlantis**   *80 ft (25 m)   E5 6c*
FA: *R. Campbell and G. Latter, 1995*
The crack up the central black streak with the crux at the top.

The Second Geo
There are some smaller walls in the headland between the First and Second Geo. A small rocky island lies just off the north end of the headland separated from the start of the Second Geo by a deep gulch. The south wall is an immaculate orange wall above a sea cave and is the most atmospheric of the cliffs here. The north side of the geo is an easy slab (containing a huge sandstone 'erratic' boulder sitting at its top). The entire south face of Second Geo can be seen from here. On the R are black corner lines. A cave cuts under the centre and the wall abuts the slab on the L. In the upper L end is a hanging corner, below and R of which is a big 'hole'. There are numerous climbs criss-crossing this wall at about the same grade. This is a selection.

   Access – Routes L of cave are started from the slabs. Routes R of cave are started from a pedestal in the biggest black corner, gained by abseil. Routes are described L to R.

373 **Juggernaut**   *80 ft (25 m)   E1 5a*
FA: *R. Anderson and C. Greaves, 1989*
Start on slab below hanging corner. Short steep wall to ledge. Pass L of big hole and finish up cracks in L arete of hanging corner.

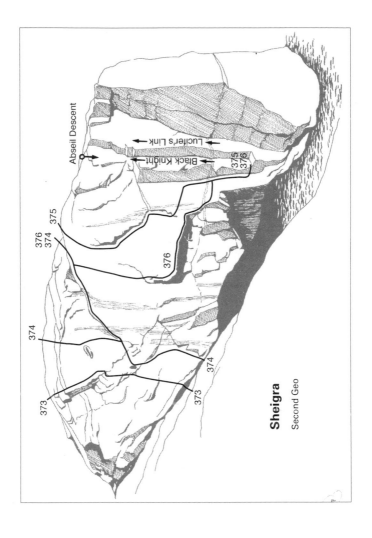

Sheigra

Second Geo

374 **Bloodlust** *80 ft (25 m)* *E1 5b*
FA: *P. Nunn and P. Fearnehough, 1978*
Follows natural line diag. R across wall. Start where slab meets
top of cave. Climb shallow corner then up to big hole. Steep
moves R to small ramp and continue along diag. line R to top.
Direct Finish (E2 5b) From big hole follow normal route R to
small ramp then climb back L onto upper wall and climb this
up R side of red section (passing curious 'eye').

The bigger (R-hand) black streak R of Bloodlust gives line of
May Tripper, 80 ft (25 m) E1 5b and finishes direct above the
diag. line of Bloodlust. The following routes climb above cave
and are started from good pedestal stance in large black corner
R of cave. The arete bounding R side of black corner is
Lucifer's Link, 120 ft (35 m) E1 5b. The black corner above
pedestal is **Black Knight HVS 5a** and smaller black corner to
L is **Dark Angel E1 5b.** Routes described R to L.

375 **Presumption** *130 ft (40 m)* *E1 5b*
FA: *P. Nunn and R. Toogood, 1983*
Climbs stepped L-curving groove in centre of wall above cave.
Climb corner of Dark Angel past bulge. Tr. horizontally L into
base of groove and follow to top. Spectacular line.

376 **Geriatrics** *130 ft (40 m)* *E2 5c*
FA: *R. Carrington and M. Boyson, 1987*
Another spectacular line across lip of OH above cave. Step L
from pedestal stance into Dark Angel. Tr. L along quartz band
then up to R end of OH. Tr. lip to L end then wall above direct
to top.

Treasure Island Wall
To the north of the slabs with the huge erratic boulder is a wall
cutting back into another geo formed by the headland of Na
Stacain (which is almost an island). 150 ft (45 m) further north
from the bare slabs containing the erratic boulder, a tiny burn

drains down to the cliff's edge. Beyond this is the main section of Treasure Island Wall.

Access – A steep descent on big holds (D) just R (looking out) of the burn gains a platform below the wall.

Just L of the descent are steep steps up orange rock sandwiched between black rock. The crackline through these steps is **Sun Spot, 60 ft (20 m) MS**. Above the L end of platform is conspicuous easy v-groove leading to big recess.

377 **The Nook**   *80 ft (25 m)   VS 4c*
FA: *A. Nisbet, 1989*
Climb v-groove for 15 ft (5 m). Take ramp up R. Climb two steep walls then hard move L gains narrow curving ramp. Move L from top of ramp until above the recess, then cracked wall to finish. Sensational.

378 **Tall Pall**   *100 ft (30 m)   S*
FA: *P. Nunn, 1975*
From the base of the v-groove, ascend middle of black slab diag. L. Continue on pink rock finishing up arete.

379 **Plum McNumb**   *100 ft (30 m)   MVS 4b*
FA: *P. Nunn and R. Toogood, 1976*
Move L from base of v-groove onto small ledge. Tr. L onto broad rib (not obvious from below). Climb rib direct (crossing Tall Pall) then steep blunt nose above on massive holds.

AM BUACHAILLE   (202652)
On the coast N of Sheigra is the remote Sandwood Bay. 1 mile (1.6 km) S are two rock stacks, A' Chailleach and Am Bodach – the Old Woman and Old Man. Guarding the entrance to the bay itself on the S side is the prominent sandstone stack of Am Buachaille (the Herdsman). It is separated from the mainland by a 30 ft (9 m) channel.

Geriatrics, 2nd Geo, Sheigra: climber, Tim Carruthers

Approach – A peat track leaves motor road between
Blairmore and Sheigra to Loch a'Mhuillin. Path leads to
Sandwood Bay: 3½ miles (5.6 km). Descend to shore N of stack
and tr. round at low tide. The channel must be crossed at low
tide by swimming, then allowing 4 hours to return before the
shore is awash: see map, p. 321.

380 **The Herdsman**   *180 ft (34 m)   HVS*
FA: *T. W. Patey, J. Cleare and I. Clough, 1967*
Start: On landward face at L of centre.
1. 85 ft (25 m) 4c Climb OH-wall on large jugs up and R to
    prow. Straight up to ledge under steep wall. Tr. L to ledge.
2. 95 ft (29 m) 4c Tr. back R and climb wall R of obvious
    corner via thin crack on good rock (original climbed crack
    above corner on poor rock) to gain deep OH-corner crack.
    Tr. L below it till a mantelshelf between two large 'soup
    plates' can be made. Cross slab into crack. Awkward pull
    out at top.

9   OUTER HEBRIDES

Introduction
The Outer Hebrides are a 130-mile (200 km) archipelago of
hundreds of islands stretching almost the full length of the
north-western seaboard of Scotland. In the north are the largest
islands of Lewis and Harris (joined as one) with mountains
reaching 2,000 ft (625 m) and offering spectacular mountain and
sea-cliff venues and a sparse population of crofters. In the
centre of the archipelago are the Uist Isles which are generally
low-lying and composed more of water than land. At the
southern end are the Barra Isles. Barra itself being inhabited.
The Southern tip is Barra Head and the collection of uninhabited
islands here offer some of the most remote climbing in the UK.

The Isles of Lewis and Harris
These islands contain some of the most astounding cliff-faces in
Britain. The routes on Sron Ulladale in Harris, and Creag Dubh
Dhibadail near Uig in Lewis justify the effort involved in
getting to the Outer Hebrides, which are more remote than France
and more expensive to get to. The weather patterns can be
extreme, but the recently developed Uig sea-cliffs, which
generally miss the bad mountain weather, have also been included.

Access
Air – Inverness or Glasgow to Stornoway (Lewis).
Ferry – Ullapool to Stornoway (Lewis); and Uig (Skye) to
Tarbert (Harris).
Bus – Inverness to Ullapool; Glasgow to Uig (Skye), Skyebus;
Stornoway to Timsgarry by Uig, post bus.
Taxi – From Stornoway: very useful for a short stay.

Accommodation
Rough camping – Anywhere outside the crofting areas.
Bivvy site – Large howff under Sron Ulladale.
Bunkhouses – Drinishader Bunkhouse, approx. 4 miles (10 km)

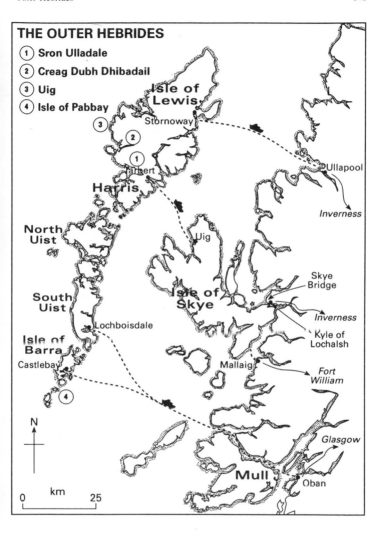

THE OUTER HEBRIDES

1. Sron Ulladale
2. Creag Dubh Dhibadail
3. Uig
4. Isle of Pabbay

Isle of Lewis

Stornoway

③

②

①

Tarbert

Harris

North Uist

Uig

South Uist

Lochboisdale

Isle of Barra

Castlebay

④

Isle of Skye

Skye Bridge

Inverness

Kyle of Lochalsh

Mallaig

Fort William

Ullapool

Inverness

Glasgow

Mull

Oban

N

km

0   25

from Tarbert, tel: (01859) 511 255; Galson Farm Bunkhouse, 20
miles (65 km) from Stornoway, tel: (01851) 850 492.
Bothy – Derelict House (034214), at the end of Loch
Tamanavay.

Provisions
Stornoway is the 'capital' with all usual amenities; early closing
Wednesdays. Tarbert has a post office/shop, café and petrol
station; early closing Thursdays. There is a caravan shop at
Timsgarry, Uig. Everything closes Sundays.

Mountain Rescue
Post: police station, Tarbert, Harris (151001).

Guidebooks
Skye and the Hebrides, Rock and Ice Climbs, Vol 2., D.
Cuthbertson, R. Duncan, G. E. Little and C. Moody, SMC,
1996

Map
Landranger Series, West Lewis, North Harris, 13.

SRON ULLADALE   (080134) Alt. 660 ft (200 m) West
facing 🦋 🦋
This is the N summit of the NS Ridge of Oreval, Ullaval and
Muladal. It lies in North Harris just N of Tarbert, the 'capital'
of Harris. The W face is a continuous wall for ½ mile (800 m),
enlarging as it leads L into a massive prow. In the nose of this
is a giant fault line (The Scoop). Originally the preserve of aid
men, now it boasts some incredible free routes. The rock is a
solid grey gneiss.
    Approach – The single-track B887 leaves the
Tarbert-Stornoway road and heads only to Hushinish. A
motorable track leaves it at Amhuinnsuidhe to the dam at Loch
Chliostair. A good path leads down loch to Glen Ulladale 2.5
miles (4 km): 1 hr.

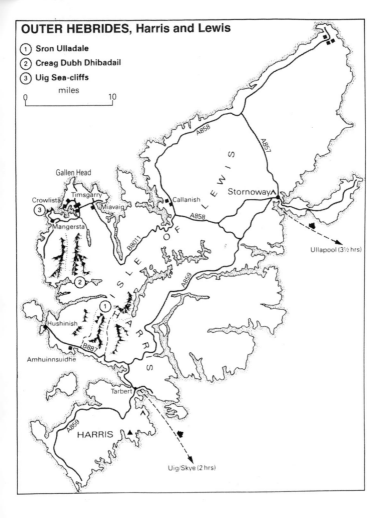

OUTER HEBRIDES, Harris and Lewis

1. Sron Ulladale
2. Creag Dubh Dhibadail
3. Uig Sea-cliffs

miles
0   10

Gallen Head
Crowlista
Timsgarry
Miavaig
Mangersta
Callanish
Stornoway
Hushinish
Amhuinnsuidhe
Tarbert
HARRIS

A858
A857
A858
A859
B8011
B887
A859

ISLE OF LEWIS
HARRIS

Ullapool (3½ hrs)
Uig/Skye (2 hrs)

Topography – The W face's most obvious features are, from the R, the South Buttress with a conspicuous L-to-R diag. gangway; an area of black stained wall, whose most obvious feature is a tongue of rock 100 ft (30 m) L of the base of gangway; and beyond this an obvious inverted staircase roof. To L the wall drops down to form a lower section, the ledge above it dwindling into slabs.

The lowest point of the W face is split by a huge corner (Stone), the upper half of the wall here being gouged by huge corners. The Scoop lies further L.

381 **Eureka**   *440 ft (132 m)   VS*
FA: *J. Grieve and E. Jones, 1967*
A good route on great rock directly up the front of South Buttress, starting up the groove line below gangway, then the bulging nose above top of gangway.
Start: Directly under nose, at line of thin cracks a few feet R of brown bulge at L end of lower tier.
1. 70 ft (21 m) Straight up grooves for 60 ft (18 m). Tr. L to O H-slab.
2. 80 ft (24 m) Move R, climb short wall to small ledge beneath steep brown groove. Groove to heather gangway.
3. 150 ft (45 m) Climb directly up steep nose above. Move L to pull over bulge to gain recessed slab. Climb to its top R corner.
4. 40 ft (12 m) Climb alarmingly O H-crack on magnificent holds.
5. 100 ft (30 m) Easy walls and ledges above.

381 **Prelude**   *600 ft (180 m)   S*
FA: *M. A. Reeves and J. Grieve, 1967*
Running across the black streaked wall diag. from R to L is a split ramp line (Midguard, V D). This climbs the wall between this and the gangway. Start just L of light-coloured tongue of rock 100 ft (30 m) L of the gangway.
1. 120 ft (36 m) Climb obvious cracked groove L of pillar, then up R to ledges.
2. 120 ft (36 m) Go R a few feet, then back L up a sort of gangway to a weakness in bulges above. Step up. Tr.

horizontally R by smooth sloping ledge to easy groove. Up
this and L on slabs.

3. 360 ft (108 m) Go straight up with increasing interest
keeping to centre of a clean ribbon of slabs.

383 **Palace of Swords Reversed**   *300 ft (91 m)   E5*
FA: *C. Waddy and R. Rogers, 1989*
Climbs the general line of the big corner to R of inverted
Staircase. Start below corner.

1. 80 ft (24 m) 5c Climb corner to ledge on R.
2. 70 ft (21 m) 6b Climb wall round OH above and L of ledge.
Continue to further ledge. L-hand groove above (PR) to
ledge.
3. 70 ft (21 m) 6b Step L off ledge, boldly up wall round OH
into groove leading beneath further OH.
4. 80 ft (25 m) 6a Tr. R along slab, go up L above OH and
continue round OH-arete. Easy to top.

384 **Kismet**   *495 ft (150 m)   E5*
FA: *C. Waddy and R. Rogers, 1989*
Climbs big hanging corner in upper wall between corner of
Stone and huge corner of The Chisel, gained from grass terrace
L of the inverted staircase, crossing Stone at mid-height. Start at
extreme L end of grass terrace at start of obvious horizontal
break. High in grade with crux OH on pitch 2.

1. 135 ft (40 m) 5c Climb short wall above past inverted flakes,
then easily L to niche. Step under bottom R corner of orange
quartz wall. Continue to thin crack leading to ramp on Stone
(pitch 4). Belay on ramp level with razor-thin flake.
2. 80 ft (25 m) 6a Follow flake L to its end. Groove to ledge
under OH of main horizontal break. Climb flakes across OH
and gain big corner for belay.
3. 80 ft (25 m) 5c Step R and climb crack in arete which joins
corner on R and follow this to its top. Tr. R to ledge.
4. 70 ft (21 m) 6a Shallow groove above to blank section at
40 ft (12 m). Hand tr. round blank pillar to gain spectacular
belay 'seat'.

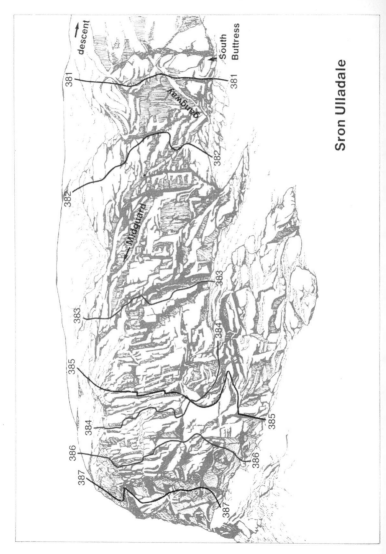

Sron Ulladale

5. 50 ft (15 m) 6a Step L into open groove leading to cracks leading to perfect square ledge.
6. 70 ft (21 m) 5b Tr. R 18 ft (6 m) past large corner. Follow good holds up arete of a groove to finish.

385 **Stone**   *670 ft (201 m)*   E5
FA: *J. Porteous and K. Spence, 1969*
FFA: *M. Fowler and A. Meyers, 1981*
A splendiferous route up a big quartz intrusion. Start at the lowest rocks below the big corner.
1. 80 ft (24 m) 5a Up the corner to large flake on R wall.
2. 110 ft (33 m) 4a Descend a little. Tr. R beneath overlap on slab then up obvious break to slab under further roof.
3. 90 ft (27 m) 5c Tr. L under roof on slab to ledge; tr. L into quartz corner. Up this. Exit out L just below its top and gain ledge.
4. 90 ft (27 m) 4a Easy quartz ramp up to ledge beneath big corner with twin cracks.
5. 150 ft (45 m) 6a Corner crack to big bulge. Tr. R along bulge into R-hand crack. Follow it with increasing lack of strength to grass ledge. Up to bigger grass ledge below corner (O H S by 30 ft (9 m)!).
6. 150 ft (45 m) 5b/c Corner strenuously till small ledge on R arete allows a tr. R round arete into easier grooves leading to top.

386 **The Chisel (Gloaming Finish)**   *495 ft (150 m)*   E7
FA: *C. Waddy, B. Drury and J. Biddle, (1 rest) 1989*
FFA and Gloaming Finish: *G. Smith and C. Waddy, 1994*
A fierce route in a spectacular position. Takes largest corner (with obvious undercut flake in L wall) in upper section to L of Stone. Start almost directly below big corner, L of orange wall midway between corner of Stone and start of Scoop.
1. 70 ft (21 m) 5b Up and R through overlaps until a wide break leads down R onto hanging wall. Continue R to belay in central crack.
2. 130 ft (35 m) 6a Climb crack which becomes groove curving

R. At its top tr. R to arete which leads to ledges (bold).
Alternative, harder but protected, climbs shallow groove 10 ft
(3 m) L of arete.

3. 30 ft (10 m) 5c Climb flakes on L. Tr. R to large ledge.

4. 100 ft (30 m) 6b Up R to main horizontal break under OH.
   Step L, pull into main corner and climb it (The Chisel) to
   gain undercut flake leading out L to arete. Over OH above to
   foot ledge belay. Exposed, strenuous but well protected.

5. 70 ft (21 m) 6a Climb short groove, tr. L along break till it
   eases and belay.

6. 70 ft (20 m) 6a Step L, climb OH into obvious corner.
   Follow this until short tr. across hanging wall leads to ledge.

7. 50 ft (15 m) Gain slab above, step R to groove. Climb this
   (steep) and continuation double grooves until a rail leads to top.

387 **The Scoop**   *500 ft (150 m)   E7*
FA: *D. Scott, J. Upton, G. Lee and M. Terry, 1969 (6 days)*
FFA: *J. Dawes and P. Pritchard, 1987 (6 days)*
A route that OHS by 150 ft (45 m), making retreat somewhat
complex. The free line deviates from that taken by D. Scott.
Start: Up easy slabs below the nose L of Stone, to belay on
earth ledge below rush platform.

1. 70 ft (21 m) 6b Step down from belay and up to OH. Pull
   over, then past flake on R to shallow bay (2 PRS). (Nut belay.)

2. 30 ft (9 m) 6a Tr. R and up on to ledge in cave (PRS).

3. 50 ft (15 m) 6b Climb blocks out R and up into groove to big
   ledge.

4. 80 ft (24 m) 6a Up to roof. Tr. L and up to hanging belay
   below main corner.

5. 80 ft (24 m) 6b Take flying groove out L and groove above
   out L to finger crack, leading to stance.

6. 50 ft (15 m) 6b Tr. L past blocks to below roof (PB).

7. 80 ft (24 m) 6a Enter groove above and take L arete to slab
   (PR). Out R in groove to ledge below capping roof (2 PRS).

8. 70 ft (21 m) 6b Tr. R (2 PRS) up over bulge (PRS) to
   hanging belay on lip of cave (nut, Friend belay).

9. Tr. L on lip and up easy rocks.

CREAG DUBH DHIBADAIL   (046238) Alt. 660 ft (200 m)
East facing 🦋🦋
A remote cliff hidden in the W mountains of Lewis. It lies
directly below the summit of Tamanaisval, and is about ½ mile
(800 m) long. The average angle is 85° and the rock is lovely
smooth gneiss. Requires about three days of dry weather after
heavy rain. One can always escape up to Uig and play on the
sea-cliffs.

Approach – Take the B8011 to Uig Sands Bay. A motorable
track leaves road just S of Carnish and heads towards Loch
Raonasgail. A good path continues along the W bank and up
the glen to the col. Bear L over the Tamanaisval-Teinnasval col
to Coire Dhibadail, 3 miles (4.8 km): 1 hr 30 mins.

Topography – In the centre a tongue of rock descends as
slabs down the hillside below the face. This central wall is
flanked on either side by prominent vertical crack faults. The L
one is a deep chimney crack (Via Valtos, E1). L of this are
more inclined slabs. The R-hand crack is indefinite in the
middle (Solitude, HVS).

388 **South Buttress**   *520 ft (156 m)*   VS
FA: *J. Grieve and M. Reeves, 1968*
Generally easy but good slabs, with one pitch a little harder. L
of the chimney line of Via Valtos are two obvious slanting
rakes. L again is a less obvious slanting line starting up slabs.
1. 120 ft (36 m) Up slabs trending R to ledge (flake belay above).
2. 100 ft (30 m) 4a Up slabs slanting R to beneath bulging wall
   (thread belay).
3. 90 ft (28 m) 4c Move L of prominent small OH. Step back R
   and up bulging wall.
4. 100 ft (30 m) 4a Climb up to corner slanting R; up this; exit
   L at top to ledge.
5. 110 ft (33 m) 4a Direct up steep wall to easier ground.

389 **The Big Lick**   *600 ft (180 m)*   E3
FA: *M. Fowler and A. Meyers, 1981*
Climbs the steepest section above the tongue. Start on its L side.

1. 90 ft (27 m) 5c Move on to front of tongue. Diag. L via a shallow groove from excellent hand ledge beneath a bulge move up L (hard) to short crack and ledge.
2. 70 ft (21 m) 5b Groove above L end of ledge to OH. Turn on R to ledge and up to further ledge.
3. 150 ft (45 m) 5b Surmount OH directly above on to slabby rock. Direct to stance at upper R side of black shaped depression on the face.
4. 70 ft (21 m) 5b Gain pinnacle/flake on R. Step off it to climb quartz wall direct (bold) to ledge 30 ft (9 m) below OH.
5. 80 ft (24 m) 5c Step down L, tr. horizontally L on exposed sloping ledge. Up corner 15 ft (5 m) then L again to ledge beneath light-coloured rock.
6. 140 ft (42 m) 5c Gain sloping ledge in R-hand groove above by awkward move. Up it with difficulty till possible to transfer to L groove, leading easier to top.

390 **Panting Dog Climb**   *600 ft (180 m)   E2*
FA: *M. Fowler and A. Strapcans, 1980*
Another climb for dog lovers, exiting off the R side of the tongue more or less direct.
Start: On highest grass ledge R of tongue.

1. 120 ft (36 m) 5b L on to tongue. Up to short black groove. Exit L zig-zag up slabby wall above to short groove. Climb this and step R to rock niche.
2. 100 ft (30 m) 5b A black corner above, then easy crack. Move R. Climb up under slanting OH till possible to tr. R to grass ledge.
3. 100 ft (30 m) 5b Tr. R 20 ft (6 m) to weakness in wall above; up 20 ft (6 m) to OH. R on to slab. Pull through bulges to good stance in foot of obvious corner.
4. 80 ft (24 m) 5a Corners to beneath R-slanting corner with OH L wall.
5. 100 ft (30 m) 5b/c Ascend corner avoiding rocking block on

Climbing in Painted Zawn, Uig Sea-cliffs

R (crux), to good ledges on L. Step R. Undercut and layback easy angled slabs to next ledge.
6. 100 ft (30 m) 4c easier to top.

UIG SEA-CLIFFS
Much has been done along the cliffs either side of the huge sandy bay known as Camas Uig on the W coast of Lewis. The main activists were members of the Lochaber Mountaineering Club. The peninsula of Ard More Mangersta immediately S and W of Uig Sands holds the most developed cliffs, there being more than 100 routes contained within the geos here. (Geo is a norse name for a zawn.)

Approach – Take the B8011 out to Timsgarry on Uig Sands, then the small road through Mangersta village. The road continues out to the head of the peninsula at a disused RAF Warning Station, now a radio station. There are numerous geos.

The Painted Zawn (006334) West facing
A sheltered geo lying just N of the ruined buildings at the road-head. Walk due NE. The geo has a striking coloration of wavy quartz and gneiss: 2 mins.

Topography – It is not a true zawn, comprising only an East and South Wall. A small island lies below it, nearly forming a West Wall. The main East wall begins from ledges about 40 ft (12 m) above sea level. Approach it by abseil. The open corner at L end of face is **Mick's Corner (VS 4c)**. The next corner to R is **Director's Corner (VS 5a)** in centre of wall. The following climbs are concentrated on the central face of bright-coloured rock:

391   **Dauntless**   *80 ft (24 m)*   *E5 6a*
FA: *G. Latter and D. Cuthbertson, 1985*
Start: 30 ft (9 m) R of Director's Corner, just R of the pink quartz wall. Up wall direct past several breaks, heading for L-hand side of twin diag. breaks. Tr. these R to top.

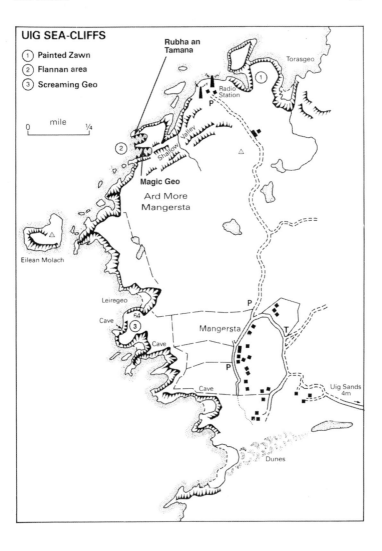

UIG SEA-CLIFFS

① Painted Zawn
② Flannan area
③ Screaming Geo

0 ———— mile ———— ¼

Rubha an Tamana

Torasgeo

Radio Station

P

Shallow Valley

Magic Geo

Ard More Mangersta

Eilean Molach

Leiregeo

Cave

S4

③

Cave

Mangersta

P

T

P

Cave

Uig Sands 4m

Dunes

392 **Motion Control**   *80 ft (24 m)   E2 5b*
FA: *M. Tighe and B. Newton (1 rest), 1980's*
FFA: *G. Latter and D. Cuthbertson, 1985*
The OH-crack in the centre.

393 **The Painted Wall**   *80 ft (24 m)   E4 5c*
FA: *D. Cuthbertson and G. Latter, 1985*
A diag. line up the pink wall on R side.
Start: Below L end of pink vein just R of last route. Climb up
into shallow scoop to gain vein. This and obvious line to finish.

394 **The Dreaded Dram**   *100 ft (30 m)   E4 5c*
FA: *D. Cuthbertson and G. Latter, 1985*
The obvious short black groove to the R, and wall above to
finish at top of Painted Wall.

Flannan Area (001329)
This is name given to area containing two deep geos just south
of headland of Rubh'an Tamana. They are Aurora Geo to north
and Magic Geo to south.
    Approach – From disused huts, follow a shallow grassy
'valley'-cum-terrace running N to S parallel with the coast and
R of the summit plateau. Its R side begins to rise to form a
rocky rib. The geos lie below this: 5 mins, tidal.

Magic Geo
Lying just at the south end of the crest of the approach ridge.
The geo runs NE to SW. The back wall is very steep, as is the
E wall. The W is slabby and turns seaward to form the
SW-facing Red Wall. On the E face directly opposite the rocks
at the foot of the Red Wall is an open slabby bay, its S side
defined by a black wall.
    Descent – By abseil or by climbing down easy groove in S
end of slabby bay.

The West Face
The corner at the back of the E wall is **Queen's Freebie (E4
6b** *). 20 ft (6 m) R of the corner are impressive cracks up
OH-wall:

395 **The Magician**   *130 ft (39 m)*   E5 6a
FA: *J. Moran and D. Pearce, 1985*
The massive OH-crack of the E wall. Gain it and climb it with
continual interest, veering L at top.

The East Face
The opposite corner to Queen's Freebie is **In the Pink (E1 5b)**.
The next route climbs the deceptive W wall opposite The
Magician. Either abseil into it or cross boulders in base of geo
at low tide:

396 **Flannan Slab**   *160 ft (48 m)*   VS
FA: *M. Tighe and J. Paterson, 1978*
Start: At the R side of wall just R of L-trending ramp.
1. 80 ft (24 m) 4c Steep initial moves lead up and R to thin
   crack. Up crack to ledge. Go easily L on ledge, then steeply
   to another.
2. 80 ft (24 m) 4c Gain groove above on L. Up this to obvious
   handrail followed L to finish.

The Red Wall
Gain base of wall by jumping gap in geo from foot of descent,
or by abseil.

397 **Flannan Crack**   *90 ft (27 m)*   VS 4c
FA: *M. Tighe and J. Paterson, 1979*
The obvious R-slanting diag, hand crack at the L end of the wall.

398 **Campa Crack**   *110 ft (33 m)*   VS 4c
FA: *P. Moores and D. Cuthbertson, 1985*
The next crack system to the R is followed in its entirety.

Aurora Geo (002329)

To the W of Magic Geo is another running parallel with it, and of similar shape. At the SE edge of the geo is a huge block boulder sitting at the base of a blank-looking slab. This is the E wall known as the Cioch Wall, which is not as steep as the W wall and has a series of slim ledges approx. 40 ft (12 m) above the sea, cutting back into the geo from the block boulder (the Cioch). The Cioch Wall is tar black and unmistakeable. The back of the geo forms an arch over the sea. Two routes which follow crack lines are described on the West Wall in the back of the geo near the arch – Star of the Sea and Newton's Law. The remaining routes are on the Cioch Wall.

Access – To get to the climbs on Cioch Wall abseil down the wall near the huge block boulder. To get to the West Wall either descend or abseil down seaward end and tr. slab into geo (VS) to reach ledges below climbs, or abseil down the routes themselves.

The Cioch Wall

At L end of ledges at base is obvious chimney (VD). Beyond this the wall drops into sea and holds obvious corner on L. Routes described from L to R. The first route is reached by awkward tr. L from ledges under two flat walls.

399 **Cormorant's Corner**   *80 ft (24 m)   E1 5b*
FA: *M. Tighe, I. Sutherland and I. Sykes, 1975*
Tr. L and belay about 10 ft (3 m) R of corner. Up and L in to hanging ramp corner. Over OH and corner crack to top.

The slabby wall gives up good range of graded routes all worth doing. From L to R these are: **Immaculate Crack 70 ft (21 m) HS (1970s)**, climbs obvious and sustained crack to R of big chimney. **Things Are Looking Up 80 ft (25 m) E1 5c (1993)**, is crackline and fault to R of Immaculate Crack; **The Roaring Foam 80 ft (25 m) E3 5c (1994)**, thin crack in centre, slanting R in upper half and finally **Chicken Run Direct 80 ft (25 m) HVS 5b (1979)** climbs thin crack between slimy wide crack and Cioch block.

The West Wall
On the W wall are two prominent corner cracks about 30 ft
(9 m) apart.

400 **Star of the Sea**   *100 ft (30 m)   E1 5b*
FA: *M. Tighe and B. Newton, 1974*
Gives great jamming and laybacking up the R-hand crack.

401 **Newton's Law**   *100 ft (30 m)   E1 5b*
FA: *B. Newton and M. Tighe, 1974*
The L-hand crack is in a large corner facing S. Another good
route.

Screaming Geo (002317)
This geo is very impressive. It consists of several facets, a huge
sea-cave, a two-tiered wall and a steep granite slab.
   Approach – From gate just north of road junction to Mangersta
village follow fence west. Cross a fence and head south west. On
a shoulder L of point height 64 (1:50 000 map)
sits a distinct small circular stone. Go straight past this and
slightly
L down a clean rock ramp leading to big ledge: 10 mins.
   Topography – A huge cave skulks in the back of the open
geo facing NW towards Eilean Molach. Its two tiered R wall
(North West Wall) runs out to the headland. The ledge splitting
it continues round on to the South West face and enlarges to
meet the descent ramp off the plateau. Beyond its S end are the
Mangersta Slabs. To L side of cliff is ridge forming Lighthouse
Arete. The wall below this and L of sea cave is the West Wall,
known as The Screaming Wall.
   Descent – Down the ramp to the big ledge. For North-West
Face: Follow the ledge R (looking out) round the edge. Abseil
off it (large boulder). Tidal. For South West Face (slabs), abseil
diag. down face off S end of big ledge to small ledge at base.
Tidal. For The Screaming Wall, abseil off boulders on ridge
above centre of face to good ledge at sea level.

North-West Face, Lower Tier
Routes are described L to R.

402 **The Screaming Abdabs/Prozac Link**   *315 ft (95 m)*   *E4*
FA: *D. Cuthbertson, L. Clegg and C. Henderson, 1988*
FA: *(The Prozac Link) H. Jones and G. Huxter, 1996*
A mixture of two routes up R side of cave and across the lip of
the headwall above, giving a serious out-there experience with
almost no options for failure.
Start: At L end of lower tier.
1. 60 ft (18 m) 5b Climb undercut groove, go L to white crack.
   This to ledge.
2. 80 ft (24 m) 5a Tr. L along horizontal break and up to ledge
   on R. Rising tr. L across orange wall (surprisingly easy) to
   belay at girdle ledge.
3. 165 ft (50 m) 5c Move R. Pull over bulge on to wall. Line of
   black pockets leads L to large block under roof. Tr. L
   around block then beneath curious down-pointing flake to
   gain pink quartz wall (hard). Climb direct up quartz wall to
   gain easy R-slanting ramp to top. (**Screaming Abdabs
   original finish** (**E6 6c**), move R, pull over roof via ramp
   hold (good Friend under roof). Go L (Friend again). Still
   hard to good holds under next OH. Use horizontal crack to
   breach it then corner to top.

R of Screaming Abdabs is an OH-face. Immediately R is an
obvious hanging slab at mid-height. **Killer Fingers (E5 6a)**
climbs a groove to R side of slab, and crosses it to layback
crack on L. **Suffering Person (E4 5c)** climbs jamming crack
and bottomless groove to L of the obvious L-facing corner to R
of Killer Fingers. R of this is a raised diag. platform.

If all Else Fails, (VD) gains a ledge above R end of raised
platform at R end of wall. Trends R and up short crack up R
side of slab to ledge. An exposed tr. R before finishing up steep
wall. A good escape route.

North-West Face, Upper Teir

The following route starts from far L end of girdle ledge overlooking upper section of Screaming Abdabs, best reached direct by abseil. A large corner is most prominent feature here.

403 **Paranoid Slippers**   *100 ft (30 m)   E4 6b*
FA: *G. Farquhar, R. Campbell and N. Clement, 1996*
A wildly positioned route L of large corner. Start up fine pink crack (**Hughy's Cocktail Mixture, E3 5c**) in L wall of corner over O H. Tr. L along lip (crux), move up and L to better holds. Continue in same line to sentry box and finish up L past horizontal break, L of wide crack and on spectacular O H-arete.

South-West Face (the Mangersta Slab)
The abseil gains a ledge below a L-leaning corner.

404 **Hundred Pipers**   *150 ft (45 m)   E3 5c*
FA: *D. Cuthbertson and G. Latter, 1985*
Start: Just R of previous route, directly beneath large open groove high on the face. Pull over bulges and up cracks in slab to finish up groove. Some loose rock near top.

405 **Moscow Mule**   *100 ft (30 m)   E2 5b*
FA: *D. Cuthbertson, L. Clegg and C. Henderson, 1988*
Start as for Claymore ascending R-facing corner to ledge at 20 ft (6 m). Follow obvious hand tr. line to L edge. Climb crack a short distance then hard move L over O H to jug. Easier groove above.

The Screaming Wall
The following route starts from the ledge at the base of the wall, reached by abseil.

406 **The Dark Crystal**   *165 ft (50 m)   E2*
FA: *S. Mayers and G. Lovick, 1993*
1. 80 ft (25 m) 5b Trend up L to base of two grooves. Climb L-hand groove to ledge.
2. 80 ft (25 m) 5b Up and slightly L to obvious corner.

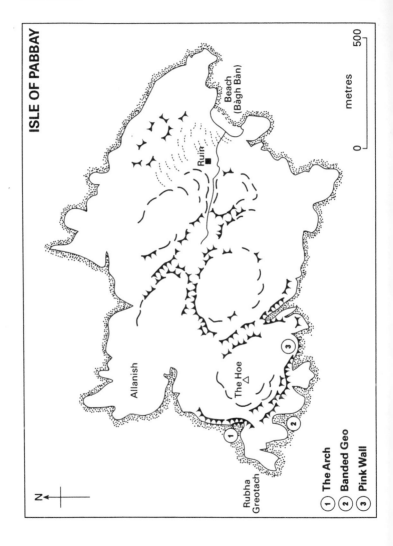

ISLE OF PABBAY

① The Arch
② Banded Geo
③ Pink Wall

The Barra Isles

Introduction
These are made up of 6 main islands with the biggest, Barra and its neighbour Vatersay (connected by a causeway) the only ones being inhabited. Further south lie Sandray, Pabbay, Mingulay and Berneray. The sea-cliff architecture here is amongst the best in Scotland and although many cliffs are plastered in guano there are areas of clean rock on all the islands which offer great adventures. The climbing ethic adhered to by those responsible for these islands' development (excepting two parties) is that of on-sight ascents without the use of pegs or bolts. If true adventure is not your cup of tea, then search elsewhere. Be prepared to get marooned in bad weather. Only Pabbay is described here.

Pabbay
Remains of settlements can be seen in the bay on the east side. This bay offers the only landing point under normal circumstances. There are climbs round the north and south shores, however The Arch and Banded Geo in the south west tip offer unrivalled climbing.

Access
There is no ferry. Sailing from the mainland would be the most satisfying approach.

Accommodation
Camp in the bay (avoid the lazy beds as Corncrake sometimes nest here).

Provisions
Take everything with you. The small stream on Pabbay can dry to a trickle in good weather.

Mountain Rescue
There is none and portable phones don't work here.

Guidebooks
Skye and the Hebrides, Rock and Ice Climbs, Volume 2, by D. Cuthbertson, B. Duncan, G. E. Little and C. Moody, SMC, 1996

Map
Landranger Series, Barra and surrounding Islands, 31.

Conservation Information
These islands have been designated under the EU Habitats Directive as a Special Protection Area for their bird nesting importance. There are numerous rare species on the island. If visiting during the nesting period the main colonies are obvious (and smelly). Smaller groups of Shag and Cormorant are less obvious. There are also numerous ground nesting birds so be careful where you are treading. Best to visit in the autumn if possible.

ARCH WALL   (592 873) South West Facing
Rubha Greotach is the most westerly headland on Pabbay (in south west corner). Just to north lies great rock arch comprising huge horizontal lower OH and arching OH near the cliff's top. A Boulder field lies at base of arch area. To its L lies a 100 m high open corner (vegetated and unclimbed). Between these two features lies a massive pillar, narrow at its base, widening with height and holding twin corners capped by a big OH near top. The L edge of big open corner is bounded by another pillar. This area drops into deep water. The two routes described climb the central pillar.

   Access – By 330 ft (100 m) abseil down the line of the huge unclimbed corner. Take a belay on the lowest possible ledge near the R side of the slab. The arch can be viewed from the headland – descent by small zig-zag path to south of The Arch.

407 **The Priest**   *365 ft (110 m)   E2*
FA: *G. E. Little and K. Howett (alt), 1995*
Climbs arete then L side of pillar between great arch and big
open corner, finishing up the left hand of the twin OH-capped
corners high on the crag. It has great character and atmosphere
with big route commitment.
1. 165 ft (50 m) 4b From tiny ledge some eight metres above
   sea climb slabby R wall of corner just L of edge to gain
   small ledge and belay on very edge.
2. 80 ft (25 m) 5b Move up into groove, step R then enjoy
   sustained and intricate climbing via cracks and grooves, well
   right of edge, leading to belay on rusty slab under OH.
3. 120 ft (35 m) 5b Move up to OH, step R then climb to base
   of L-hand corner. Climb fine corner to big OH then make
   short, difficult tr. L to finish.

408 **Prophesy Of Drowning**   *380 ft (125 m)   E2*
FA: *K. Howett and G. E. Little, 1996*
One of finest routes in Hebrides, climbs line parallel and to R of
The Priest. Low in grade. Start on lowest small ledge on R side
of slab.
1. 135 ft (40 m) 5b Up R edge of slab passing to R of larger
   ledge to reach small block about 20 ft (7 m) above. Swing
   wildly round OH-R arete into base of hanging groove with
   distinctive projecting ledge in base. Up groove and larger
   continuation above in excellent position to exit R onto
   shattered ledged rock, level with lip of great OH.
2. 65 ft (20 m) 5a From edge of the OH climb up and R across
   immaculate wall to enter small R-facing groove. This
   becomes a ramp. Belay at its top below main corner line.
3. 100 ft (30 m) 5c Climb superb corner with hard moves
   through its steepest section. Up easy corner above to OH and
   exit L onto large ledge below final corner.
4. 80 ft (25 m) 5a Excellent final corner to capping OH. Exit R
   in a great position.

BANDED GEO   (592 870) West Facing
Just to south of Rubha Greotach, lies a geo holding a 60 m
high, long, west facing wall. It starts on dry land on L, near
headland and curves round back of geo above easy angled slabs
which dip into sea.

Topography – Where slabs dip into sea (tidal) wall increases
in height with brown coloured lower section and corners near
the top guarded by OHs. Large boulders sit in back of geo
below here. Shattered ledges at 30 ft (10 m) continue R-wards
around base of wall into deep chimney/corner capped by OHs. R
again (beyond the OH-corner topped by OH) is the cleanest
section of wall which has long OH at 2/3 height and a deep
corner above slab on R with long ledge at high water level.
Most conspicuous feature here is L to R diag. quartz band.

Access – At most states of tide, climb very steep wall
covered in jugs to L of boulders in back of geo to gain
shattered ledges. Routes up to Spring Squill, can be accessed by
tr. these ledges (VS to gain Spring Squill). Routes described
L to R.

409 **Ship of Fools**   *150 ft (45 m)   E5 6b*
FA: *R. Campbell and P. Thorburn, 1998*
Climbs acutely OH-wall R of deep chimney/corner R of brown
wall. From easy ramp below wall climb boldly up Biotite to
gain slanting OH 12 ft (4 m) L of its lowest point. Gain flake
above lip with difficulty, move up L to cross bulge by flakes.
Continue up until rock becomes noticeably compact (Alcite !).
Up and R, then back L through bulge, then up R again to pull
through another bulge to gain flake. Step R past a detached
flake into black niche. Step R and climb direct to belay on slab.
Scramble to the top.

410 **Endolphin Rush**   *200 ft (60 m)   E4*
FA: *K. Howett and G. E. Little, 1997*
A magnificent and strenuous route on excellent rock. Start on
long low ledge below and L of start of Spring Squill.
1. 80 ft (25 m) 5c Climb up to and follow R diag. wide, band of

pink pegmatite across OH-wall. As steepness relents move up
and R to gain crackline that trends back L slightly with
increasing difficulty to reach small stance beneath big OHS.

2. 120 ft (35 m) 5c From just above belay move down and L
between big OH above and another below. Pull through OH
which is a leaning wall at this point via conspicuous fat
spike to gain ledge below another OH. Move L to bypass
this and direct to top.

411 **Spring Squill**   *215 ft (65 m)   E1*
FA: *A. Cunningham and G. Nicoll, 1995*
Stunning. From R end of long ledge move up R to smaller ledge
with flake/thread belay.

1. 135 ft (40 m) 5b Follow flake line R-wards to ledge and then
trend steeply back L and into R-hand of two short cracks
leading to easier climbing. Move into vague depression, past
huge downward pointing flake, to climb crack through bulge
(crux) on L and then up to belay on L under break in long OH.

2. 80 ft (25 m) 4b Pull through narrowing in OH and continue
directly to top.

To R is obvious chimney-corner. This is line of **Corncrake
Corner** 215 ft (65 m) HVS 5a, which climbs chimney, then R
wall of corner above. Gain base by abseil.

412 **Spooky Pillar**   *215 ft (65 m)   HVS*
FA: *A. Cunningham and G. Nicoll, 1995*
Tackles pillar to R of Corncrake Corner (and L of less well
defined unclimbed corner). Abseil to tiny ledge at base of
Corncrake Corner.

1. 135 ft (40 m) 5a Climb straight up keeping slightly L of edge
through bulges until a move R round edge at top bulge leads
into crack. Follow this to good ledge and belay.

2. 80 ft (25 m) 4a Easier climbing straight up to finish.

To R of Spooky Pillar wall diminishes slightly in height with
large grass ledge at 2/3rds height. An unclimbed flaky corner

separates two long smooth walls from Spooky Pillar. These walls are separated by an obvious L-facing corner.

413 **Hyper-ballard**   *180 ft (55 m)   E2*
FA: *G. Nicoll and L. Hughes, 1997*
Takes line up wall just R of L-facing corner. Abseil to foot-ledge 12 ft (4 m) R of base of corner, calm seas preferred.
1. 100 ft (30 m) 5b From foot-ledge climb directly up to OH. Tr. 20 ft (6 m) L and pull spectacularly through OH at crack. Continue to grass ledge.
2. 80 ft (25 m) Easy cracks and slabs to top.

414 **Mollyhawk**   *180 ft (55 m)   HVS*
FA: *L. Hughes and G. Nicoll, 1997*
Abseil to foot-ledge of Hyper-ballard
1. 100 ft 30 m) 5a Move up and R to climb R-facing groove. Move L to obvious break in OH, pull through and continue to grass ledge.
2. 80 ft (25 m) Easy cracks and slabs to top.

About 100 ft (30 m) R of Spooky Pillar main section of wall finishes. Crag becomes more disjointed and most obvious feature is a worrying looking off-width chimney and flake crack. Abseil approaches.

415 **Blo' Na Gael**   *165 ft (50 m)   E1*
FA: *A. Cunningham and F. Fotheringham, 1996*
1. 115 ft (35 m) 5b The R edge of wall R of off-width chimney. Pull through undercut and climb up and L into curving flake. Move R into thin crack and up this to bulge on edge. Go R through bulge and back L into deep cracks on wall leading to ledge.
2. 50 ft (15 m) 4a Climb through gnarly ground and corners to finish.

Right again is wide corner crack leading to an unstable bulge.

416 **Wind Against Tide**   *165 ft (50 m)   E1*
FA: *A. Cunningham and F. Fotheringham, 1996*
Climb R wall of wide corner crack R of Blo' Na Gael to gain
large horizontal break. Tr. break R-wards until level with large
OHS and climb thin crack, then up and R to good ledge. Finish
more or less direct.

THE PINK WALL   (596869) South Facing
The amazing big wall to the east of Banded Geo. It presents the
biggest vertical wall on the island although its lower half below
a huge middle ledge (inhabited by fulmars in the breeding
season) is broken. Above this lies an excessively steep pink
wall. Two continuous parallel corner lines starting from sea
level, define its R side. The central ledge steps down at the west
side of the wall where it forms a more shattered ledge system
just above a conspicuous black glacis that sits at the top of the
overhanging lower wall at this point.
   Approach – For routes on front face make a free 330 ft
(100 m) abseil from a big flat block at the top of the wall down
the general line of a central crack/groove that splits the wall
(**Raiders of the Lost Auk, 80 m E3**) to gain the halfway
ledge. To gain ledge in the bay at base of the corner lines
on R make a free 330 ft (100 m) abseil down L-hand corner.
From top of wall descend to east a little way and tr. out
toward the sea on obvious grass terrace which ends above the
large OH above corners. Abseil from boulders above the end of
the OH.

417 **The Tomorrow People**   *365 ft (110 m)   E4*
FA: *G. E. Little and K. Howett, 1997*
Climbs line of least resistance up west side of front face to L of
abseil line. A route with serious feel and some strange rock!
Start at cluster of big spikes just above black glacis down and L
of ledge about 30 ft (10 m) in from L side of crag.
   1. 80 ft (25 m) 5b Trend up and L on weird rock to large spike
      where wall bulges. Shallow chimney through bulge then
      immediately hand tr. R into another chimney. Climb this to

its top then tr. R across ledge to L-facing corner with strange 'pillar' in back.

2. 80 ft (25 m) 5c Step up L and make hard move L to gain thin crack up steep wall. Up this to jug then step R to gain big flake edge. This leads into big corner (of belay) below capping OH. Tr. hard L below OH to hanging belay on 'fired' rock just after blind downwards moves.

3. 65 ft (20 m) 5c Move L into shallow chimney line to capping OH. Pull over via deep crack into recess. Trend L 10 ft (3 m) to belay by big semi-detached block.

4. 135 ft (40 m) 5b Step R and climb immaculate crack up flying 'edge' above to top.

Most distinctive feature on front face is large L-facing, hanging corner-line of next route.

418 **A Cormorants Out of the Question Then?** *245 ft (75 m) E5*
FA: *R. Campbell and P. Thorburn, 1998.*
Start below and R of series of strange flakes under corner.

1. 65 ft (20 m) 5c Gain and climb flakes, then follow diminishing flake-line on R to break. Tr. L, gain large but easy corner and belay half-way up it.

2. 80 ft (25 m) 6b From top of corner, tr. L to crack in OH. Up this and gain pegmatite flakes (hard). From vertical flake, undercut L to gain diag. line of jugs which lead to break.

3. 100 ft (30 m) 5b Step L, climb steepening to make awkward pull L onto shelf. Continue up groove to further shelf. Tr. L below steep wall with loose flake and step L around lichenous arete. Climb direct to top.

419 **The Guga** *245 ft (75 m) E6*
FA: *R. Campbell and P. Thorburn, 1997*
Climbs spectacular line up OH-corner on the immediate R side of R arete of front face, starting from halfway ledge. Start from belay below corner 30 ft (10 m) R of arete.

1. 65 ft (20 m) 6b Climb wall into corner and follow it with

difficult exit L onto ledge. Move up OH-wall on R to ramp
and belay.
2. 80 ft (25 m) 6b Climb corner on R, then make hard moves
   through bulge to gain L-arching pegmatite bulge (capping
   OH). Follow this to crack, then move up R-wards to gain
   ledge.
3. 100 ft (30 m) 4c Climb up L from belay then direct line to
   top.

420 **U-Ei** *365 ft (110 m)* *E2*
FA: *R. Gantzhorn and S. Wacker, 1995*
Start on platform at base of parallel corners.
1. 165 ft (50 m) 5b Climb L side of slabby wall on perfect
   holds for 80 ft (25 m) to step L into short hanging corner. Up
   to this OH. Step out L to comfortable ledge.
2. 100 ft (30 m) 5a As above.
3. 100 ft (30 m) 5b Climb up to OH. Tr. R under it to gain base
   of OH-corner system. Climb this to finish by L-slanting
   ramp.

Prophesy of
Drowning, Outer
Hebrides: climber,
Graham Little

10   HOY, ORKNEY ISLES

Introduction
Hoy is the second largest of the Orkney Islands off the N coast
of Scotland. It is also the highest and wildest. On its NW coast
is a 12-mile (19 km) stretch of cliff whose highest point is
St John's Head, 1,141 ft (342 m) – one of the highest sea-cliffs
in the British Isles. The Old Man of Hoy lies nearby.

Access
Air – Edinburgh or Glasgow to Kirkwall Airport, Orkney
mainland, via Aberdeen and Inverness.
Rail – Edinburgh to Thurso.
Bus – Inverness to Scrabster near Thurso, Citylink daily.
Ferry – P & O Ferries. Scrabster (near Thurso, John O'Groats)
to Stromness on Orkney Mainland, daily (2 hrs) not Sunday, tel:
(01224) 572 615; or from Aberdeen (weekly). Orkney to Hoy
either by private passenger ferry Stromness to Moaness, north
Hoy, tel: (01856) 850 624; or Orkney Isles Shipping Company
ferry from Houghton, Orkney Mainland to Lyness and
Longhope on Hoy, tel: (01856) 852 044.
Taxi – Longhope to Rackwick Bay.

Accommodation
Camping – At Rackwick Bay (197997).
Youth hostels – Linksness and Glen, Rackwick Bay (200998),
an unattended open hostel; Stromness and Kirkwall (mainland).

Provisions
All usual amenities at Kirkwall and Stromness on mainland
(early closing Thursdays); and at Longhope on Hoy (early
closing Thursdays).

Old Man of Hoy, Orkney Isles: climber, Rusty Baillie

Mountain Rescue
Post: police station at Wick (362511), tel: 999. Nearest
telephone, Rackwick Bay (200998).

THE OLD MAN OF HOY   (175009)
The Old Man was connected by an arch to the mainland which
collapsed nearly a century ago. The pile of boulders leading out
to the stack's base bears testimony to its demise.

Approach – The stack lies 1.5 miles (2.4 km) NW of
Rackwick. Walk diag. up hillside just beyond the old
schoolhouse: 30 mins.

Descent – From summit, abseil down line of East Face Route.
Requires extra rope to leave in place down Pitch 2 (there may
be one in situ).

421 **East Face Route**   *460 ft (138 m)   E1*
FA: *R. Bailie, T. W. Patey and C. J. S. Bonington, 1966*
The original route up this pre-eminent British sea-stack.
1. 70 ft (21 m) 4b Climb shattered pillar above the boulder
   ridge leading out to the stack to large ledge (the Gallery).
2. 120 ft (36 m) 5b Descend a little and tr. R to gain foot of big
   corner crack. Step R at top to triangular alcove.
3. 80 ft (24 m) 4c Step R and move back L over easy ledges to
   regain crackline. Follow this to large ledge.
4. 120 ft (36 m) 4b Climb wall on R then direct up to base of
   final crack or chimney in corner on L.
5. 70 ft (21 m) 4b The final crack.

11 CENTRAL HIGHLANDS OUTCROPS

Introduction
Five separate cliffs are included in this section. Although they are some distance apart, each lies not far from the main (A9) road from Perth to Aviemore. They give distinctly different types of climbing in very contrasting surroundings.

History
The first recorded climbs appeared in an early SMC journal when Harold Raeburn described the ascent of a vegetated gully on Creag Dubh. After this nothing was climbed until the late 1950s. In 1959 Terry Sullivan, aware of the potential of Scotland's outcrops, was already developing Glen Nevis. He set the ball rolling at Creag Dubh with his ascent of The Brute, now a popular route. Edinburgh climbers Robin Smith and Robin Campbell visited Polney Crag at Dunkeld, and the plums were snatched in a very short time. Campbell and others went on to explore Cave Crag. Many lines were added including Rat Race, but the best free climb was Smith's Coffin Corner (5a).

Creag Dubh then became the focus of attention. In 1964 Dougal Haston climbed the impressive Inbred (HVS 5a), one of his few rock climbs before his obsession with big mountains took him abroad. Inbred became a test piece. The following year the Edinburgh Squirrels besieged Creag Dubh, bringing the total number of routes to 30, before the publication of a new guidebook. However, controversy raged with the SMC as their route names were sometimes blatantly rude, and it led to a SMC decision not to record such routes in journals and guides. Tom Patey meanwhile climbed the first route on Binnein Shuas – the upper section of The Fortress. Strangely, the guide did not immediately arouse interest, until Kenny Spence and J. Porteous forced The Hill on the Great Wall in 1967. This bold, serious route still sees the odd epic and long fall. Dirc Mhor was discovered at this time by 'Bugs' McKeith when the party climbed Holy Smoke (VS) up the edge of the impressive

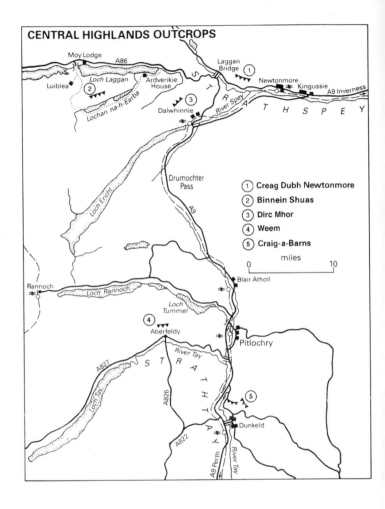

CENTRAL HIGHLANDS OUTCROPS

Moy Lodge A86 Laggan Bridge ①
Luiblea Loch Laggan Ardverikie House ② Newtonmore Kingussie A9 Inverness
Lochan na-h-Earba ③ STRATHSPEY
Dalwhinnie River Spey

Loch Ericht Drumochter Pass A9

① Creag Dubh Newtonmore
② Binnein Shuas
③ Dirc Mhor
④ Weem
⑤ Craig-a-Barns

miles
0   10

Blair Atholl

Rannoch Loch Rannoch Loch Tummel
④ Aberfeldy A9
Pitlochry
A827 STRATHTAY River Tay
A826 ⑤
Loch Tay Dunkeld
A822 A9 Perth River Tay

Sentinel Rock. Dougie Lang and Grahame Hunter visited Binnein Shuas that same year and must have wondered why Patey had missed the great slab. Ardverikie Wall (S), became an instant classic and the pair capitalized on their new discovery, producing several more excellent routes during 1967 and 1968.

The most striking events of the early 1970s were many solos at Creag Dubh, particularly Ian Nicholson's ascent of Inbred, while George Shields was engrossed in the second ascent of The Hill. Shields, living in Aviemore, also contributed Niagara and Jump so High (both E1). Later several significant free ascents occurred at Cave Crag. Dave Cuthbertson, a young Edinburgh laddie, freed Rat Catcher and Murray Hamilton did likewise with Rat Race (E3), only using one point of aid. The latter was possibly one of Scotland's most impressive free ascents at the time, and the final aid point was finally eliminated by American Mike Graham. In 1976 Derek Jameson created the brilliant Warfarin (E2), crossing the steep central face of Cave Crag, and Cuthbertson freed High Performance with a desperate 6a move. He went on through the late '70s and early '80s to monopolise development of the untouched lines of Creag Dubh and Cave Crag. Lady Charlotte was established at Cave Crag by him and was the area's first E5. Mousetrap was freed at 6b, Case Dismissed, Ruff Licks, Wet Dreams and Acapulco at Creag Dubh were also due to Cuthbertson's insatiable appetite. The next rise in interest in Dirc Mhor was in 1980. Alan Fyffe visited first with Keith Geddes to produce Slow Hand and then the pair were accompanied by Addo Liddell to bag the superb hanging corner of Working Class Hero (E1). Fyffe returned the next year with Martin Burrows – Smith to climb Positive Earth (E2). In 1984 Binnein Shuas was rudely awakened when Mark Charlton made the first breach of the fortress with Storming the Bastille, a route which chimneys through a 15-ft roof. While he was engaged on this, John Griffiths was busy fighting his way up cracks to the right, only to be defeated by loose gravel and grass. He did however manage to clean it a little and a few days later teamed up with Charlton and Alan Moist to give the stunning Ardanfreaky.

In 1987 the last line on Creag Dubh's Great Wall was nabbed by Steve Monks, narrowly beating Grant Farquhar from Dundee. Cuthbertson meanwhile placed two bolts on Cave Crag producing Marlina. It was still bold, however, and required natural gear too. Several sport climbs have become established and accepted here now.

Further developments in this area included a concerted effort in the mid 1990s by Kevin Howett in the company of Graham Little and others, to climb the remaining lines at Dirc Mhor resulting in three fine E5's on Sentinel Rock, including Fanfare For the Common Man, and a host of others further up the defile. Various people added hard lines to Binnein Shuas with Howett's Wallachian Prince (E5), Rick Campbell's Turning a Blind Eye (E6) and Neil Craig's Wild Mountain Thyme (E4).

The immaculate schist crags hidden in the forest above the village of Weem were developed as a sports climbing venue over the winter and spring of 1997 by George Ridge, Janet Horrocks and others to produce the areas best bolted climbing at all grades.

Access

Both Dunkeld and Newtonmore are roadside crags (for Scotland), so are easily reached by public as well as private transport. Binnein Shuas however requires private transport, or a lengthy journey by rail, limited post bus service and foot-slogging. Hitch-hiking down the A68 Laggan road can take days!

Rail – Glasgow or Edinburgh to Inverness, via Perth, Dunkeld, Pitlochry, Newtonmore and Aviemore.

Bus – Glasgow or Edinburgh to Inverness (Citylink and Stagecoach), stopping at all main towns and villages.

Post bus – Newtonmore to Ardverikie House and Kinlochlaggan post office, once daily all year.

Accommodation

Camping – Dunkeld campsite (016421) at Inver, ½ mile (1 km) W of Dunkeld on the A822 Crieff road; campsite (036416) at Birnham, 1 mile (2 km) S of Dunkeld.

Rough camping: in forest at car-park for Cave Crag, or under the crags themselves (fresh water at Lady Charlotte's Cave). At Newtonmore permission is usually given to camp below the crag or by the river – enquire Creag Dubh hotel (fresh water just W of crag). At Binnein Shuas, rough camping by Lochan na-h-Earba may be possible outside stalking season – enquire at Luiblea Lodge.

Club Huts – 'Jockspot' (Map 35, 667947), Edinburgh JMCS, ½ mile (1 km) W of Newtonmore crags on N side of road: good base for Creag Dubh or Binnein Shuas; Raeburn Hut SMC (on A889 Dalwhinnie to Laggan Road).

Bivvy sites – Dunkeld – Myopic's Cave (Polney Crag), sleeps 6, reached via small track to L of Polney Crag, from which a path cuts up hillside to cave; Lady Charlotte's Cave (Cave Crag), dank with in-situ stream; Binnein Shuas – large basic boulder howffs below the fortress.

Youth hostel: nearest is at Pitlochry or Kingussie.

Provisions

Dunkeld – usual shops and cafés (Dunkeld bakery is good value) early closing Thursdays. Petrol. Newtonmore – chip shop, good café, several hotels, early closing Wednesdays. Kingussie – Spar shop and hotels, giving good value; also petrol: early closing Wednesdays.

Mountain Rescue

Local police – dial 999.

Guidebooks

Highland Outcrops, K. Howett, SMC, 1998

Maps

Landranger Series: for Binnein Shuas-Loch Rannoch, 42; for

Craig-a-Barns, Dunkeld-Pitlochry and Aberfeldy, 52; for Creag
Dugh, Newtonmore-Kingussie, 35.

BINNEIN SHUAS   (468827) Alt. 1,500 ft (500 m) South
facing 🦋 🦋 🦋
A unique crag, famous for its classic slab climb, Ardverikie
Wall. The true potential however is realized in the hard routes
on the roofs of The Fortress. The whole face catches the sun all
day, and the routes on The Fortress stay mainly dry, but those
on the Eastern Sector have continual weeps. The rock is a
strange micro-granite and feldspar – coarse-grained where newly
exposed and in cracks, giving painful jamming. It becomes
horribly greasy when wet.

Approach – From the A86 Spean Bridge – Newtonmore road
near Moy Lodge, a track crosses a concrete bridge over the
River Spean (432830) to Luiblea. Cars can be parked just
before the bridge. Follow the bulldozed track off L (gate
usually locked), to gain older track leading R to the beautiful
sandy bay on Lochan na-h-Earba. A faint path runs up N side
of the loch to the cliff: allow 1 hr 30 mins.

Topography – The huge OHS of The Fortress are obvious, set
above a hanging slab. The L side is a slab tapering up the
hillside to a gully. The most obvious feature here is a white
streak running down the centre of this slab (Kubla Khan). To
the R of The Fortress are the 500 ft (150 m) slabs of the Eastern
Sector. Routes are described L to R.

Descent – The Fortress routes finish on a terrace two-thirds of
the way up the cliff. Above are easy slabs. Either continue up the
cliff and walk well W of it, or follow the terrace L into easy gully.
Descend here, keeping R (looking out) in lower section.

The Fortress
The Gully Wall on the L contains the excellent steep slab of Kubla
Khan. The routes through the central roofs begin from 'the Garden'
above the Lower Slab. Gain the Garden up the grassy corner ramp
bounding the L side of the slab. The R side of The Fortress is
formed by the lower Right Wall containing Delayed Attack.

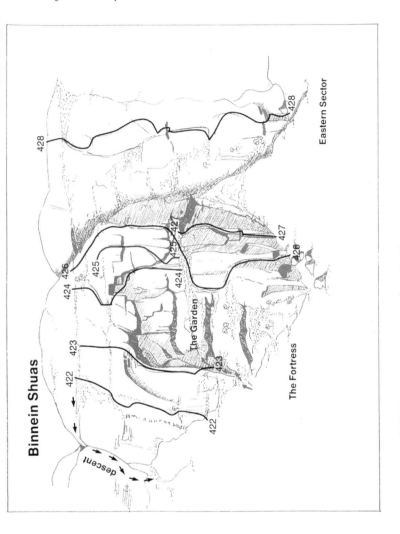

422 **Kubla Khan**   *395 ft (120 m)*   S
FA: *D. F. Lang and G. N. Hunter, 1967*
This climbs the white streak up the slabs on the L side of The
Fortress. A superb second pitch.
Start: Directly below the pale streak down and R of a prominent
vertical dyke.
1. 60 ft (18 m) Climb a steep grooved wall to a grass ledge
   beside the dyke.
2. 150 ft (45 m) The slight grooved slab with a pale streak is
   followed until a scoop can be gained on L.
3. 45 ft (14 m) Leave scoop and climb direct to terrace.
4. 140 ft (42 m) A final pitch can be done on the upper tier if
   desired. From behind obvious large boulder climb an OH,
   then easy slabs to top.

423 **The Keep**   *400 ft (120 m)*   HVS
FA: *D. F. Lang and G. N. Hunter, 1967*
This superb exposed route follows the L edge of the OH-section
of The Fortress. Scramble up the grassy corner/ramp bounding
the L side of lower slabs, which leads to the Garden. Nut belay
beside the rowan tree just below entrance to the Garden.
1. 40 ft (12 m) 4c Above is a crack in L wall of corner, climb
   it to stance on edge.
2. 140 ft (42 m) 5b Continue by grooves in buttress edge to
   gain two parallel cracks. Use both cracks to gain fault
   above. Then past loose block to gain slab. Continue to grass
   ledge.
3. 60 ft (18 m) Slabs above to terrace.
4. 150 ft (45 m) Slabs to top if desired.

424 **Ardanfreaky**   *350 ft (105 m)*   E3
FA: *M. A. Charlton, J. Griffiths and A. A. Moist, 1984*
A stunning climb through some surprising ground, which takes
the line of the R-bounding corner and roofs of the main face of
The Fortress above the Garden. Climbed on sight, so still some
fragile holds.
Start: Below cracks running down from corner.

1. 70 ft (21 m) 5c Up the steepening cracks until possible to move R into corner. Layback up OH-corner to ledge.
2. 60 ft (18 m) 6a Over jug-rich roof above (NR). Tr. L under roof to strange down-pointing spike. Step up to main roof. Tr. L in wild position across wall into base of short hanging corner, which succumbs after a struggle. Exit L on to ledge on arete.
3. 130 ft (39 m) 5a/b Follow diag. crack above to R with interest, then slab to tree belay.
4. 90 ft (27 m) Corner crack above to top.

425 **Wild Mountain Thyme** *150 ft (45 m)   E4 6b*
FA: *N. Craig, G. Latter and R. Campbell 1995*
Climbs a short (but steep) hanging diag. crack to R of Ardanfreaky. Start 15 ft (5 m) R of corner of that route below shallow groove. Climb groove to a bulge. Undercling L to gain base of diag. crack above. The crack succumbs with one huge span and leads into vertical crack on R. Follow this through small OH to top.

The next two routes start up the lower R wall of The Fortress.

426 **The Fortress** *420 ft (126 m)   HVS*
FA: *T. Patey and party, 1964 (lower tier)*
FA: *R. Carrington and J. Marshall, 1970 (upper tier)*
Fine sustained climbing up the R edge of The Fortress. R of the toe of buttress is a jumble of huge boulders next to a large roof, and just above them is a hanging groove guarded by another roof (sapling over lip). Start here.
1. 70 ft (21 m) 5a Up to roof. Layback round L into groove. Up this till possible to tr. L on to large grass ledge.
2. 100 ft (30 m) 5a L of a short R-facing corner are twin cracks. Up these to diag. crack leading R to gain 'the Garden'. Belay near R end.
3. 100 ft (30 m) 5a Gain triangular OH-niche up and R. Exit up fine crack issuing from its roof. R at top and up to large ledge.
4. 150 ft (45 m) Climb the edge to top.

427 **Delayed Attack**   *150 ft (45 m)*   *E3 6a*
FA: *G. Goddard, 1983*
The lower R wall of The Fortress is O H and capped by a roof.
A diag. crack runs down from L end of this roof into hanging
corner. Start below the corner of this crack. Up crack to roof
under corner. Pull over and R into corner (crux). Up this and
fine crack. Fist ripping jams, to gain the R end of 'the Garden'.
Ardanfreaky gives obvious continuation.

Eastern Sector
The next route climbs the line of the coloured streak running
down the huge slab of the Eastern Sector:

428 **Ardverikie Wall**   *620 ft (186 m)*   *S*
FA: *D. F. Lang and G. N. Hunter, 1967*
One of the best routes in the country.
Start: 25 ft (8 m) L of obvious boulder lying against the slab R
of base of hidden gully.
1. 45 ft (14 m) Climb a rib, then into corner line on R to ledge
    under O H. Large flake belay.
2. 120 ft (36 m) 4a Tr. L to rib up steeply on to slab. Take
    easiest line, first R then diag. back L to ledge (flake belay).
3. 120 ft (36 m) 4a Follow flake groove on R to bulge. Step R
    on to ledge. Pull over bulge. Continue up 10 ft (3 m) to small
    ledge and large flake.
4. 110 ft (33 m) 4a Move out R across slab below obvious diag.
    crack (crux), to gain good holds. Slightly L up ill-defined rib
    into shallow L-trending ramp/groove to spike belay in base
    of large scoop.
5. 75 ft (23 m) Climb L side of scoop, then line of R-leading
    overlap to its top. Pull over and L, then slab to terrace.
6. 150 ft (45 m) Finish up easy slabs.

Ardverikie Wall, Binnein Shaus: climber, Billy Hood

CREAG DUBH, NEWTONMORE   (673958) Alt. 1,100 ft
(366 m) South facing 🦋 🦋
Creag Dubh is a justifiably popular crag, offering a multitude of
excellent climbs on generally good rock. This extensive
half-mile mass comprises three apparently broken sections.
Closer scrutiny reveals surprisingly large clean walls, which
offer steep wall climbing on flat or horribly sloping holds, some
well protected, some very bold. The extreme grades here offer
the best quality, and there are plenty to choose from. The lower
grades tend to be vegetated and give few good-quality routes,
but there are some long, enjoyable routes on offer in the middle
grades.

Year-round climbing is possible as the walls tend to dry
quickly, but weeps, particularly in Sprawl Wall and Central
Wall, often result after bad weather.

Approach – 4 m (6.5 km) W of Newtonmore, on the A86,
there is a small car-park below the crag.

Topography – A small path runs from the car-park up the
hillside just R of a fence to the base of Central Wall. The
impressive sheet of contorted coloured rock up to the L is Great
Wall. It continues L, diminishing in height before finally rearing
up as a smooth OH-wall bounded on the L by a waterfall.
Broken ground with several short walls continues L for 200 yds/
metres to reach the lowest buttress (Bedtime Buttress). R of the
fence Central Wall comprises several buttresses, each getting
smaller. Lying in a diag. line R to L above this section is
Sprawl Wall, whose R end is a conspicuous black streaked face.

Great Wall
Steep grass and rocks lie below its base, but directly below the
wall is a palatial ledge to R of a silver birch tree. Routes are
described R to L (see diagram opposite).

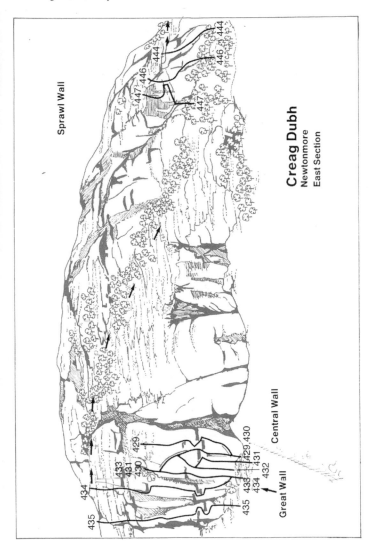

Sprawl Wall

Creag Dubh
Newtonmore
East Section

Central Wall

Great Wall

429 **Strapadicktaemi**   *160 ft (48 m)   E1*
FA: *D. Cuthbertson and R. Anderson, 1976*
This route is varied and well protected.
Start: At R end of ledge 15 ft (5 m) R of a large boulder on the
ledge and below a thin crack leading to a triangular niche
(Inbred).
   1. 75 ft (23 m) 5a Over initial bulge via crack, then follow
      R-slanting crack to a ledge. Short crack above to long narrow
      ledge. Climb through bulging wall above, and L-wards to
      large ledge (old bolt belay).
   2. 85 ft (26 m) 5a Move R to gain L-slanting crack. Up this to
      small OH. Tr. L to gain vertical crack leading to top. Belay
      well back.

430 **Inbred**   *160 ft (48 m)   HVS*
FA: *D. Haston and T. Gooding, 1964*
A tremendous first pitch.
Start: As for Strapadicktaemi, below thin crack.
   1. 70 ft (21 m) 5a Up crack to PR. Move L and then up
      into niche. Pull out R via crack in lip and up wall to
      ledge.
   2. 90 ft (27 m) 4b Over bulge at L end of ledge and follow
      L-trending ledges and ramp to tree.
      Either abseil off or climb slabby wall on L to top (4a).

431 **The Hill (Variation)**   *160 ft (48 m)   E2*
FA: *K. Spence and J. Porteous, 1967*
FA: *D. Cuthbertson and R. Kerr, 1980 (variation)*
The best route on the wall, and very bold for its time.
Start: From the boulder just L of Inbred.
   1. 120 ft (36 m) 5b Climb the orange-coloured wall via slight
      scoop on jugs. Where it gets extra steep there's a PR (poor).
      Straight up into slight groove (the original line tr. R from
      here into triangular niche of Inbred to belay, the exits L
      along lip of bulge back into line of route). Continue over
      bulge into recess. Climb down L into second recess. Exit L
      and then back R and up on good holds to Inbred ledge.

(**Over the Hill E3 5c**, climbs directly up bulging wall above
first recess.)
2. 40 ft (12 m) Follow ramp L to tree. Abseil off.

432 **The Final Solution**   *150 ft (45 m)   E5 6a*
FA: *S. Monks and W. Todd, 1987*
An intimidating line up centre of orange wall just L of The
Hill. The second should remain firmly belayed – jumping into
the void to save a falling leader would be doubly fatal. Gain
blocky ledge at 10 ft (3 m) (just L of The Hill) from the L,
with hard moves. Leave L end of ledge up slight rib. At its top,
step L, then trend R into base of small recess. Place the first
good N R. Stop shaking, and wander with ease directly above to
join The Hill, at its second recess. Finish up this to tree. Abseil
off.

433 **The Fuhrer (Variations)**   *140 ft (42 m)   E4 5c*
FA: *D. Cuthbertson and I. F. Duckworth, 1979*
FA: *D. Cuthbertson, C. Henderson and G. Latter, 1986*
(Variations)
A combination of The Fuhrer and Colder than a Hooker's Heart
gives a route of sustained seriousness and quality, with never
enough protection.
Start: 10 ft (3 m) L of obvious diag. quartz seam to L of
Incubus. Up steeply to tiny ledge (loose block). Up into quartz
seam and try hard to gain sloping holds above and L, follow
these up to block-O H. Stand on block, then R to gain ledge
(P R). Up straight groove above and L to large hold at its top,
and in base of huge expanse of featureless quartz. Up this direct
to ledge. Pull direct through roof above and up faint groove to
tree. Abseil off.

To the L, Great Wall increases in height and forms narrow
buttresses. Directly above the silver birch tree, L of The Fuhrer,
are twin roofs. In the wall above these is a further roof. The
next route is a combination of two climbs giving sustained
climbing wandering across this area from near The Fuhrer,

passing between the twin roofs and finishing beside the upper roof.

434 Organ Grinder/LMF *300 ft (90 m)* *E1*
FA: *K. V. Crocket and C. Stead, 1971 (pitch 1 and 3 – Organ Grinder)*
FA: *F. Harper and B. March, 1971 (pitch 2 – LMF)*
Start: Just L of The Fuhrer.
1. 70 ft (21 m) 5b Up thin crack to handrail. Follow L for 20 ft (6 m) till possible to climb wall above to ledges below R-hand roof.
2. 100 ft (30 m) 5b Skirting L side of roof is a shattered crack. Climb crack, then up wall and slab to large ledge (bolt belay).
3. 130 ft (39 m) 5a Up wall to ledge below prominent roof. Tr. L to niche in L end of roof. Turn on L and up groove in fine position to tree. Belay. Abseil descent.

Defining the L side of the buttress tackled by Organ Grinder is a tree-choked chimney fault. It starts just L of the silver birch tree, and is well defined at first but undistinguished in its upper section (Nutcracker Chimney). The next route climbs the slender buttress L of Nutcracker Chimney.

435 King Bee *450 ft (135 m)* *VS*
FA: *D. Haston, J. Moriarty and A. Ewing, 1965*
The classic of the crag, giving continuous excitement despite some vegetable patches. Start at a rib of rock just L of the chimney.
1. 80 ft (25 m) 4c Up rib to tree. Move L and up corner to roof. Tr. R through roofs, then move back L above lip, then up wall to small stance.
2. 120 ft (36 m) 5a Move L and up wall diag. to gain thin crack in bulge. Move L on to edge (exposed). Climb slight arete to expose belay.
3. 70 ft (20 m) 4c Step R to OH. Pass on R to easy grass ledges.
4. 100 ft (30 m) 4b Climb wall above R tree, then diag. L up good rock to top.

Waterfall Wall

The L-hand section of Great Wall becomes more broken and vegetated to end in an open grassy fault. Waterfall Wall continues L from here, firstly as a two-tiered wall, then rearing up into an 150 ft (45 m) OH-wall, bounded by an impressive free-falling waterfall. The next route starts up the centre of the two-tiered section (see diagram on p. 392):

436 **Smirnoff** *200 ft (60 m)   HVS*
FA: *D. Bathgate and J. Brumfitt, 1965*
A technical route on good rock up a tapering stepped corner facing L above the R end of the tree-lined middle ledge.
Start: Below the centre of the lower tier, below quartz blotch.
1. 50 ft (15 m) 4c Up wall to quartz. Over arch roof to ledge, belay below corner.
2. 150 ft (45 m) 5a Bridge up between wall and tree if you're a gibbon, or up the wall if you can climb a bit harder! Pull over roof and up into base of corner. This leads to terrace. Abseil off trees is recommended, as upper section is broken and horrible.

The stepped OH-corner facing Smirnoff on the L is the general line of **Take Off (VS)**. The prominent quartz streak just L is **Show Off (E1 5a/b)**, which climbs the OH-quartz wall via a groove (PR), and slab above to R end of horizontal roof. It then escapes R to a large block and a groove, above and L of the upper continuation corner of Take Off. The next routes are on the true Waterfall Wall section. They are steep and in a very exciting situation, and are some of the best at Creag Dubh. They all start on the ledge below the wall just R of stream:

437 **Independence** *130 ft (39 m)   E2 5c*
FA: *D. Cuthbertson, R. Kerr and C. Fraser, 1981*
Start: Below the quartz wall on the higher of several ledges. A steep wide crack to R of ledge leads up to ledge beneath roofs. Pull through break in roof L'wards (PR) to foot ledge. Ascend

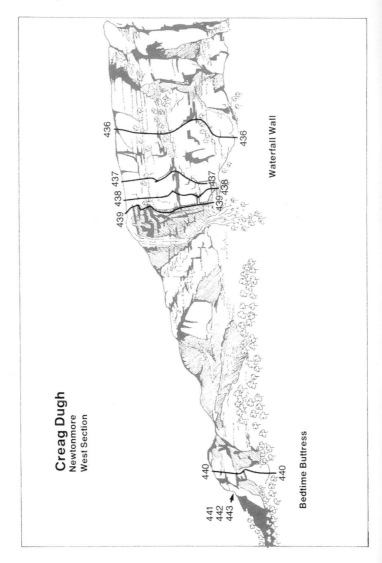

Creag Dugh
Newtonmore
West Section

436

437

439 438 437

439 438

436

Waterfall Wall

440

440

441
442
443

Bedtime Buttress

wall R to gain L-trending fault. Up this till near top, then go R to finish up quartz wall.

438 **Acapulco** *150 ft (45 m) E4 6a*
FA: *D. Cuthbertson and R. Anderson, 1981*
A big bold pitch with much atmosphere.
Start: Below quartzy wall as for Independence. Up the L diag. quartz streak to ledge (bold). Up short undercut groove in centre of wall. From its top trend L to protruding hold in lip of roof. In desperation, finger tr. R along lip to block. Pull over to ledge. Once recovered, climb diag. L into centre of wall, then direct to large ledge. Scramble above, or abseil off.

439 **Wet Dreams/Niagara** *280 ft (84 m) E2*
FA: *G. Shields and party, 1972 (Niagara)*
FA: *D. Cuthbertson and R. Anderson, 1981 (Wet Dreams)*
This climbs the big open corner line in the L edge of the wall.
Start: Below the centre of the wall on large rock ledge.
1. 30 ft (9 m) 5a Climb up a flake in a corner on the R until possible to tr. L across top of the steep quartz wall to ledge below L side of wall.
2. 100 ft (30 m) 5c Up under OH; pull through OH into corner with some difficulty, then follow corner (2 PR) to trees and ledges.
3. 135 ft (40 m) 4c Pull out L onto recessed slab at R end of OH – wall. Up slab to trees. Tr. R through these and up to ledge. Hand tr. (spectacular) L to avoid OH. Arete to top.

Bedtime Buttress
This is the buttress at the far L end of the hillside. It is in three sections: 1) a steep slab, undercut and split by a roof on the R; 2) to L of a vegetated gully, a less distinguished wall ends on a terrace above which, 3) is a long very steep upper tier of immaculate rock. The first route climbs up the steep slab of the first section:

440 **Porn**   *300 ft (90 m)   HVS*
FA: *J. Porteous and M. Watson, 1970*
The most obvious feature is the large diag. quartz streak (Succer
E1 5b). Porn climbs the centre of the wall L of the quartz,
crosses it at mid-height, then goes up wall on its R. Start: 5 ft
(1 m) L of L end of roof at base of the wall beside fallen tree.
1. 150 ft (45 m) 5a Up the short steep wall and thin crack into
   corner on R. Up this and L-trending line of holds under the
   quartz streak, until possible to tr. R into small cave.
2. 30 ft (9 m) 4c Thin crack in steep wall above and L of cave
   to tree belay.
3. 120 ft (36 m) 4a Up slab starting just R of roof and finishing
   up R side of capping roof at top.

The following routes are on the long upper tier of L section.
Gain the terrace below it by scrambling up a short gully, round
to the L of the lower tier. Routes are described L to R as you
approach.
   Descent – Either abseil off tree at top of Case Dismissed, or
descend down hill to L (W).

441 **Case Dismissed**   *75 ft (23 m)   E3 6a*
FA: *D. Cuthbertson and R. Anderson, 1978*
A large boulder sits on the ledge; just to its L is a thin crack.
Gain it direct (hard). At its top step R on to foot-ledge. Struggle
finally with quartz crack on R to block-OH and top.

442 **Ruff Licks**   *80 ft (24 m)   E3 5c*
FA: *D. Cuthbertson and R. Anderson, 1977*
About 30 ft (9 m) R of boulder a quartz crack splits wall. Gain
this via thin crack on L, and up to sapling. Step L; a thin crack
and dwindling strength gain top.

Ruff Licks, Newtonmore: climber, Andy Nelson

443 **Muph Dive**   *80 ft (24 m)   E2 5c*
FA: *D. Bathgate and R. K. Holt, 1965*
FFA: *M. Hamilton and A. Last, 1977*
30 ft (9 m) R of Ruff Licks is a stepped O H-corner. A great
pitch, technical and only adequately protected.

Sprawl Wall
Lying to the R of Central Wall, its most prominent feature is a
black-streaked O H-wall at its bottom R which contains the
routes below. It continues as a quartz-studded wall, with a
jungle-like appearance, running diag. L up hillside.
   Descent – Follow terrace above black-streaked wall well R
and gain *terra firma*, or abseil off tree down black-streaked wall
– 150 ft (45 m) (see diagram, p. 387).

444 **Tree Hee**   *270 ft (71 m)   S*
FA: *H. Small and J. Graham, 1965*
Delightful route on good rock.
Start: 50 ft (15 m) R of lowest point of buttress, R of
black-streaked wall.
   1. 120 ft (36 m) Make a L-rising tr. above an O H-wall on
      quartz knobbles. Then a shallow groove to ledge on L edge.
   2. 150 ft (45 m) Move up and R and fight past a holly tree. Up
      slab to overlap (poor protection), then head up L to gain a
      terrace.

445 **Jump So High**   *270 ft (71 m)   E1*
FA: *F. Harper, A. McKeith and A. Ewing, 1965*
FFA: *G. Shields and party, 1970s*
Start: Below vegetated corner L of lowest point of buttress.
   1. 100 ft (30 m) 4a Up deep vegetated corner to ledge on R of a
      slab.
   2. 120 ft (36 m) 5b Ascend slab L under large roof to small
      ledge at foot of O H-crack in black-streaked wall. Up crack to
      big ledge of Instant Lemon.
   3. 50 ft (16 m) 5a Up the thin O H-crack above and trend R to
      top.

446 **Instant Lemon**   *140 ft (42 m)   E3*
FA: *D. Jameson and D. Cuthbertson, 1980*
A serious wander around the black-streaked wall.
Start: Scramble up broken rocks to a spacious ledge with tree
below L end of wall.
1. 65 ft (20 m) 5b Clamber over large block up on L and
   commit yourself to the handrail leading horizontally R along
   quartz band for 20 ft (6 m). Climb up and R to broken
   ledges. Nut belay at R end.
2. 75 ft (23 m) 5c Follow slim ledge in wall down L until
   possible to stand on it. Move L on small holds and up into
   base of groove. Follow the line up R to corrugated roof and
   finish on its L. Abseil off tree.

DIRC MHOR   (591861) Alt. 2,150 (650 m) North West
Facing 🦋 🦋
This ravine cuts a slice through the hills north west of
Dalwhinnie. It is a giant meltwater channel. The ravine is ½
mile (1.5 km) long, angled north east to south west with the east
side being a virtually continuous line of cliffs and the west side
being more broken. Guarding entrance to the north end is the
most impressive buttress, the 90 m high Sentinel Rock. The rock
is a fine grained micro-granite similar to, but more compact,
than Binnein Shuas.

   Access – Follow the A889 north out of Dalwhinnie to where
the road ascends a steep hill. Park at the top of the hill opposite
a locked forestry gate. Follow the track through the gate to a
stalkers' house. Pass the house and follow the small glen of the
Alt an-t-sluie until the deep gash of Dirc Mhor is seen on the
left. Take a rising line on the left of the ravine to contour into
the base of Sentinel Rock as the base of the defile is full of
deep heather and boulders. 1 hr 15 mins.

Sentinel Rock
This barrel shaped buttress presents a fine front face. L wall is
OH and split by excellent corner of Working Class Hero.
Fanfare For The Common Man and The Scent of a Woman take

lines up front face. The R side of buttress is defined by huge corner in upper half capped by O H where Positive Earth finds a way.

Descent: The routes finish on terrace. Ascend more broken ground above before going over top of hill and walking back round N end of The Dirc.

447 **Working Class Hero**   *285 ft (85 m)*   *E1*
FA: *A. Fyffe, K. Geddes and A. Liddell, 1980*
Takes the fine ramp and corner up the left wall. Start at the toe of the buttress at the base of the big slanting slab.
1. 50 ft (15 m) 4b Climb big slab to belay at top.
2. 100 ft (30 m) 5b Gain and climb small right facing corner in overhanging wall above which leads to the corner line. Follow this spectacularly to niche and exit R onto large ledge.
3. 135 ft (40 m) 4c Step up to large ledge leading diag. R across face to corner. Up this to top of a pinnacle. Tr. diag. R using thin crack and from its end tr. back hard L. Easier rock to top.

448 **Fanfare For The Common Man**   *300 ft (90 m)*   *E5*
FA: *G. E. Little and K. Howett (alt), 1994*
A stunning line on L-hand side of front face. Start at lowest point of the crag as for Working Class Hero.
1. 80 ft (25 m) 5a Climb the easy angled slab (as for Working Class Hero) for 10 m to the point where an obvious flake crack breaks the R wall. Ascend this then traverse R along a fault to step up onto the R-hand of two sloping rock ledges. Move L to take an awkward belay at the junction of the two ledges. Climbing direct from the fault to the ledges via a short steep diag. crack is 6a.
2. 80 ft (25 m) 6b Step up onto the higher ledge then move L to the base of a slight groove. Climb this to a thin horizontal crack. Pull up bulging rock with increasing difficulty to a hairline horizontal crack then make committing moves L and up to gain better holds. A sequence of good holds lead to the large ledge. A brilliant pitch.

3. 70 ft (20 m) 5c Climb easy rock, just R of the belay, to gain
   a R-trending ramp shared with Working Class Hero. Follow
   this to the start of a less distinct L-trending ramp. Ascend
   this to a deep incut hold below bulging rock. Go straight
   over the bulge to a thin flake then move L to gain a flange.
   Move L and up to a ledge.
4. 70 ft (20 m) 4a Climb a L-trending stepped groove then
   scramble back right and up to gain a wide block strewn
   terrace.

449 **The Scent Of A Woman**   *315 ft (95 m)*   *E5*
    FA: *G. E. Little and K. Howett, 1994*
    A magnificent, central line on front face. Start at lowest point of
    crag below OH-corner.
    1. 80 ft (25 m) 6a Climb flake up corner and on up continuation
       OH-corner cutting through OH to rest above lip. Move R
       then up pod on R side of big block to rock pedestal.
    2. 100 ft (30 m) 6b Step R and up into short, shallow R-facing
       groove. Pull out L to gain thin crack which leads up to join
       the L-trending diag. crack of Positive Earth. Follow
       continuation of diag. line up L then tr. Diag. L to under
       obvious isolated OH in centre of face. Climb straight up two
       stepped OH-wall above (hard over lip), then move up R to
       gain rock ramp leading to R end of large ledge.
    3. 65 ft (20 m) 6b Move L up short slabby wall to R-trending
       ramp. From this follow less distinct L-trending rock ramp to
       deep incut hold below bulging rock (as for Fanfare For The
       Common Man). Move R and up to diag. crack in bulging
       wall then up and R again to gain sharp 'edge'. Make difficult
       contorted moves up to undercling. Undercling R-wards to
       gain poor crack in bulge leading up to ledge.
    4. 70 ft (22 m) 4a Climb short slabby corner then broken
       ground leading to block strewn terrace.

450 **Positive Earth**   *285 ft (85 m)*   *E2*
    FA: *M. Burrows Smith and A. Fyffe, 1981*
    This traces a line up R side of front face finishing up obvious

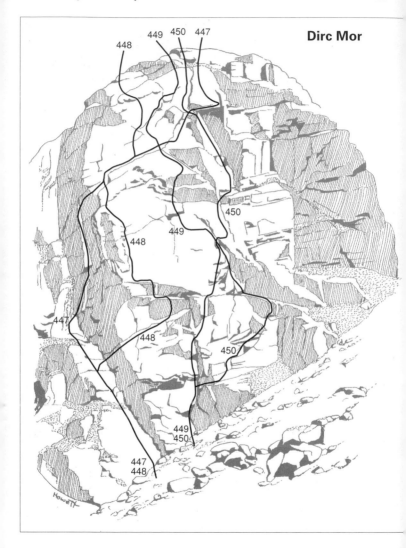

Dirc Mor

big corner. Start at toe of buttress as for Scent of a Woman.

1. 65 ft (20 m) 4c Climb corner till it steepens and escape up R wall onto large slab. Follow line diag. up wall above to belay at obvious large blocks.

2. 65 ft (20 m) 5b Move slightly L into niche. Climb thin L-diag. crack which with hard move to reach good small triangular ledge (junction with Scent of a Woman). Up wall above on good holds leading into base of big corner.

3. 45 ft (15 m) 4a Climb corner and exit L under the OH to belay on large ledge.

4. 100 ft (30 m) 4c Climb fine vertical crack above to finish.

WEEM   (840500) Alt. 700 ft (230 m) South Facing ✗
Just north of the charming holiday town of Aberfeldy in the centre of highland Perthshire, lies a steep hillside covered in ancient woodlands, above the tiny village of Weem. The woods are managed by Forest Enterprise as a Community Woodland and there is a way-marked circular walk. Hidden amongst the trees are several buttresses of fine quality schist. Some are visible from the road. The biggest and best, Weem Rock, is partially hidden. The area has become the most popular sport climbing venue in Scotland, although there is a mixture of sport and gear routes here. The crags are home to a very rare pink flower. Although presently none exist on the routes, climbers are asked to avoid damage to them if seen (information board at Weem Rock).

Crag Layout – There are five developed buttresses in two separate groups. The Secret Garden area at the west end above Menzies Castle and the main Weem Rock at the east end above the village itself. Only the two main buttresses are described here.

Access – For Secret Garden Crag start from the Forestry Commission car park near Menzies Castle. For Weem Rock park at small church in Weem village.

The Secret Garden Crag (837499)
Stays very dry even in poor weather.

Approach – From FC Forest Walks car park follow path up hill to junction (walk marker post). Go L passing behind walled garden where smaller path continues and ascends up hill. Easter Island Buttress (which can be seen from road) lies to right, whilst The Secret Garden Crag lies short slog further uphill. Routes described L to R.

451 **100 Ways To Be a Good Girl**   *30 ft (10 m)*   *6b+*
FA: *J. Horrocks, 1997*
Up limestone-like grey streak at L end.

452 **Batweeman**   *30 ft (10 m)*   *6b+*
FA: *I. Watson, 1997*
Pleasant moves up corner to ledge. Thinner technical wall above with crux near top.

453 **Forbidden Fruit**   *45 ft (15 m)*   *6c+*
FA: *I. Watson, 1997*
R of corner. Up slopey holds to ledge, then steep crimpey journey up blank wall to grasp 'forbidden fruit'.

454 **Faithless**   *45 ft (15 m)*   *6c*
FA: *G. Ridge, 1997*
Follow diag.-seam up to OH, then (illogically) pull R through OH. Finish direct.

455 **The Watchtower**   *45 ft (15 m)*   *6c+*
FA: *C. Miln, 1997*
Up lower 'blank' wall to OH, pull through direct, then slab to finish.

456 **Caledonia Dreaming**   *45 ft (15 m)*   *6c+*
FA: *N. Sheperd, 1997*
Follow thin crack all the way, with wild moves through OH.

Weem Rock
Approach – From church follow small lane past houses. At

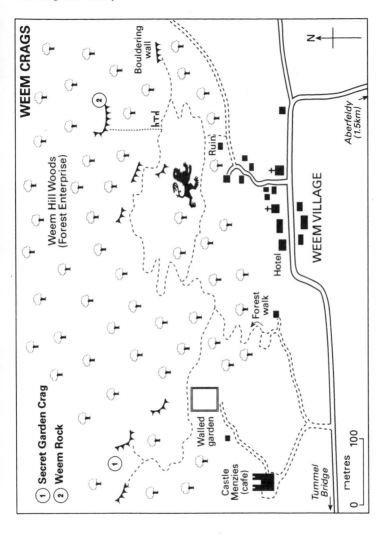

entrance into private garden (gate) take track on R. Just beyond derelict shack small path branches L to gain main 'forest walk' paths. Turn R and follow zig-zag path to small wood carving of table and chairs. Just past this indistinct stony path heads direct up steep hillside, through thick trees to crag.

Topography – Front wall is steep black slab. Round its L arete is viciously OH-wall slanting up hillside above easy-angled rock slab. Main feature is large hanging corner. Further R from black slab wall is more broken, ending in vertical corner capped by OH. All routes are equipped with lower-offs. Routes are described L to R with first routes up centre of OH-wall L of corner starting from raised ledge on rock slab. Extreme L line of bolts starting directly off ledge gives 7a route. Same start but direct is **One Peg One 30 ft (10 m) 7a+**. First route climbs off R end of ledge.

457 **High Pitched Scream**   *45 ft (15 m)*   *7a*
FA: *N. Shepherd, 1997*
Pull slightly R from ledge, then climb direct to the OH, then direct to top.

458 **The Screaming Weem**   *60 ft (20 m)*   *7b*
FA: *G. Ridge, 1997*
Parallel line to High Pitched Scream up faint crack just L of corner. Start at base of rock slab. Strenuous moves gain semi-detached block (handle with care). Use block to gain flake, then pocketed crackline leads to better holds. Hard move gains OH then jugs to top.

459 **The Last Temptation**   *60 ft (20 m)*   *E2 5c*
FA: *G. Ridge and J. Horrocks, 1997*
The excellent hanging corner. Climb steep crack to enter corner with difficulty. Corner to OH. Pull out L and step R to follow crack behind small tree to top.

The following routes are on front face with main black wall containing three excellent lines.

460 **The Real McKay**   *80 ft (25 m)*   *6a*
FA: *D. McKay, 1997*
Line up immediate R side of arete into short corner in arete to
ledge. Wall above to lower-off.

461 **Back To Basics**   *80 ft (25 m)*   *HS*
FA: *G. Nicoll and W. Wright, 1997*
Climbs obvious flake and corner crack to R of arete to reach O H
near top. Step R and finish up hanging crack.

462 **The Long Good Friday**   *80 ft (25 m)*   *6b+*
FA: *I. Watson, 1997*
Climbs L side of black slab. Start from boulder. Up lower slab
followed by thin balance moves through main overlap. Easier to
top.

463 **Confession Of Faith**   *80 ft (25 m)*   *6b+*
FA: *J. Horrocks, 1997*
Excellent route directly up centre of slab with thin moves to
gain very welcome side hold under larger overlap. Blind and
difficult moves above lead to easier ground.

464 **Mannpower**   *80 ft (25 m)*   *6a*
FA: *D. Pert, 1997*
Climbs up wall just L of a small corner to gain line of faint and
intermittent crack line marking R side of black section. Passing
main overlap proves to be crux.

Just R is long L-facing vegetated groove. The wall to R has
some fine easier climbs.

465 **The Soup Dragon**   *60 ft (20 m)*   *5+*
The wall R of corner provides easiest route on crag.

466 **Scoobie Snacks** *60 ft (20m)* *6a+*
FA: *G. Ridge and D. Johnson, 1997*
Immediately R of Soup Dragon and L of raised grass ledge.
Climb steep wall direct onto slab. Follow slab to small OH at
steepening. Pull up R to near top and lower-off on R.

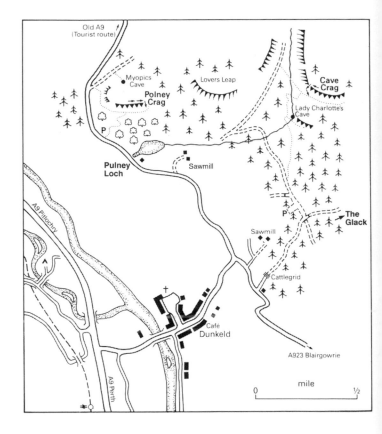

CRAIG-A-BARNS, DUNKELD

Three cliffs, composed of a peculiar mica-schist, lie above Dunkeld on the slopes of the hill known as Craig-a-Barns. Polney Crag, generally slabby on coarse, solid rock, lends itself to pleasant, easy climbing; in particular there are some excellent VS routes. Cave Crag, however, is consistently overhanging with rock varying from solid and angular, as at Polney, to deceptively suspect, and now sports some strenuous and athletic climbs. The cliffs of Lovers' Leap, higher on the hill between the aforementioned crags, are disappointingly vegetated, although routes have been done here. Again climbing is possible all year round.

Approach – See map opposite.

Polney Crag   (435014) Alt. 2,000 ft (600 m) South facing ✘
Topography – This can be clearly seen from the road, and is split into five sections. At the L-hand end, Myopics Buttress OHS above the start of the track branching R off the main road. 50 yds/metres further R is the Ivy Buttress area, characterized by what looks like a huge OH-boulder. Set back to its R are corner lines. Above these lies Upper Buttress containing the hide-out of a local cattle-rustler, Duncan Hogg's Hole. The main crag lies a further 50 yds/metres up and R and continues for approximately 200 yds/metres. It ends at a buttress lying above a huge rockfall, and is split centrally by Hairy Gully.

The first route starts at the Ivy Buttress.

467 **Consolation Corner/Hogg's Hindquarters**   *200 ft (60 m)*   VD
FA: *P. Brian and R. Campbell, 1950s*
An excellent combination of routes on Ivy Buttress and Upper Buttress.
Start: R of the projecting buttress is an obvious clean-cut corner, which is **Ivy Crack** (VS 4b), a well-polished classic. 10 ft (3 m) R of this is a short wall formed by a large boulder.
1. 50 ft (15 m) Up the short wall of the boulder, move L and up a corner to a ledge. Tree belay.

2. 50 ft (15 m) Climb up the two little ribs above. Steep but juggy. Follow the descent path down L to reach another buttress surrounded by trees. The crevasse in its base enlarges to form a cave.
3. 100 ft (30 m) From this recess (Duncan Hogg's Hole) climb a groove. Exit R and move back L on to a rib which is followed to the top. At first strenuous, and then delicate.

Main Crag, Left Hand

As one approaches from the L, one encounters first a recessed area with slabs on the L wall and a rib to the R. Just R of this is a large beech tree next to wall, R of which is an attractive wall crossed with roofs and split by an obvious groove. The lowest horizontal roof contains an obvious break just R of a broken tree stump, leading above to the groove. Three routes share a start through this break which has the name 'Wriggle' painted on it, complete with an arrow for the myopic. The first route begins behind the beech tree.

Descent – Walk R to descend a steep but easy gully between L- and R-hand sections of crag (Hairy Gully).

468 **Beech Wall**   *115 ft (35 m)*   *HS*
FA: *R. N. Campbell (solo), 1959*
Start directly behind beech tree at corner.
1. 50 ft (15 m) 4c. Up corner, then continuation corner on R. Exit L at top to ledge. Up to long ledge and belay on flake on L.
2. 80 ft (20 m) 4a Climb L and up clean wall direct into grass bay. Finish up L-facing groove in L side of wall above.

469 **The Way Through**   *100 ft (30 m)*   *E2 5b*
FA *K. Spence and R. Sharp, 1967*
Climbs through twin OHs between the beech tree and break of Wriggle. Start below OHs. Climb steep wall to lip. Pull diag. R through bulge onto slab beneath next OH. Pull over this direct to cracked blocks below prow above. Climb thin crack through OH of prow then easily to top.

The Groove, Polney
Crag, Dunkeld:
climber, Ben Ankers

470 **The Groove**   *100 ft (30 m)*   *VS 4c*
FA: *R. Smith, 1959*
One of the best routes on the crag.
Gain break by tr. from R, past little bush. Enter groove above
and follow it for a few feet until possible to climb L across wall
to cracked block above L-hand roof. Climb clean-cut groove
leading R to top.
   A variation, **The Rut (VS 5a)**, continues up the vertical
central groove where the last route tr. L. It finishes by last few
moves of that route.

471 **Wriggle**   *100 ft (30 m)*   *VS 4c*
FA: *R. N. Campbell, 1959*
The most popular route on Polney. Climb through the break as
for The Groove, then tr. horizontally R on slab above roof to
gain exposed edge. Follow this edge, joining a final short crack
to top.

472 **Twilight**   *100 ft (30 m)   E1 5b*
FA: *D. Cuthbertson and R. Kerr, 1980*
A fine open route up the impressive wall L of the edge of
Wriggle.
Start: Below holly bush at R side of lower roof. Climb short
groove to L of holly bush and swing out L on to face to join
Wriggle. Step L and climb direct up wall over small bulge, and
finish up bulging nose at top. Poor protection.

473 **Holly Tree Groove**   *100 ft (30 m)   VD*
FA: *R. N. Campbell, 1959*
Pleasant diagonal wander up slabs to R of holly bush. From the
bush follow slanting groove under concave wall to ledge.
Chimney leads to top.

474 **Cuticle Crack**   *80 ft (24 m)   S*
FA: *P. Brian, 1959*
The classic 'VD' of the crag, seeing much traffic. It climbs a
disjointed crack line over blocky bulges just R of the descent of
Hairy Gully.

Main Crag, Right Hand
The buttress continues past Hairy Gully, broken a little with a
huge rockfall lying below it. Beyond this the wall is split into
two tiers by a slim ledge system. The lower tier has a hanging
R-facing groove down its centre and a diag. yellow slab on its ·
L, topped by two prominent noses of rock.

475 **The End**   *110 ft (33 m)   VS*
FA: *R. N. Campbell, 1960*
1. 50 ft (15 m) 4b Up diag. yellow slab L to below bulging
    nose. Step L then up and R on to nose. Then L under second
    nose, and over on to its top. Up L to ledge.
2. 60 ft (18 m) 5a Pull over bulging wall by vertical fault.
    Follow thin crack up slab to roof. Step R then pull over via
    break; easy slabs to top.

476 **Barefoot/Beginning** *110 ft (33 m) E2*
FA: *D. Cuthbertson and P. Hunter, 1980/1976*
One of the best routes at Polney. Both pitches are serious.
Start: Just L of the hanging corner in the lower tier.
1. 50 ft (15 m) 5b/c Up easy slabs to overlap. Pull over to thin flake. Up this, and gain tiny holds leading R to arete. Pull on to small ledge then finish up R arete.
2. 60 ft (18 m) 5b Short R-facing tapering corner on R to its top. Step up and R over lip of steep wall on to slab. Up to roof and pull over. Step L and up to top.

Terminal Buttress (HS 4b) climbs the corner in the lower tier and pulls over the bulging upper tier L of the end into a grass recess, then finishes up the roof crack above.

Cave Crag (439018) Alt. 2,200 ft (700 m) South-west facing 🦋
Although it is hidden in trees, close inspection reveals clean rock and some of the best single-pitch hard routes within easy reach of the big cities. There are two crags. The lower lies just beside Lady Charlotte's Cave, and can be gained by a faint path to its R. The upper, more impressive, tier is described below.

Approach – From Lady Charlotte's Cave take the path up the hillside to its L, which then turns to the R to base of the crag – see map, p. 406.

Topography – There are two sections, the main face (approached first) and a R-hand wall round the prominent prow (High Performance). At the L end a large ramp runs diag. L up the wall. Below the ramp the rock is vegetated; above it, lies Lady Charlotte.

R of The Ramp (HS) a spruce tree grows very close to the crag. R again is a large groove leading to large roofs near top of crag (Mousetrap). R again is the prominent crack of Rat Race. The steep central section now sports numerous bolts and six interconnecting variations on three routes, and sees a constant queue of would-be gymnasts. It is a home from home for visiting limestone lemurs.

477 **Lady Charlotte**   *140 ft (42 m)   E5 6a*
FA: *D. Cuthbertson and M. Duff, 1980*
A serious pitch up the steep blank wall above the base of The
Ramp.
Start: Just R of its base. Step on to wall and up to flat hold at
top of R-leaning groove. Stand on it and hard moves up diag. L
to gain horizontal break (PR on R). Direct up to undercling,
then continuation flake. From its top up and L to ramp, then to
ledge. Thin crack in wall on L above to top.

478 **Ratcatcher**   *150 ft (45 m)   E3 5b*
FA: *A. Petit and K. J. Martin, 1969*
FFA: *D. Cuthbertson and M. Hamilton, 1976*
A badly protected and steep line up the black-streaked groove R
of Lady Charlotte.
Start: At small corner to L of spruce tree. Up wall and corner to
small ledge (PR); up R, then back L to horizontal fault (PR).
Continue up groove to exit R at top.

The big R-facing groove just R of the tree is **Mousetrap (E4
6b)** with the crux through the roof at top. It remains wet a lot
of the time, and has some loose rock.

479 **Warfarin**   *180 ft (54 m)   E2*
FA: *D. Jameson, G. Nicol and M. Duff, 1978*
A brilliant journey L to R under the roofs at the top of the crag.
Start: Beneath a R-facing corner R of Mousetrap.
1. 80 ft (24 m) 5c Up the undercut groove (PR), exit L at its top
   and go L into Mousetrap. Up this for 10 ft (3 m), until
   possible to tr. R to hanging stance.
2. 100 ft (30 m) 5b Step R and climb to corner under roof (PR);
   continue R under roofs with tricky moves in spectacular
   position to finish.

480 **Rat Race** *140 ft (42 m)   E4*
FA: *B. Robertson, 1963*
FFA: *M. Graham (USA), 1978*
A magnificent climb in exhilarating position up crack in centre
of wall R of Mousetrap.
1. 60 ft (18 m) 6a The crack to hanging stance of Warfarin,
   (PR)
2. 80 ft (24 m) 5c Up and R into corner under roof as for
   Warfarin (PR), pull out L through roof on to wall, then up to
   top. Or easier, tr. R out of corner and then up through roof
   on large flange holds (5b).

The Sport Wall
The section of very steep wall R of Rat Race has been
developed as the only part of the crag accepted as a sport
climbing venue. There are 7 variations based on two main lines,
leading to two separate lower-offs. The main lines only are
described.

481 **Marlina** *65 ft (20 m)   7b+*
FA: *D. Cuthbertson, 1986 (Original)*
FA: *M. Hamilton, 1986 (L-hand variation)*
Start up L-hand line of bolts. Move L from 2nd bolt to take
biggest holds up to flange. Tr. R then slightly up into R to L
diag. crackline. Follow this (hard) to lower-off.
Variation: **Hamish Teddy's Excellent Adventure 80 ft (25 m)**
7b+, climbs soaring arete above base of diag. crack mainly on L
side. A popular route and the easiest.

482 **Silk Purse** *80 ft (25 m)   7c+*
FA: *M. Hamilton, 1986 (as Fallout Direct)*
FA: *G. Livingston, 1987 (a linking section to produce Silk
Purse)*
Takes the R-hand line of bolts. At the 4th bolt make hard moves
up and L to join Marlina at base of diag. crack. Follow crack L
to further bolt then pull up R into shallow groove leading to
lower-off

483 **Corpse** *150 ft (45 m)   E2 5c*
FA: *N. MacNiven, 1960 (3* PA*)*
FFA: M. Hamilton and A. Taylor, 1976
A fine pitch; A good introduction to the rock and the harder
routes. Start just R of a brown scoop below R facing corner.
Climb wall into corner. Up this to a slab under roof (PR), tr. R
and climb awkward crack to the top.

484 **Coffin Corner** *100 ft (30 m)   HVS 5a*
FA: *R. Smith, 1960*
The steep section is bounded on the R by this obvious corner.
Climb diag. to enter corner. This gives well protected jamming
and bridging.

485 **High Performance** *100 ft (30 m)   E4 6a*
FA: *G. and R. Farquhar, 1960*
FFA: *D. Cuthbertson, 1978*
This climbs the solitary prow at the R end of the face sitting
above some large boulders. Well protected gymnastics.
Start: From top of boulder gained through cave. The crack in
roof is wild and leads to small OH-ledge. Step R and up to
groove (PR) to top.

Rat Race, Cave Crag, Dunkeld: climber, Duncan McCallum

12   CAIRNGORMS

Introduction
The granite mass of the Cairngorms is split into two separate sections by the long E-W valley of Royal Deeside. The N Cairngorms are essentially a high mountain plateau intersected by deep glaciated valleys, with a distinctly remote feeling. The sheer scale of the area makes climbing here quite serious. This Northern range is renowned for the superb horseshoe of cliffs at the head of Loch A'an (including Shelter Stone and Hell's Lum) but there are numerous others.

The S Cairngorms are dominated by two major mountains, Lochnagar (of 'Old Man' fame) and Broadcairn. The magnificent NE coire of Lochnagar, revered by local Aberdonians, contains a range of routes, including some great low-grade classics, but the huge Creag an Dubh Loch on the E flanks of Broadcairn dominates, with the best middle- and upper-grade routes in a mountain setting in Britain.

In contrast to these remote cliffs the short roadside crags of the Pass of Ballater, located a mere 5 mins drive from Ballater village, gives a dry alternative when the mountains are hidden in mist.

History
In the late 1800s the attention of the SMC was drawn naturally to the broken buttresses of Lochnagar, it being the most accessible and prominently visible cliff from Deeside. Harold Raeburn attempted several lines, even employing abseil inspections, and his main reward was the gully bearing his name. He and other early visitors such as G. R. Symmers and W. A. Ewan of the local Cairngorm Club concentrated on the evil, rotten gullies. However, after beavering away in these and equally appalling chimneys, they realized the possibilities of the ridges. But it was left to James H. B. Bell to complete the classic Eagle Ridge in 1941. This, and the equally fine but overlooked Mitre Ridge of Beinn a' Bhuird (1933) by M. S.

Cumming and J. W. Crofton, were the first milestones in
Cairngorms development.

Bell also visited the Dubh Loch and climbed Labyrinth Route
with Nancy Forsyth, but it wasn't until the 1950s, when a new
and enthusiastic group of Aberdeen climbers appeared, that
climbing development accelerated. They included Mac Smith,
Bill Brooker, Tom Patey, Ken Grassick and Jerry Smith. Whole
untouched cliffs awaited them, but they concentrated on the
winter potential and became masters at mixed climbing in
tricounis nails. Smooth Cairngorm granite must have been very
hostile in such footwear, and consequently rock standards
lagged behind those of the rest of Scotland.

Brooker grovelled up Deep Cut Chimney on Hell's Lum in
1950, and Patey produced the brilliant Square Face in the
remote Garbh Choire of Beinn a'Bhuird, but the first big line on
the open faces was Vertigo Wall on the Dubh Loch. Climbed
by Patey, G. McLeod and A. O'F. Will in 1954 in tricounis and
the rain, it must have been a frightening experience. Their
success fuelled attempts by various parties on the ridiculous
wall to the right, ending when Dick Barclay and Alec 'Sticker'
Thom reached the base of the Giant corner. As they were then
trapped, friends had to haul them to safety from the rim. Their
pegs led to much confusion in the future.

A year later Jerry Smith forced Lochnagar's Pinnacle Face,
using rope-soled shoes – a breakthrough in footwear for the
East Coasters, who all but hung up their tricounis. Brooker and
Grassick repeated it a year later using vibram-soled
kletterschuhe. Gaining confidence, they tackled the Dubh Loch
in 1958 to give Waterkelpie Wall (VS). Another Aberdonian,
Ronnie Sellers, climbed Citadel on the Shelter Stone that same
year and later visited Hell's Lum with G. Annand (Brimstone
Grooves, Hellfire Corner and Devil's Delight resulted). As visits
to the Loch A'an Basin entailed a 10-mile (23 km) arduous
walk from the Derry Gates, the pace of development was
surprising. Patey developed the Crimson Slabs on Creagan a'
Choire Etchachan, with Dagger and Talisman, and later
Djibangi fell to John Hay.

1959 saw the first intrusion from 'outsiders' when J. R. Marshall from Edinburgh climbed the Mousetrap (VS), up the front face of the Dubh Loch (an obvious plum missed by the locals). Soon this became the trade route, despite being regarded as the hardest in the area. Mac Smith produced a guidebook in 1960, but the impetus had left the Aberdeen group by then. Their greatest feats remained their winter routes, and rock standards lagged behind those achieved by the Creagh Dhu. The Cairngorm ski complex was built in 1960, consequently easing access to Loch A'an. Robin Smith paid a social call in 1961 and did the brilliant Clean Sweep on Hell's Lum. But his direct ascent of the Shelter Stone's Bastion in 1962 pushed the grades up two full notches to E1. The Needle was the first of the new breed.

By now the Aberdeen scene had changed, the new generation christening themselves 'The Spiders'. Prominent members were Mike Forbes, Brian Lawrie and Mike Rennie. PA shoes and chrome molly pegs were accepted as standard, and every face in the massif came under fire. Forbes and Rennie succeeded with some aid on the thin crack of the Crimson Slabs to give Stiletto, then Scabbard, as well as a repeat of the Needle in 1966. Rennie also climbed Cougar on the Dubh Loch, but he used sixteen pegs for aid on this committing excursion across the central Gully Wall. Dave Bathgate and other 'Squirrels' from Edinburgh forced the Giant here in an epic ascent with lots of aid and a bivvy, and King Rat fell to Alan Fyffe and J. Bower, again with some aid. However the biggest event of the 1960s was the ascent of Culloden (E2) on the awesome Broad Terrace Wall. Snatched by the English Barley brothers with only four aid points, it was kept secret for many years. Not long before Fyffe produced a new guidebook in 1970 the Dubh Loch had an unprecedented day of activity when Black Mamba, False Face and Goliath fell stimultaneously to rival teams.

After the new guidebook the Shelter Stone was blitzed by 'outsiders', Rab Carrington giving The Pin (E2), Kenny Spence Steeple (E2) and Carrington and Ian Nicholson Haystacks (E2). The latter especially gained a reputation for difficulty. Over the next five years Aberdonians Dougie Dinwoodie and Bob Smith accounted for most of the remaining natural lines up to E2. This was a strong partnership, Smith noted for his power and lack of fear, Dinwoodie for caution and tenacity. Smith's premature death in 1983 was a sad loss to the Aberdeen scene. In 1977 Dave Cuthbertson and Murray Hamilton made a free ascent of Cougar, battling with the ungardened cracks; and the following year Dinwoodie completed Cupid's Bow on the Shelter Stone, also in traditional style with a little aid. This was to be the end of the on-sight era. As the lines became steeper and harder and gardening 'en route' became impractical, abseil inspection took its place. Hamilton's ascent of Sans Fer on the Dubh Loch was a result of this style – a hard free route, which then led to some soul-searching in the Aberdeen camp which didn't even use chalk.

1982 and 1983 were dry summers. Hamilton and Pete Whillance spent days gardening at the Dubh Loch and were rewarded with a selection of climbs of stunning quality and unheard-of difficulty for the area. Startibartfast started it all off in May 1983, and was the first E5. Others followed – Run of the Arrow (E5), a free ascent of Cupid's Bow (E4), Naked Ape (E5), Ascent of Man (E4), Flodden and Cannibal (E6), Dinwoodie finally adopted this style and produced Perilous Journey (E5). He later returned with partner Graeme Livingston to attempt a line on the False Gully Wall: Livingston finally succeeding to produce The Improbability Drive, (E6). A new guidebook in 1985 by Fyffe and Andy Nisbet now contained a healthy selection of modern hard routes.

Developments over the past few years have seen some of the most audacious lines completed. In 1989, on the Central Slabs of Shelter Stone Crag, Rick Campbell free climbed Thor at E5 and began to make an impression on the seemingly blank sections remaining. His on-sight ascent of the blankness left of Run of the Arrow was first to fall as Aphrodite (E7). Free climbing the formerly aided roof of Snipers at 6c he boldly led into the unknown above. Reaching an impasse well above protection when the rope ran out he had to return the next day to complete this scary excursion. He went on to really push the boat out with Realm of the Senses (E7) again on-sight and on which some long falls were taken. This was followed by L'Elisir d'Amore another nasty E7.

On Crag an Dubh Loch Campbell and Paul Thorburn and Neil Craig, over several visits, on-sight led a complete ascent of a line partially climbed by Dinwoodie in 1987 to give The Web of Weird / Hybrid Vigour at E6. Dinwoodie also produced Fer de Lance (E6) in 1987. Lochnagar remained neglected by all but a handful of local enthusiasts who were at home with the dirtier rocks. They produced several good climbs including Wilson Moir's The Existentialist (E6). In 1995 Wilson Moir with Neil Morrison and Niall Ritchie, climbed The Shetlander (E6) on Central Gully Wall and finally in 1997 Thorburn with Gary Latter climbed another line here, on-sight, called The Origin of the Species (E7).

Access
The access points for approaching each cliff differ considerably, and travelling between them would be a problem if relying on public transport. The following is a guide:
Hell's Lum, Shelter Stone Crag – Aviemore
Creagan a' Choire Etchachan, Coire Sputan Dearg and Beinn a' Bhuird – Braemar.
Lochnagar and Broadcairn – Ballater
Rail – Glagow/Edinburgh to Aviemore, daily via Perth and Pitlochry; Glasgow/Edinburgh to Aberdeen, daily via Dunfermline, Perth and Dundee.
Bus – Edinburgh to Inverness (stagecoach) via Perth and Aviemore; Glasgow to Inverness (express coach); Edinburgh to Aberdeen (stagecoach); Pitlochry to Braemar/Ballater (local bus), connection with BR at Pitlochry; Aberdeen to Ballater (local bus – 'heather hopper'); Ballater to Linn of Dee (post bus, once daily); Aviemore to ski complex (local bus daily).

General Accommodation (see also under cliff headings)
Camping – **Northern Cairngorms**: Glenmore Forest site

(975097), Forestry Commission, Loch Morlich; Aviemore
(896124), numerous sites in area. (*Rough camping* – the central
massif is unrestricted; National Nature Reserve – leave no
litter.) **Southern Cairngorms**: Ballater (370953), outskirts of
village by River Dee; Coilachriech (318968) on A93 between
Ballater and Balmoral. (*Rough camping* – by Creag an Dubh
Loch and Lochnagar is tolerated outside the stalking season;
consult the Ranger, Glen Muick.)

Huts – **Southern Cairngorms**: Muir of Inverney (076896),
Cairngorm Club hut. **Northern Cairngorms**: Mill cottage
(844047) MCofS hut, Feshiebridge near Kincraig. Milehouse
(839043) Ladies Scottish Club hut also near Kincraig.

Bunkhouses – **Northern Cairngorms**: Glenmore Lodge,
National Outdoor Training Centre (987095) near Loch Morlich
below Cairngorm offers B&B or self-catering chalets, tel:
(01479) 861 212. Glen Feshie Hostel (849009) Balachriock Ho.
near Feshiebridge, Glen Feshie, tel: (01540) 651 323.
Newtonmore Independent Bunkhouse (713990) in centre of
Newtonmore, tel: (01540) 673 360. Speyside Backpackers in
centre square of Grantown-on-Spey, tel: (01479) 873 514.
Bothan Airigh Bunkhouse (815017) in Insh Village near
Kincraig, tel: (01540) 661 051. **Southern Cairngorms**: Gulabin
Lodge at the Spittal of Glenshee (freephone 0800 783 0423).
Rucksacks Braemar (149914) in centre of Braemar village, tel:
(01339) 741 517.

Bothys – **Northern Cairngorms**: see Crag Introductions.
Southern Cairngorms: Gelder Shiel (256900), 3 miles (4.8 km)
N of Lochnagar.

Youth hostels – **Northern Cairngorms**: Aviemore (893119),
centre of village; Glenmore (976099), by Forestry campsite.
Southern Cairngorms: Ballater (369955), village centre;
Braemar (155910), village outskirts towards Glenshee; Inverey
(078896), nr Linn of Dee, 5 miles (7 km) W of Braemar.

Provisions
Usual amenities in Aviemore (early closing Wednesdays),
Ballater (early closing Thursdays) and Braemar (Spar shop open
all week). Excellent outdoor shop in Braemar. Petrol available
on Sundays at most towns. Cafés at Ballater, Aviemore and
Glenmore (next to Forestry Commission campsite). Bar and
food at Glenmore Lodge, Climbing wall also available here.

Mountain Rescue
Cairngorm Rescue Team – Post: Achnatoul, Aviemore
(897142).
Glenmore Lodge Rescue Team – Posts: Glenmore Lodge
(986094); White Lady Shieling, Coire Cas (995053).
Grampian Police/Braemar Rescue Team – Posts: police station,
Braemar (149914); police station, Ballater (369955); Ranger
Service, Spittal of Glenmuick (308850).

Guidebooks
The Cairngorms Rock and Ice Climbs, Vol. 1, A. Fyffe and A.
Nisbert (Northern Cairngorm) and Vol. 2, A. Nisbert and A.
Fyffe (Southern Cairngorm), SMC. 1995

Maps
Landranger Series: for Lochnagar and Broadcairn – Ballater, 44;
for Northern Cairngorms – Grantown and Cairngorm, 36, and
Braemar, 43.
Outdoor Leisure Series: High Tops of Cairngorm, 3.
Harvey Map Series, Walker and Super Walker, Cairngorm
(covers the northern Cairngorm massif). Super Walker Map
Lochnagar.

Northern Cairngorms
Loch A'an Basin
Loch A'an is surrounded by the mountains Cairngorm, Cairn
Lochan, Ben Macdhui and Beinn Mheadhoin. Around the head
of the loch are four cliffs: Stag Rocks, disappointingly broken,

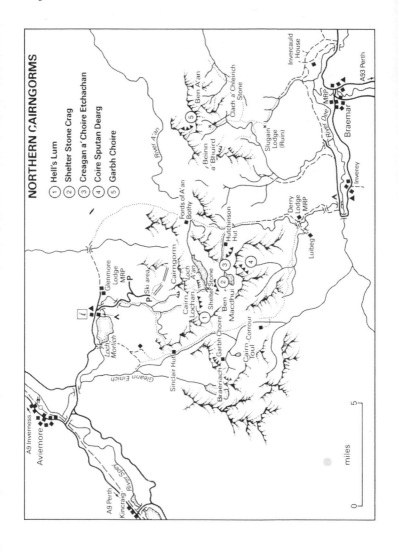

NORTHERN CAIRNGORMS

1. Hell's Lum
2. Shelter Stone Crag
3. Creagan a'Choire Etchachan
4. Coire Sputan Dearg
5. Garbh Choire

and the excellent Hell's Lum lie on the S slopes of Cairn
Lochan. Opposite, the glen is dominated by Shelter Stone Crag,
whose apron of slabs culminates in a huge tower nearly 900 ft
(270 m) above the screes. It is separated from the incoherent
mass of Cairn Etchachan on the L by the deep, obvious
Castlegate Gully.

Approach – From Aviemore (N): via ski car-park in Coire
Cas, then follow the Faicaill a' Choire Chais to the plateau.
Then either down Coire Raibert (path down L bank) to Loch
A'an, or contour SE over the flanks of Cairn Lochan and down
Coire Domhain (passing Hell's Lum Crag to the R): 3 miles
(4.8 km), 2 hrs.

Accommodation – Camping at the head of Loch A'an; The
Shelter Stone (001016), cave under largest boulder below
Shelter Stone Crag; other howffs in the jumble of boulders.
Fords of A'an Refuge (032042), E end of the loch, is
somewhere to run to if a storm brews up!

HELL'S LUM CRAG   (995017) Alt. 2,800 ft (850 m) South
facing
Hell's Lum Crag lies at the end of a vague spur between the
Feith Buidhe and Allt Coire Domhain, the two W-most feeder
streams of Loch A'an. It takes its name from the deep gully of
the Hell's Lum on the L, which cuts diag. into the cliff, and
gives an excellent selection of lower-grade routes. Dries very
slowly.

Topography – The most prominent feature of the cliff when
viewed from below is the deep chimney of Deep Cut. To its R
is the frontal face of steepening slabs and corners. To its L is
the Grey Buttress, a prominent, almost detached tower whose L
side is defined by the deeply indenting Hell's Lum Gully. L of
this are scrappy slabs. The climbs are described L to R: see
diagram, p. 370.

Descent – Down Coire Domhain to the R.

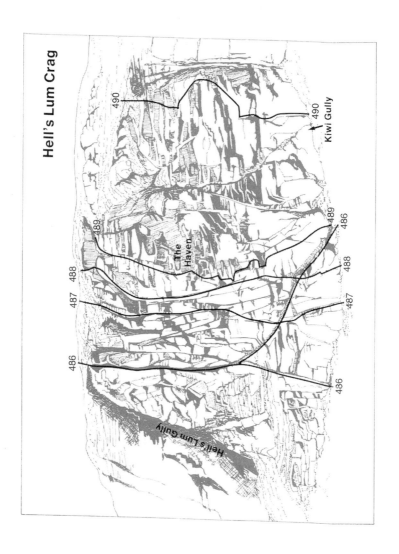

Hell's Lum Crag

486 **Deep Cut Chimney** *450 ft (135 m)* *VD*
FA: *I. M. Brooker and Miss M. Newbigging, 1950*
An impressive slit. Much vegetation in the lower half, but this
is avoidable in the upper chimney by wild back and footing.
Start: By either climbing directly from below chimney, or by
easy terraced fault cleaving slabs from the R. Once in chimney,
climb back and foot, thus avoiding the jungle. About 150 ft
(45 m) from the top the chimney cuts deep into the bowels of
the cliff and chockstones are wedged out in space. Back and
foot outwards below final chockstone-OH, and reach the pile of
jammed boulders. The finish comes with startling suddenness.

Frontal Face
Steepening from bottom to top with sound clean rock. Some of
the routes are persistent drainage lines, but the climbs are
graded for dry conditions (only fast-drying routes are included).
From Deep Cut Chimney the first obvious feature is the long
L-facing Hell Fire Corner (VS) in the centre of the face.
Further R is Kiwi Gully, slanting L in its lower section and
deepest at two-thirds height, then fading near top. R again are
slabs with a more horizontal structure of overlaps leading
towards a shallow watercourse fault near R end (The Escalator).

487 **Salamander** *475 ft (143 m)* *HVS*
FA: *D. Dinwoodie and J. Tweedle, 1971*
A direct line, L and parallel to Hell Fire Corner. Fine climbing
but slow drying.
Start: Below an obvious R-facing corner in lower slabs about
150 ft (45 m) L of start of the diag. terraced fault of Deep Cut
Chimney.
1. 130 ft (39 m) 4b Climb into corner which leads to ledge.
   Continue in same line through steeper section by bulging
   slab to reach platform.
2. 60 ft (18 m) Easy rocks to diag. terraced fault.

Salamander, Hell's Lum Crag, Cairngorms: climber, B. Williamson

3. 60 ft (18 m) 5a Twin cracks up steep slabs L of an obvious corner to a platform.
4. 60 ft (18 m) 4b Through overlap by short black corner then follow crack to obvious recess.
5. 90 ft (27 m) 4b Continue up to shallow groove and follow this break through upper OHS, by a striking chimney slit.
6. 75 ft (23 m) Continue up open funnel to easy ground.

Next is **Hell Fire Corner (VS 4b)**, the large L-facing corner line with small subsidiary corners just L of its main line, then a chimney through the overlap at the top. Unfortunately it is a drainage line. Moving R from Hell Fire Corner is the cleanest and highest sweep of rock. The next route is considered as the finest here:

488 **Clean Sweep**   *570 ft (171 m)   VS*
FA: *R. Smith and G. Tiso, 1961*
A route of many adjectives, taking the pink leaning corner overlooking Hell Fire.
Start: at a green whaleback buttress just L of the base of the diag. terraced fault of Deep-Cut Chimney.
1. 90 ft (27 m) 4c Take the corner on the L of the buttress a short way to gain a groove. Up the groove to cracks which lead to top of buttress and the diag. fault.
2. 150 ft (45 m) 4a Step over the fault and climb slabs and corners to a huge block belay below the prominent pink corner.
3. 150 ft (45 m) 4c The corners past two cracks, and a couple of small roofs and the continuation fault. Superb technical crux, well protected on rough clean rock.
4/5. 180 ft (54 m) 4b Continue by cracks, corner and bulges up the round grey edge above to top. Continuously interesting.

489 **The Omen**   *525 ft (157 m)   HVS*
FA: *A. Liddell and M. Burrows-Smith, 1976*
A fine climb up a good natural line just to R of Clean Sweep.
Start: At base of diag. terraced fault of Deep Cut Chimney.

1. 90 ft (27 m) 5a Gain the slab above the short vertical wall and follow it in a L-rising tr. to a ledge system.
2. 110 ft (33 m) 5a Go L up, then back R on the ledge above. Climb a thin crack in slab to below obvious L-facing corner (just L of huge block in triangular niche). Climb corner (unprotected) to gain huge block belay of Clean Sweep.
3. 145 ft (45 m) 4b Climb crack 15 ft (4 m) R of Clean Sweep. Move up and R over a bulge, then a quartzy crack to reach the Haven (a series of grass ledges).
4. 90 ft (27 m) 4c Climb to the top of a huge block, then cracks in pink rock. Easy rocks to top – 90 ft (27 m).

Between here and Kiwi Gully lie several routes. The best known is **Devil's Delight (HS)** which climbs a vegetated fault to obvious L corner, then through a large triangular niche and the Haven to a shallow chimney fault in steep upper rocks. R of Kiwi Gully the slabs are clean and drier, crossed by overlaps. On their R is wet gully of **The Escalator (M)**.

490 **Auld Nick**   *510 ft (153 m)*   S
FA: *G. Brown, I. Houston and I. Small, 1963*
A pleasant route up R centre of clean slabs.
Start: 30 ft (9 m) R of Kiwi Gully, at obvious crack.
1. 150 ft (45 m) The crack and continuation corner to below first overlap.
2. 150 ft (45 m) The R-facing corner in the overlap and crack in slab to next bulge. Go R in horizontal crack, then diag. R to belay.
3. 60 ft (18 m) Climb L-facing corner by series of steps to nut belay below R tapering roof.
4. 150 ft (45 m) Go past the roof on R. Continue L, passing big block to gain large ledge. Climb wall above by a thin crack, and finish either side of big grey block. Scramble to finish.

SHELTER STONE CRAG   (001013) Alt. 1,980 ft (600 m)
North-east facing
This is split into three distinct sections. The highest, on the R, is

the Bastion; in the centre is a smooth area of undulating slabs bounded on the L by the grassy fault of Sticil Face, and separated from the Bastion by the vertical fault of Citadel. L of Sticil Face is the long, broken Raeburn's Buttress, then Castlegate's Gully which separates Shelter Stone Crag from Cairn Etchachan.

Central Slabs

This magnificent sheet of rock now forms the centrepiece of the cliff, and contains the best routes.

Topography– They hang in the middle of the face with grass terraces above and below (High and Low Ledge). A broken tier of slabs guards entry to Low Ledge. The huge diag. diedre of Thor dominates the slabs, its lower end finishing in an overlap running L. A L-facing corner descends from the base of the diedre to Low Ledge, and several routes start here. Gain Low Ledge from the L, up grass.

Descent – 1) Scramble up the grass fault of Sticil Face in the wall above High Ledge, to gain deep 100 ft (30 m) chimney to finish. 2) Two long abseils down Pin. 3) Abseil down Run of the Arrow.

491 **The Missing Link**   *395 ft (119 m)   E4*
FA: *D. Cuthbertson and D. Jameson, 1981*
This free climbs the bottom half of Thor and branches out R up a lower diverging overlap that saw many free attempts and was provisionally named Loki. Sustained and serious on the crux pitch.
Start: At base of L-facing corner of Thor.
1. 110 ft (33 m) 5a Climb the corner to a small OH. Move L, then up to below main overlap. Nut belay above loose flake.
2. 70 ft (21 m) 5b Up the Thor diedre past a niche (Run of the Arrow belay) to a hanging belay just at base of start of the subsidiary overlap on R.
3. 150 ft (45 m) 5c Tr. R to gain the start of thin overlap. Up with difficulty and boldly to junction with large roof. Pull

Shelter Stone Crag

over and follow continuation fault (2 PR – poor) to reach hollow horizontal flake. Tr. R on this and swing round rib into Pin. Belay a few feet higher.

4. 65 ft (20 m) 5a Up the continually interesting crackline of Pin to High Ledge.

492 **Run of the Arrow**   *330 ft (99 m)*   E5
FA: *P. Whillance and T. Furnace, 1982*
Hard and serious, up some surprising ground. It takes a faint crackline in the slab above the Thor diedre L of Cupid's Bow. Start: From Low Ledge as for Missing Link below corner.

1. 30 ft (9 m) Easily up R to ledge, poor belay.
2. 105 ft (31 m) 5a Move L round rib and follow crack in the rib into base of Thor diedre. Up this for 15 ft (4 m) into a small niche (PB).
3. 110 ft (33 m) 6b Swing out of diedre L through the break. Move L across slab to gain thin crackline, follow this past loose hold. Up and R across slab to small ledge. Up to gain flake. Hard moves L and up on to small ledge in scoop. Step L round rib and up crack to sloping ledges (PB).
4. 75 ft (23 m) 5b Follow obvious R line to join Cupid's Bow and finish up its flake and slabs above.

493 **Cupid's Bow**   *275 ft (83 m)*   E4
FA: *D. Dinwoodie and R. Renshaw, 1978, (4 pa)*
FFA: *M. Hamilton and R. Anderson, 1982*
A superb and much sought-after line up the bow-shaped corner above the upper part of Thor diedre. Technical and only adequately protected.
Start: As for Run of the Arrow.

1. 30 ft (9 m) Up R to a ledge. Poor belay.
2. 125 ft (38 m) 5b Gain a grassy bay above and climb out of this via cracks on L. Move R to a shallow corner which is climbed to pull out L on to rib. Go up and L to Thor diedre. (Hanging PB as for Missing Link.)
3. 100 ft (30 m) 6b Climb up the diedre past small ledge until the diedre forms a short section of a corner. Swing out L on

to ledge below The Bow. Climb The Bow (PR) with
difficulty, then the L arete. Intricate and absorbing climbing.
Up to the bulging section where good holds appear. Above
The Bow tapers and curves over R. Step out L on to a very
small ledge, and up very thinly to good break (Run of the
Arrow). Step R a little to belay.
4. 50 ft (15 m) 5a Climb the flake out L and slabs to top as for
Run of the Arrow.

494 **Thor** *425 ft (125 m)* E5
FA: *R. Campbell and N. Craig, 1989*
A stunning route both in the climbing and the line. Start at base
of L-facing corner leading to main diedre.
1. 145 ft (40 m) 5b Climb the corner till under OH. Tr. R into
main diedre and up this to small stance (PB).
2. 80ft (25 m) 6b Continue up diedre to below overlap. Gain
good side-pull in alcove (PR) and cross it (crux) to reach
flake (PBS).
3. 150 ft (45 m) 6a Continue R under overlap (PR) to jug and
good horizontal crack (PR) above overlap. Hand tr. lip of
overlap to gain series of rising ledges (old PRS) leading R
into crack-line of The Pin. Up this to belay.
4. 50 ft (15 m) 4c Continue up crackline to high ledge or abseil
off down The Pin.

495 **Realm of the Senses / L'Elisir d'Amore** *460 ft (139 m)* E7
FA: *R. Campbell and G. Latter, 1993 (Realm.)*
FA: *R. Campbell (unseconded – top roped first), 1994
(L'Elisir . . .)*
A combination of two very hard routes giving one of the
hardest routes of its type in Scotland. Start as for Cupid's Bow.
1. 30 ft (9 m) Up R to ledge below steep wall.
2. 100 ft (30 m) 5c Gain grassy bay and pull out R to follow
natural R-curving line leading into The Pin first belay.
3. 120 ft (35 m) 6c Climb L-facing corner up and L to overlap
(hard). Move L (2PRS but no holds!) to join Missing Link.
Follow this above overlap to PRS and hollow flake. Place

runners above OH above. Reverse couple moves and tr. L above overlap to flake leading to Thor. Belay.
4. 45 ft (15 m) 6a Follow Thor diedre to belay at the R side of alcove.
5. 165 ft (50 m) 6c Tr. under OH to PR and hard span R as for Thor to easy ground then follow white scar above OH gain PR in pocket 20 ft (6m) above. Move R and up to hanging flake (place crucial NR). Move back to PR then hard moves up L to pale streak. Move L up a flake to its top. Desperate L again to foothold in red streak. Precariously up streak to poor pockets leading L to short groove. L wall of groove, then easy ground. Tr. 65 ft (20 m) L to belay at top of Run of the Arrow.

496 **The Pin**   *280 ft (84 m)   E2*
FA: *R. Carrington and J. Gardner, 1968 (2 PA)*
FFA: *B. Campbell-Kelly and M. Kosterlitz, early 1970s*
The striking crackline near the R-hand side of the slabs. Excellent route.
Start: High up on the R of Low Ledge, immediately below the steep crack.
1. 60 ft (18 m) 5b The crack to a stance on L.
2. 70 ft (21 m) 5b Continue up the crack, crossing an awkward bulge. Trend R then back to the crack and good thread belay.
3. 150 ft (45 m) 5a Go up and climb the OH-wall to the poor stance of Missing Link. Continue up to High Ledge.

The Bastion
A very impressive tower of clean rock, unfortunately split at several points by grass terraces allowing some interconnection of routes, but not detracting from the stature of the climbs. Reasonably quick drying.
  Topography – Separating the central slabs and the Bastion, a fault (Citadel, VS), runs from just L of the toe to the summit and is generally scrappy except for its final pitches bounding the

The Pin, Shelter Stone Crag, Cairngorms: climber, Alan Russell

L edge of the upper section. To the R are two R-facing corners, Steeple taking the L-hand one. The R-hand corner is the finish of the Needle which starts up the boiler-plate slabs R of the corners at the base. The main cliff is bounded further R by more broken and grassy rock, before turning into the deep Pinnacle Gully.

Descent – Down the hillside well to the N (Castlegate's and Pinnacle gullies are loose).

497 **Steeple** *815 ft (246 m) E2*
FA: *K. Spence and M. Watson, 1968, (P. 1–6)*
FA: *J. Porteous, K. Spence and M. Watson, 1968 (P. 7–9, 2 PA)*
FFA: *J. Lamb and P. Whillance, 1975*
The initial attempt was thwarted below the final bastion and the team returned to climb it later in the rain. That's keen! Sustained, at a reasonable grade.
Start: Below the second R-facing groove 10 ft (3 m) up the small grassy gully on R.
1. 100 ft (30 m) 5a Climb the corner crossing two small overlaps and belay beyond the second, R of the step in corner.
2. 85 ft (26 m) 5a Climb the slabby groove surprisingly strenuously and with much interest. Exit L at top to grassy terrace.
3. 150 ft (45 m) Follow walls and grass ledges to belay on terrace below a steep line of weakness at L end.
4. 115 ft (35 m) 5c Follow steep fault line to below OH. Move R with difficulty to gain ramp. Follow this to ledges below corner with many cracks in L wall.
5. 150 ft (45 m) 4c Climb the obvious layback cracks up and R to foot of obvious and impressive corner. Large ledge with large blocks. Boulder belay.
6. 140 ft (42 m) 5b Climb the corner, initially most awkward, to its top. Exit L to ledge.
7. 75 ft (23 m) 5a Above is thin crack, surprisingly difficult, which leads to easier cracks and ledges to top.

498 **The Spire**   *730 ft (219 m)   E4*
FA: *M. Hamilton and R. Anderson, 1982*
Excellent climbing between Steeple and The Needle, starting
from the grass terrace at the top of their 3rd pitch.
Start: Below the obvious slim groove midway between Steeple
and Needle's crux pitches on the terrace (about 30 ft (10 m) R
of Steeple).

1/2. 185 ft (56 m) 5a as Steeple.
3. 150 ft (45 m) 5c Gain the groove and follow to bulge at top.
   A crack leads out R on to ledge (Needle belay). Intricate.
4. 30 ft (9 m) Directly above over ramps to belay by large
   pointed block.
5. 150 ft (45 m) 6a Above is obvious hanging ramp leading R.
   Gain it and follow to cracks. These lead to grass ledge.
6. 140 ft (42 m) 5b An airy and spectacular pitch. Trend up
   R'wards across wall via grooves, to the arete overlooking
   Steeple. Up to ledges.
7. 75 ft (23 m) Finish as for Steeple.

499 **The Needle**   *840 ft (252 m)   E1*
FA: *R. Smith and D. Agnew, 1962*
A fine achievement for its time and the first of the long modern
routes: a classic. Low in the grade, but good.
Start: At easy angled slabs about 100 ft (30 m) R of Steeple
directly below the L end of an obvious L-to-R diag. fault that
runs steeply through the slabs.

1. 100 ft (30 m) 4b Climb straight up the slabs with a step L on
   to a nose and up a flake to a ledge.
2. 150 ft (45 m) 5b Excellent pitch. Climb diag. L up the slab
   to gain the R of two converging cracks which form the
   conspicuous fault. Continual interest, to a short steep wall
   near top. Climb the L rib of the recess above to gain R end
   of the terrace.
3. 75 ft (23 m) Cross the terrace and up a slab slightly L till a
   flake leads to a huge block.
4. 110 ft (30 m) 5b Climb up L for 15 ft (4 m) then move R on
   to flake crack in corner. From its top a narrow ledge leads L

to a crack up the bulging wall. Strenuous moves gain the recess above, and then a stance.

5. 65 ft (20 m) Exit from L end of stance to gain ramp of Steeple. Follow to ledges below a corner. Step down R on to ledges, to belay.

6. 110 ft (33 m) 5a From R end of ledge climb L-facing corner by crack for thin fingers, and break out R to ledge. Up by blocks and ledges L'wards to long ledge.

7. 65 ft (20 m) Go up the grooves L'wards to foot of impressive main corner.

8. 105 ft (31 m) 5a The Needle – a chimney – to ledge.

9. 70 ft (21 m) Continue up the continuation gully threading a pile of chockstones to emerge on the plateau.

CREAGAN A'CHOIRE ETCHACHAN   (016997) Alt. 2,500 ft (850 m)   East facing

A fine crag situated on the E slopes of Creagan a'Choire Etchachan, a N satellite of the broad mass of Derry Cairngorm. It is just off the well-trodden path up to Ben MacDhui from Deeside. It presents a striking bold face of granite about 350 ft (105 m) high and contains some classic routes. Receives early sun, but takes a few days to dry out completely.

Approach – From Braemar: 700 yds/metres beyond Derry Lodge turn R at the public telephone and cross a bridge. The path climbs up Glen Derry through the forest. Beyond the woods, follow the main path branching L into Coire Etchachan: 5 miles (8 km); 1 hr 45 mins. From Aviemore: From the ski complex follow walk to Shelter Stone. Follow path over the Beinn Mheadhoin – Cairn Etchachan col to the outflow of Loch Etchachan, and descend to the cliff: 5.5 miles (8.9 km), much ascent and descent unless the chairlift is used; 2 hrs 45 mins.

Accommodation – Hutchinson Memorial Hut (024998), at base of crag, earth floor but ideally situated; Bob Scott's bothy (043931), on bank of river, 100 yds/metres S of Derry Lodge, 3 miles distant from crag.

The Steeple, Shelter Stone Crag, Cairngorms: climber, Murray Hamilton

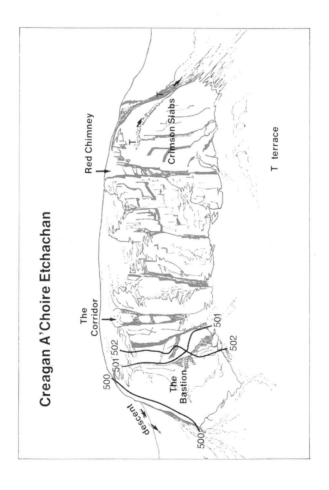

Topography – The large buttress at L side is the Bastion and its R-hand side is a slabby trench, the Corridor. R of this the crag is a less attractive series of buttresses and gullies. Above and R of the third buttress are prominent OHS. Beyond these is a deep chimney (Red Chimney) beyond which comes the finest feature of the cliff, the Crimson Slabs.

The Bastion
There are two major features, the easy angled crest on the L, overlooking a loose horrible gully (Forked Gully) and a very impressive gable wall overlooking the corridor. Between these, the Bastion is a mass of slabby ribs and grooves.

Descent – Avoid Forked Gully. Try grass and scree further L.

500 **Quartzvein Edge** *360 ft (108 m)* M
FA: *K. Winram, G. C. Greig and M. Smith, 1952*
Popular on reasonable rock up the crest.
Start: At the foot of Forked Gully beyond a detached block.
Climb a 10 ft (3 m) wall characterized by an inset piece of quartz.
Follow edge at first, then wander up slabs which develop into a shelf skirting a false tower on L. Scree funnel leads to top.

501 **The Talisman** *300 ft (90 m)* HS
FA: *W. D. Brooker and K. A. Grassick, 1956*
This excellent route, steep and clean, follows the R edge of the Bastion up the gable wall. Dries quickly.
Start: At platform beside huge block set against the wall 30 ft (9 m) up The Corridor.
1. 110 ft (33 m) Climb crack behind belay to ledge. Move R and up till possible to tr. L across huge slab to crest.
2. 60 ft (18 m) 4a Detour L round an OH and up corner to regain crest. Move L to groove and up short OH-corner above to stance (block belay).
3. 130 ft (39 m) Follow crest directly starting on R side. Scramble to plateau.

502 **Talking Drums** *345 ft (104 m)   E2*
   FA: *A. Nisbet and S. Kennedy, 1981 (Pitch 1)*
   FA: *C. MacLean and A. Nisbet, 1986*
   Sustained and well protected with sensational finish across the
   Talisman head-wall.
   Start: At lowest rocks L of Talisman.
   1. 120 ft (36 m) 5b Climb corner to overlap (PR), then
      continuation corner on L. Tr. R immediately across
      steep wall on good holds to arete. Up this to Talisman
      stance.
   2. 110 ft (33 m) 5a Obvious thin crack leading diag. R past
      triangular block and through girdling bulge. Move slightly L
      and up to poor stance under head-wall. Gain base of
      R-slanting shallow groove R of Talisman arete direct via two
      small scoops. Climb groove to good foothold at top. Move R
      and up on hidden holds to hand tr. line R to mantelshelf.
   3. 115 ft (35 m) 5b Make delicate move up to gain small ledge
      (PR). Swing down R and across wall to base of corner.
      Follow this to top.

   Crimson Slabs
   A spectacular 400 ft (120 m) sweep of clean pink slabs
   providing some of the best rock-climbing in the area. Bounding
   the L side is Red Chimney. The slabs are split by two corners,
   Dagger on R and Djibangi on L. These are slow to dry, being
   drainage lines, but the others are quicker.
      Descent – R of the slabs beyond a line of small crags. For
   those wishing to avoid the sometimes inferior upper tier, exit R
   along steep terrace beginning from the platform above the top
   of Dagger corner: see diagram, p. 444.

503 **Scalpel Direct** *350 ft(105 m)   E1*
   FA: *D. Dinwoodie and G. S. Strange, 1977*
   Between Red Chimney and Djibangi is large bow-shaped
   overlap. Sprouting from its lower R-end, shallow tilted grooves
   run up the wall, the line of the route.
   Start: 10 ft (3 m) R of Red Chimney.

1. 90 ft (27 m) 4b Climb arete just R of twin grooves to large platform belay below overlap.
2. 150 ft (45 m) 5b Step on to edge of overlap. Straight up over bulge, then step R to small ledge. Continue directly up shallow groove to overlap. Step R to place N R S then return and make rising tr. L (crux) to an arete formed by a large curving corner. Go up cracks directly above to grass ledges.
3. 130 ft (39 m) Easier rocks lead up and R to grass at top of Djibangi Pitch 3. Ascend broken rock to terrace.

504 **King Crimson**   *410 ft (123 m)   E3*
FA: *A. Ross and G. S. Strange, 1984*
A fine serious eliminate on perfect rock between Scalpel and Djibangi.
Start: At grassy alcove beneath main corner, as for Djibangi.
1. 110 ft (33 m) 4c Climb diag. up flake/crack on L to bulge. Turn it on L and gain small corner set in centre of slabs (Djibangi). Follow it, then easy rocks R to ledge below main corner as for Djibangi.
2. 150 ft (45 m) 5c From L end of ledge climb direct up pink rock to under shallow curving overlap (N R). Go L on to grey rock, then up to below notch in main overlap. Move R through it just R of notch. Straight up and pull L into small groove. Belay above on cracked slabs.
3. 150 ft (45 m) 5a Up cracked slabs direct going through break in overlap and passing R of large block. Scrambling leads to top.

505 **Djibangi**   *420 ft (126 m)   VS*
FA: *J. Y. L. Hay, R. Wiseman and A. Cowie, (2 PA) 1956*
FFA: *Unknown*
The L-hand of the big corners is incorporated in this wandering route which is slow to dry.
Start: In grassy bay below corner line.
1. 125 ft (38 m) Follow diag. line out L to large platform of Scalpel. Trend R into short corner set in centre of slab

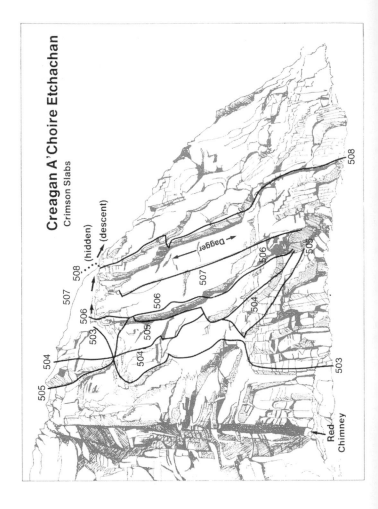

Creagan A'Choire Etchachan
Crimson Slabs

(junction with King Crimson), then out R to ledge below corner.

2. 110 ft (33 m) 4c The corner over overlap. Exit R near top to stance.
3. 80 ft (24 m) Step back L into corner. Up a short way, then trend L, heading for obvious large L-facing corner in upper tier.
4. 115 ft (35 m) The groove to huge block. Pass it, then rib to easy ground.

506 **Sgian Dubh**   *330 ft (100 m)   HVS*
FA: *A. Nisbet and M. Bridges, 1978*
This climbs directly into Djibangi corner then up its R arete. Exposed, and dries quickly.
Start: In Djibangi recess.

1. 105 ft (32 m) 4c Exit from recess on its L side following a series of L-facing shallow corners leading to ledge below corner.
2. 105 ft (32 m) 5a Climb the arete with a short excursion of 5 ft (1½ m) out R at mid-height, to stance on rib.
3. 120 ft (36 m) Scramble up grassy grooves R to terrace.

507 **Stiletto**   *330 ft (100 m)   E1*
FA: *M. Forbes and M. Rennie, 1966*
FFA: *D. Dinwoodie and A. McIvor, 1976*
Well protected but sustained thin crack between Djibangi and Dagger. A weep on the second pitch is slow to dry.
Start: Below the crack.

1. 75 ft (23 m) 4b Up lower broken crack to below main crack.
2. 130 ft (39 m) 5c The Crack with two particularly 'tricky bits'.
3. 125 ft (38 m) 4a Tr. R into Dagger, then up to terrace.

The corner to R is **The Dagger (VS 4c)**. Grassy and usually wet.

508 **Scabbard/Delicatessen**   *455 ft (135 m)*   *VS*
FA: *M. Rennie and M. Forbes, 1966 (Scabbard)*
FA: *A. Nisbet, R. F. Allen, B. Davison, S. Kennedy, G. P. Muhlemann, 1983 (Delicatessen)*
Fine exposed route up rib R of Dagger. Dries very quickly.
Start: At clean-cut R-facing corner directly below the rib.
1. 65 ft (20 m) 4c Move a little L to a stance level with the Dagger corner.
2. 105 ft (31 m) 4c Climb obvious finger crack. Further cracks up rib to small overlap. Continue up edge to gain huge spike belay of Dagger.
3. 165 ft (50 m) 4b Move R. Descend a little and pull out R on to edge of secondary corner system. Climb series of cracks and blocks on R of edge to terrace.
4. Walk down terrace for 60 ft (18 m) to below clean cracked arete on R side of upper slabs.
5. 130 ft (39 m) 4c Climb the arete direct.

COIRE SPUTAN DEARG, BEN MACDHUI   (003991) Alt. 3,300 ft (990 m) South facing
The S-facing crag is a rarity in the Cairngorms, and along with Hell's Lum 'Sputan' has an unusually friendly atmosphere. The coire lies at the head of Glen Luibeg high on the S flank of Ben Macdhui; the cliff base is one of the highest in the area, but, catching the sun in spring, it is quickly stripped of snow and dries rapidly. There are numerous good low-grade routes with easy descents.
   Approach – Follow the B road to Linn of Dee from Braemar. A locked gate (Derry Gates) 700 yds/metres on L past Linn of Dee marks the start of the track to Derry Lodge, car park in trees. Follow good track to the Lodge. Take L track from the Lodge up Glen Luibeg and keep R at a junction. The path continues up side of burn and peters out. Continue to crag: 8.5 miles (13.7 km), 4 hrs
   Accommodation – Hutchinson Memorial Hut (024998), 1½ m (2.5 km) distant. Gain the crag up the L side of Creagan a 'Choire Etchachan and through col to gain Coire Sputan Dearg;

Bob Scott's bothy (043931), by Derry Lodge is 5 miles (8 km) from the coire; campsite at Robbers' Copse (015938) is 3½ miles (5.5 km) distant; bivvy boulders in the coire (poor).

Topography – On approaching the coire high on L are seen red slabs (continually wet); to their R are a series of buttresses divided by wide scree gullies gradually descending and merging into broken rock near low col to Loch Etchachan. The second buttress from L is the biggest and cleanest, Grey Man's Crag, containing the best routes.

Descent – The central scree gully in the face (Glissade Gully), or the second gully R of Grey Man's Crag.

509 **Crystal Ridge**   *300 ft (90 m)   D*
FA: *R. Still and J. E. Lawrence, 1948*
One of the few excellent easy routes in the Cairngorms. It follows, as closely as possible, the crest of a great slab angling into and bolstering up, the upper L flank of Grey man's Crag. The ridge has a steep L wall overlooking the gully on L.

Grey Man's Crag
It is defined by an obvious deeply cut 'Y' chimney (Slab Chimney) on L and Anchor Gully on R. The wall is characterized by L-leaning slabby grooves on the frontal face, and the L wall overlooking Slab Chimney is steep and split by a remarkable crack.

510 **Amethyst Pillar**   *300 ft (90 m)   HVS*
FA: *R. W. P. Barclay and W. D. Brooker, 1956*
The best route in the coire. A direct line up the steep wall overlooking Slab Chimney. Start at the foot of the prominent slanting chimney fault in L end of the wall.
1. 120 ft (36 m) 4c Climb up into prominent round niche. Exit R on to steep slabs. Climb up wall above. Go L and pull over a bulge into obvious hanging corner. Step L at small roof, then down L and tr. along a flake-ledge to belay at its end.
2. 75 ft (23 m) 4c Above is a shallow cracked groove with bulge. Climb the groove and exit R on to ramp. (Or climb

wall diag. R from flake belay to gain ramp lower down.) Up ramp L to top.

3. 105 ft (31 m) 5a Up R to obvious vertical crack above rock pedestal. Loose jammed flake is used to pass final bulge, then crack to slabs, then top.

Just L of centre of buttress a well-defined groove develops higher into a chimney (Pilgrim's Groove, HS), but is vegetated and wet. The fault to its R, joining Pilgrim's Groove at the chimney, is Lucifer (S), again usually wet.

511 Grey Slab   *360 ft (108 m)   HS*
FA: *M. Higgens, J. C. Innes and B. T. Lawrie, 1963*
A lovely route up the conspicuous L-trending corner in centre of buttress leading to a large slab near top. Scramble up broken rocks to good platform 30 ft (9 m) below corner.

1. 30 ft (9 m) Shallow depression above, then awkwardly R to below corner.
2. 60 ft (18 m) Corner to grass ledge (crux).
3. 120 ft (36 m) Continue up corner to OH. Turn it on L and up to ledge. Climb corner up R side of Grey Slab until forced L at its top.
4. 150 ft (45 m) Step down L and enter chimney of Pilgrim's Groove, which proves to be manky. Better to continue up short slab to enter the chimney higher up (4c).

512 Ferlas Mor   *350 ft (105 m)   HS*
FA: *J. Mothersele, G. S. Strange, D. Stuart, B. T. Lawrie and D. Dinwoodie, 1971*
A direct line R of Grey Slab. Good climbing.

1. 30 ft (9 m) As for Grey Slab to stance below corner.
2. 90 ft (27 m) Swing up R and follow grooves and ribs on edge overlooking Grey Slab.
3. 120 ft (36 m) Move L and continue up grooves. Exit on to crest on R, level with top of the Grey Slab.
4. 110 ft (33 m) Follow the continuation of the dyke up L via short chimney in crest and arete, as for Hanging Dyke.

513 **Hanging Dyke**   *360 ft (108 m)   VD*
FA: *A. Parker and J. Young, 1949*
A popular route following the basalt dyke up the backbone of
the crag. Delicate exposed crux.
Start: R of lowest rocks at foot of the broad slab.
1. 80 ft (24 m) Follow the dyke up centre of the slab to small
   ledge. Then a grassy crack to a good stance. Dyke runs out L.
2. 110 ft (33 m) Climb a wide slab inclining L by a series of
   parallel cracks to a sloping corner, rejoining the dyke where
   it steepens below a rib.
3. 60 ft (18 m) Climb the rib on small holds until the dyke falls
   back into a chimney (crux).
4. 110 ft (33 m) Follow the continuation of the dyke up L via
   the chimney and an arete to top.

THE GARBH CHOIRE, BEINN A'BHUIRD   (111012) Alt.
2,900 ft (900 m) North facing
Beinn a'Bhuird is the highest summit of the E Cairngorms. It
forms an almost separate massif set in the vast remoteness of
the forest of Glen A'an. Its E side drops violently into a series
of rugged coires and, although each contains great stretches of
clean granite, the routes in general lack continuity. The
definitive guidebook (see p. 422) is recommended for those who
wish to explore this area fully. Included here are the cliffs of
the Garbh Choire, the remotest cliffs in the Cairngorms, hidden
from civilization on the slopes at the head of the Slochd Mor.
They require at least one day to dry in summer.
   Approach – From Braemar: leave the A93 Braemar-Aberdeen
road 100 yds/metres E of the gates to Invercauld House
(signpost to Keiloch). Follow track past house (locked gate),
passing Altdourie Cottage, and enter Glean an T'Slugain. Path
passes Slugain Lodge ruin, then goes over col into upper Glen
Quoich. Continue up glen for some distance before branching
up R to a huge boulder (Clach a'Chleirich). Follow stream up to
sneck between Ben A'an and Cnap a'Chleirich. Contour L into
Garbh Choire: 9½ miles (15.5 km); 4 hours 30 mins. The easiest
method of approach is by mountain bike to the ruin.

Accommodation – Smith/Winram Bivouac (097996); the howff at foot of dividing buttress between Coire an Dubh Lochan and Coire nan Clach in upper Glen Quoich, is a recess under second largest boulder immediately below short belt of pink granite slabs that sleeps 3. Otherwise camping in coire.

Topography – Main area extends NW of sneck. Two main buttresses are situated one at each end of this main face, Squareface on the L and Mitre Ridge on the R. Between them are broken cliffs and gullies, one enclosing a large stream.

Squareface Buttress

Broken rocks from the sneck lead to the North Face, which is imposing, capped by foul rock, and remains virgin. To its R and hidden from view from below is the 300 ft (90 m) rectangular West Face overlooking a large grassy amphitheatre, the High Bay. This slabby face gives the buttress its name.

Descent – Wide grassy rake slanting R from lowest rocks into the high bay and up to the plateau.

514 **Squareface** *320 ft (100 m)   VD*
FA: *T. W. Patey and J. M. Taylor, 1953*
The superlative of superlatives, continuously exposed and in a remarkable situation. Gain base via grassy rake from coire or plateau. The L side is a stepped arete bordering the North Face. Start: R of crest of arete near foot of back bay gully.

1. 120 ft (40 m) Up cracks and grooves in slab with awkward step over bulge to first platform. Follow ridge to smaller stance beneath undercut crest of arete.
2. 100 ft (30 m) Launch out R on to slab and tr. R to vertical crack; up this to second platform.
3. 100 ft (30 m) Delicate tr. R to gain deep cracks leading to top. The deep crack is severe, so layback a flake 12 ft (4 m) R, then leave it for gangway leading out R to top.

The Mitre Ridge

One of the most striking pieces of rock architecture in the
Cairngorms. It juts proudly from the plateau, the East and West
walls meeting at an acute angle to form the ridge. This topped
by three towers leading back to plateau. The East Wall is slabby
and vegetated; the West Wall is liberally endowed with holds,
but very steep. When viewed head-on, the towers on the crest
are obvious. Directly below the notch between the first and
second tower is the triangular Cuneiform Buttress. Its L side is
defined by an obvious corner gully (Cumming-Crofton Route).
To its R is a recessed area with two deep chimney/corner lines
(Commando Route and Ghurka). R of these is another bigger
buttress (The Slochd Wall) whose top is the third tower.

515 **Cumming-Crofton Route** *530 ft (160 m)* S
FA: *M. S. Cumming and J. W. Crofton, 1933*
FA: *J. H. B. Bell, 1930s (Variation finish)*
The classic of the coire, dirty in places but worthwhile
nonetheless.
Start: Directly below the deep corner and chimney line down
the L side of Cuneiform Buttress. Scramble up to platform
below chimney.

1. 100 ft (30 m) Climb chimney with its hanging flake at
   mid-height. Stance is on small pinnacle flanking the ridge.
2. 50 ft (15 m) Go R across steep wall via smooth groove till
   holds on top edge of wall lead airily back L to base of
   groove system.
3. 75 ft (23 m) The groove, difficult at first on R wall, leads to
   a platform.
4. 100 ft (30 m) Crack in L wall, then tr. R and follow a
   sloping ledge to a short wall. Continue in same line up loose
   gully to notch between first and second towers.
5. 75 ft (23 m) Bell's variation takes the best of three choices up
   the second tower. Follow a shelf R and up exposed crack in W
   face. Step L from crack and finish direct to top of tower.
6. 130 ft (39 m) Scramble along narrow horizontal arete to final
   tower and plateau.

Southern Cairngorms
LOCHNAGAR   (246857) Alt. 2,900 ft (900 m) North-east
facing 🦋 🦋

The forested slopes of Royal Deeside rise into the complicated
mass of low-lying foothills of the Balmoral Deer Forest.
Crowning them all is Lochnagar, a bulky mountain with two
main coires on its N flank. Its odd name was coined by the
Victorians in preference to its possible original, Beinn nan
Ciochan (the Hill of the Breasts), which is much more apt. The
climbing is centred around the NE Coire, a sombre place. The
main face is split by great gullies into distinct buttresses;
considerable areas of cliff are loose and grassy, but the
exceptions in this 'Citadel of Vegetatious Granite' give classic
mountain routes.

Approach – Best from Spittal of Glenmuick car-park. Pass
the Ranger centre, turn R on track crossing Glen Muick to
junction beside an outbuilding of Allt-na-Giubhsaich Lodge.
Follow path by the fence W from S end of building, through
pine trees, to join bulldozed track on to open ground. This leads
over the Muick/Gelder col to Gelder Shiel (bothy) and Easter
Balmoral. At the col a path branches L past Meikle Pap, and on
to the summit plateau. Leave the path by Meikle Pap and
descend into the coire: 5¼ miles (12 km); 2 hrs 30 mins.

Topography – The coire is split into two sectors. The S,
closest to Meikle Pap, forms a fringe of rock under the plateau,
and on its R is Central Gully, an open chute sending scree to
the loch below. To R of this is the N sector, a great
amphitheatre of buttresses and gullies.

Descent – The main (R) branch of the Black Spout Gully on
the R of the coire: see diagram on p. 455.

516 **Eagle Ridge**   *750 ft (225 m)   S*
FA: *J. H. B. Bell and N. Forsyth, 1941 (1 PA)*
This is Bell's most significant route, inspiring further
generations of Cairngorm devotees. It was reputedly his only
use of ironmongery, ever. Popular, and it dries quickly.

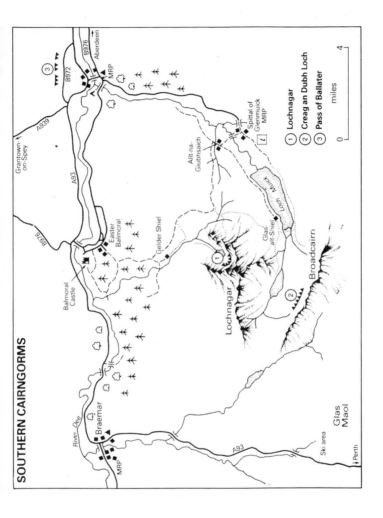

SOUTHERN CAIRNGORMS

① Lochnagar
② Creag an Dubh Loch
③ Pass of Ballater

miles
0   4

Start: Just inside the screes of the Douglas Gibson Gully (see diagram) at the first, most obvious groove.

Climb the groove for 60 ft (18 m). Easier climbing leads up a shallow gully bending R to short chimney with jammed blocks leading to buttress face. Regain ridge crest in 100 ft (30 m) pitch by choice of routes L. The crest is rounded and inclines easily to slabby nose, where the way rounds corner on R. Go up a 30 ft (9 m) inset corner to crest again.

The ridge here steepens as a 50 ft (15 m) tower. Swing up into a recess on R. Continue up steep rock and slightly L to gain sentry box at top of tower (exhilarating pitch). Follow a smooth arete to finish up a little corner to ledge on crest (try not to be forced out to R here). Follow crest over the 'whaleback' for 60 ft (18 m) to ledge, and belay in short slab/corner. The top of this ends in an airy knife-edge forming the crest. A vertical 12 ft (4 m) wall abutting the edge gives the crux, which is climbed via a short corner and continuation crack out L on upper slab to another level arete. Climb crest to projecting square-cut OH. Swing up on to the coping slab above and from some cracked blocks mantelshelf into a V recess. Finish up final slabs which dip into DG Gully.

CREAG AN DUBH LOCH   (234825) Alt. 2,500 ft (750 m)
North-east facing 🦋 🦋

Situated in the upper reaches of Glen Muick on the N slopes of Broadcairn, the Dubh Loch presents a nearly continuous line of 900 ft (270 m) cliffs for nearly a mile. It is the biggest single face in the Cairngorms, and receives its name from the black lochan at its base. The rock is a good solid pink or grey granite sculpted into overlapping roof-tile slabs. Major faults which gave early easier routes tend to be vegetated, and the Dubh Loch's brilliance emerges in the Extreme climbs it now boasts.

The face receives early-morning sun, so early starts are worth the effort, but several days are required to dry it out. Broad Terrace Wall in particular usually doesn't dry out until after a drought.

Approach – From Spittal of Glenmuick follow a track along

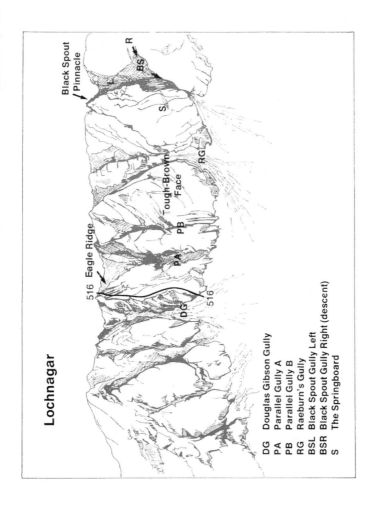

Lochnagar

DG   Douglas Gibson Gully
PA   Parallel Gully A
PB   Parallel Gully B
RG   Raeburn's Gully
BSL Black Spout Gully Left
BSR Black Spout Gully Right (descent)
S   The Springboard

the N shore of Loch Muick to Glas-alt-Shiel (a mountain bike is handy). The path leads up by a cascading stream to Dubh Loch: 2 hrs on foot.

Accommodation – Howff (234825) beneath Black Mamba on central slabs.

Descent – Usually easiest via Central Gully. If this is full of snow early in the season, then the ridge on R (looking down) gives access to a tr. L into lower part of the gully. The line is not obvious on first acquaintance.

Topography – There are four separate sections to the face. On the L above broken rocks the steep Broad Terrace Wall which peters out in a huge amphitheatre on R (the Hanging Garden). The central section of the crag is split by the huge Central Gully. On its L is the Central Slabs, on its R the Central Gully Wall. The latter extends R to form a frontal face whose R end is crossed by a diag. fault (False Gully). Above this is False Gully Wall.

Broad Terrace Wall

Broken rocks lead up to a large grass balcony ledge (Broad Terrace) below an horrendously steep face of dark smooth granite. Cleaving the L side is the huge corner fault of Sword of Damocles (E1). To the R of the smooth section it continues steeply, but with more features, before disappearing into the Hanging Garden. Gain the Broad Terrace by a zig-zag path up L side of lower crags by vegetation starting near foot of SE gully. To the L of Sword of Damocles is another vertical fault taken by The Last Oasis (VS 4c). L again is an area of water-washed rock which although slow to dry offers excellent climbing. Directly up the centre L of Last Oasis is a conspicuous crackline.

517 **Alice Springs**   *300 ft (95 m)   E2*
FA: *M. Hamilton and P. Whillance, 1983*
Start below fault of The Last Oasis.
1. 80 ft (20 m) Climb fault easily to steepening.

Eagle Ridge, Lochnagar, Cairngorms

2. 135 ft (40 m) 5c Climb over steepening. Step L onto rib.
   Follow thin crack L to ledges. Climb prominent crack above
   to belay ledge.
3. 120 ft (35 m) 5b Gain base of corner above. Step R to rib
   and gain crack on R. Follow this to groove leading to top.

Sword of Damocles (E1) climbs the huge corner on the L
gained directly up small ledges and a crack (5b). The corner
proves easier but the hanging chimney above is also hard.
Finish out R up a further chimney.

518 **Flodden**   *450 ft (135 m)   E5*
FA: *M. Hamilton, R. Anderson and K. Spence, 1983*
A stunning natural line diag. across the steepest section. In the
centre are two big roofs, one above the other. Scramble up L
then tr. R to below a L-leaning corner up L side of roofs.
1. 135 ft (40 m) 6a Up corner till it leans. Climb a flake,
   step up and L across wall to crack. Up this to below large
   roof.
2. 50 ft (15 m) 6a Crack round L side of roof leads to ledge.
   Tr. this to faint crack. Up crack and scoop above to R end of
   Grass Balcony. Tr. L to a corner (PB).
3. 35 ft (10 m) 5a Tr. L round a corner and climb crack to
   pinnacle top.
4. 80 ft (24 m) 6b Tr. L off pinnacle and up to under L end of
   roof. Step L and follow ramp, passing flake. Step down from
   its top to possible shake out. Up slim groove above. L across
   slab to corner. Up this steeply to belay.
5. 150 ft (45 m) 5a Corner behind, then L to scramble to top.

519 **Culloden**   *410 ft (125 m)   E2*
FA: *A. D. and R. R. Barley, 1967, (4 PA)*
FFA: *J. Lamb and P. Whillance, 1974*
Superbly positioned but a little dirty. Climbs a big V-groove R
of twin roofs. Highest ledge of Broad Terrace contains blocks at
highest point.
Start: L of these. Climb up L to big platform.

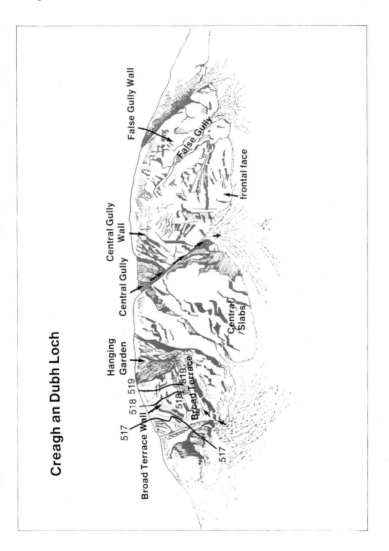

Creagh an Dubh Loch

1. 150 ft (45 m) 5a Climb up grooves, cracks and flaky wall. Move R to top of big flake.
2. 120 ft (35 m) 5c O H-crack above and big hanging V-groove to ledges. Straight up shallow grooves above. Avoid bulge at 30 ft (10 m) on L and continue to small perch.
3. 115 ft (35 m) 4a Continue up short groove and greasy walls to top.

Central Slabs
The huge sweep of overlapping slabs in centre of face is about 1,000 ft (300 m) high, and is seamed by vertical cracks and split by a terrace above half-height (can be escaped along R to Central Gully Buttress). Route-finding can be a problem.

520 **Dinosaur/Pink Elephant**   *1,090 ft (330 m)   HVS*
FA: *J. W. Stenhouse and B. T. Lawrie, 1964 (Dinosaur, 1* PA*)*
FA: *J. Grieve and A. Fyffe, 1969 (Pink Elephant)*
A combination giving sustained climbing up L side of slabs.
Start: At the lowest rocks just R of pink streak and climb broken cracks to grass rake coming in from the R.

1. 135 ft (40 m) 4c Follow main crack system above to stance 15 ft (5 m) below long lower overlap.
2. 135 ft (40 m) 4c Surmount overlap and go up slab over awkward bulge, then up slightly higher to a toe tr. L (careful not to go too high). Step up L, then down L into obvious shallow corner. Up this, using L arete to top of big flake. Dinosaur Gully lies to L.
3. 150 ft (45 m) 4c Gain a grassy niche above. Up bulging corner above and break R over big L-slanting overlap on to slabs. Follow obvious line up into Dinosaur Gully.
4/5. 280 ft (94 m) Climb up this to the terrace.
6. 70 ft (21 m) 4c Obvious corner on R side of sea of slabs to belay under bulges.
7. 150 ft (45 m) 4c Continue up grooves above, through O H by short bulging slot, then slabs to block.
8. 120 ft (36 m) 5a A tapering slab leads L on to R end of big

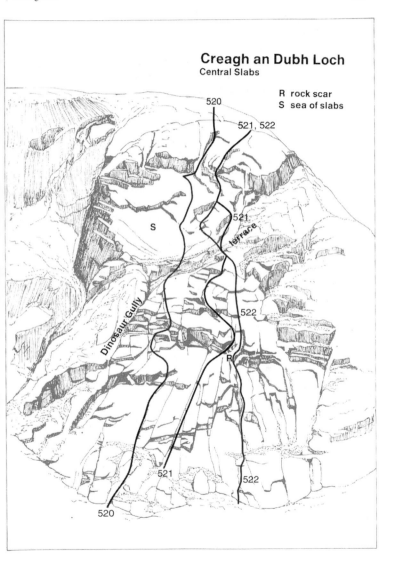

Creagh an Dubh Loch
Central Slabs

R rock scar
S sea of slabs

grass ledge below upper OHS. Tr. R on to slabby knife-edge drop into upper groove.

9. 150 ft (45 m) 5a Climb groove, negotiating steep step on L, and so to top.

521 **Blue Max**   *995 ft (300 m)   E1*
FA: *B. W. Robertson, A. G. Fyffe and W. T. Wilkins, 1967*
FFA: *J. Fraser and party, 1975*
Great climbing up centre of slabs breaking through main overlap at obvious rockfall scar. Scramble up grass rake R of Dinosaur to large block.

1. 135 ft (40 m) 5a Up crackline above block over difficult bulge. Continue up cracks, then R into long corner.

2. 115 ft (35 m) 5a Corner to small ledges. Above, make thin tr. R over a smooth slab to nut belay below main overlap.

3. 83 ft (25 m) 4c Break through overlap by R tr. across wall immediately above recent rockfall scar. Then go up cracks to belay.

4. 135 ft (40 m) 5b Abandon crackline (Cyclops VS) by L tr. to below huge diamond block in next overlap. Climb R side of block to upper bulge. Over this to groove then to next bulge. Step R and pull over by crack twisting back into groove. Up it to belay on rib.

5. 160 ft (48 m) Continue up rib and succeeding crack and corner to OH; the continuation corner is blank. Turn OH on R by cracks to small ledge; up walls on L to bigger ledge. Scramble up to R end of upper slabs.

6. 135 ft (40 m) 4c Most obvious feature above is big crescent-shaped groove (Cyclops). This gives best finish. Up it to short twin grooves. Climb L-hand groove and up L by short cleft and cracks above to grass stance below obvious nose.

7. 150 ft (45 m) 4c Up just R of nose, then L over slab to quartz corner. Up corner for 15 ft (5 m) and exit R to rib. Up this to grassy grooves and up to belay.

8. 83 ft (25 m) finish up big groove on R by tr. R wall to broken ground.

522 **Black Mamba**   *1045 ft (310 m)   VS*
FA: *A. Fyffe and J. Grieve, 1969*
Classic of slabs. Start R of distinctive slabby tongue circled by
grass R of base of grass rake.
1. 80 ft (20 m) 4c Climb delicate shallow crack to gain grass
    ledge.
2. 150 ft (45 m) 4b Directly up cracks into long corner. Climb
    this and pull L to stance under main OH.
3. 150 ft (45 m) 4b Climb OH using cracked groove on R and
    follow cracks to ledges.
4. 150 ft (45 m) 4b Step round big flake and climb cracked
    slabs to shallow gully containing large pointed block. Easy
    slabs lead to The Terrace.
5. 65 ft (20 m) Scramble up R to edge of upper slabs.
6. 135 ft (40) 4b Obvious crescent-shaped groove lies above.
    Climb up diag. L under small bulges L of this groove to gain
    pink rib and slabs above to belay (close to Pink Elephant).
7. 150 ft (45 m) 4b Tr. back R to gain crackline leading to grass
    stance below obvious nose. Up R of nose, then L to base of
    quartz corner.
8. 165 ft (50 m) 4c Climb corner for 15 ft (5 m), then step R
    onto rib. Climb this to grassy grooves leading into larger
    groove on R. Tr. R wall to finish on broken ground.

Central Gully Wall
The showpiece of the S Cairngorms, this is a frightening wall
hanging over Central Gully. On the L, up inside the gully, is a
huge open corner (Giant); then follows a maze of roofs and
hanging slabs extending out of the gully on the R before turning
into the long frontal face. This is split by vertical cracklines, the
most famous being King Rat. On the R-hand side of this the
wall is topped by False Gully Wall.
    To the L of the Giant corner are two prominent hanging
corner lines. The L-most is the huge recessed scoop of Vertigo
Wall (VS), characterized by a big rockfall scar. The next route
climbs the wall between Vertigo and the Giant, finishing up the
central corner line: see diagram, p. 465.

431 **Goliath Eliminate**   *350 ft (105 m)   E2*
FA: *B. S. Findlay and M. Rennie, 1969 (4 PA)*
FFA: *I. Nicholson and party, 1970*
FA: *S. Docherty and N. Muir, 1971 (4 PA) (Direct Start)*
FFA: *B. Davison and A. Nisbet, 1983 (Direct Start)*
FA: *J. McArtney and B. T. Lawrie, 1967 (Shelf Variation)*
A brilliant route. Low in grade. Up the gully from Giant a huge
slab cuts back across the face (original route). The vertical wall
below contains a vast wedged block. Start: 30 ft (10 m) L up
and L of block.

1. 65 ft (20 m) 5b Tr. R to a grass ledge. Hand tr. R and
    mantelshelf before the ledge becomes rounded. Step R to
    base of block. Chimney up the back and belay on top.
2. 50 ft (15 m) 4c L up flake, and pull over bulge to gain the
    normal start slabs. Belay on R below small corner in steep
    wall above.
3. 135 ft (40 m) 5a Steep corner and move up to shelf (hard).
    Follow this R to wall. Go up and R across wall and easy
    groove then R to gain large platform below final corner of
    Giant.
4. 100 ft (30 m) 5b Climb corner as for Giant to top. Scramble
    to plateau.

524 **The Giant**   *330 ft (100 m)   E3*
FA: *D. Bathgate, A. Ewing and J. Brumfitt, 1965*
FFA: *N. Escourt and P. Braithwaite, 1974*
Climbs the huge corner in the fiercest section of the wall. It has
a short hard crux, well protected by a new PR. Climb easily R
up obvious sloping ramp to foot of first corner.

1. 65 ft (20 m) 5c Up cracks above to base of two parallel
    grooves. A flake gains L groove, and so to ledge.
2. 65 ft (20 m) 6a Climb L-hand of twin grooves above (RP
    runners and RP in R groove). Grooves swing L, then up
    vertical flake crack to ledge.
3. 100 ft (30 m) 5a Over blocks to groove with steep slab on L.
    Gain its top, go L on to slab, then up L to grass ledge. Tr.

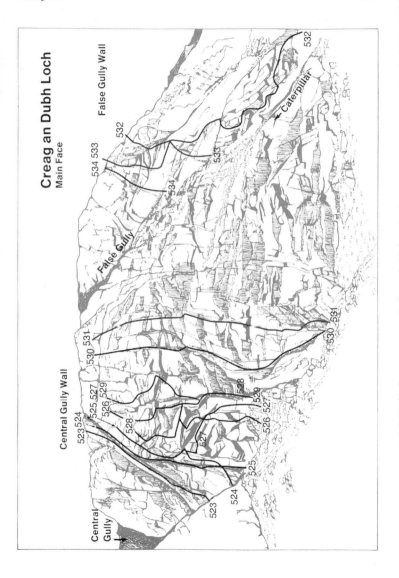

Creag an Dubh Loch
Main Face

False Gully Wall

Central Gully Wall

False Gully

Central Gully

Caterpillar

523 524 525 527 526 529 528 521 525 524 523

530 531 530 531

532 533 534 533 532

back R and step on to OH-nose. Crack above, go L, then, up
to big platform below main corner.

4. 100 (30 m) 5b The corner and easy ground to grass ledge.
Scramble to top.

525 **The Naked Ape**   *430 ft (130 m)   E5*
FA: *P. Whillance, M. Hamilton, P. Botterill and R. Anderson,
1982*
Stunning climbing up big arete R of Giant. Bold.
Start: Below groove heading directly up to main corner of
Giant, down R of that start.

1. 115 ft (35 m) 5b Up groove and R fork via flake crack to
ledge at top of initial ramp of Giant.

2. 100 ft (30 m) 6b Above is smooth groove R of Giant crux.
Climb its L rib, then cross it R to PR. Move up R on to steep
slab. Tr. R to arete and step up (PR). Tr. R along footledge
to gain good ledge in corner.

3. 83 ft (25 m) 6a Follow L-leaning slabby corner to niche
below OH (NR in lip). Go down L to arete. Up L and over
break in OH to gain sloping ledge. Short steep wall (PR) to
ledge in niche.

4. 135 ft (40 m) 5c OH-crack above the ledge. Step R into
cracks, and so to groove system. Follow this to grassy
terrace. Scramble R to plateau.

526 **Cannibal**   *470 ft (140 m)   E5*
FA: *M. Hamilton and R. Anderson, 1984*
Well below Naked Ape is big OH-alcove. Start at prominent
cracked arete to the R.

1. 100 ft (30 m) 5c Crack just L of arete, then turn it to crack
on other side. Up this till it fades, then crack in crest on L
steeply to slab stance.

2. 35 ft (10 m) 6a L, and gain holds leading to PR below roof.
Out R until crack above roof leads to higher slab (PB).

3. 100 ft (30 m) 6b Gain L-slanting corner above leading to OH.
Tr. L to loose flake. Crack behind to recess (PR), pull over R
wall to big slab (Cougar Slab). Belay at R end.

4. 135 ft (40 m) 6b Above and R is stepped corner. Up first step. Swing R on to arete and up till corner can be regained. Up it and out R below steep nose. Wall R of nose to short crack, then pull on to block on nose. Slab L below roof to stance.
5. 100 ft (30 m) 5a Crack above, then scramble to top.

527 **Voyage of the Beagle**   *530 ft (160 m)   E4*
FA: *M. Hamilton and R. Anderson, 1983*
A real voyage across the main face via prominent diag. slab line beneath that of Cougar, to finish up Naked Ape. Generally slabby. R of Cannibal at base of Central Gully is a big grassy mound with embedded blocks (start of Cougar).
Start: 15 ft (5 m) L at a groove.
1. 90 ft (27 m) 5c Climb flake crack on R to gain groove. Up it to small ledge.
2. 45 ft (14 m) 6a L across wall then regain corner. Step down L and gain crack leading back to fault and so to slab (nut belay).
3. 50 ft (15 m) 4c Cross slab to (PB).
4. 135 ft (40 m) 6a Step down to lower slab. Cross to arete. Step L round arete and up to enter groove. Up to its top (NR on upper slab on R for second); L to gain groove leading to ledge in corner joining Naked Ape at its 2nd pitch belay. Follow Naked Ape to top in two pitches: 83 ft (25 m), 6a; 135 ft (40 m), 5c.

528 **Cougar**   *450ft (135 m)   E2*
FA: *M. Rennie and P. Williams, 1968*
FFA: *D. Cuthbertson and M. Hamilton, 1977*
Another diag. line up R edge of monolithic wall, then curving L over the top. Sustained but well protected.
Start: At top of grassy mound with blocks at foot of Central Gully. Difficult route-finding on last pitch.
1. 100 ft (30 m) 4c Short R tr. into initial corner. Up it to notch. Up L and gain ledge under OH.
2. 135 ft (40 m) 5b/c Cracks leading L over bulge, and go up steep corner line to the R end of big slab.

3. 115 ft (35 m) 5b/c Tr. slab L by crack. Step down into recess below short OH-corner crack. Up this, then L by flakes to belay under short impending recessed wall.
4. 100 ft (30 m) 5c Climb wall to gain girdling slab under final bulging overlap. Move R and mantel on to block. Climb crack above past protruding stone to overlap. Tr. L under it past a gap to reach good rounded spike. Step up, tr. L along bulge, then up and L to ledge below roof. Scramble to plateau.

529 **Vampire** *600 ft (180 m)   E1*
FA: *D. Dinwoodie and G. S. Strange, 1972*
FFA: *B. T. Lawrie and A. Nisbet, 1977*
Sustained and one of the best of its grade hereabouts, but described variously from HVS to E3!
Start: As for Cougar.

1. 100 ft (30 m) 4c Short tr. R into corner and up to notch, then L to good ledge under OH.
2. 135 ft (40 m) 5a Bulge is split on R by OH-crack with jammed flake at base. From flake pull R round bulge and up corner to grass ledge. Stance above.
3. 135 ft (40 m) 5b Big corner above is dirty (E3 5c). Step back down, then on to slabs on R. Diag. R over them, and a bulge to reach ledge. Toe tr. L across tiny dwindling ledge to corner. Up this to bulges, and out L by short wall and slab to grass stance. Poor gear.
4. 100 ft (30 m) 5b Move L up slab and climb short recessed corner. Climb the slot above and go up slab to exit R on to ledge.
5. 130 ft (39 m) 4c Move L round cracked blocks and work direct to easy ground, staying just L of grass-choked groove.

At the R end of the grassy mound starts the frontal face. The next route starts from the toe of the face. The most obvious feature is a R-facing recess at the toe, and a horizontal band of roofs above:

530 **The Mousetrap** *600 ft (180 m)   VS*
FA: *J. R. and R. Marshall and R. Anderson, 1959*
A well-protected classic, and the easiest line up the front face.
Start: At deep easy groove at toe, leading up to an array of
cracks L of the recess.
1. 120 ft (36 m) 4a The groove then tr. L over slab. Up to belay
   below and L of main crack.
2. 150 ft (45 m) 4c Up R and climb crack to recess above.
   Continue up recess to belay near top.
3. 90 ft (27 m) 4a Climb steep flake corner on L. Move up to
   cracks and continue to stance.
4/5. 180 ft (54 m) Follow crackline for two pitches to big
   grassy ledge.
6. 60 ft (18 m) 4a Slab above leads to broken ground. Scramble
   to top.

531 **King Rat** *730 ft (220 m)   E1*
FA: *A. Fyffe and J. Bower, 1968 (5PA)*
FFA: *P. Thomas and M. Fowler, 1977*
A long crack system emanating from recess at toe of crag and
cutting through obvious OH at 165 ft (50 m). One hard section
through this OH. Start at L wall of recess.
1. 135 ft (40 m) 4b Steep rocks in back L of recess gains tr. L
   on flakes round edge to ledge. Cracks in slab to grass ledge.
2. 80 ft (20 m) 5b From R end of ledge climb cracked slab to
   cave under OH. Climb up steep cracked wall on L into
   corner (crux, VS with aid). Climb corner to ledge.
3. 165 ft (50 m) 4b General line of cracked ribs above till under
   short steep wall. Climb L up slabs to below short leaning
   corner.
4. 30 ft (10 m) 4b Corner to ledges.
5. 100 ft (30 m) 4c Up short wall on L to slab under OH. Tr.
   10 ft (3 m) L. Surmount bulge, tr. back R on narrow slab,
   then climb direct to ledges.
6/7. 230 ft (70 m) 4b Climb discontinuous crack and shallow
   groove systems to top. Scramble to plateau.

To the R of the frontal face False Gully slants up L to peter out in upper reaches. The next route is a combination up buttress at lower R end of frontal face and up the False Gully Wall, above False Gully. Caterpillar Crack (a slanting runnel) splits the roof-seamed buttress from the main face.

532 **Sous les Toits/False Face**   *800 ft (240 m)   E2*
FA: *D. Dinwoodie, B. T. Lawrie, 1976 (Sous les Toits)*
FA: *G. N. Hunter and D. F. Lang, 1969 (False Face)*
FFA: *R. Smith and D. Dinwoodie, 1977*
Good sustained climbing.
Start: At a grass bay at R side of buttress.
1. 65 ft (20 m) 6a Climb obvious chimney, then take tr. L (Hard) to hanging slab (or up and L to then tr. L to ledge under jutting nose and abseil and to hanging slab, E1 5b).
2. 100 ft (30 m) 5b Tr. slab to L end round corner and up to delicate slab under bulge. Over wall above on R of OH. Move up R to recess. Direct over roof to slab under more roofs.
3. 35 ft (10 m) 5a Turn OHS on R. Up L to lip of L-hand roof. Up slim ramp above and swing R to stance below final roof.
4. 135 ft (40 m) 5a Turn by corner on R of roof. Up and L to belay under short wall.
5. 15 ft (5 m) Wall to False Gully. The most obvious feature in False Gully Wall is a huge corner bounding the R edge of the smooth section in the centre. From just below it climb slightly R to grass shelf leading into the corner (V D).
6. 120 ft (36 m) 5c (crux) The big leaning corner to sloping ledge on L. Strenuous.
7. 150 ft (45 m) 5b Up short wall above. Move R into hidden chockstone chimney leading to ledge below overlap. Gain ledge above, then over overlap (PR). Tr. R across OH-slab. Then up and L to grooves and so to big ledge.
8. 150 ft (45 m) 5a Move back L and up into big corner. Up till near its top, then R wall leads R and up by detached flake to ledges. Broken ground to top.

False Gully Wall

False Face bounds the R edge of the most impressive, smooth
section of the wall. To its L are several thin crack and groove
lines. The prominent line in the centre 100 ft (30 m) L of False
Face is Startibartfast. Between these two climbs are other thin
cracks.

533 **Sans Fer**   *485 ft (145 m)   E4*
     FA: *M. Hamilton and K. Spence, 1979*
     Excellent climbing up thin crack in wall between False Face
     and Startibartfast. Start 30 ft (10 m) L of leaning corner of False
     Face.
     1. 135 ft (40 m) 5b Climb to niche and slab. Gain prominent
        finger crack and follow this to sloping ledge and belay
        shared with False Face.
     2. 65 ft (20 m) 6b Walk L along ledge for 30 ft (10 m) to base
        of crack. Climb it to belay.
     3. 135 ft (40 m) 6a Tr. 15 ft (5 m) L to groove leading through
        bulge. Follow grooves up slightly R, then move L to ramp.
     4. 150 ft (45 m) 5c Tr. L on ramp to niche. Exit L through OH.
        Tr. L then up into further niche. Direct through OH to easy
        ground and block belay.

534 **Startibartfast**   *240 ft (80 m)   E5*
     FA: *M. Hamilton, P. Whillance and R. Anderson, 1982*
     The most prominent crack is very serious.
     Start: From slanting grass terrace below crack in centre of wall.
     1. 65 ft (20 m) 6b Ledge on wall R of crack gives access to
        small groove. Up this till it fades (NR high R). Up L across
        wall to crack. Follow it and shallow corner, moving R at top
        to sloping ledges.
     2. 65 ft (20 m) 6a Obvious corner with three small OHS to slab.
     3. 135 ft (40 m) 5c Same line by steep cracks to top.

PASS OF BALLATER   (367971) Alt. 825 ft (250 m) South facing

The granite crags of the Pass of Ballater provide by far the best outcrop climbing on the E side of the Cairngorms (with the exception of the Aberdeen sea-cliffs) and offer an excellent alternative to Creag an Dubh Loch or Lochnagar in doubtful weather. Well developed since the mid-1970s, the cliffs are very popular, especially with Aberdeen climbers and give a fine day's climbing in their own right, mostly in the middle and upper grades. Being on clean granite, most routes dry quickly.

Approach – The cliffs are located just above the road on the N side of the pass. Soil erosion is a major problem, especially on the approach slopes to the Central Section. Climbers are requested to approach the climbs described by a vague path at the L end of the W section.

Topography – The cliffs divide themselves into three main sections when viewed from the road: Western, Central and Eastern. The Western section consists of two tiers – the Upper Tier contains the easily identified corner of Little Cenotaph, while the main features of the Lower Tier are a prominent steep buttress bounded on the R by a huge slab. The Central section contains the obvious soaring roofed corner of Anger and Lust at the L end, and the equally obvious groove of Bluter Groove in the centre of the cliff. No routes are described on the smaller Eastern section, although a number of good short problems exist.

Western Section, Upper Tier
The routes described are on either side of the obvious right-angled corner of Little Cenotaph.

535 **Little Cenotaph**   *25 ft (8 m)   HVS 5a*
FA: *G. Strange, 1975*
The R-angled corner. Painful bridging for those short of stature (direct finish, 5b).

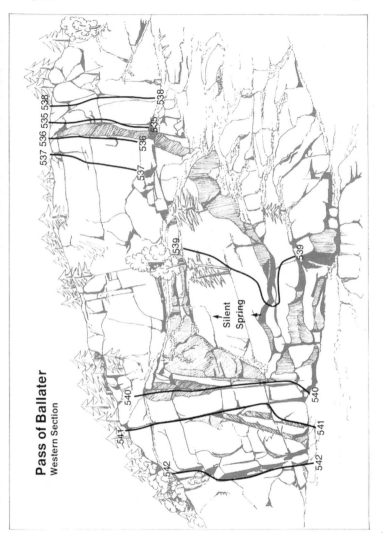

Pass of Ballater
Western Section

538
535
537 536 535 538
537
536
539
39
Silent Spring
540
541
540
541
542
542

536 **Smith's Arete** *40 ft (13 m)* *E5 6a*
FA: *R. Smith, 1983*
The vertical arete immediately L of Little Cenotaph. A serious on-sight lead.

537 **Peel's Wall** *40 ft (13 m)* *E4 5c*
FA: *J. Peel and A. Barley, 1977*
Takes a line up the beautiful wall L of Smith's Arete. Gain an undercut flake and climb strenuous crack to an obvious horizontal break. Arrange protection in the break and climb straight up to reach a narrow ledge. Make difficult and precarious moves up and R to finish.

538 **Pink Wall** *25 ft (8 m)* *HVS 5a*
FA: *G. Strange and D. Stuart, 1972*
A fingery but well protected route up the R wall of Little Cenotaph. Awkward start.

Western Section, Lower Tier
Characterized by an impressive wall with a vertical seam of quartz up its R edge, immediately L of a large slab. Routes are described R to L.

539 **Medium Cool** *60 ft (18 m)* *VS 4c*
FA: *B. Lawrie and G. Strange, 1979*
This climbs the large slab mentioned above.
Start: In a crevasse directly beneath the slab and climb to a large overlap. Tr. L under the overlap to a ledge before moving back R to negotiate the overlap. Climb the slab above to a large tree. Continue up the slab behind the tree on small holds. Popular.

Silent Spring (E1 5a) climbs the niche above ledge at end of L tr. of Medium Cool to gain small scimitar-shaped crack. Then gains upper slab. A mantel leads to horizontal break, another follows. Then gain tree (R), follow L-trending runnel on L to top.

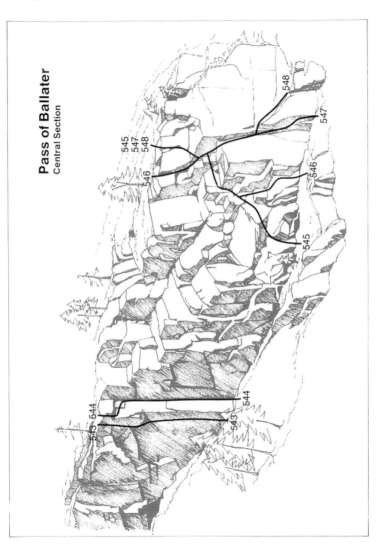

540 **Rattlesnake**   *60 ft (18 m)   E2 6a*
FA: *D. Dinwoodie and B. Lawrie, 1981*
This climbs the obvious quartz fault on the R edge of the wall.
Approach from the L by a grassy terrace. Start up a short hard
corner (crux) to gain the fault.

541 **Pretzel Logic**   *50 ft (15 m)   E3 5c*
FA: *B. Sprunt and N. Macdonald, 1980*
Starts 20 ft (6 m) L of Rattlesnake, just R of a sharp arete.
Climb a short corner for 20 ft (6 m) and move R across the wall
into a finger crack using a flat ledge. Easier climbing leads to
an obvious, slanting corner which leads with some difficulty to
the top. An OH-groove a few feet R of the normal start gives a
good, strenuous direct start (E2 6a).

542 **Lucky Strike**   *40 ft (13 m)   VS 4c*
FA: *M. Freeman, G. Strange, D. Stuart and R. Simpson, 1971*
Takes the steep, black streaked corner 15 ft (5 m) L of the start
of Pretzel Logic. An awkward start leads into the corner. Finish
up a short corner next to a tree.

Central Section
This is composed of a tapering L wall, split by corners and
roofs turning R on to a front face. Routes on tapering wall are
described first.

543 **Cold Rage**   *60 ft (18 m)   E4 6a*
FA: *D. Dinwoodie and C. Maclean, 1983*
Climbs the crack line up the wall L of the roofed corner.
Follow the thin crack (crux) starting just L of the corner to
reach a niche at 30 ft (9 m). Move L and continue straight up to
a small nose which forms the R side of a prominent slot. Climb
the slot and wall to finish. Strenuous.

Anger and Lust, Pass of Ballater: climber, Brian Sprunt

544 **Anger and Lust**   *60 ft (18 m)*   *E2 5c*
FA: *R. Smith and A. Williams, 1980*
A magnificent, sustained route taking the huge roofed corner on
the tapering L wall of the cliff. Climb the corner directly to the
roof. Tr. L under the roof to finish by a deep crack in a
breathtaking situation.

Climbs on the front face now follow:

545 **Giant Flake Route**   *90 ft (27 m)*   *MVS 4b*
FA: *G. Strange and D. Mercer, 1966*
Follows a rising flake line slanting diag. R 'wards across the
centre of the cliff. Start up a short corner (awkward),
approximately 25 ft (8 m) L of Bluter Groove to reach the
flakeline which is followed in short steps.

546 **Convoy**   *80 ft (24 m)*   *VS4c*
FA: *J. McCartney, D. Piper and A. Corbett, 1960s (2 P A)*
FFA: *J. McCartney, D. Mercer and B. Lawrie, 1966*
12 ft (4 m) R of Giant Flake Route is another groove (Bluter
Groove lies to R again) – climb this to join the Giant Flake
Route. Follow it R to above Bluter Groove; climb direct to
obvious alcove. Direct over roof on good holds.

547 **Bluter Groove**   *50 ft (15 m)*   *E3 6b*
FA: *M. Hamilton, P. Whillance and R. Anderson, 1982*
A local test-piece taking the obvious groove in the centre of the
cliff. Climb the R arete for a few feet before moving back into
the groove. Desperate, but good protection can be arranged.
Continue up the easier upper groove on excellent jams.

548 **Blutered**   *50 ft (15 m)*   *HVS 5a*
FA: *D. Wright, A. Hyman and G. Muhleman, 1976*
Avoids the lower section of Bluter Groove. Start 15 ft (5 m) R
of the groove and follow an obvious tr. line across the wall (P R)
into the upper part of the groove with your hands by your feet.
Finish up the groove.

13   GALLOWAY

These are the dramatic but often overlooked hills in the south
west of Scotland. They offer a complicated mixture of rough
walking over tussock grass and craggy ground, numerous lochs
and lochans surrounded by sometimes-impenetrable Forestry
Commission plantations of foreign trees. However, the hills in
the core of the range, the highest being The Merrick and The
Rhinns of Kells (also known as 'The Range of the Awful
Hand') are remote and beguiling with evocative names
conjuring images of elves, pixies and goblins.

   The rock varies with some huge crags containing large
amounts of vegetation but the magnificent granite crags of The
Dungeon of Buchan deep in the heart of the hills offer by far
the best climbing in the entire south west of Scotland due to
their scale, quality and surroundings. As an alternative to the
hill venue when the weather is inclement, there are now several
seaside crags which, although short, offer excellent (and until
now, fairly unknown) climbing.

History
Climbing interest has a long pedigree with descriptions of crags
in SMC Journals as early as 1906 but strangely there were no
routes recorded. The first was Cooran Buttress (VD) on the
biggest crag, The Dungeon of Buchan, climbed by J. Simpson
and J. Ratcliffe in 1955. Graham Little, living locally, climbed
The Highwayman (HVS) here in 1968 but left it unrecorded
and made impressions on nearby Craigencallie in the 1970's.
From then on, excepting the odd visit from Scots from Glasgow
(who mainly concentrated on nearby sea-cliffs) it was activists
from the nearby English Lake District who developed the
Dungeon crags. Pete Whillance and J. Fotheringham unwittingly
repeated Highwayman but did add Cyclopath (E1) in 1982.
There was a further lull until Steve Reid and Joe Grinbergs,
again from The Lakes, made numerous visits through 1991 to
establish over 15 excellent routes.

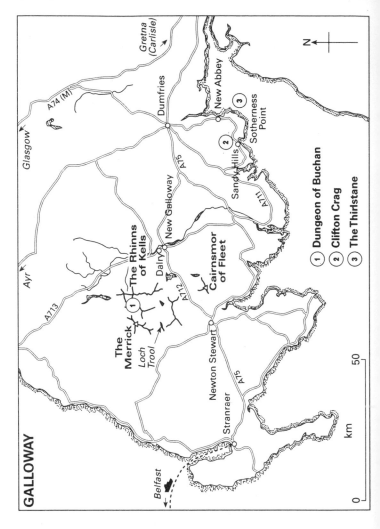

Access
A car is essential, although there are local bus services if time
is not important.

Accommodation
As the mountain crags are quite remote from main roads either
very long day visits or camping nearer the crags themselves are
the options.

Camping – Wild camping can be had over most of the
interior. Glen Trool Campsite run by The Forestry Commission
(400790) on the shores of beautiful Loch Trool. For the seaside
crags there are several campsites near the crags in Sandyhills
(890 550) and Southerness (975 552).

Bothies – The Backhill of Bush Bothy (480842) only 2 km
from Dungeon of Buchan is an excellent base although it has
suffered from vandalism at times and so do not rely on it being
weatherproof.

Provisions
St. John's Town of Dalry and New Galloway are closest
habitation and offer the usual amenities.

Maps
Galloway Hills – Landranger Series: No 77 Dalmellington to
New Galloway. Harvey Map Super Walker Series: Galloway
Hills.
Lowland crags – Landranger Series: No 84 Dumfries and Castle
Douglas.

DUNGEON OF BUCHAN   (462848) South West facing
This is a northern satellite top of the hill, Craignaw between
The Merrick and The Rhinns of Kells. It lies near the head of
the glen of The Black Water of Dee.

Approach – From any direction, this involves a long walk.
From Glen Trool over the back of Craignaw is 8 km of rough
walking. Easier option is to cycle along a forestry track from
Clatteringshaws Loch (a reservoir) to Backhill of Bush, then

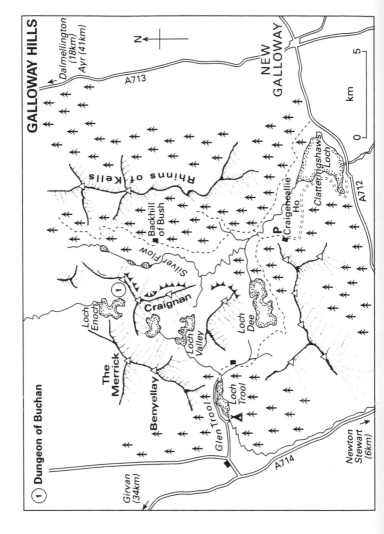

GALLOWAY HILLS

Dalmellington (18km)
Ayr (41km)

A713

N

NEW GALLOWAY

5

km

0

A712

Rhinns of Kells

Backhill of Bush

Silver Flow

Craigencallie Ho

P

Clatteringshaws Loch

Loch Enoch

① Craignan

Loch Valley

Loch Dee

The Merrick

Benyellary

Loch Trool

Glen Trool

Newton Stewart (6km)

A714

Girvan (34km)

① Dungeon of Buchan

escape the plantations onto The Silver Flowe. Skirt this to the N. Distance is 11 km of which 9 km is track.

Topography – The main crag running the full height of the hillside is obvious offering clean granite tiers separated by small heather ledges. This is Cooran Buttress. The rectangular wall of Dungeon Buttress is near the L hand side of the hill.

Conservation Information – Please avoid the Dungeon of Buchan buttresses during the nesting season of 1st April to 31st July. The Silver Flowe – a huge raised bog, Site of Scientific Interest and Nature Reserve, sits at the base of the crag and is best avoided at all times – it's a bog!

Dungeon Buttress
Defined on L by gully. Terrace cuts across crag at ⅔rds height. Routes described L to R.

549 **Carrick Corner**   *120 ft (35 m)*   *VS 4c*
FA: *S. Reid and J. Grinbergs, 1991*
The obvious corner near L hand side leading to awkward exit and detached block. Slab leads L into niche and difficult exit.

550 **Scots Wha' Hae**   *120 ft (35 m)*   *E1 5b*
FA: *S. Reid and J. Grinbergs, 1991*
R of corner is steep crack with jammed flakes just R of arete. Climb crack to tiny ledge. Hard move up R to shallow niche. L over OH to gain arete. Follow arete to slabs then up R to finish.

551 **Incy Wincy Spider**   *120 ft (35 m)*   *E2 5b*
FA: *S. Reid and J. Grinbergs, 1991*
Super route. Climb steep jam crack 6 ft (2 m) R of last route to niche below and R of that on last route. Pull over OH R-wards. Tr. R to pinnacle (hollow). Use this to pull L then up L to thread. Up to terrace and finish up corner just R of cracked arete.

552 **Parcel of Rogues** *120 ft (35 m)* *E3*
FA: *D. Wilson, W. O'Connor and S. Reid, 1991*
Start below OH-niche R of Incy Wincy Spider.
1. 100 ft (30 m) 6a Climb crack to small ledge up R of OH.
    Follow hard crack tr. L into undercut groove Up this and
    exit R at top to terrace.
2. 15 ft (5 m) 5b Impending slanting crack in narrow arete to top.

Cooran Buttress
The crag presents a front face with a series of fine corner-lines
in its lower R half. Routes described L to R.

553 **The Highwayman** *430 ft (130 m)* *HVS*
FA: *G. E. Little and J. Dykes, 1968*
Climbs front face L of main huge corner-line. Start 30 ft (10 m)
L of corner, near toe of buttress.
1. 150 ft (45 m) 5a Climb shallow groove to gain central crack
    leading to ledges. Tr. R 10 ft (3 m) to groove with large
    spike at top. Up L onto upper slab. Climb crack just L of
    rib, then L over bulge to heather terrace. Belay at R end
    under small OH.
2. 120 ft (35 m) 4c Up crack just L of OH to narrow terrace.
3. 60 ft (20 m) 4c Crack in short wall to next terrace.
4. 100 ft (30 m) 4a Crack-groove line up and L.

554 **Heir Apparent** *430 ft (130 m)* *E1*
FA: *S. Reid and J. Grinbergs, 1991*
Excellent route. Start at foot of huge corner.
1. 150 ft (45 m) 5b Steeply up L wall to flake, then up L onto
    small ledge. Groove above and continuation groove in L
    arete of corner. Follow this then up L to large spike. Back R
    into corner leading to belay below small OH at R end of
    terrace.
2. 120 ft (35 m) 5a Pass OH on R. Continue up, slightly R to
    gain sloping ledge. Easier via niche to terrace.
3. 60 ft (20 m) 4c Short wall above and scramble to upper
    terrace.

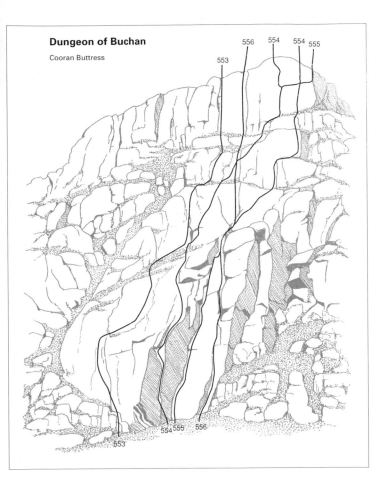

Dungeon of Buchan

Cooran Buttress

4. 100 ft (30 m) 5b Gain long thin flake in smooth wall (hard). Follow it past small ledge. Just before its top step R and swing R into groove. Finish up OH-crack.

4a. **Direct Finish**: E2 5b Follow the thin flake to its top. Up L to gain good holds, then direct up slight flake above to further good holds. Tr. L into scoop and finish more easily.

555 **The Colonel's Corner** *430 ft (130 m)* *HVS*
FA: *S. Reid and J. Grinbergs, 1991*
Another excellent route climbing huge corner.

1. 150 ft (45 m) 5a Climb corner to steep exit L by poised flake. Cracks above lead to two short grooves. Climb R groove to stance.
2. 120 ft (35 m) 4b Up to R-slanting groove leading to narrow ledge. Up L to grass ledge and up again to higher ledge. Climb wide crack on R until possible to gain arete on R. Climb this to spike (spectacular).
3. 60 ft (20 m) Scramble to terrace above.
4. 100 ft (30 m) 5a Climb overhung groove on R past two poised blocks. Tr. R into another groove leading to top.

556 **Cyclopath** *430 ft (130 m)* *E1*
FA: *J. Fotheringham and P. Whillance, 1982*
Bold slab climbing. Start at foot of slabby wall R of huge corner.

1. 150 ft (45 m) 5a Climb groove in slab. Move L onto wall and up flakes to crack. Follow this to belay on R.
2. 120 ft (35 m) 4c Wall behind stance to blunt spike in R-slanting groove of Colonel's Corner. Follow thin crack in bulge above to belay on terrace.
3. 60 ft (20 m) Easiest line up short wall and scramble to below obvious central crack in upper tier.
4. 100 ft (30 m) 4c The central crack just R of top pitch of Highwayman.

CLIFTON CRAG   (909 571) South West Facing

Clifton is one of Southern Scotland's best kept secrets. Quick drying, close to the road, and in a beautiful location; its only weak point is the diminutive stature of the climbs. However, they pack such a punch into their short length that they are guaranteed to leave you just as drained as a 50 m pitch would on most other crags. They lie on a small forested hillock (Fairgirth-hill) about 20 km south of Dumfries, overlooking the Solway Firth.

Approach – via the A710 south from Dumfries. A few miles before reaching Sandyhills Bay, there is a narrow lane on the R (west) and some outcrops can be seen on the hillside to the north of this lane. Follow the lane for about 2 km to a small lay-by on the L just past Upper Clifton Farm. A granite stile leads into a field. Walk straight across this, well to the L of the farm buildings, to an angle in the far wall. A second stile is hidden some 15 m to the R. Cross the next field to a gate in the far corner, under Hollowstones Wall; rather boggy. Please keep dogs on a lead when in the fields. Climbs described from L to R.

Conservation Information – The Main Area or Red Slab buttresses should be avoided during the nesting season if raptors are in residence.

Hollowstones Wall

At far L hand end of crag is yellow wall, flanked on L by a hawthorn tree, and with pleasant gearing up area below.

557 **Sidekick**   *50 ft (15 m)*   *HS 4b*
Take the groove behind tree, finishing up steep crack.

558 **Jeune Ecole**   *50 ft (15 m)*   *S*
Superb. Start at shallow, blocky, chimney-crack just R of tree. Climb crack to a platform on the R. Climb steep crack in the wall to gain standing position on ledge on L Tr. to arete and finish up groove.
Direct Variation: **Overground** Severe.

Start just R of Jeune Ecole and climb the wall to the platform.
Climb the crack of Jeune Ecole to the ledge and continue
directly up the crack and groove above.

Dirl Chimney Area
A path leads up and R to a bay behind an oak tree.

559 **Gramercy**   *40 ft (13 m)   Severe 4a*
An enjoyable pitch gained either from foot of Dirl Chimney, or
from the top of Jeune Ecole. Climb short crack on the very L
edge of bay (to the L of start of Dirl Chimney) and follow easy
ramp up L to huge block. (The same point can reached from
below the short wall at the top of Jeune Ecole by tr. R 10 m.)
Climb the crack forming L side of block to ledge. Follow crack
on R onto front of buttress and climb directly to top with
difficulty when it peters out.

560 **Dirl Chimney**   *40 ft (13 m)   VS 4c*
A classic! Dirl means 'A tremulous stroke; a sharp blow; a
resonating sound; an anxious haste or hurry; a twinge of
conscience; an exhilarating pleasure of mind and body'. All
these, and more, may happen when you undertake this
interesting exercise in back and footing up the chimney on the
L side of bay. Start below and L of chimney at crack with
wobbly block in it. Climb crack without hesitation, deviation or
repetition and move R into chimney. Follow it over OH to
easier slabs.

561 **Gibbon in Wonderland**   *40 ft (13 m)   HVS 5a*
A classic of the ilk! Start opposite oak tree. Tr. up and R across
slab to finish up fist-sized crack.

562 **Blazing Apostles**   *50 ft (15 m)   E2 5b*
Good, strenuous climbing up twin cracks in OH-arete just R of
oak tree. Finish up OH groove, just R of Gibbon's crack.

563 **Tour de Force**   *50 ft (15 m)   VS 4c*
Quality climbing. Start as for Blazing Apostles, but tr. R below overhang for 2 m, then go over bulge and up short corner.

Main Wall
A large beaked roof dominates this area which is defined by steep corner on L and fine arete on R. Gain foot of wall by scrambling up from R to 'Low Ledge'. Another move up and L leads to 'High Ledge' from which the following routes start.

564 **Liplet**   *30 ft (10 m)   Severe 4a*
Start to L of tree on L end of High Ledge and climb short groove to OH which is overcome with difficulty.

565 **Ratten's Rest**   *30 ft (10 m)   HVS 5b*
The short corner behind tree is worth the considerable struggle.

566 **Wall Street**   *40 ft (13 m)   E1 5b*
FA: *C. Macadam and G. Macadam, 1977*
A truly superb route – strenuous, technical and well protected. Follow thin crack just L of centre of wall to break and then finish up awkward hanging groove immediately L of OH.

567 **The Groove**   *40 ft (13 m)   HVS 4c*
The V-Groove just R of centre, exiting R. Beware of dubious blocks at top.

568 **Kenny's Chimney**   *25 ft (8 m)   Ungradeable*
A classic thrutch, the grade dependant on one's girth. The crux is avoiding getting one's head stuck.

569 **The Arete**   *50 ft (15 m)   E1 5b*
FA: *C. Macadam, 1978*
Exciting climbing up arete with prominent spike on it. Start down and R from 'Low Ledge' at the foot of Elder Crack. Climb up to OH and tr. L under it. A difficult move leads round

arete and into groove on L. Climb short corner until it is possible to move R to the spike. Move up with difficulty and finish by short crack up on R.

570 **Elder's Crack** *50 ft (15 m)* *VS 4b*
FA: *Unknown*
A great little climb up crack to R of The Arete. Start down and R of Low Ledge directly under the crack.

The Red Slab
To R of The Esplanade is complex area of walls and OHs half hidden behind some pinnacles. The crack flanking the red slab on R is DIY (HVS).

570 **Toddamundo** *50 ft (15 m)* *E4 6a*
FA: *C. Macadam, 1978*
Climb blunt arete R of DIY to break. A thought provoking reach from sharp fingerhold on lip of OH gains strenuous and exposed upper wall. A further hard move (crux) leads to jug at top. A Friend 4 is advisable.

571 **Fingerlust** *35 ft (12 m)* *E4 6a*
FA: *C. Macadam, 1978*
The thin crack in leaning tower on R gives another tremendous route; short, but very strenuous and technical with excellent protection (provided you can hang around and place it).

Jugular Vein Buttress
About 100 m R of the Red Slab is Twin Cracks Buttress marked by a blasted tree in the centre near the top and a large detached pinnacle below. A short bushwack down and to the R leads to a steep buttress with a double tier of OHs on the L and contains three excellent routes.

572 **Moonshine**   *50 ft (15 m)   E2 5c*
FA: *Unknown*
At the L side of buttress, 3 m L of central crackline of The
Slash, is a slab topped by crescent shaped OH. Climb desperate
slab R under first OH to resting place. Continue tr. R, crossing
The Slash and stepping onto Jugular Vein. Continue tr. to finish
up short crack in R arete.

573 **The Slash**   *50 ft (15 m)   HVS 5a*
FA: *Unknown*
The central crack.

574 **Jugular Vein**   *50 ft (15 m)   E1 5b*
FA: *C. Macadam and G. Macadam, 1977*
Fine climbing up wall to R of The Slash. Start up and R of that
route. Climb wall L-wards to resting position on arete. Step R
and climb crack above. Low in grade.

THE THIRL STANE   (993 568) South Facing
The Thirl Stane is a small standstone outcrop, about 10 m high,
located on a shingle beach not far from Southerness, east of
Clifton Crags. It is an excellent bouldering venue centred
around a cave and is very sheltered and quick to dry. Some of
the lines may require a rope to top-out.
    Approach – From Dumfries, follow the A710 Solway Coast
road and take the first signed road to Southerness. Take the first
left then just past a sharp left-hand bend take the road to
Powillimount. Park at the end of the road and a short walk east
along the beach gains the crag.
Descent – The normal descent leads to the far right end of the
crag, from whence a good low level traverse leads back to the
arete, crossing the cave en route.

The steep landward side of the cave is split by a roofless cave
which offers numerous technical problems on the smooth 'Thirl
Walls', most of which finish by squirming up through the chimney
above. Grades range from 5b to 6c and are about 8–10 m high.

All the obvious lines on the walls either side of the cave have been climbed – a rope is advisable. L of the cave, the very L arete of the crag gives an excellent juggy V Diff. 2 m left of the cave is a fine 10 m route (**Goodnight Irene**, E2 5c) through a lower roof then L under the higher roof and an E5 6b direct variation (**Thank You Irene**).

APPENDIX

Useful Addresses
Mountaineering Council of Scotland (MCofS)
The Old Granary, West Mill Street, Perth PH1 5QP, tel:
(01738) 638 227, fax: (01738) 442 980.
The Representative Body for Mountaineering, Hill Walking,
Climbing and X-country Skiing in Scotland. Membership is
open to clubs, associations and companies, and individuals.
Benefits include use of a mountain hut network throughout the
UK; low-cost courses in winter skills, basic winter climbing,
navigation, mountain first aid; free civil liability insurance and
competitive activity holiday insurance; Expedition Grants;
reductions on prices of outdoor equipment; regular news
magazine 'The Scottish Mountaineer'; reduced subscriptions to
Climber Magazine and TGO; and an information service
covering all aspects of the activity.
The MCofS campaigns for freedom to roam, is a member of
The Access Forum, negotiates over access problems, fights
against developments which threaten to destroy the Scottish
mountains and distributes conservation information.

Scottish Youth Hostels Association
National Office, 7 Glebe Crescent, Stirling FK8 2JA, tel:
(01786) 451 181.

Scottish Natural Heritage (Publications)
The Publications Officer, Battleby, Redgarton, Perth PH1 5EW,
tel: (01738) 627 921, fax: (01738) 441 897. The government
body with responsibility for conservation of and access to the
Scottish countryside.

The Scottish Tourist Board
23 Ravelstone Terrace, Edinburgh EH4 3EU, tel: (0131) 332
2433, fax: (0131) 343 1513.

National Trust for Scotland
5 Charlotte Square, Edinburgh EH2 4DU, tel: (0131) 226 5922.

The John Muir Trust
12 Wellington Place, Leith, Edinburgh EH6 7EQ, tel: (0131) 554 0114.
A charitable trust that owns and manages land in Scotland with an emphasis on conservation and the local inhabitants, continuing the work and ideas of the great conservationist John Muir, who was born in Scotland.

Save The Cairngorms
PO box 39, Inverness IV1 2RL.
A membership organisation open to individuals, that fights to protect the Cairngorm mountains from harmful development.

Scottish Wild Land Group
8 Hartington Place, Bruntsfield, Edinburgh EH10 4LE, tel: (0131) 229 2094.

Mountain Bothies Association
Ted Butcher, 26 Rycroft Avenue, Deeping St James, Peterborough PE6 8NT.
A charity with membership open to all who are prepared to give time, effort and help to maintain unlocked shelters in remote country in Scotland.

Glenmore Lodge National Outdoor Training Centre
Glenmore, Aviemore, Inverness-shire PH22 1AV, tel: (01479) 861 276, fax: (01479) 861 212.

Caledonian MacBrayne Ferries
Head Office: Gourock PA19 1QP, tel: (01475) 650 100, fax: (01475) 637 607

INDEX TO ROUTES AND CLIFFS